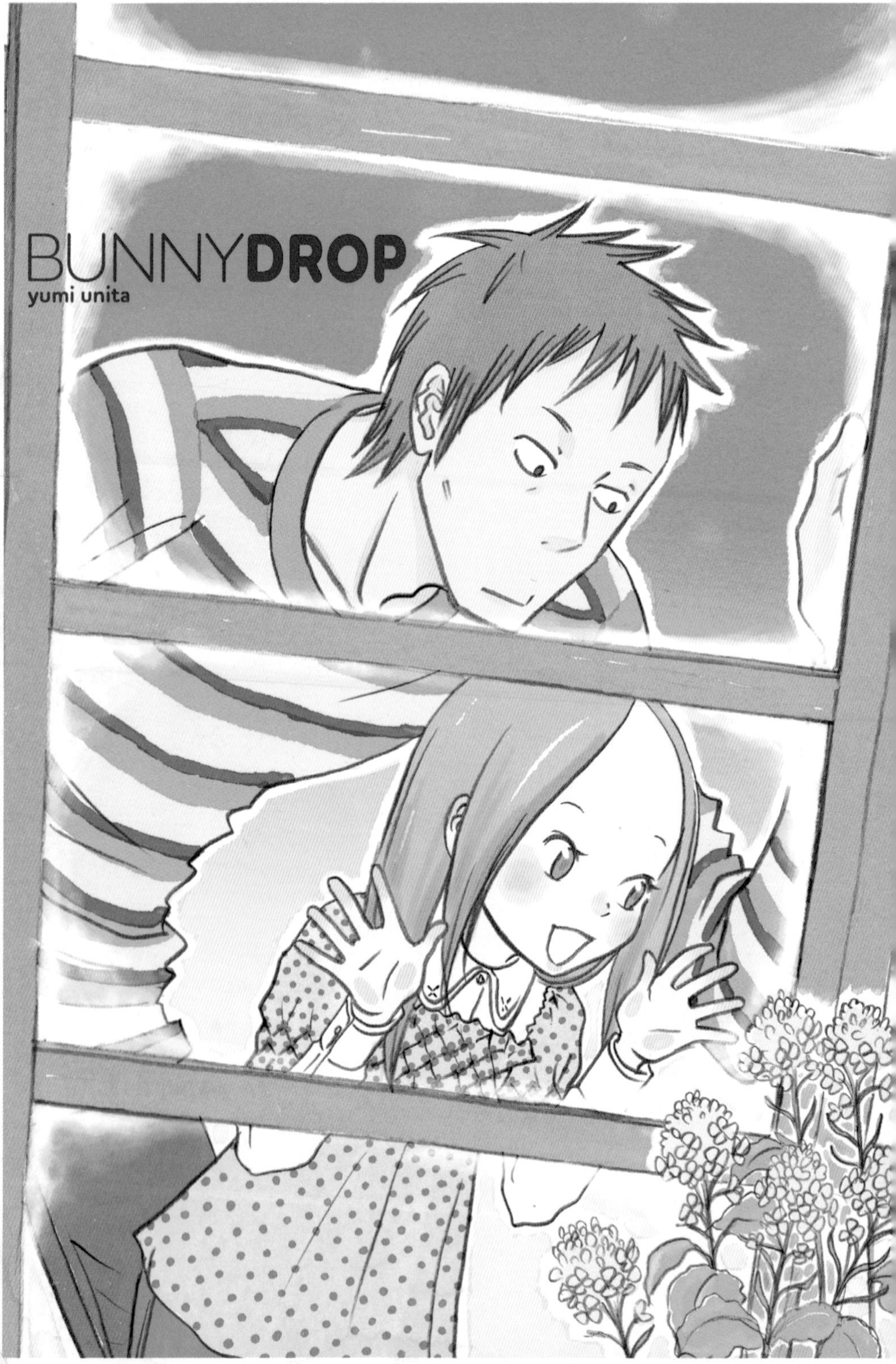
BUNNYDROP
yumi unita

BUNNY DROP 4

yumi unita

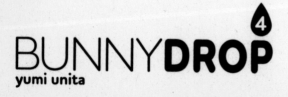

STORY

After taking in his late grandfather's love child Rin
out of necessity, Daikichi finds himself raising her.
When he finally meets Masako, Rin's biological
(and long-absent) mother, he resolves anew to
raise the little girl himself. His life with Rin, who
is now in elementary school, continues to be
full of surprises and moving revelations......

MAIN CHARACTERS

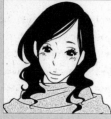 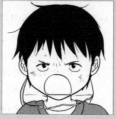

KOUKI & KOUKI'S MOM
Rin's friend from nursery school and his mother.

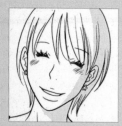 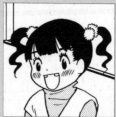

HARUKO & REINA
Daikichi's cousin and her daughter.

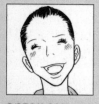

GOTOU-SAN
An energetic, enthusiastic
working mother from
Daikichi's workplace
(also his *senpai*). A
supportive confidante.

DAIKICHI KAWACHI
Thirty-year-old bachelor.
Like a fish out of water
around women and
children.

RIN KAGA
A smart, responsible
first-grader. Technically
Daikichi's aunt.

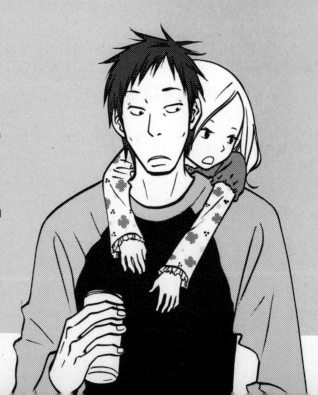

contents

BUNNY**DROP**

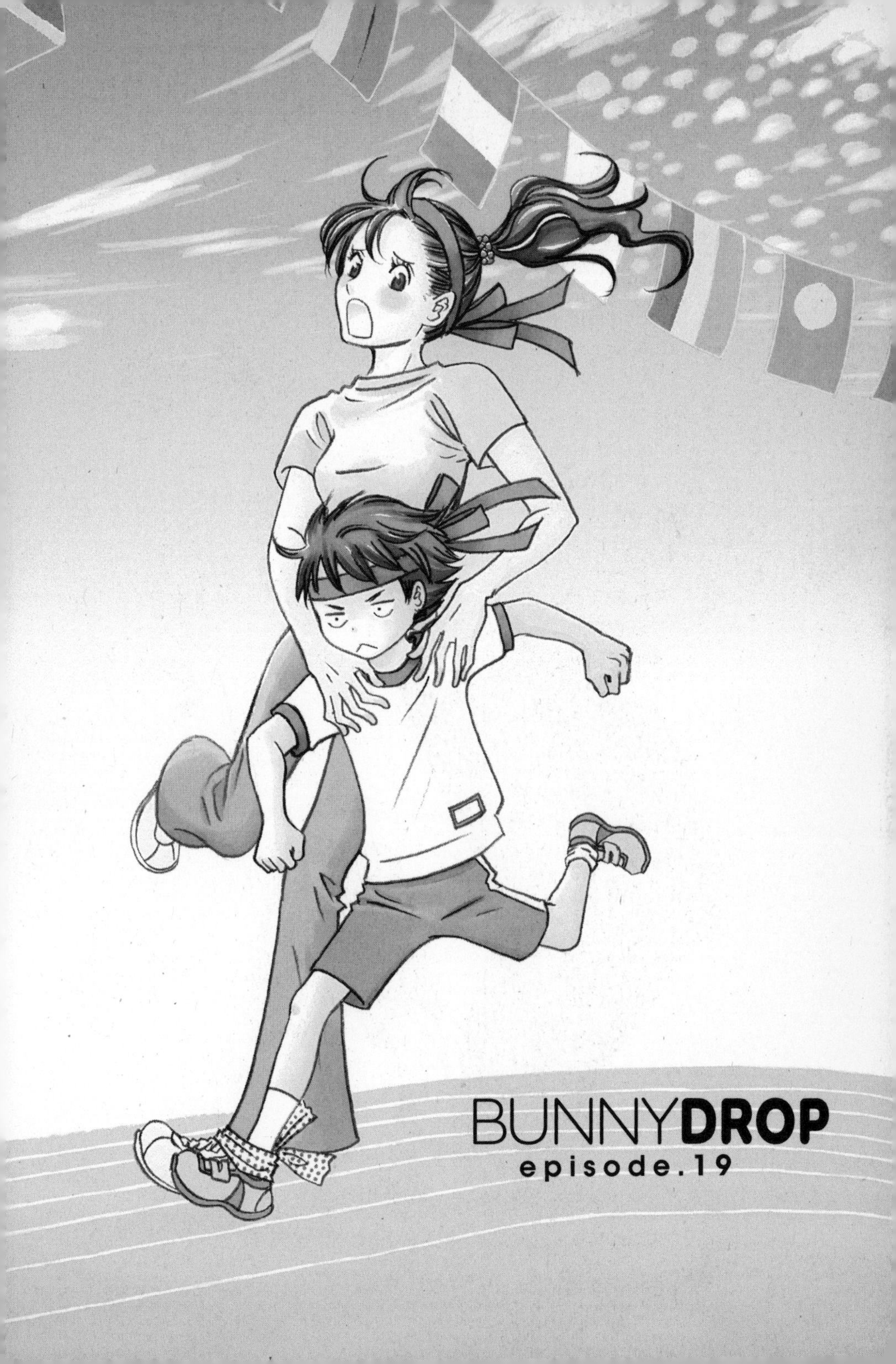
BUNNY**DROP**
episode.19

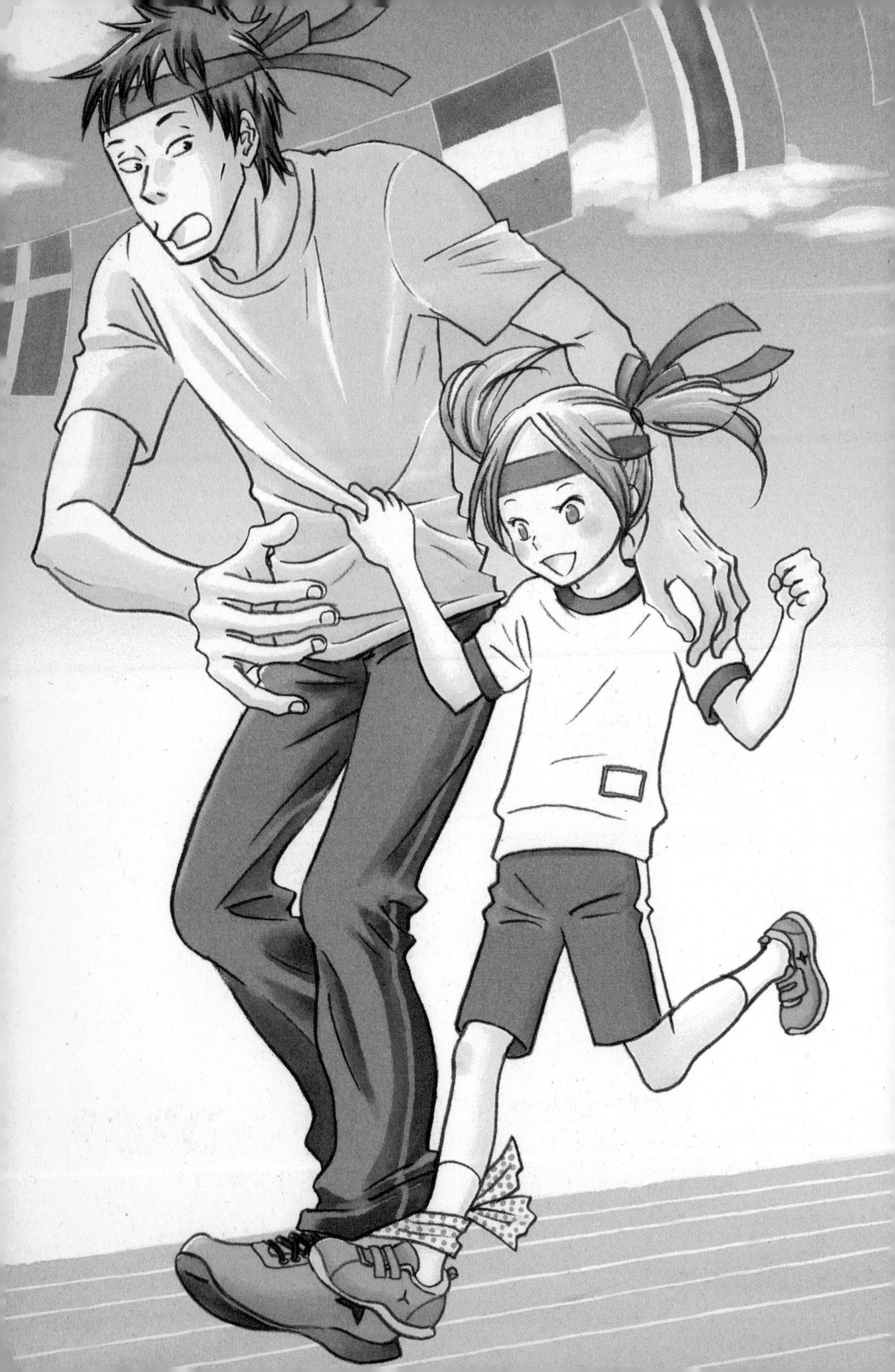

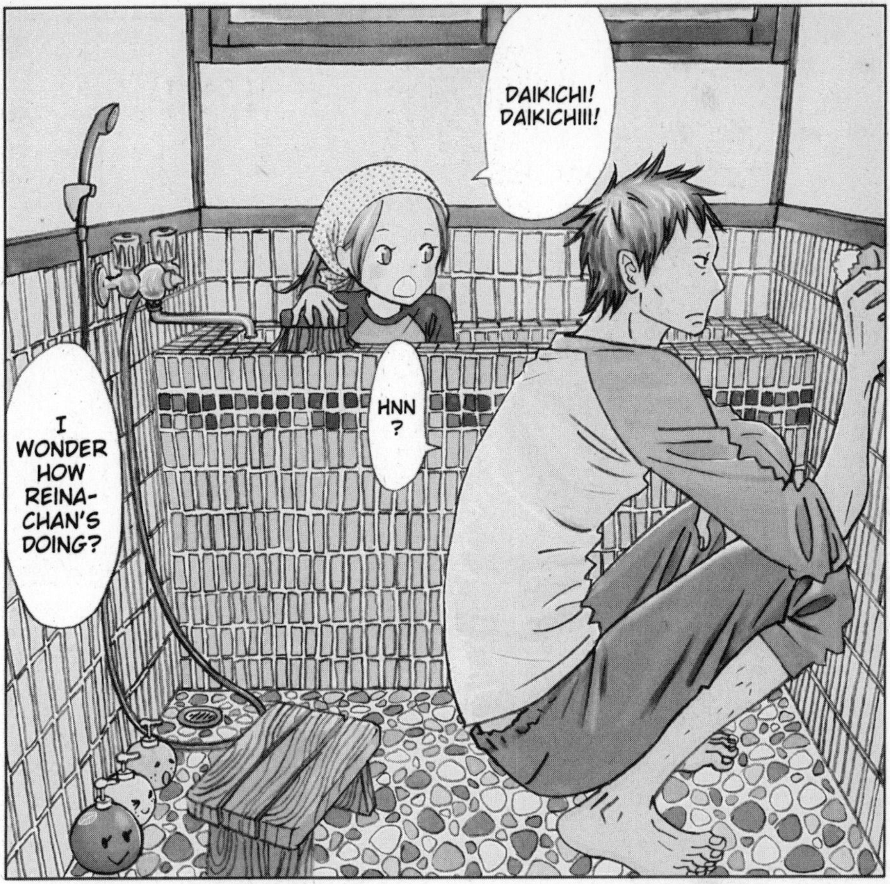
DAIKICHI! DAIKICHIII!
HNN ?
I WONDER HOW REINA-CHAN'S DOING?
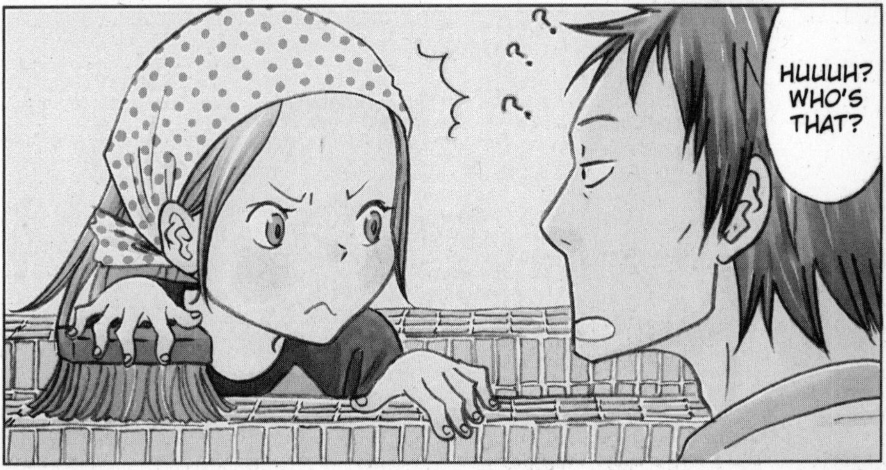
HUUUH? WHO'S THAT?

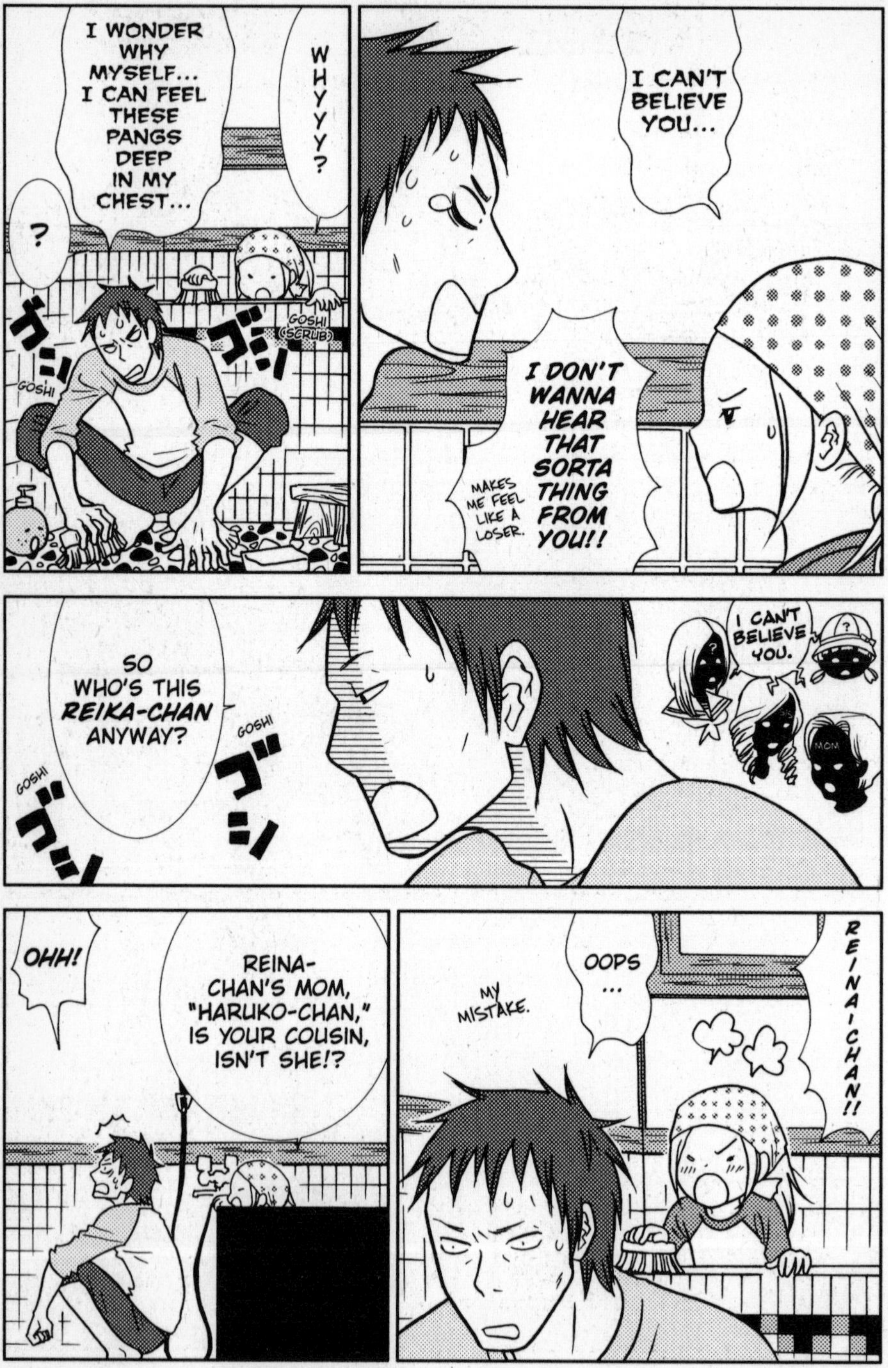
I CAN'T BELIEVE YOU...
I DON'T WANNA HEAR THAT SORTA THING FROM YOU!!
MAKES ME FEEL LIKE A LOSER.
WHYYY?
I WONDER WHY MYSELF... I CAN FEEL THESE PANGS DEEP IN MY CHEST...
?
GOSHI (SCRUB)
GOSHI
I CAN'T BELIEVE YOU.
MOM
SO WHO'S THIS REIKA-CHAN ANYWAY?
GOSHI
GOSHI
REINA-CHAN!!
OOPS...
MY MISTAKE.
REINA-CHAN'S MOM, "HARUKO-CHAN," IS YOUR COUSIN, ISN'T SHE!?
OHH!

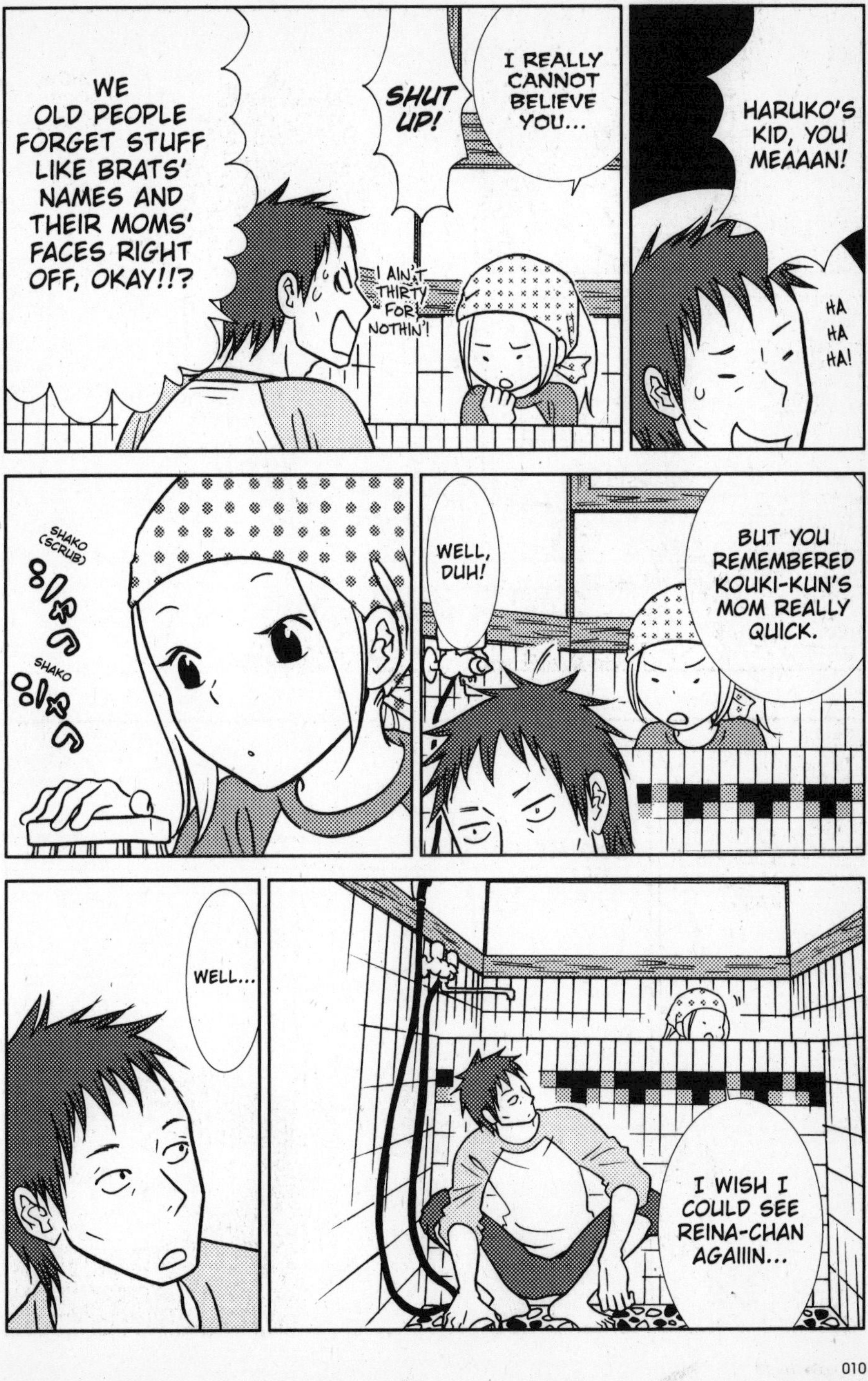
HARUKO'S KID, YOU MEAAAN!
HA HA HA!
I REALLY CANNOT BELIEVE YOU...
SHUT UP!
WE OLD PEOPLE FORGET STUFF LIKE BRATS' NAMES AND THEIR MOMS' FACES RIGHT OFF, OKAY!!?
I AIN'T THIRTY FOR NOTHIN'!
BUT YOU REMEMBERED KOUKI-KUN'S MOM REALLY QUICK.
WELL, DUH!
SHAKO (SCRUB)
SHAKO
I WISH I COULD SEE REINA-CHAN AGAIIIN...
WELL...

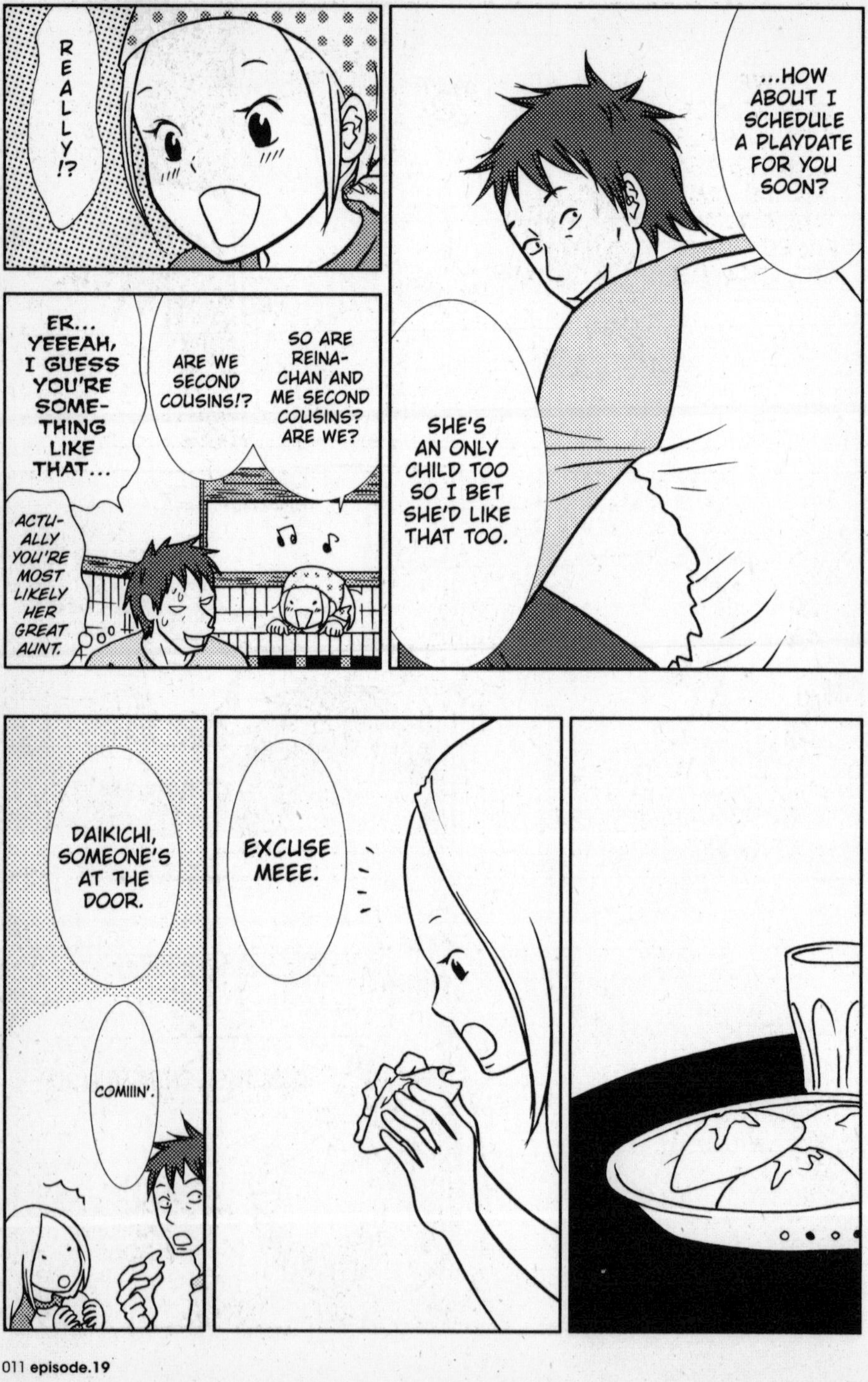
...HOW ABOUT I SCHEDULE A PLAYDATE FOR YOU SOON?
SHE'S AN ONLY CHILD TOO SO I BET SHE'D LIKE THAT TOO.
REALLY!?
SO ARE REINA-CHAN AND ME SECOND COUSINS? ARE WE?
ARE WE SECOND COUSINS!?
ER... YEEEAH, I GUESS YOU'RE SOMETHING LIKE THAT...
ACTUALLY YOU'RE MOST LIKELY HER GREAT AUNT.
EXCUSE MEEE.
DAIKICHI, SOMEONE'S AT THE DOOR.
COMIIIN'.

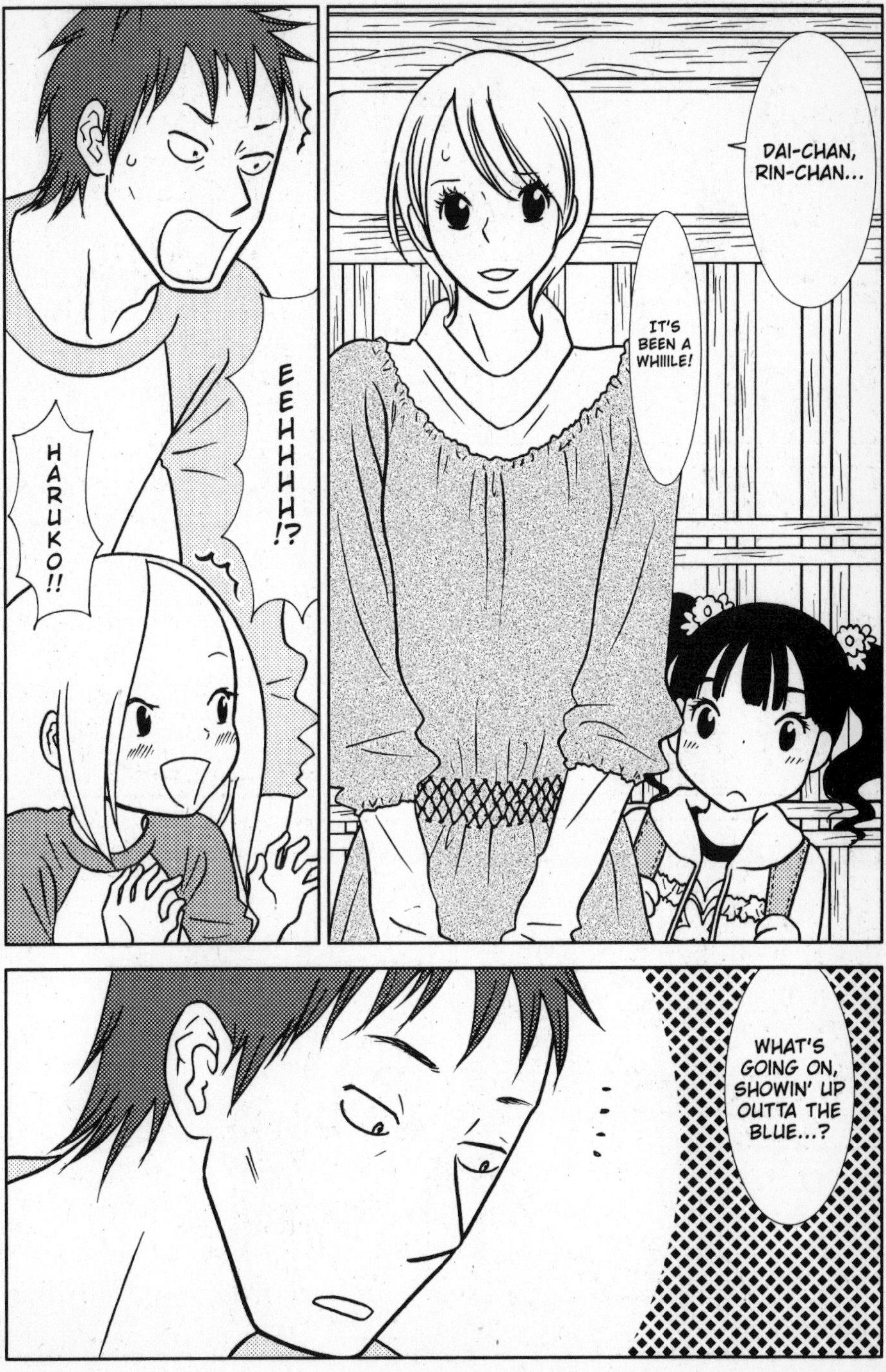
DAI-CHAN, RIN-CHAN...
IT'S BEEN A WHIIILE!
EEHHHHH!?
HARUKO!!
WHAT'S GOING ON, SHOWIN' UP OUTTA THE BLUE...?
...

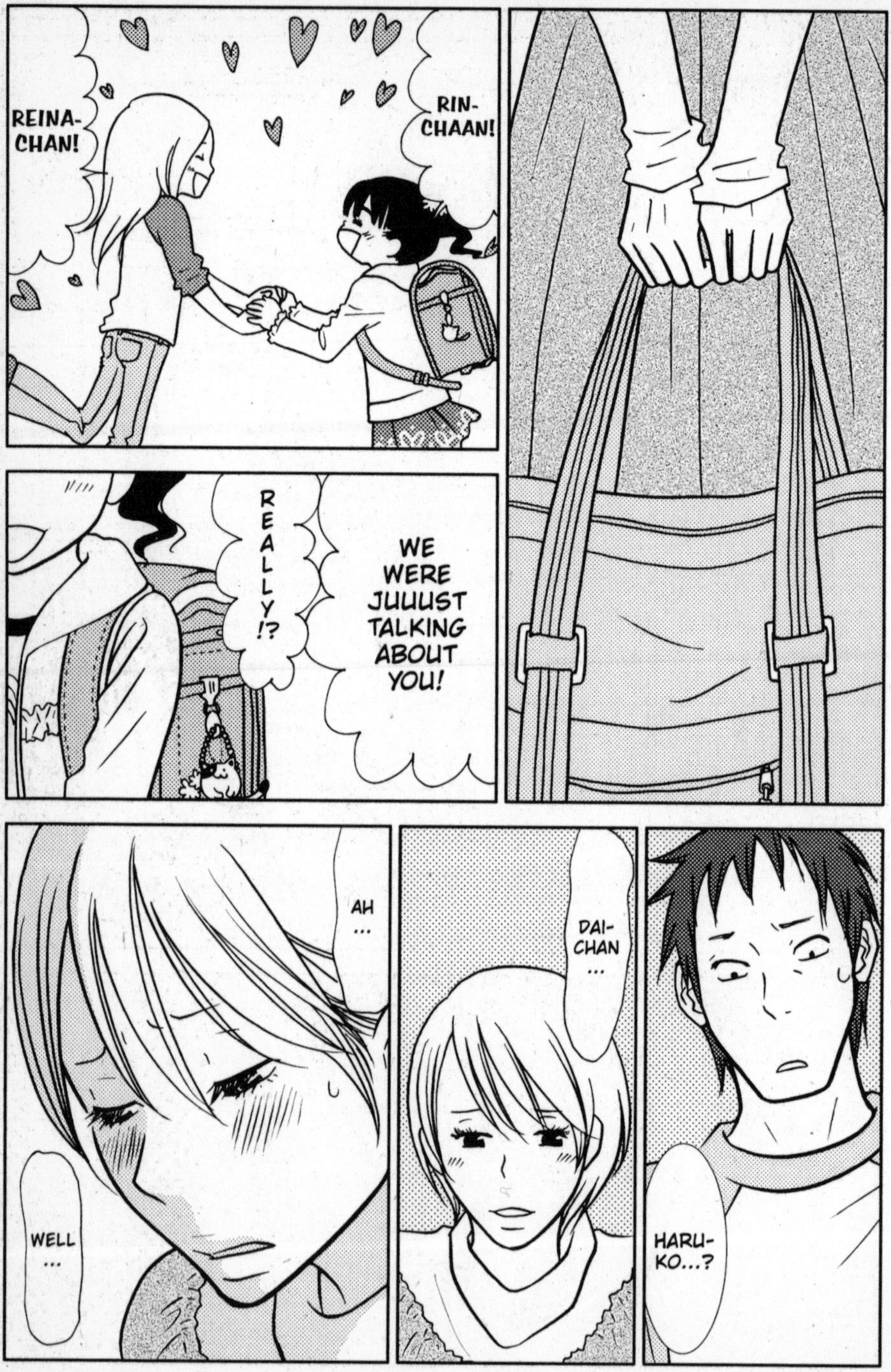
RIN-CHAAN!
REINA-CHAN!
WE WERE JUUUST TALKING ABOUT YOU!
REALLY!?
HARU-KO...?
DAI-CHAN...
AH...
WELL...

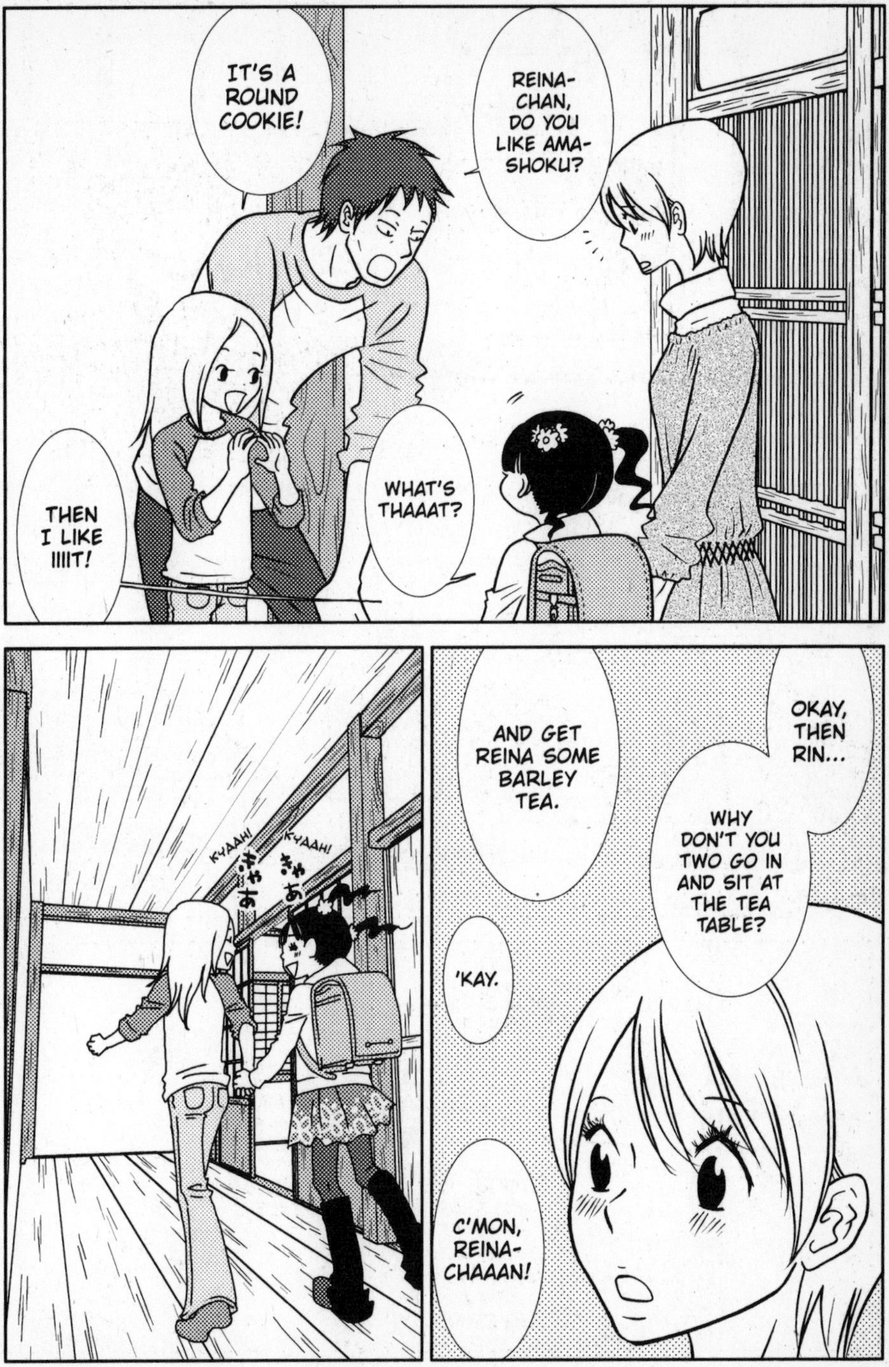
REINA-CHAN, DO YOU LIKE AMA-SHOKU?
WHAT'S THAAAT?
IT'S A ROUND COOKIE!
THEN I LIKE IIIIT!
OKAY, THEN RIN...
WHY DON'T YOU TWO GO IN AND SIT AT THE TEA TABLE?
AND GET REINA SOME BARLEY TEA.
'KAY.
C'MON, REINA-CHAAAN!
KYAAH!
KYAAH!

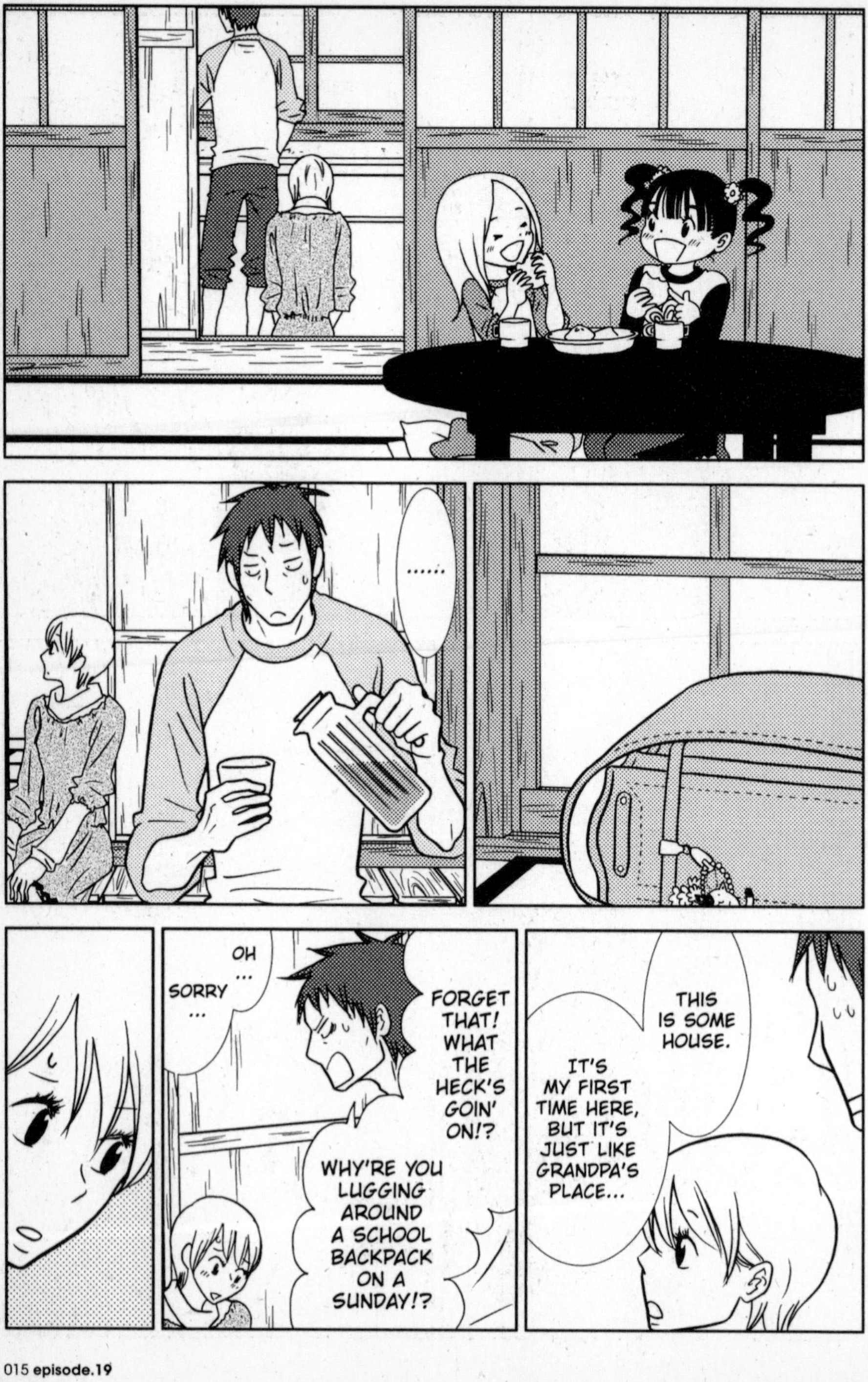
......
THIS IS SOME HOUSE.
IT'S MY FIRST TIME HERE, BUT IT'S JUST LIKE GRANDPA'S PLACE...
FORGET THAT! WHAT THE HECK'S GOIN' ON!?
WHY'RE YOU LUGGING AROUND A SCHOOL BACKPACK ON A SUNDAY!?
OH ... SORRY ...

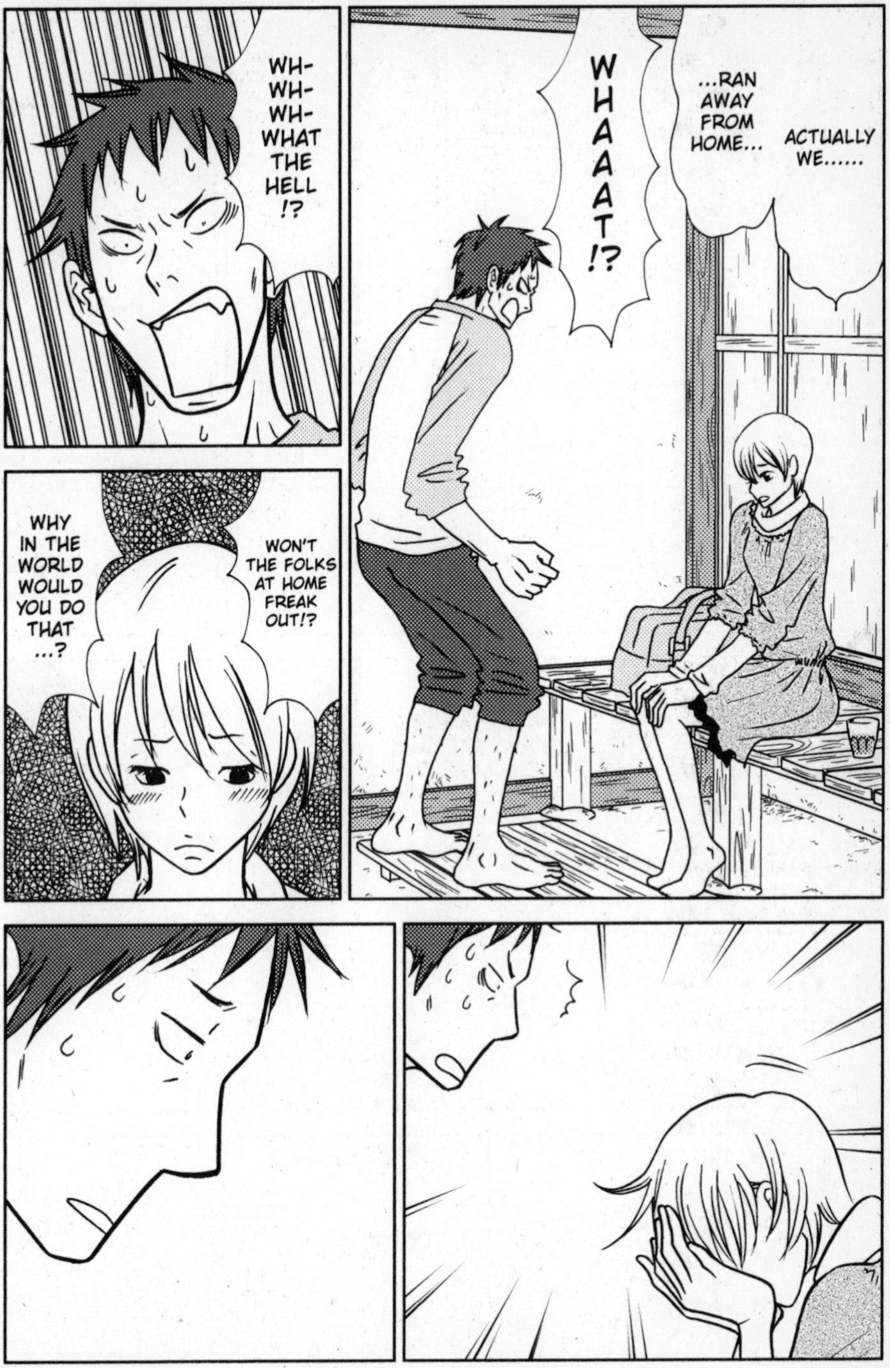
ACTUALLY WE......
...RAN AWAY FROM HOME...
WHAAAAT!?
WH-WH-WH-WHAT THE HELL!?
WON'T THE FOLKS AT HOME FREAK OUT!?
WHY IN THE WORLD WOULD YOU DO THAT ...?

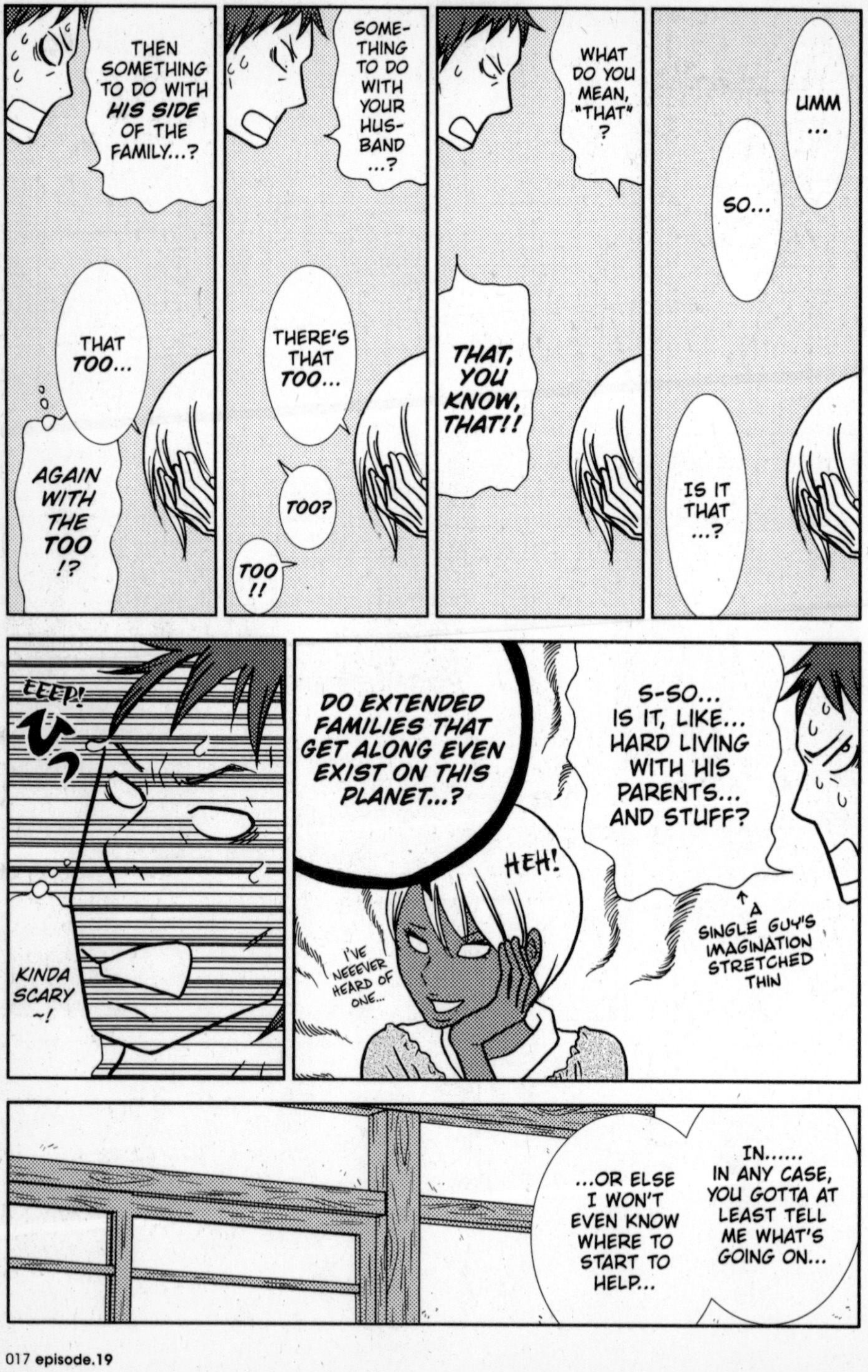
UMM ...
SO...
IS IT THAT ...?
WHAT DO YOU MEAN, "THAT"?
THAT, YOU KNOW, THAT!!
SOMETHING TO DO WITH YOUR HUSBAND ...?
THERE'S THAT TOO...
TOO?
TOO !!
THEN SOMETHING TO DO WITH HIS SIDE OF THE FAMILY...?
THAT TOO...
AGAIN WITH THE TOO !?
S-SO... IS IT, LIKE... HARD LIVING WITH HIS PARENTS... AND STUFF?
A SINGLE GUY'S IMAGINATION STRETCHED THIN
DO EXTENDED FAMILIES THAT GET ALONG EVEN EXIST ON THIS PLANET...?
HEH!
I'VE NEEEVER HEARD OF ONE...
EEEP!
ひっ
KINDA SCARY ~!
IN...... IN ANY CASE, YOU GOTTA AT LEAST TELL ME WHAT'S GOING ON...
...OR ELSE I WON'T EVEN KNOW WHERE TO START TO HELP...

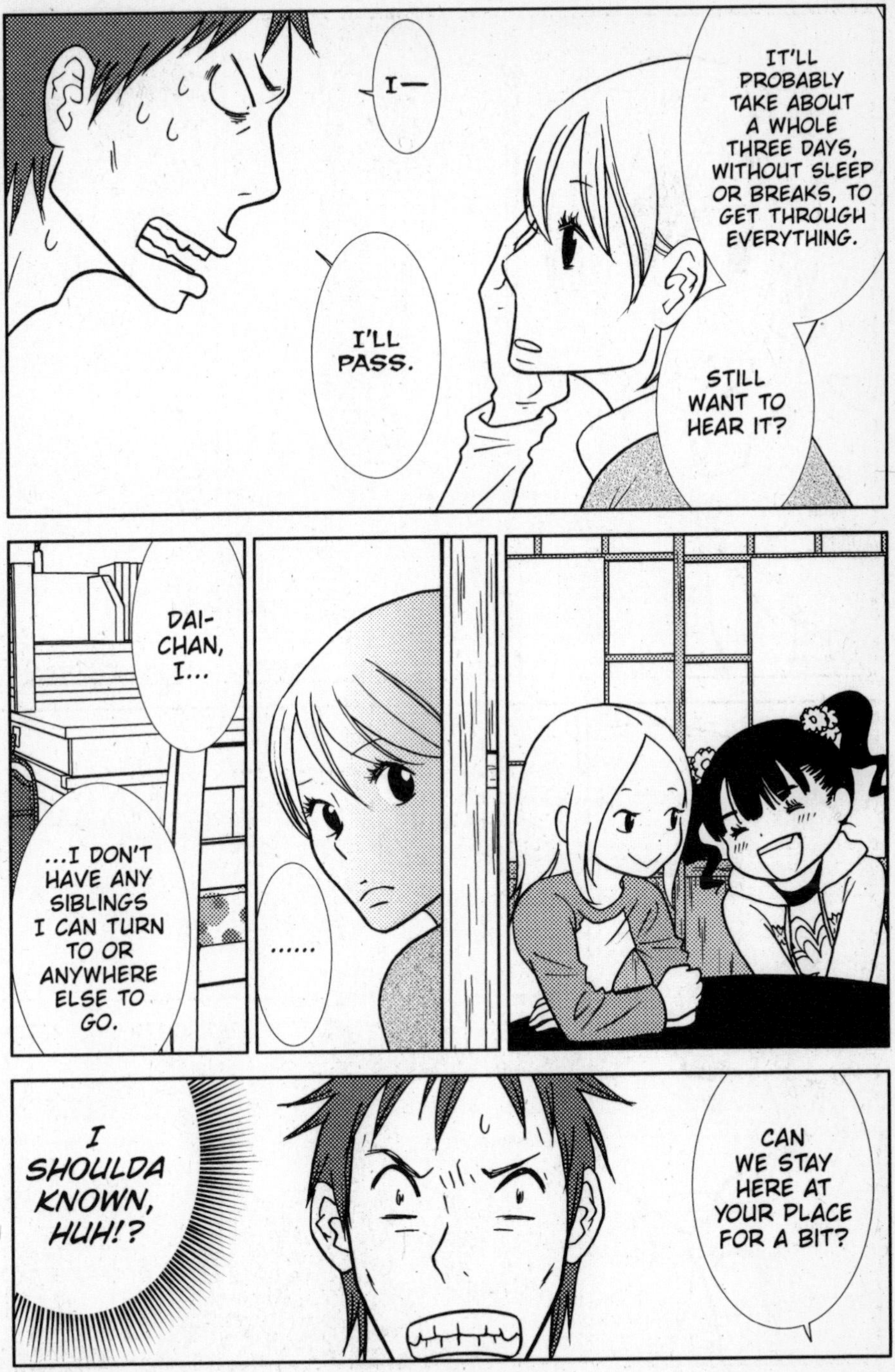
IT'LL PROBABLY TAKE ABOUT A WHOLE THREE DAYS, WITHOUT SLEEP OR BREAKS, TO GET THROUGH EVERYTHING.
STILL WANT TO HEAR IT?
I—
I'LL PASS.
......
DAI-CHAN, I...
...I DON'T HAVE ANY SIBLINGS I CAN TURN TO OR ANYWHERE ELSE TO GO.
CAN WE STAY HERE AT YOUR PLACE FOR A BIT?
I SHOULDA KNOWN, HUH!?

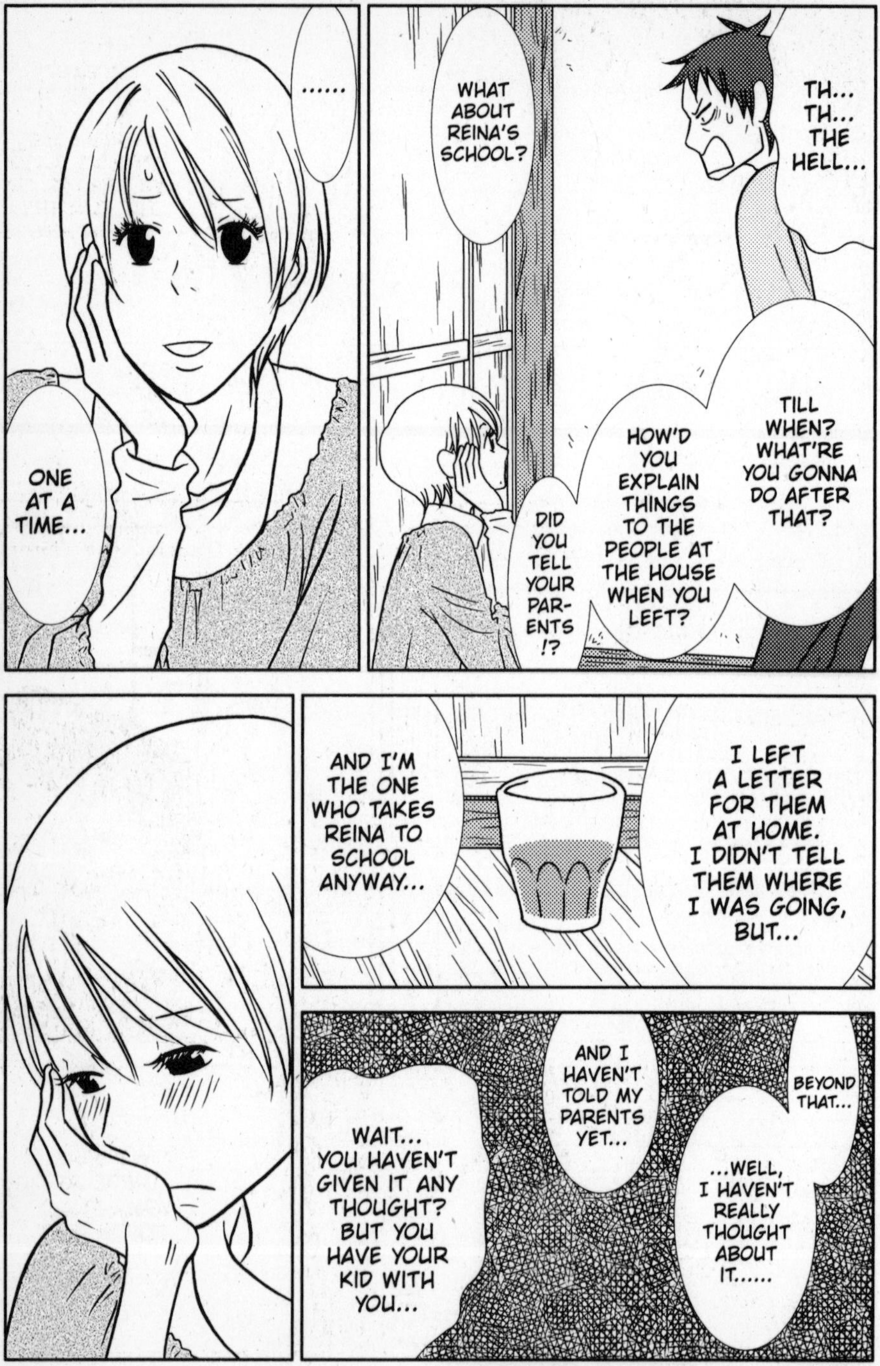
TH... TH... THE HELL...
WHAT ABOUT REINA'S SCHOOL?
TILL WHEN? WHAT'RE YOU GONNA DO AFTER THAT?
HOW'D YOU EXPLAIN THINGS TO THE PEOPLE AT THE HOUSE WHEN YOU LEFT?
DID YOU TELL YOUR PAR-ENTS!?
......
ONE AT A TIME...
I LEFT A LETTER FOR THEM AT HOME. I DIDN'T TELL THEM WHERE I WAS GOING, BUT...
AND I'M THE ONE WHO TAKES REINA TO SCHOOL ANYWAY...
AND I HAVEN'T TOLD MY PARENTS YET...
BEYOND THAT...
...WELL, I HAVEN'T REALLY THOUGHT ABOUT IT......
WAIT... YOU HAVEN'T GIVEN IT ANY THOUGHT? BUT YOU HAVE YOUR KID WITH YOU...

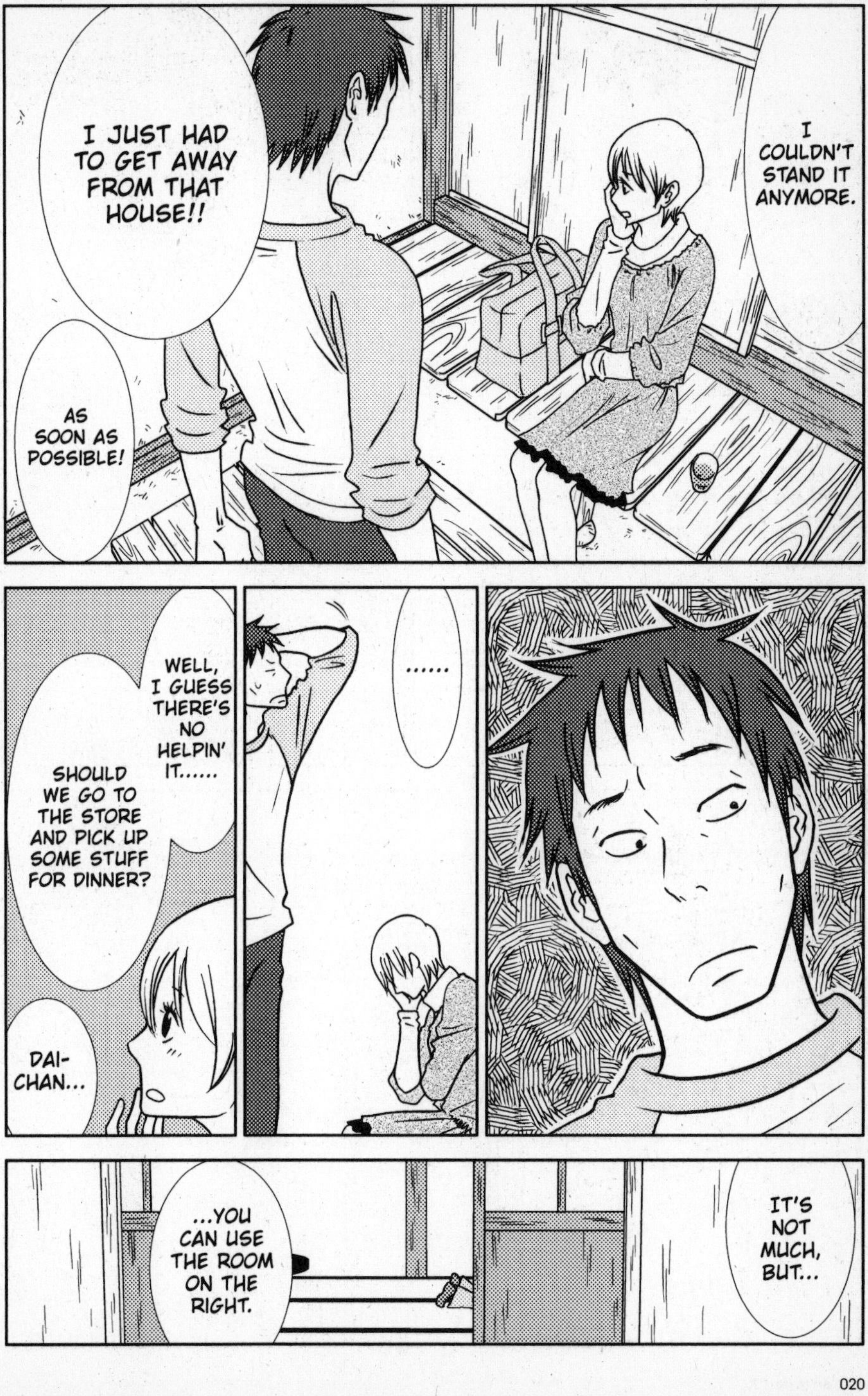
I COULDN'T STAND IT ANYMORE.
I JUST HAD TO GET AWAY FROM THAT HOUSE!!
AS SOON AS POSSIBLE!
......
WELL, I GUESS THERE'S NO HELPIN' IT......
SHOULD WE GO TO THE STORE AND PICK UP SOME STUFF FOR DINNER?
DAI-CHAN...
IT'S NOT MUCH, BUT...
...YOU CAN USE THE ROOM ON THE RIGHT.

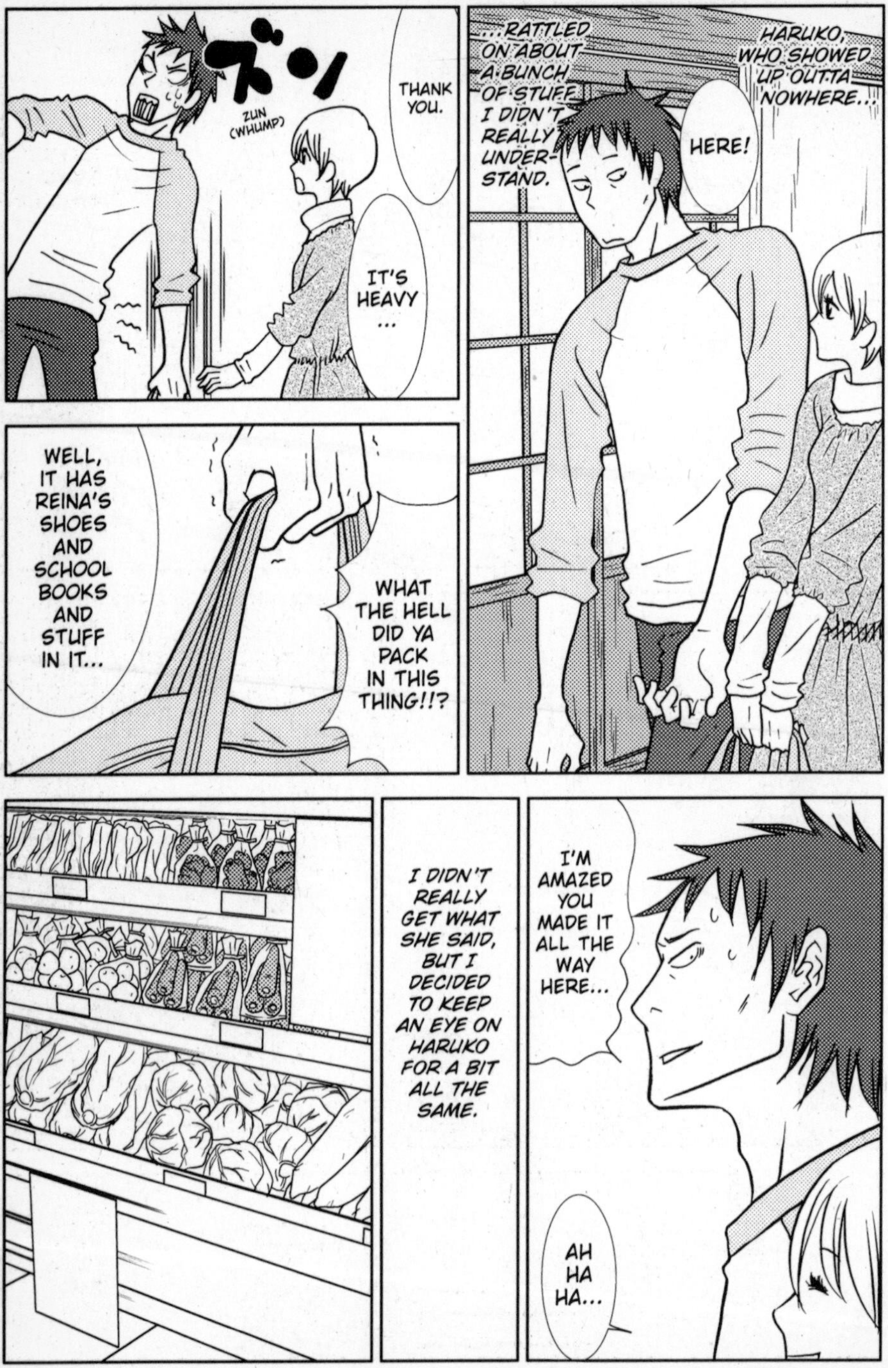
HARUKO, WHO SHOWED UP OUTTA NOWHERE...
...RATTLED ON ABOUT A BUNCH OF STUFF I DIDN'T REALLY UNDER-STAND.
HERE!
THANK YOU.
ズン
ZUN (WHUMP)
IT'S HEAVY ...
WHAT THE HELL DID YA PACK IN THIS THING!!?
WELL, IT HAS REINA'S SHOES AND SCHOOL BOOKS AND STUFF IN IT...
I'M AMAZED YOU MADE IT ALL THE WAY HERE...
AH HA HA...
I DIDN'T REALLY GET WHAT SHE SAID, BUT I DECIDED TO KEEP AN EYE ON HARUKO FOR A BIT ALL THE SAME.

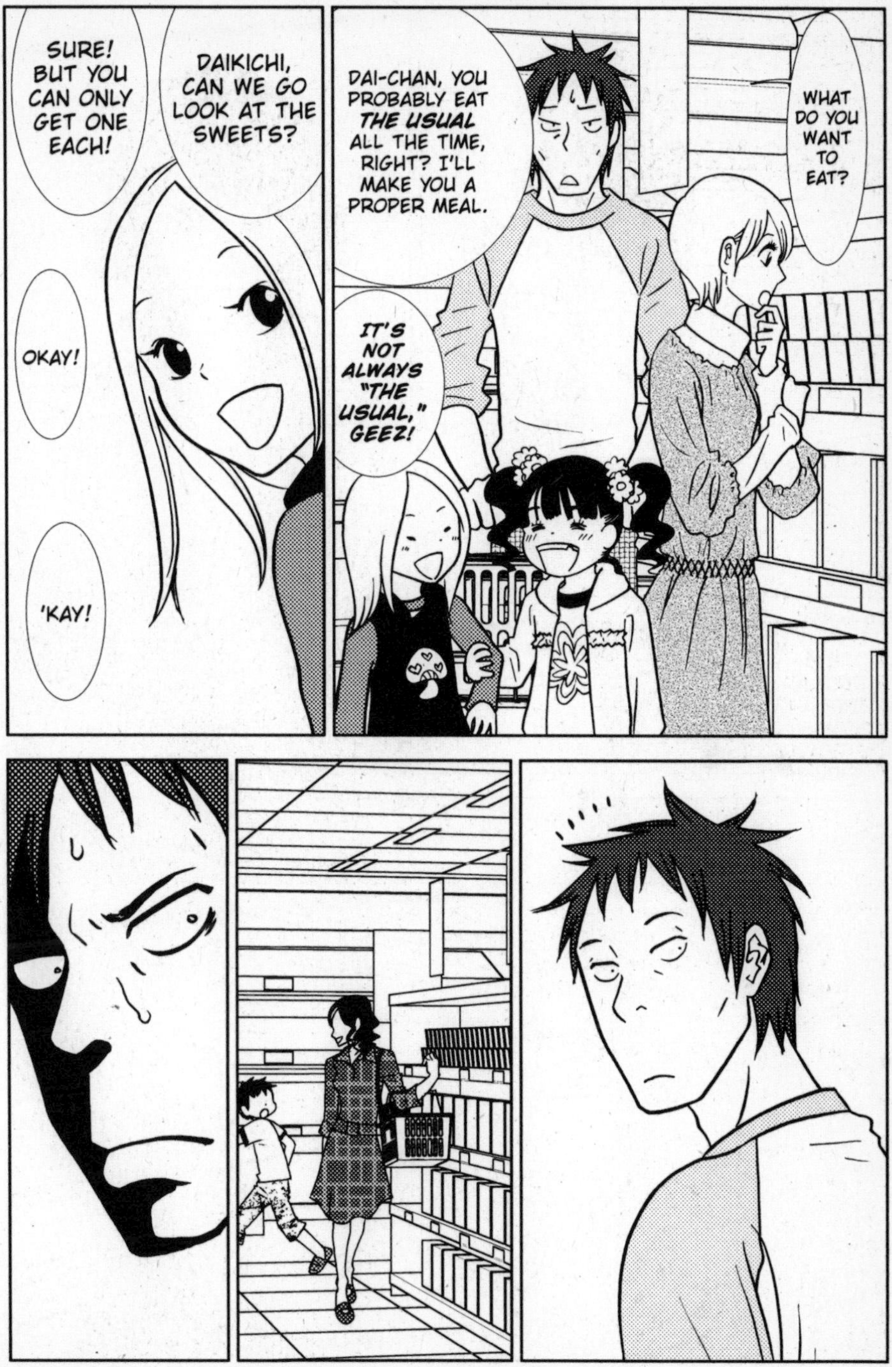
WHAT DO YOU WANT TO EAT?
DAI-CHAN, YOU PROBABLY EAT THE USUAL ALL THE TIME, RIGHT? I'LL MAKE YOU A PROPER MEAL.
IT'S NOT ALWAYS "THE USUAL," GEEZ!
DAIKICHI, CAN WE GO LOOK AT THE SWEETS?
SURE! BUT YOU CAN ONLY GET ONE EACH!
OKAY!
'KAY!

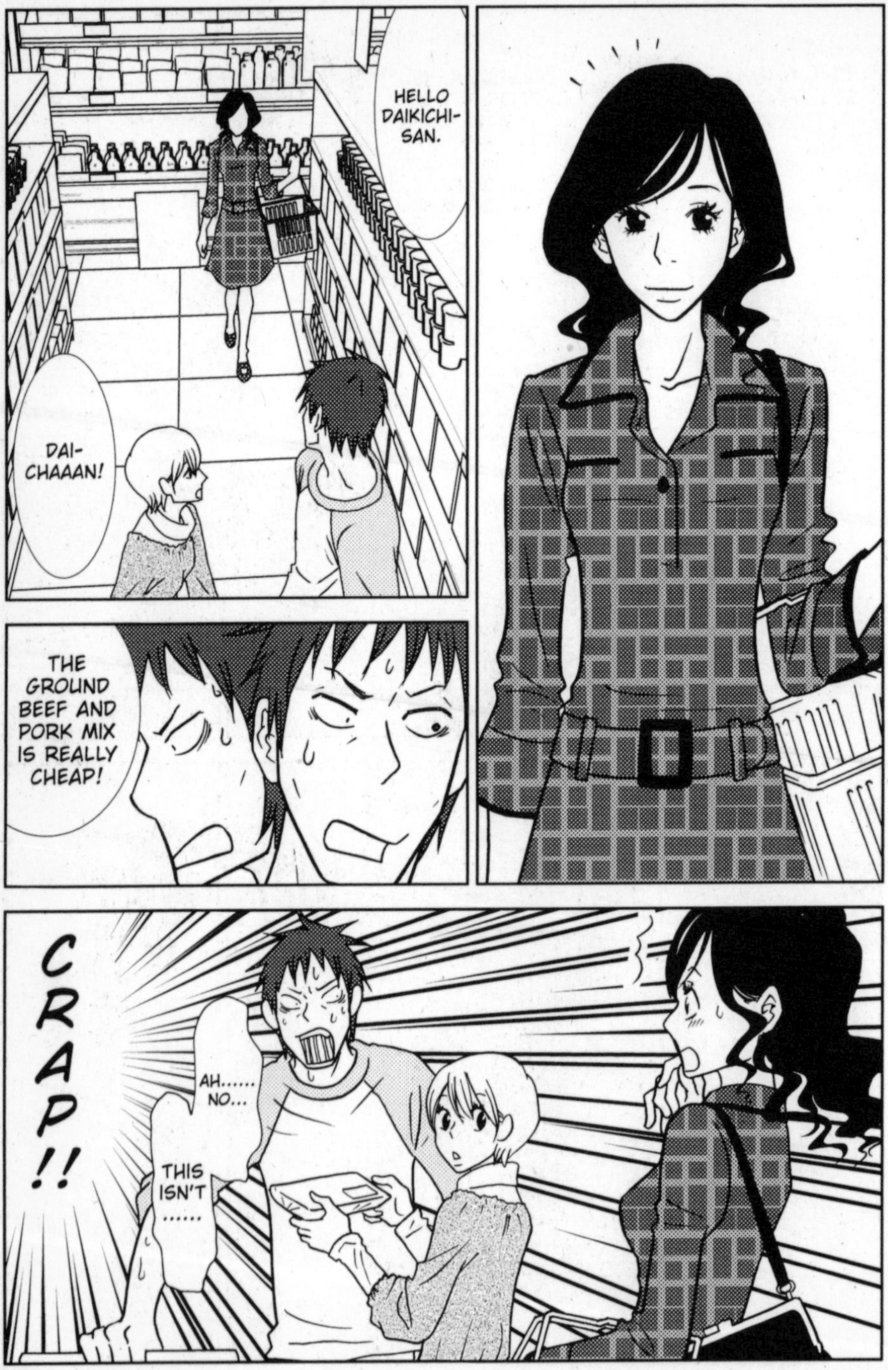
HELLO DAIKICHI-SAN.
DAI-CHAAAN!
THE GROUND BEEF AND PORK MIX IS REALLY CHEAP!
AH...... NO...
THIS ISN'T ......
CRAP!!

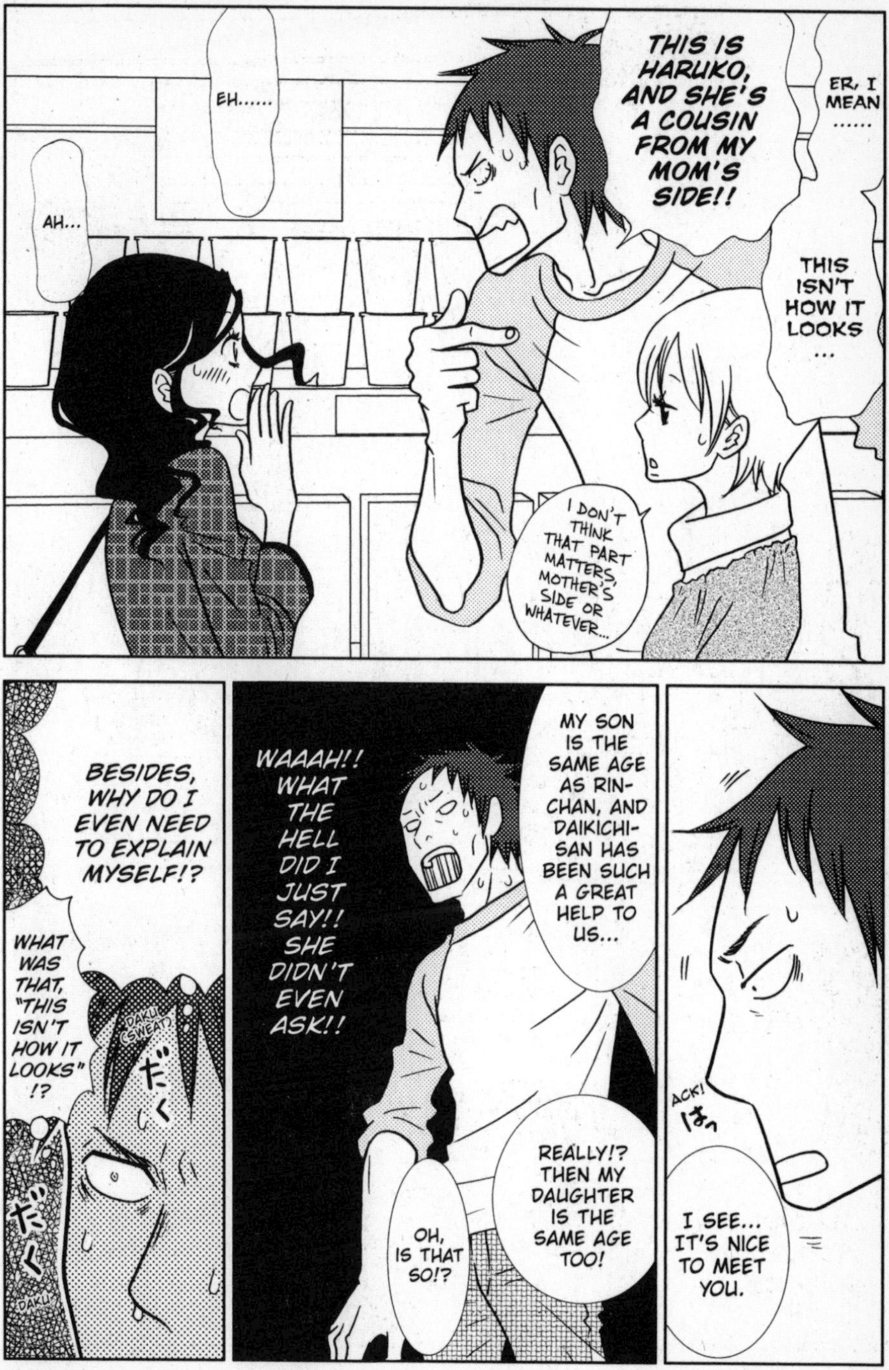
ER, I MEAN ......
THIS IS HARUKO, AND SHE'S A COUSIN FROM MY MOM'S SIDE!!
THIS ISN'T HOW IT LOOKS ...
EH......
AH...
I DON'T THINK THAT PART MATTERS, MOTHER'S SIDE OR WHATEVER...
ACK! はっ
I SEE... IT'S NICE TO MEET YOU.
MY SON IS THE SAME AGE AS RIN-CHAN, AND DAIKICHI-SAN HAS BEEN SUCH A GREAT HELP TO US...
WAAAH!! WHAT THE HELL DID I JUST SAY!! SHE DIDN'T EVEN ASK!!
REALLY!? THEN MY DAUGHTER IS THE SAME AGE TOO!
OH, IS THAT SO!?
BESIDES, WHY DO I EVEN NEED TO EXPLAIN MYSELF!?
WHAT WAS THAT, "THIS ISN'T HOW IT LOOKS" !?
DAKU (SWEAT) だく
だく DAKU

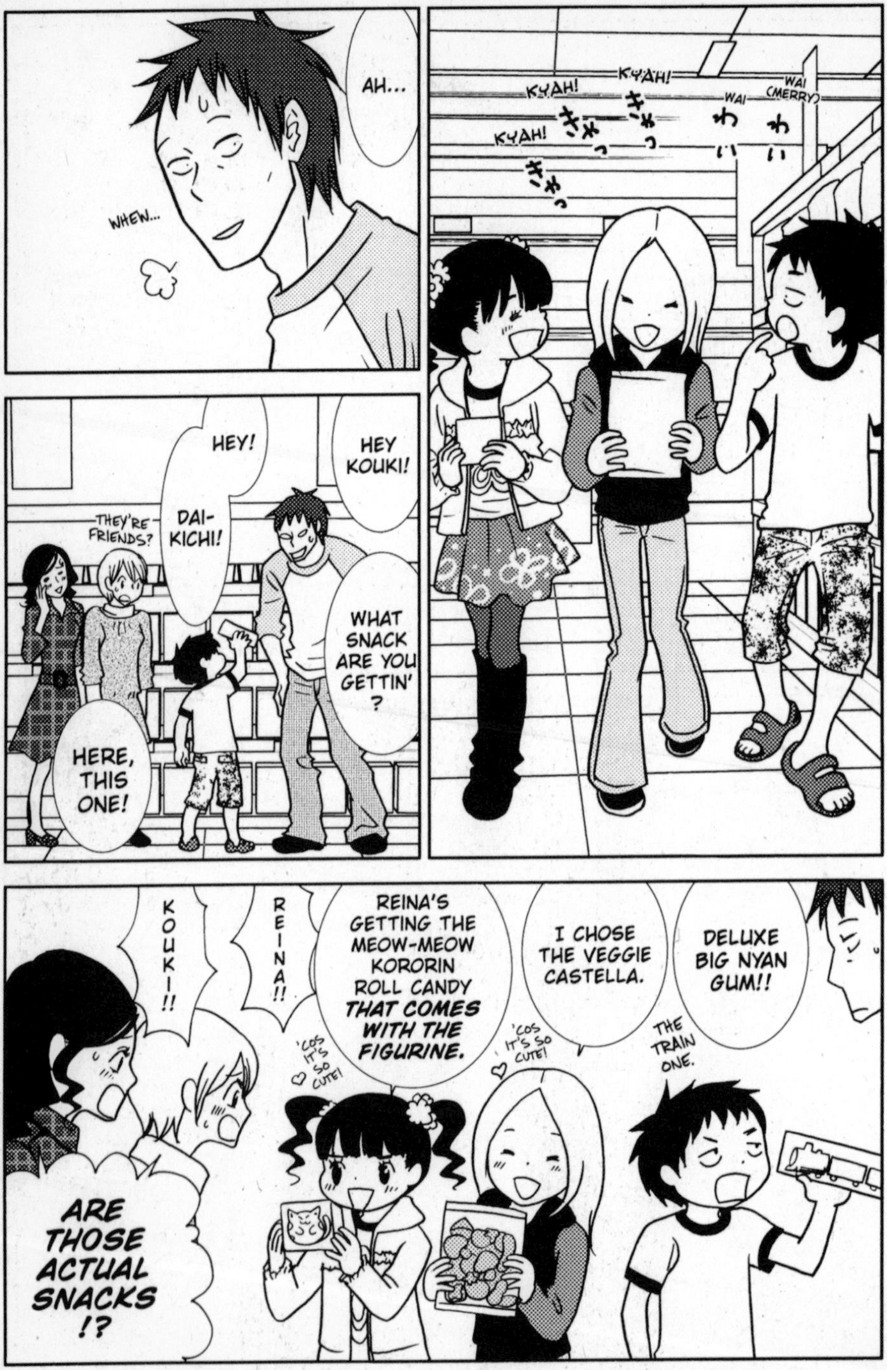
WAI (MERRY)
わい
WAI
わい
KYAH!
きゃっ
KYAH!
きゃっ
KYAH!
きゃっ
AH...
WHEW...
HEY KOUKI!
HEY!
DAI-KICHI!
WHAT SNACK ARE YOU GETTIN'?
THEY'RE FRIENDS?
HERE, THIS ONE!
DELUXE BIG NYAN GUM!!
THE TRAIN ONE.
I CHOSE THE VEGGIE CASTELLA.
'COS IT'S SO CUTE!
REINA'S GETTING THE MEOW-MEOW KORORIN ROLL CANDY ***THAT COMES WITH THE FIGURINE.***
'COS IT'S SO CUTE!
REINA!!
KOUKI!!
ARE THOSE ACTUAL SNACKS!?

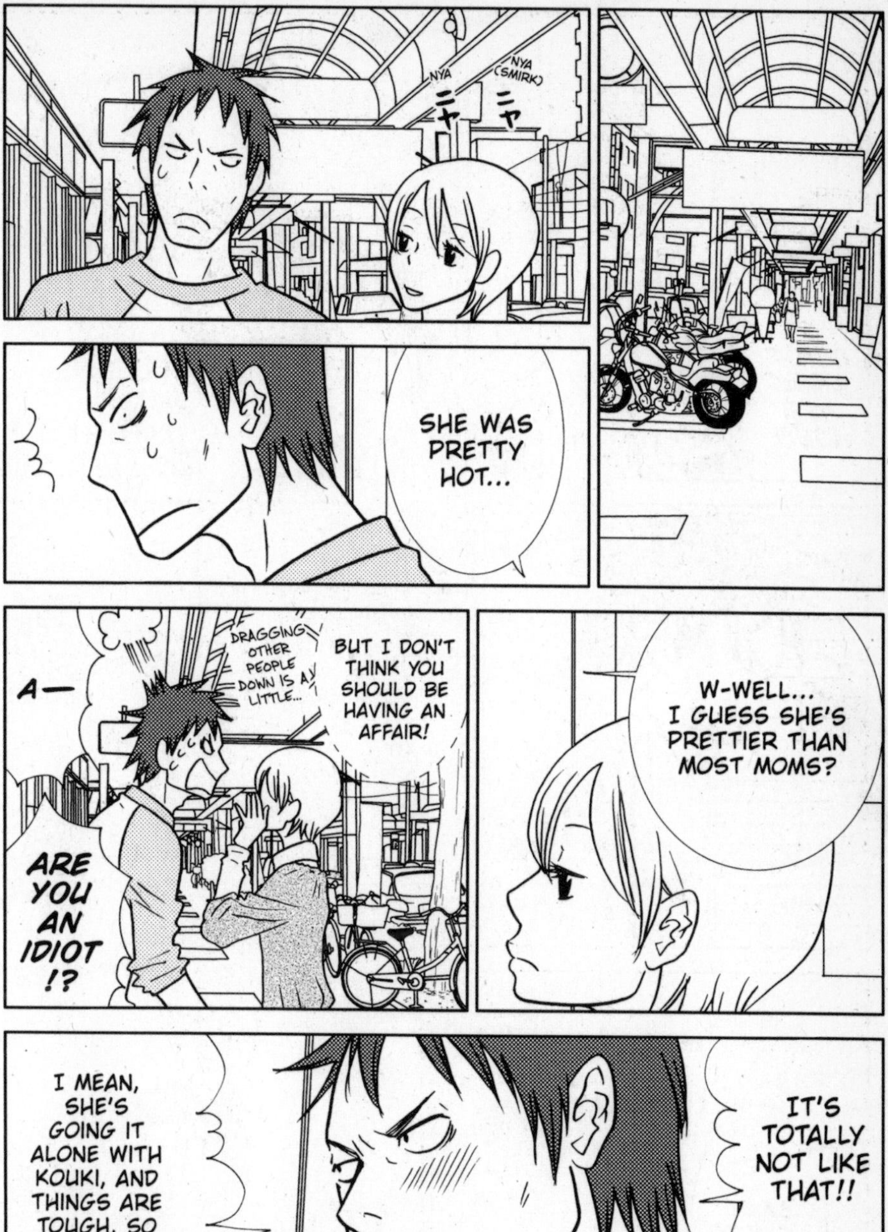

ニヤ
NYA (SMIRK)
ニヤ
NYA
SHE WAS PRETTY HOT...
W-WELL... I GUESS SHE'S PRETTIER THAN MOST MOMS?
BUT I DON'T THINK YOU SHOULD BE HAVING AN AFFAIR!
DRAGGING OTHER PEOPLE DOWN IS A LITTLE...
A—
ARE YOU AN IDIOT !?
IT'S TOTALLY NOT LIKE THAT!!
I MEAN, SHE'S GOING IT ALONE WITH KOUKI, AND THINGS ARE TOUGH, SO THERE'S NO TIME FOR THAT...

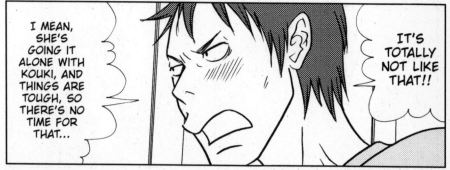

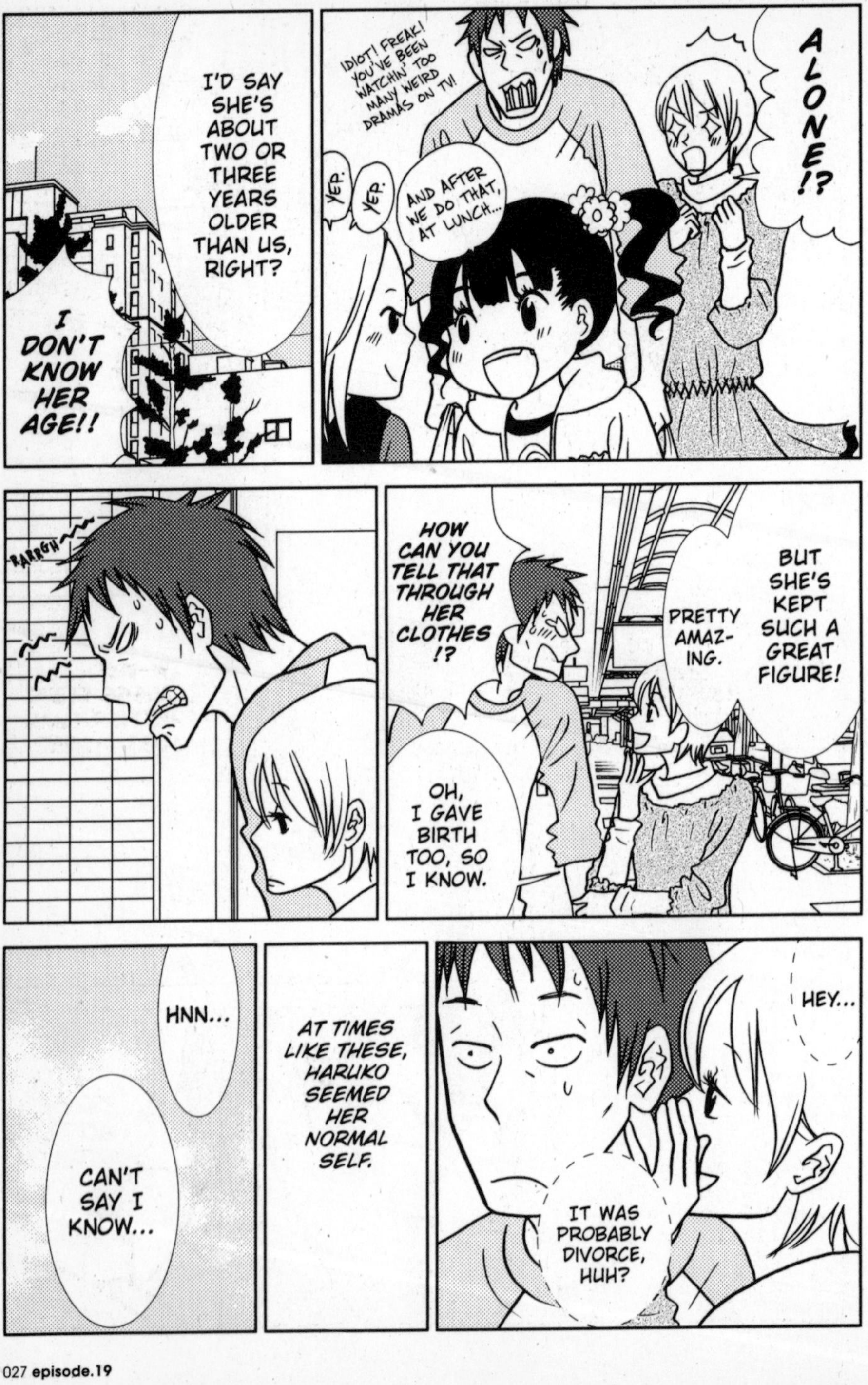
ALONE!?
IDIOT! FREAK! YOU'VE BEEN WATCHIN' TOO MANY WEIRD DRAMAS ON TV!
AND AFTER WE DO THAT, AT LUNCH...
YEP.
YEP.
I'D SAY SHE'S ABOUT TWO OR THREE YEARS OLDER THAN US, RIGHT?
I DON'T KNOW HER AGE!!
BUT SHE'S KEPT SUCH A GREAT FIGURE!
PRETTY AMAZ-ING.
HOW CAN YOU TELL THAT THROUGH HER CLOTHES!?
OH, I GAVE BIRTH TOO, SO I KNOW.
RARRGH
HEY...
IT WAS PROBABLY DIVORCE, HUH?
AT TIMES LIKE THESE, HARUKO SEEMED HER NORMAL SELF.
HNN...
CAN'T SAY I KNOW...

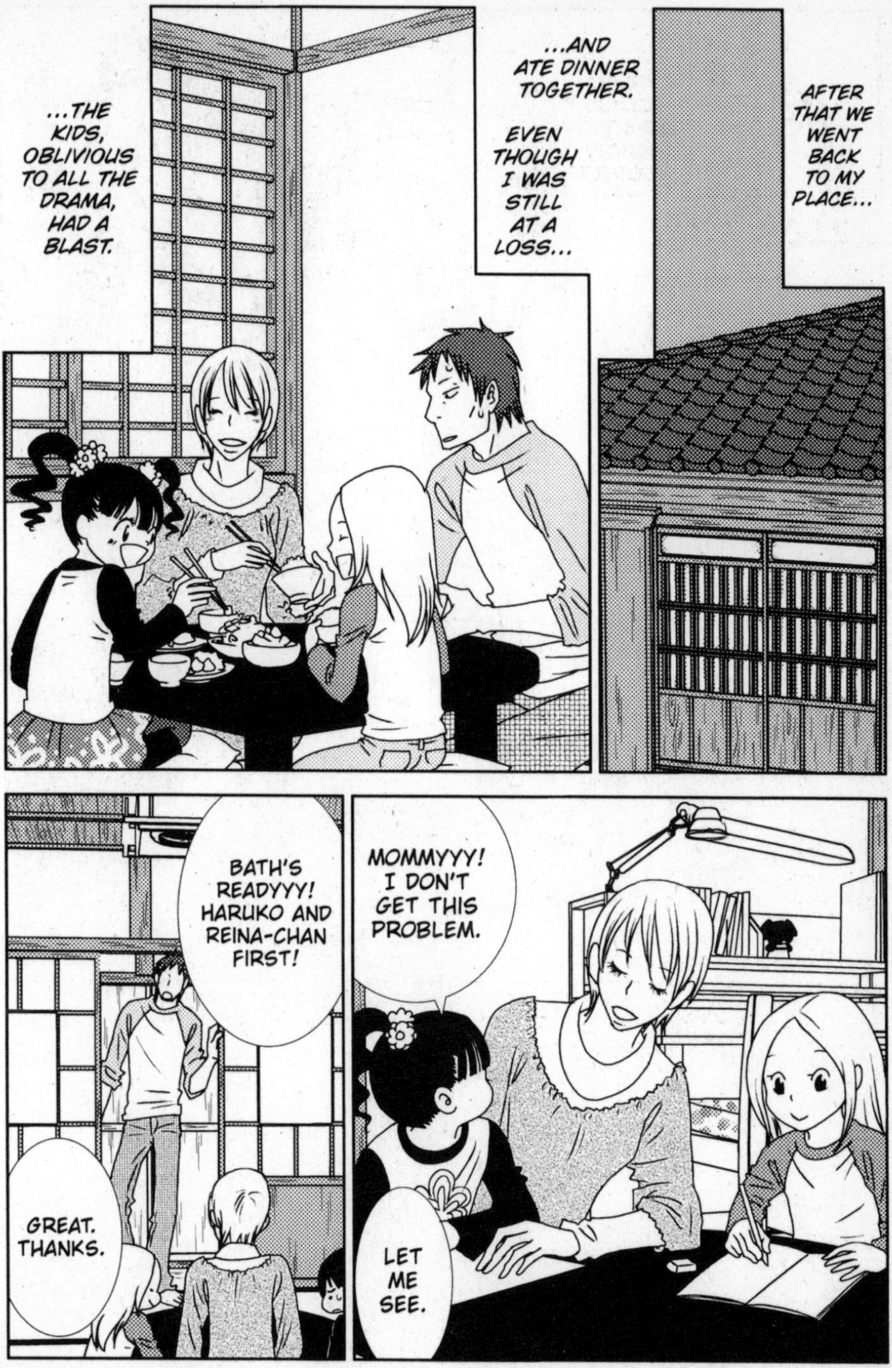
AFTER THAT WE WENT BACK TO MY PLACE...
...AND ATE DINNER TOGETHER.
EVEN THOUGH I WAS STILL AT A LOSS...
...THE KIDS, OBLIVIOUS TO ALL THE DRAMA, HAD A BLAST.
MOMMYYY! I DON'T GET THIS PROBLEM.
LET ME SEE.
BATH'S READYYY! HARUKO AND REINA-CHAN FIRST!
GREAT. THANKS.

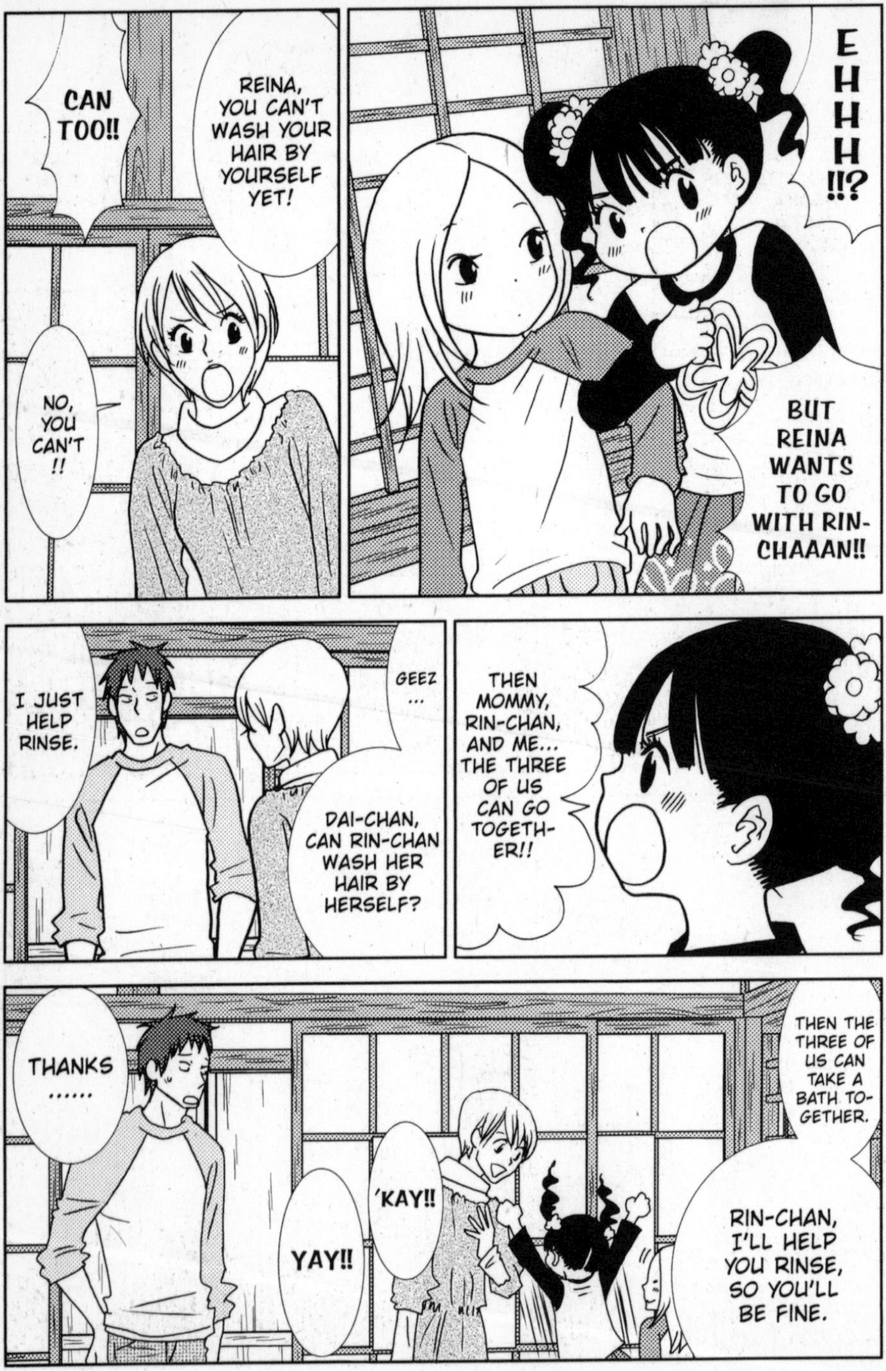
EHHHH!!?
BUT REINA WANTS TO GO WITH RIN-CHAAAN!!
REINA, YOU CAN'T WASH YOUR HAIR BY YOURSELF YET!
CAN TOO!!
NO, YOU CAN'T!!
THEN MOMMY, RIN-CHAN, AND ME... THE THREE OF US CAN GO TOGETHER!!
GEEZ...
DAI-CHAN, CAN RIN-CHAN WASH HER HAIR BY HERSELF?
I JUST HELP RINSE.
THEN THE THREE OF US CAN TAKE A BATH TOGETHER.
RIN-CHAN, I'LL HELP YOU RINSE, SO YOU'LL BE FINE.
'KAY!!
YAY!!
THANKS......

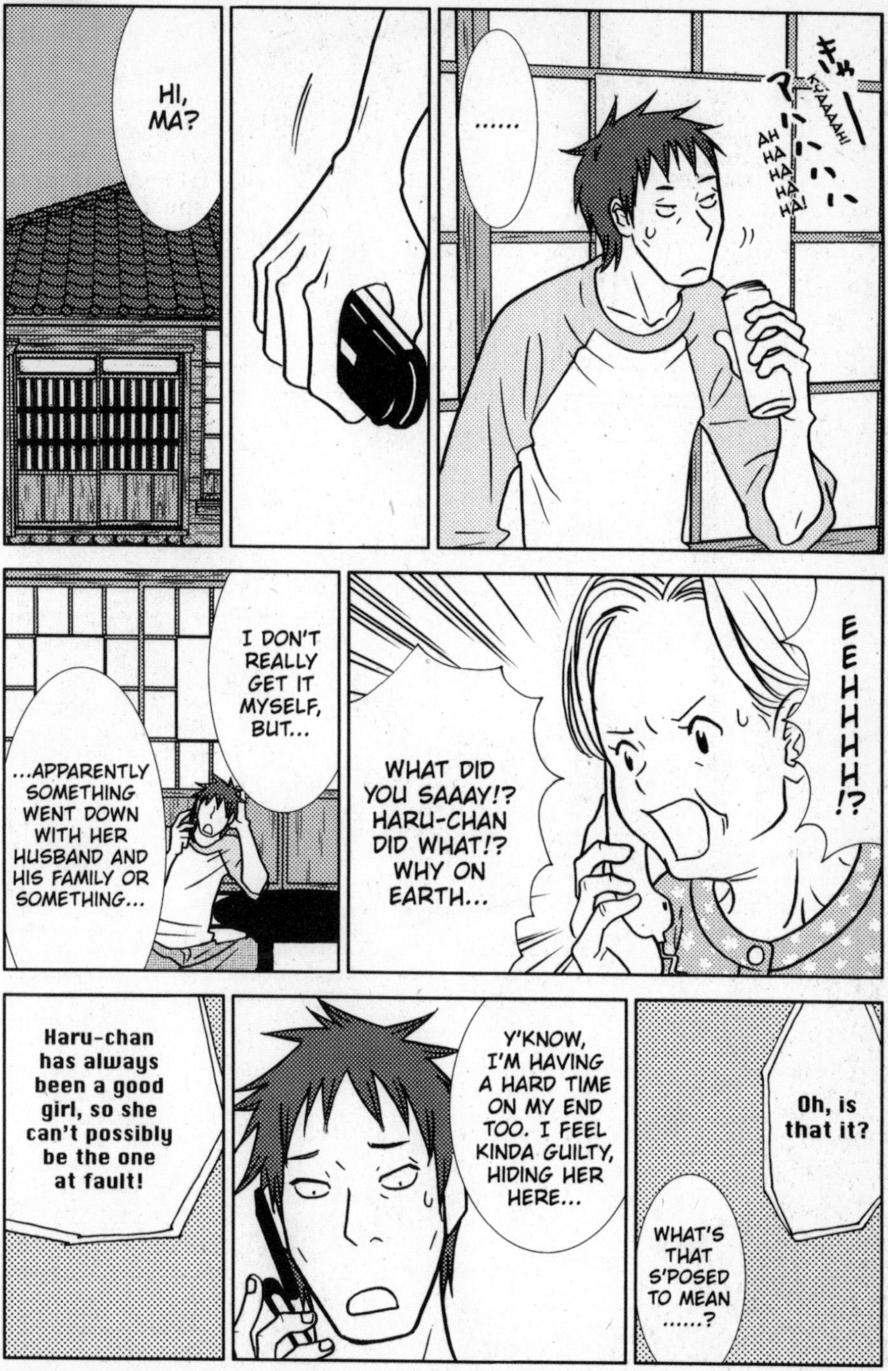

きゃー
KYAAAAAH!
アハハハハ
AH HA HA HA HA!
......
HI, MA?
EEHHHHH!?
WHAT DID YOU SAAAY!? HARU-CHAN DID WHAT!? WHY ON EARTH...
I DON'T REALLY GET IT MYSELF, BUT...
...APPARENTLY SOMETHING WENT DOWN WITH HER HUSBAND AND HIS FAMILY OR SOMETHING...
Oh, is that it?
WHAT'S THAT S'POSED TO MEAN ......?
Y'KNOW, I'M HAVING A HARD TIME ON MY END TOO. I FEEL KINDA GUILTY, HIDING HER HERE...
Haru-chan has always been a good girl, so she can't possibly be the one at fault!

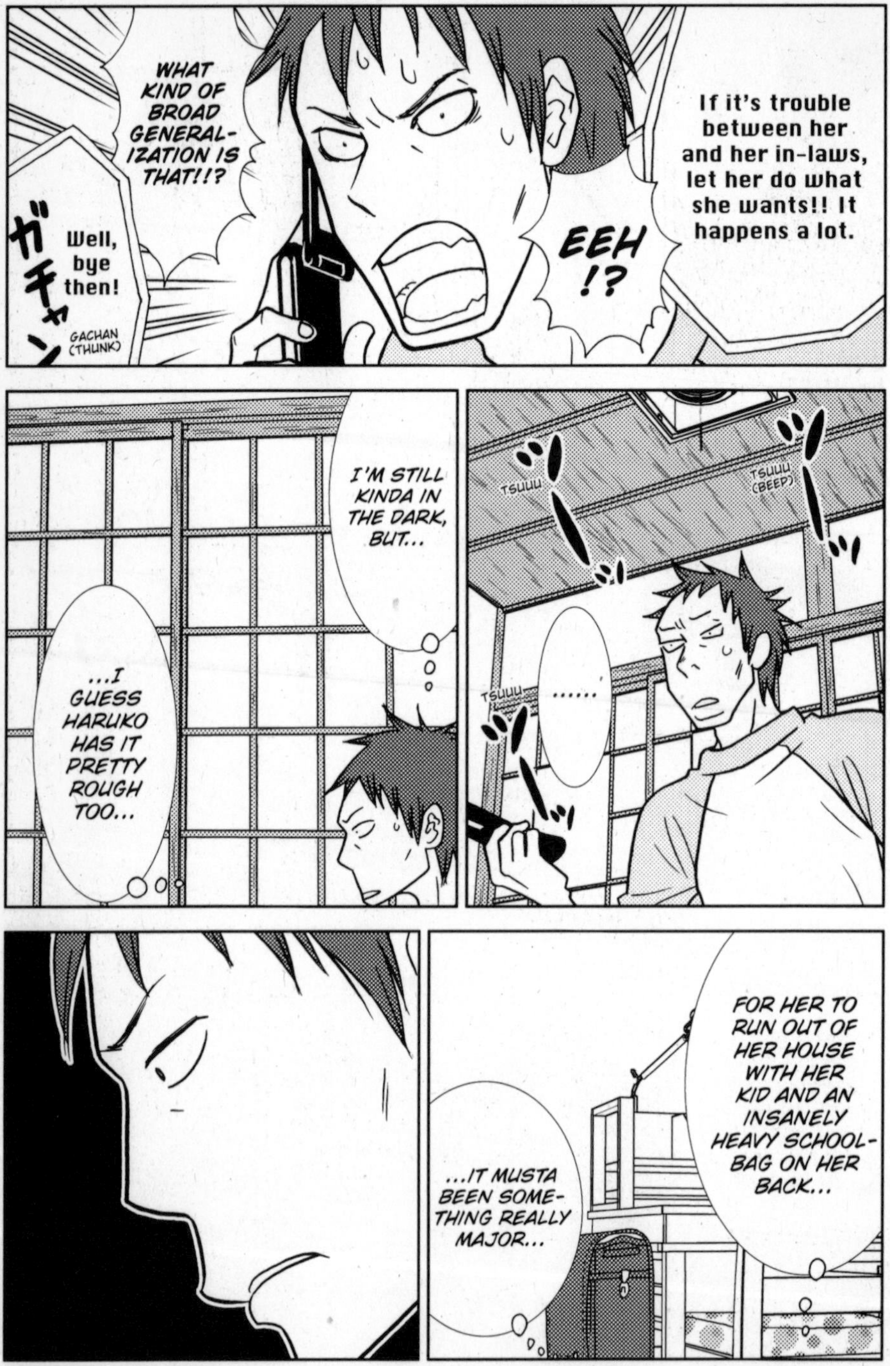
If it's trouble between her and her in-laws, let her do what she wants!! It happens a lot.
EEH!?
WHAT KIND OF BROAD GENERAL-IZATION IS THAT!!?
Well, bye then!
ガチャン
GACHAN (THUNK)
TSUUU (BEEP)
TSUUU
......
TSUUU
I'M STILL KINDA IN THE DARK, BUT...
...I GUESS HARUKO HAS IT PRETTY ROUGH TOO...
FOR HER TO RUN OUT OF HER HOUSE WITH HER KID AND AN INSANELY HEAVY SCHOOL-BAG ON HER BACK...
...IT MUSTA BEEN SOME-THING REALLY MAJOR...

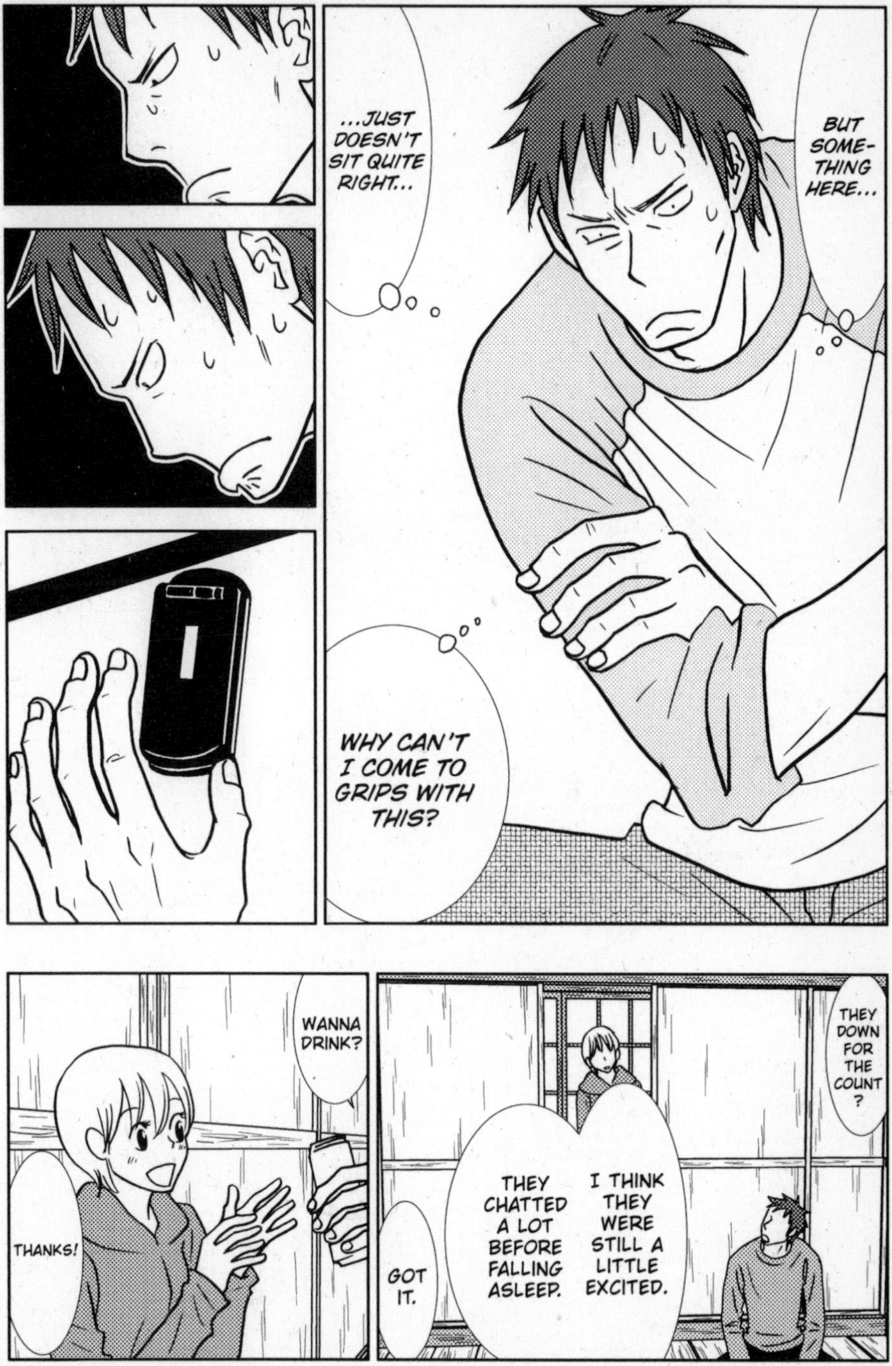
BUT SOME-THING HERE...
...JUST DOESN'T SIT QUITE RIGHT...
WHY CAN'T I COME TO GRIPS WITH THIS?
THEY DOWN FOR THE COUNT?
I THINK THEY WERE STILL A LITTLE EXCITED.
THEY CHATTED A LOT BEFORE FALLING ASLEEP.
GOT IT.
WANNA DRINK?
THANKS!

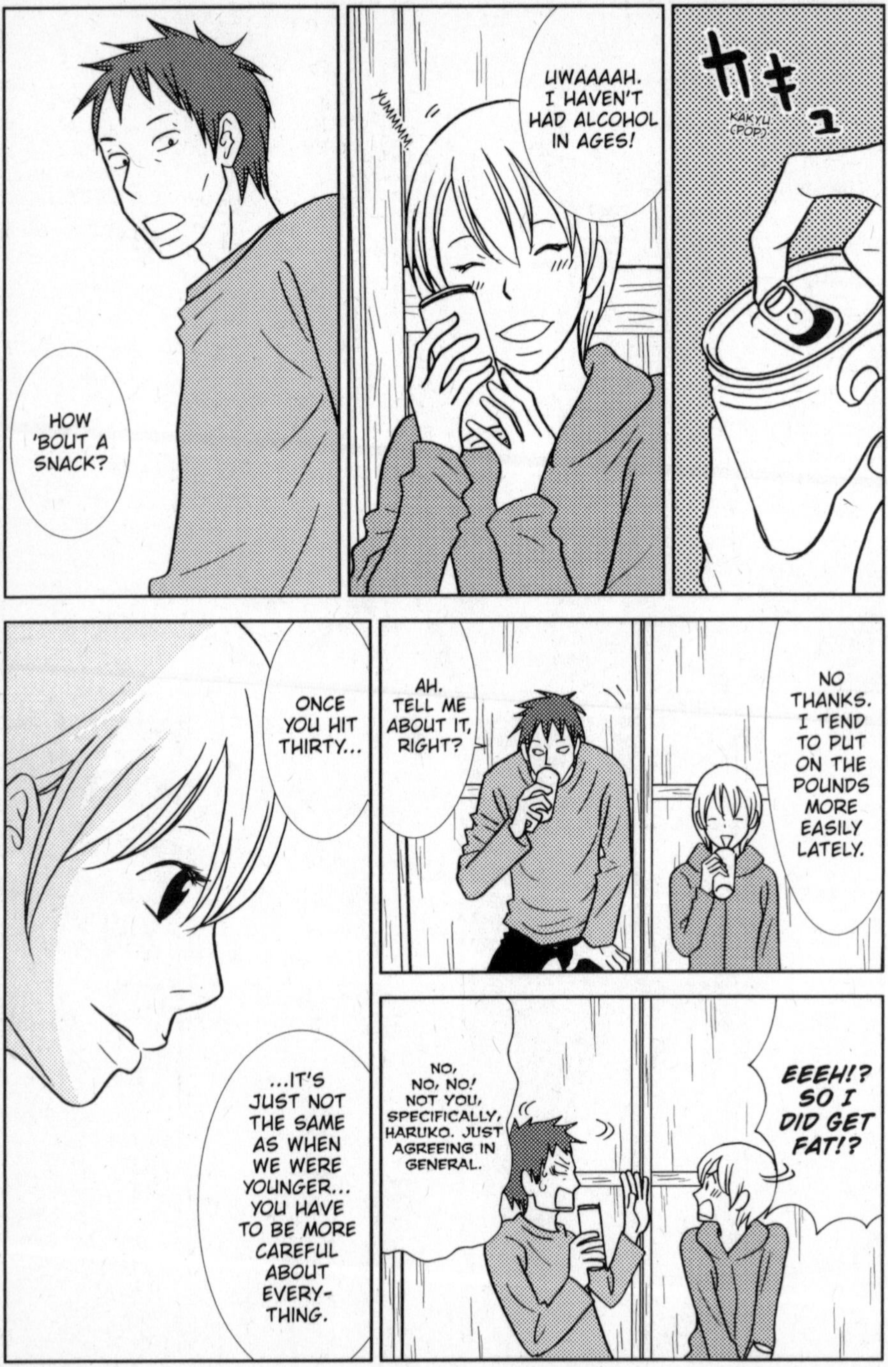
カキュ
KAKYU (POP)
UWAAAAH. I HAVEN'T HAD ALCOHOL IN AGES!
YUMMMM.
HOW 'BOUT A SNACK?
NO THANKS. I TEND TO PUT ON THE POUNDS MORE EASILY LATELY.
AH. TELL ME ABOUT IT, RIGHT?
EEEH!? SO I DID GET FAT!?
NO, NO, NO! NOT YOU, SPECIFICALLY, HARUKO. JUST AGREEING IN GENERAL.
ONCE YOU HIT THIRTY...
...IT'S JUST NOT THE SAME AS WHEN WE WERE YOUNGER... YOU HAVE TO BE MORE CAREFUL ABOUT EVERY-THING.

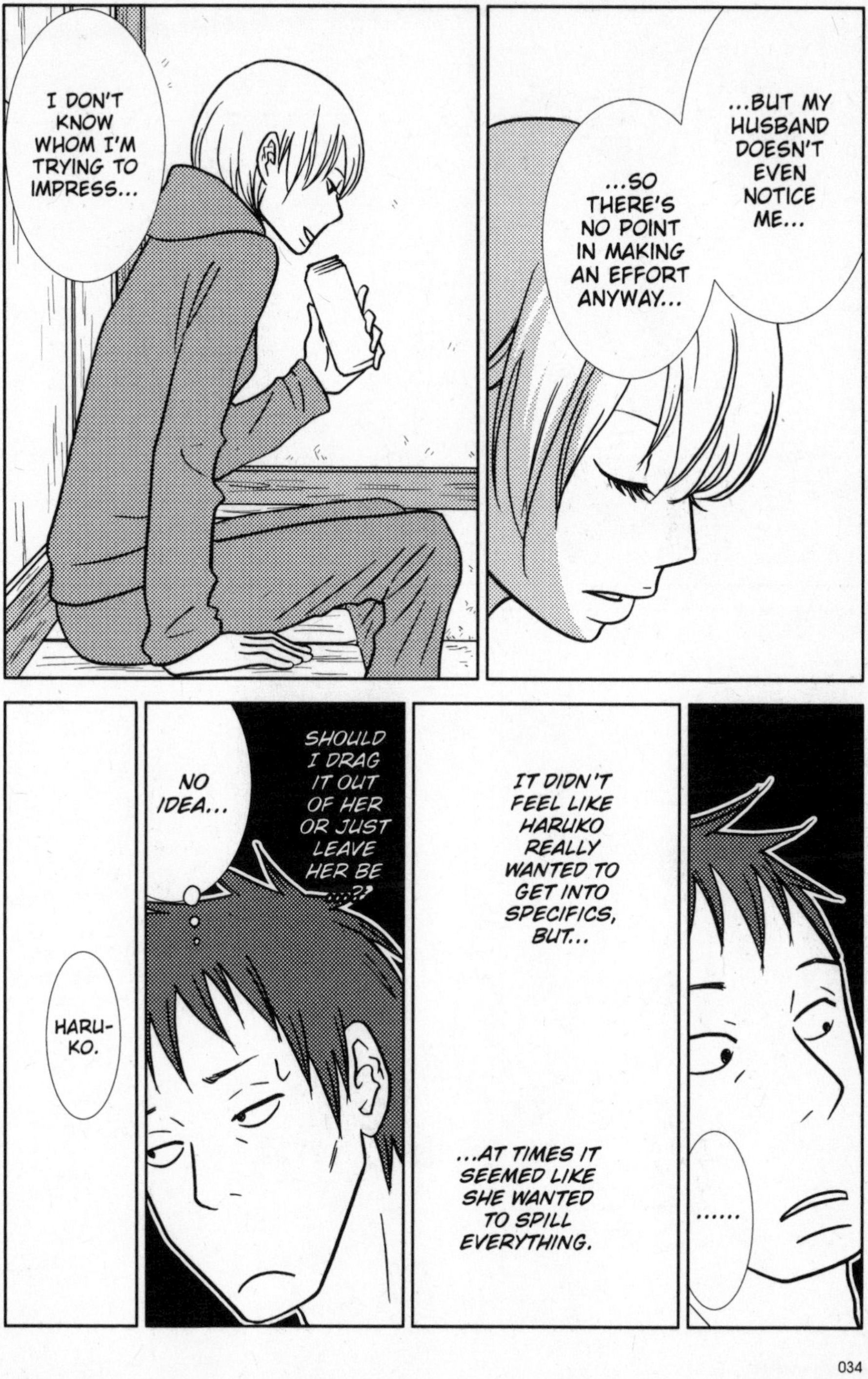
...BUT MY HUSBAND DOESN'T EVEN NOTICE ME...
...SO THERE'S NO POINT IN MAKING AN EFFORT ANYWAY...
I DON'T KNOW WHOM I'M TRYING TO IMPRESS...
......
IT DIDN'T FEEL LIKE HARUKO REALLY WANTED TO GET INTO SPECIFICS, BUT...
...AT TIMES IT SEEMED LIKE SHE WANTED TO SPILL EVERYTHING.
SHOULD I DRAG IT OUT OF HER OR JUST LEAVE HER BE ??
NO IDEA...
HARU-KO.

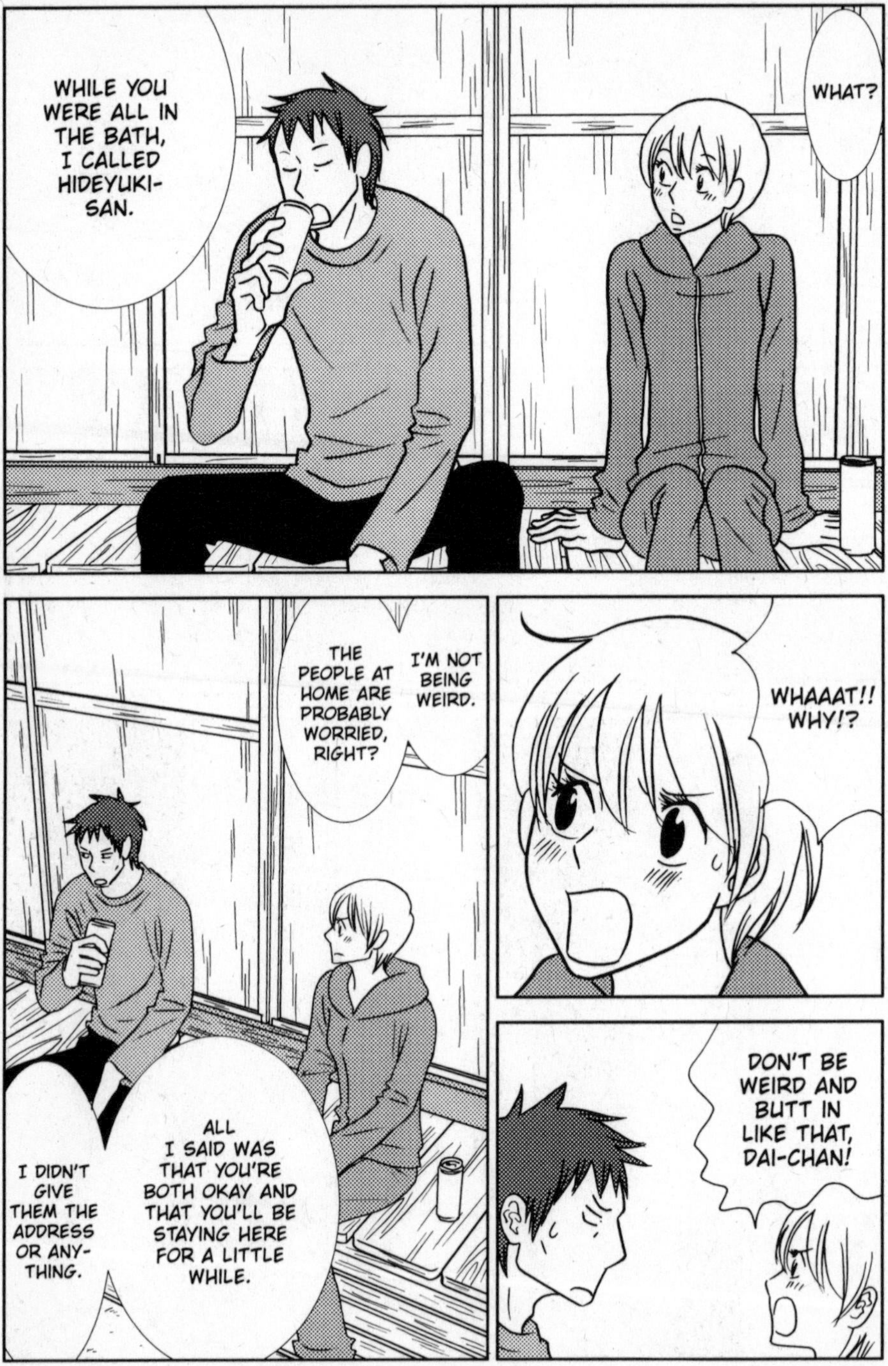
WHILE YOU WERE ALL IN THE BATH, I CALLED HIDEYUKI-SAN.
WHAT?
WHAAAT!! WHY!?
DON'T BE WEIRD AND BUTT IN LIKE THAT, DAI-CHAN!
I'M NOT BEING WEIRD.
THE PEOPLE AT HOME ARE PROBABLY WORRIED, RIGHT?
ALL I SAID WAS THAT YOU'RE BOTH OKAY AND THAT YOU'LL BE STAYING HERE FOR A LITTLE WHILE.
I DIDN'T GIVE THEM THE ADDRESS OR ANY-THING.

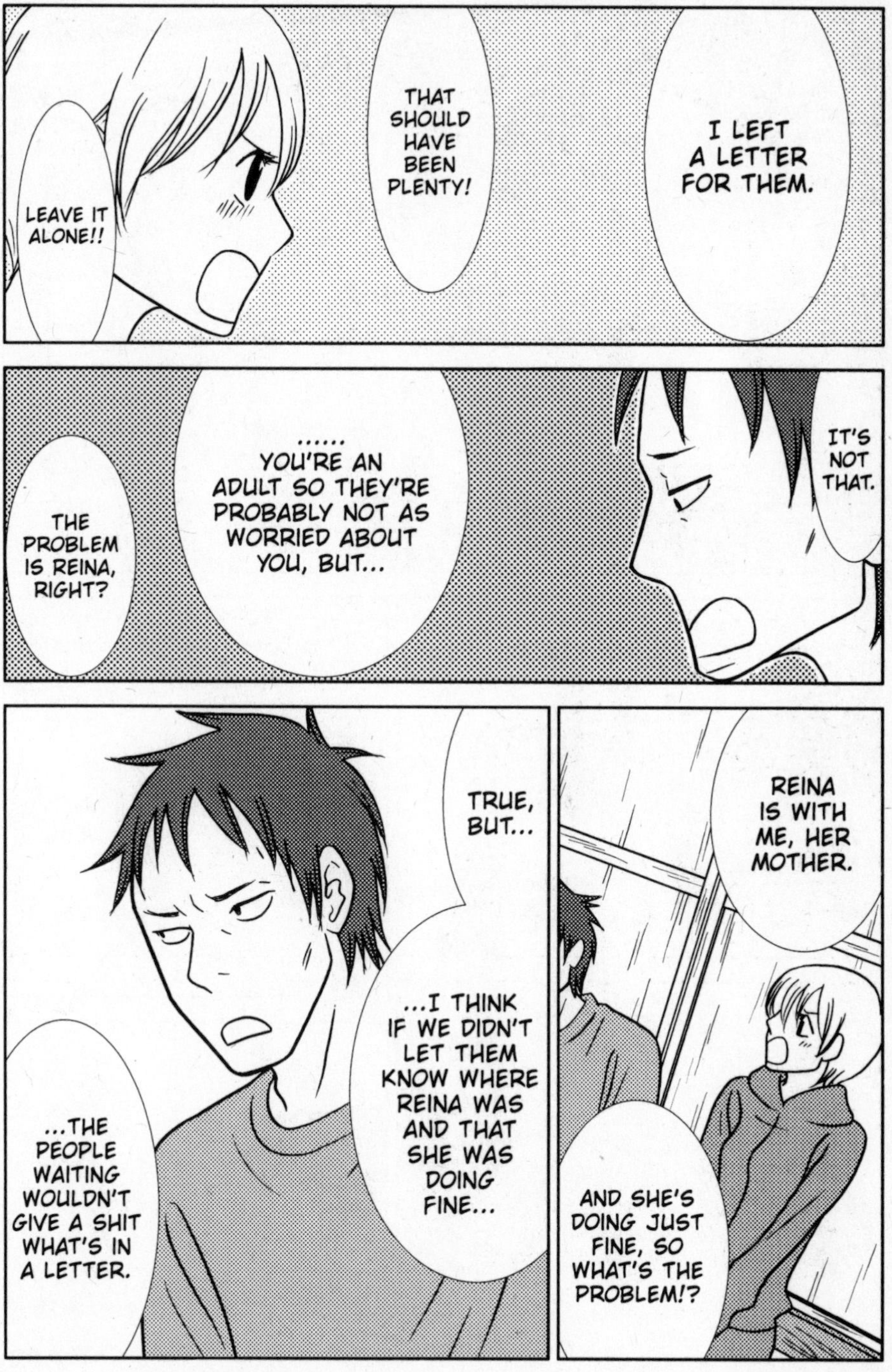
I LEFT A LETTER FOR THEM.
THAT SHOULD HAVE BEEN PLENTY!
LEAVE IT ALONE!!
IT'S NOT THAT.
...... YOU'RE AN ADULT SO THEY'RE PROBABLY NOT AS WORRIED ABOUT YOU, BUT...
THE PROBLEM IS REINA, RIGHT?
REINA IS WITH ME, HER MOTHER.
AND SHE'S DOING JUST FINE, SO WHAT'S THE PROBLEM!?
TRUE, BUT...
...I THINK IF WE DIDN'T LET THEM KNOW WHERE REINA WAS AND THAT SHE WAS DOING FINE...
...THE PEOPLE WAITING WOULDN'T GIVE A SHIT WHAT'S IN A LETTER.

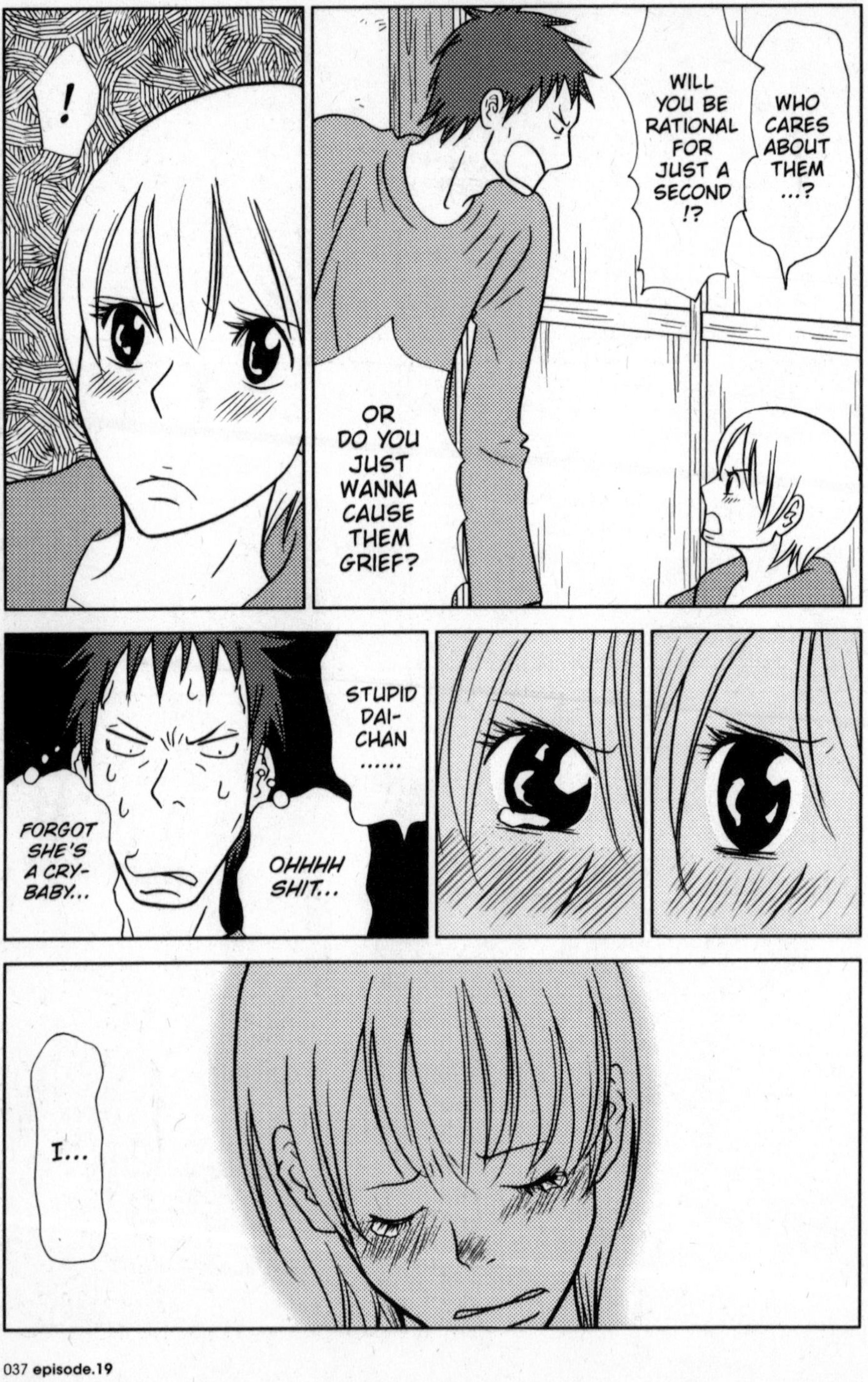
WHO CARES ABOUT THEM ...?
WILL YOU BE RATIONAL FOR JUST A SECOND !?
OR DO YOU JUST WANNA CAUSE THEM GRIEF?
!
STUPID DAI-CHAN ......
OHHHH SHIT...
FORGOT SHE'S A CRY-BABY...
I...

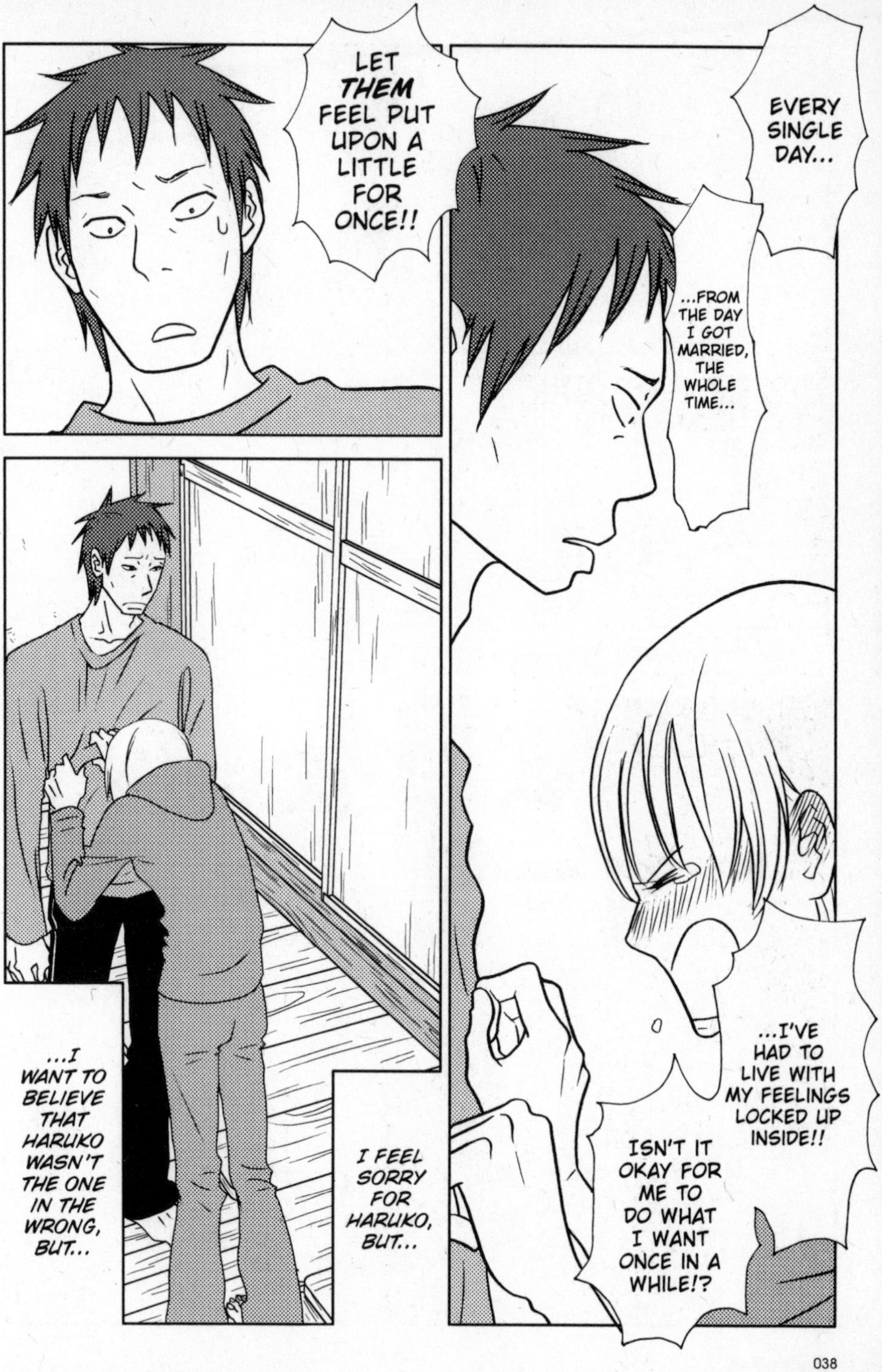
EVERY SINGLE DAY...
...FROM THE DAY I GOT MARRIED, THE WHOLE TIME...
...I'VE HAD TO LIVE WITH MY FEELINGS LOCKED UP INSIDE!!
ISN'T IT OKAY FOR ME TO DO WHAT I WANT ONCE IN A WHILE!?
LET *THEM* FEEL PUT UPON A LITTLE FOR ONCE!!
I FEEL SORRY FOR HARUKO, BUT...
...I WANT TO BELIEVE THAT HARUKO WASN'T THE ONE IN THE WRONG, BUT...

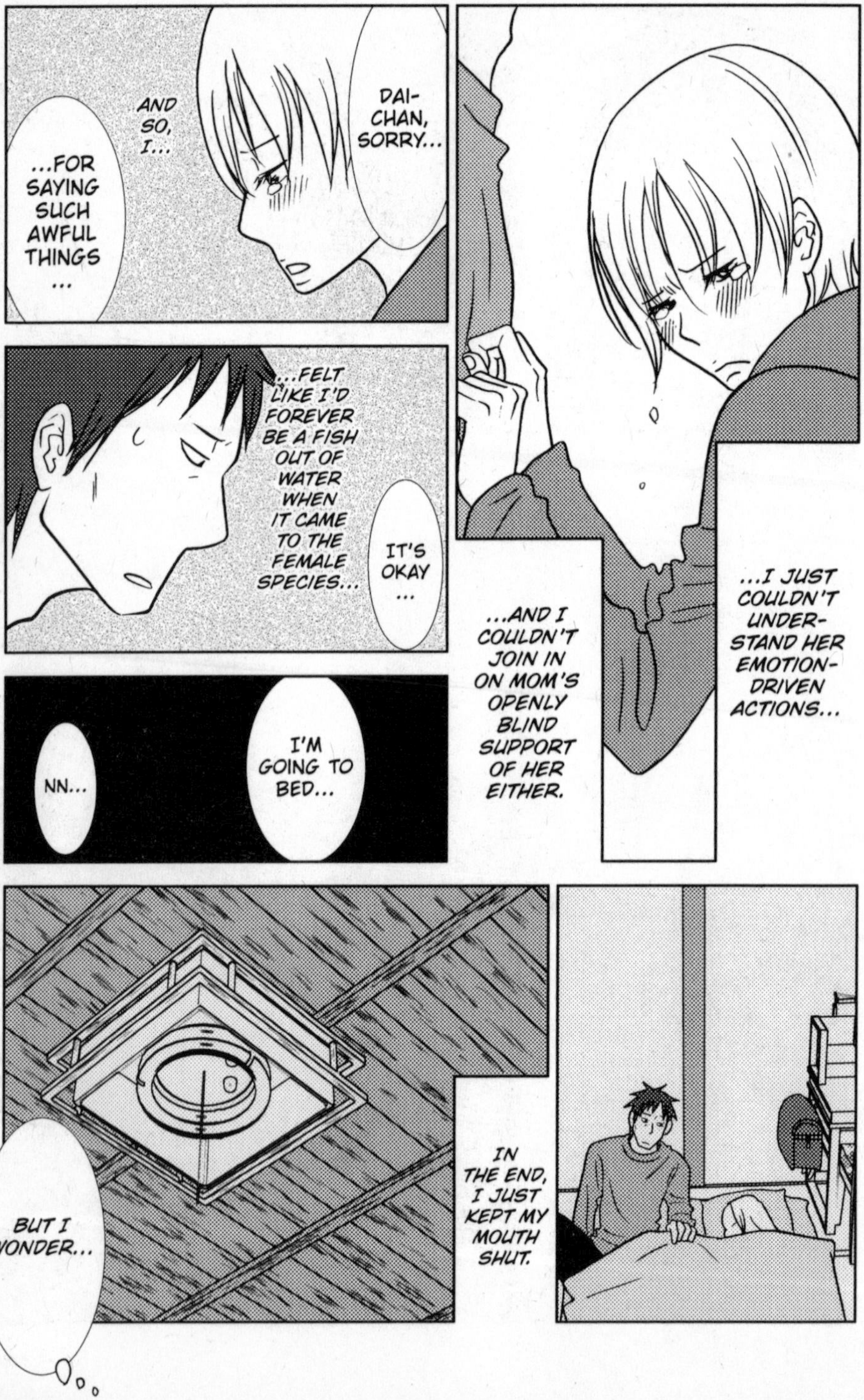
...I JUST COULDN'T UNDERSTAND HER EMOTION-DRIVEN ACTIONS...
...AND I COULDN'T JOIN IN ON MOM'S OPENLY BLIND SUPPORT OF HER EITHER.
DAI-CHAN, SORRY...
AND SO, I...
...FOR SAYING SUCH AWFUL THINGS...
IT'S OKAY...
...FELT LIKE I'D FOREVER BE A FISH OUT OF WATER WHEN IT CAME TO THE FEMALE SPECIES...
I'M GOING TO BED...
NN...
IN THE END, I JUST KEPT MY MOUTH SHUT.
BUT I WONDER...

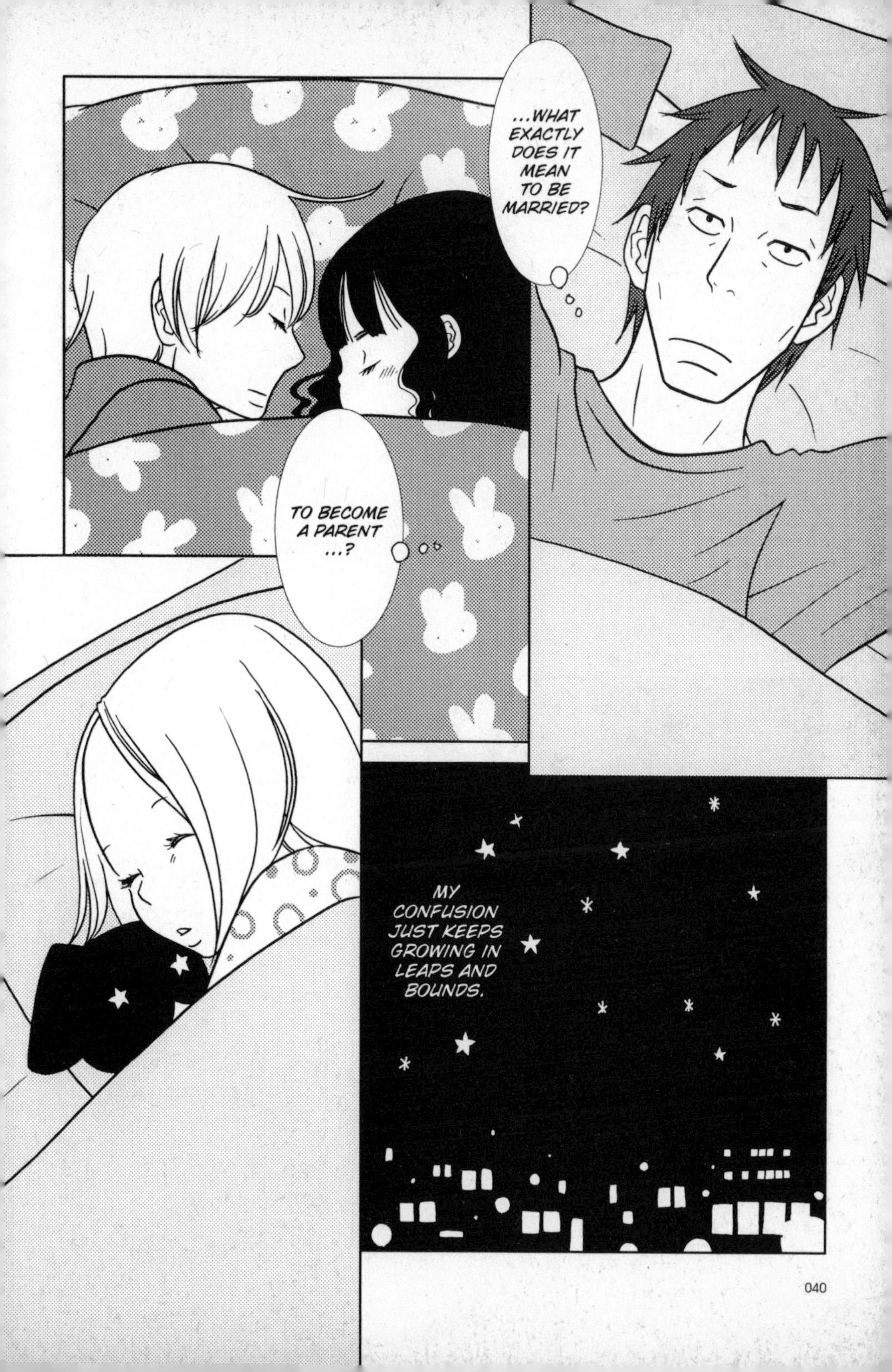
...WHAT EXACTLY DOES IT MEAN TO BE MARRIED?
TO BECOME A PARENT ...?
MY CONFUSION JUST KEEPS GROWING IN LEAPS AND BOUNDS.

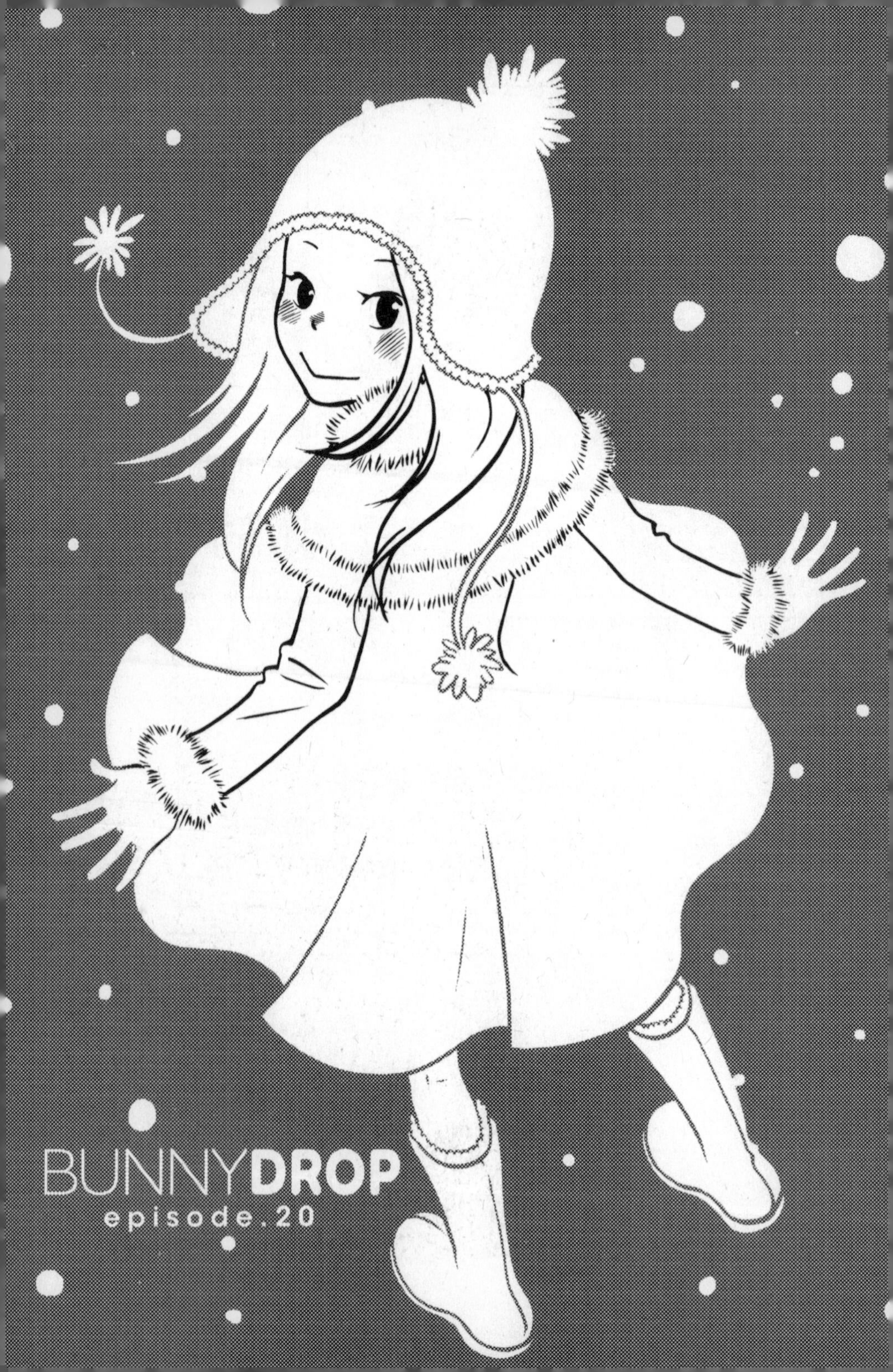
BUNNYDROP
episode.20

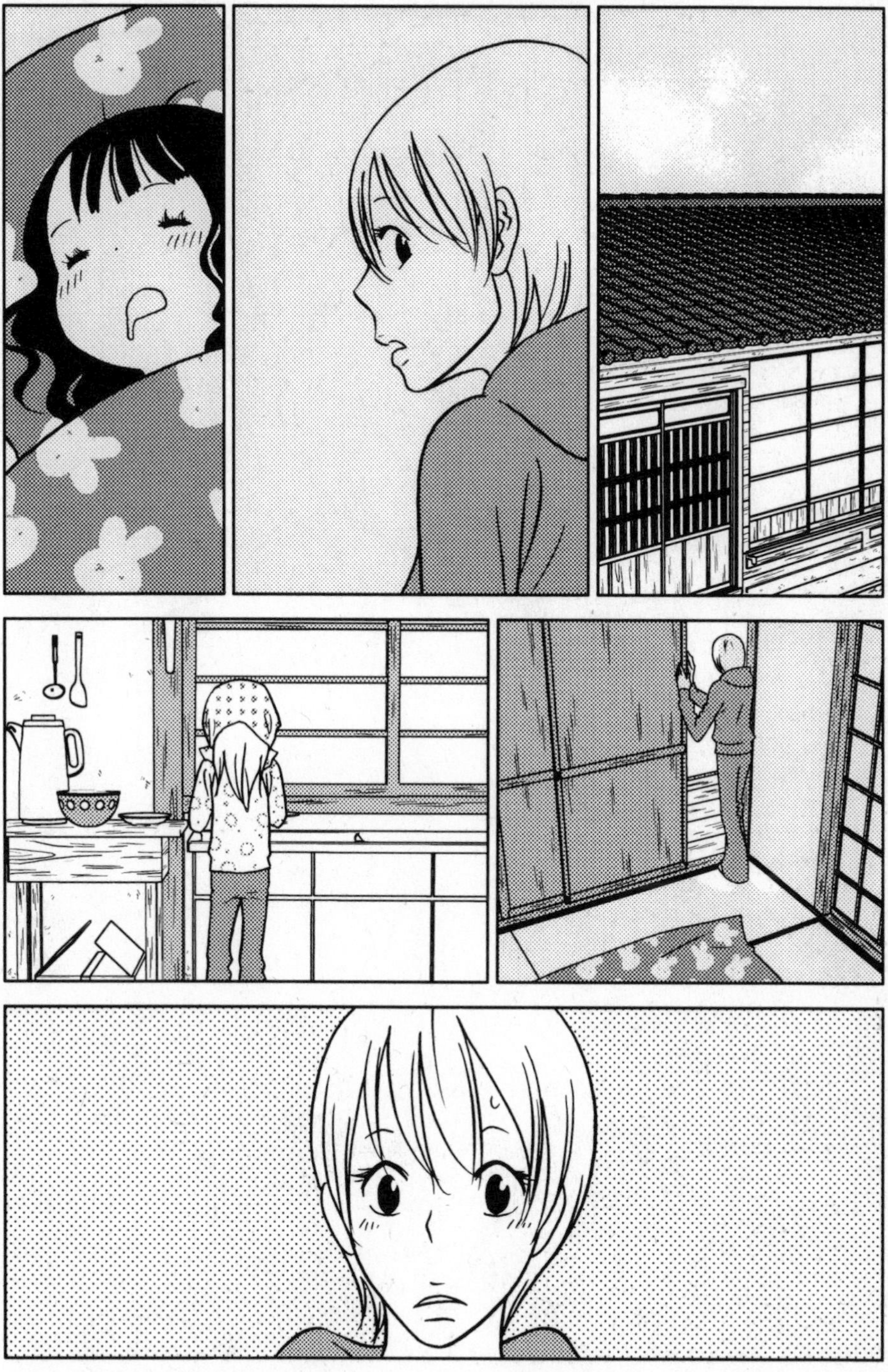

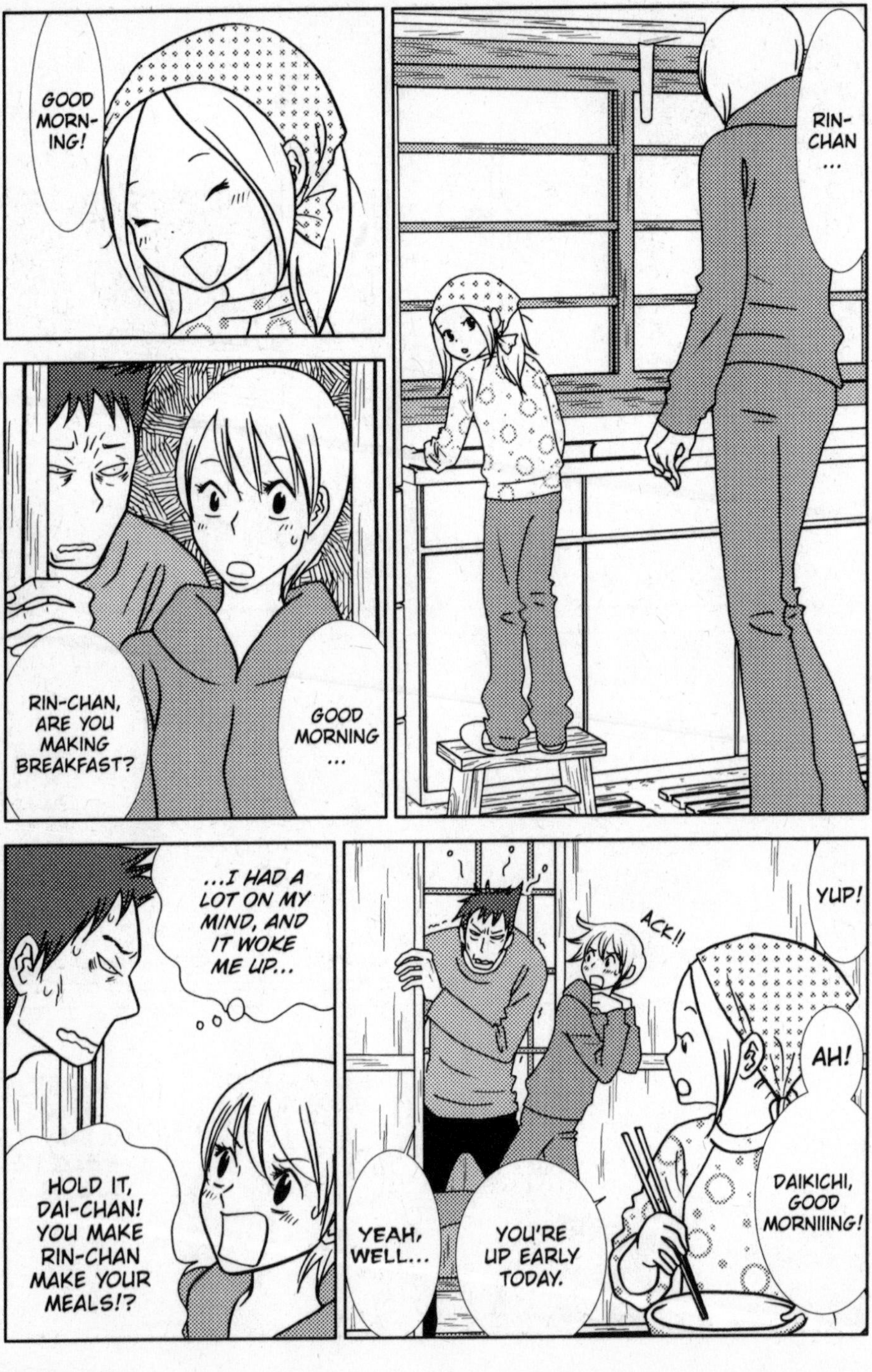
RIN-CHAN...
GOOD MORNING!
GOOD MORNING...
RIN-CHAN, ARE YOU MAKING BREAKFAST?
YUP!
ACK!!
AH!
DAIKICHI, GOOD MORNIIING!
YOU'RE UP EARLY TODAY.
YEAH, WELL...
...I HAD A LOT ON MY MIND, AND IT WOKE ME UP...
HOLD IT, DAI-CHAN! YOU MAKE RIN-CHAN MAKE YOUR MEALS!?

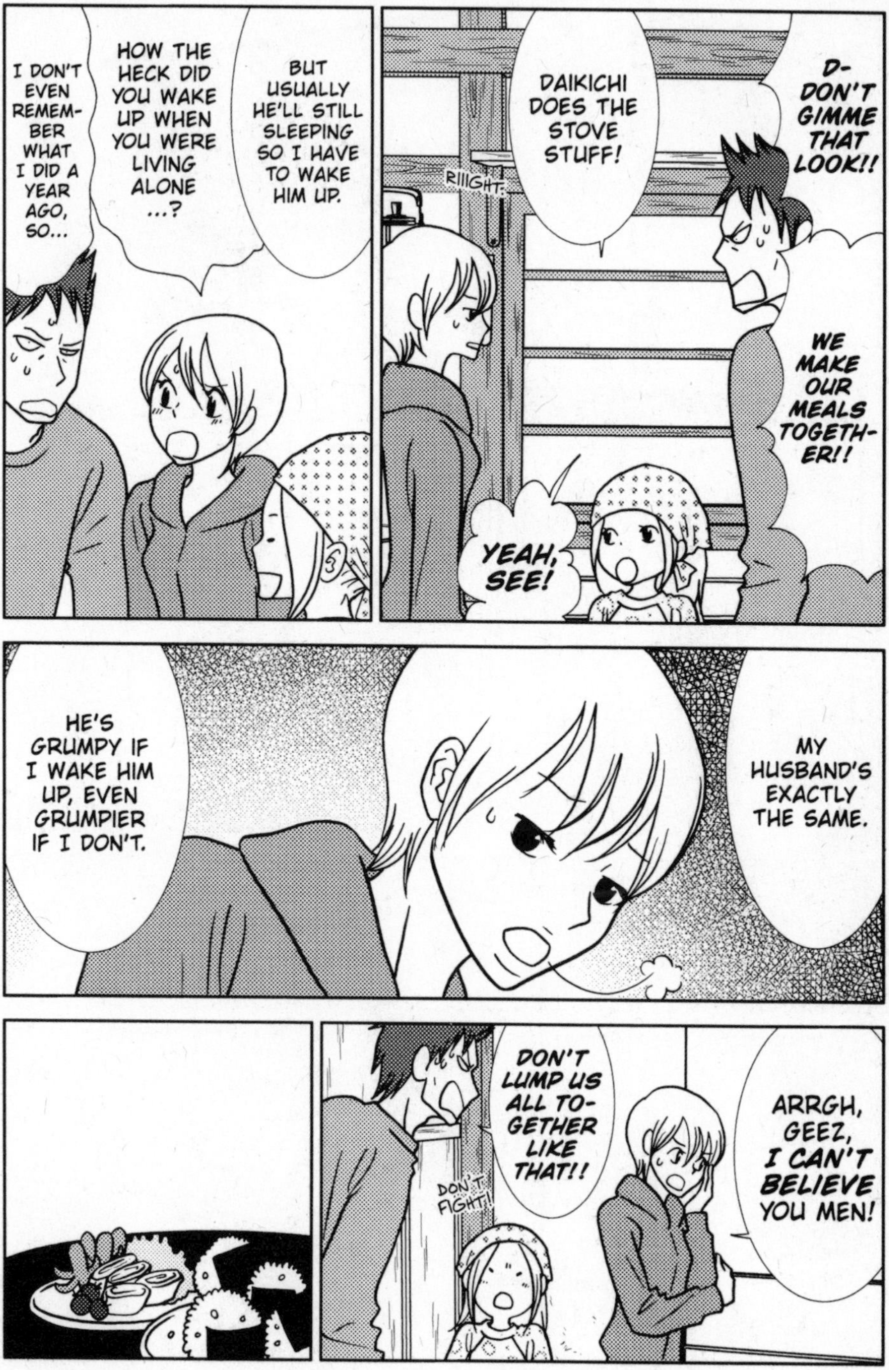
D-DON'T GIMME THAT LOOK!!
DAIKICHI DOES THE STOVE STUFF!
RIIIGHT.
WE MAKE OUR MEALS TOGETHER!!
YEAH, SEE!
BUT USUALLY HE'LL STILL SLEEPING SO I HAVE TO WAKE HIM UP.
HOW THE HECK DID YOU WAKE UP WHEN YOU WERE LIVING ALONE ...?
I DON'T EVEN REMEMBER WHAT I DID A YEAR AGO, SO...
MY HUSBAND'S EXACTLY THE SAME.
HE'S GRUMPY IF I WAKE HIM UP, EVEN GRUMPIER IF I DON'T.
ARRGH, GEEZ, I CAN'T BELIEVE YOU MEN!
DON'T LUMP US ALL TOGETHER LIKE THAT!!
DON'T FIGHT!

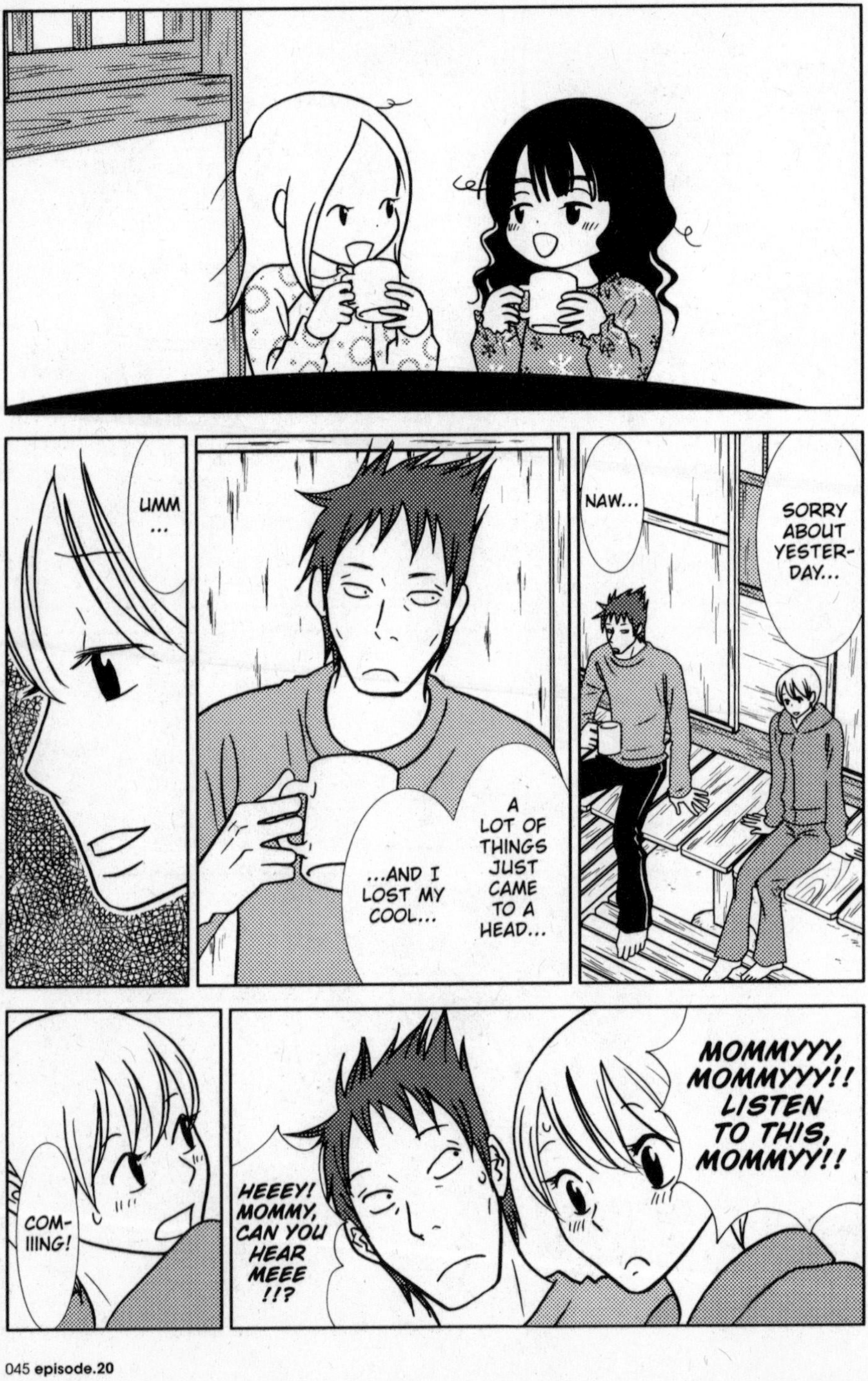
SORRY ABOUT YESTER-DAY...
NAW...
A LOT OF THINGS JUST CAME TO A HEAD...
...AND I LOST MY COOL...
UMM ...
MOMMYYY, MOMMYYY!! LISTEN TO THIS, MOMMYY!!
HEEEY! MOMMY, CAN YOU HEAR MEEE !!?
COM-IIING!

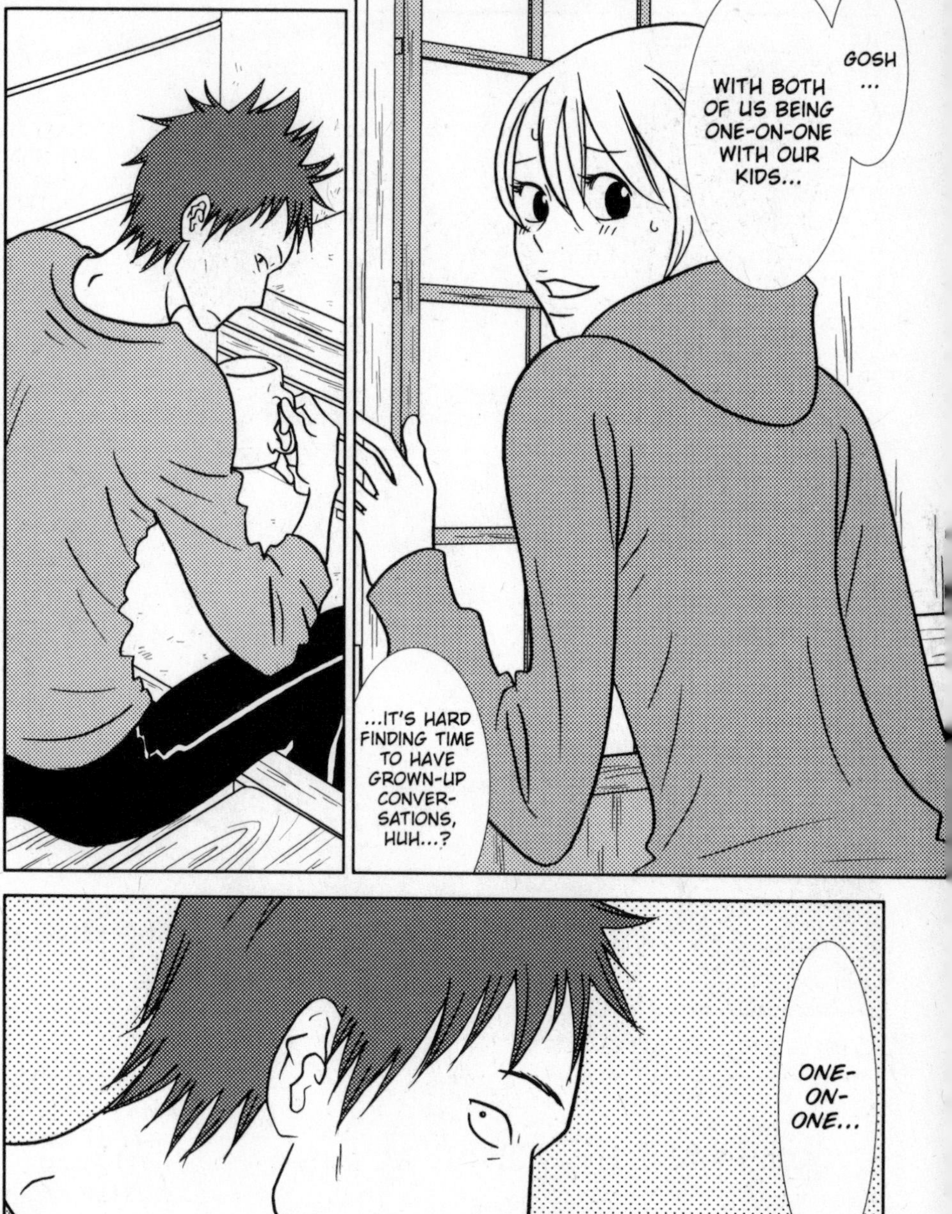
GOSH ...
WITH BOTH OF US BEING ONE-ON-ONE WITH OUR KIDS...
...IT'S HARD FINDING TIME TO HAVE GROWN-UP CONVER-SATIONS, HUH...?
ONE-ON-ONE...

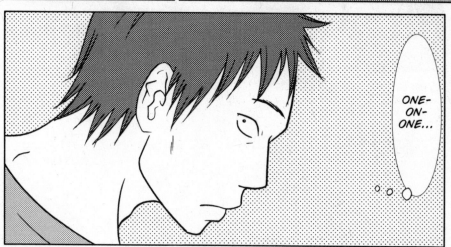

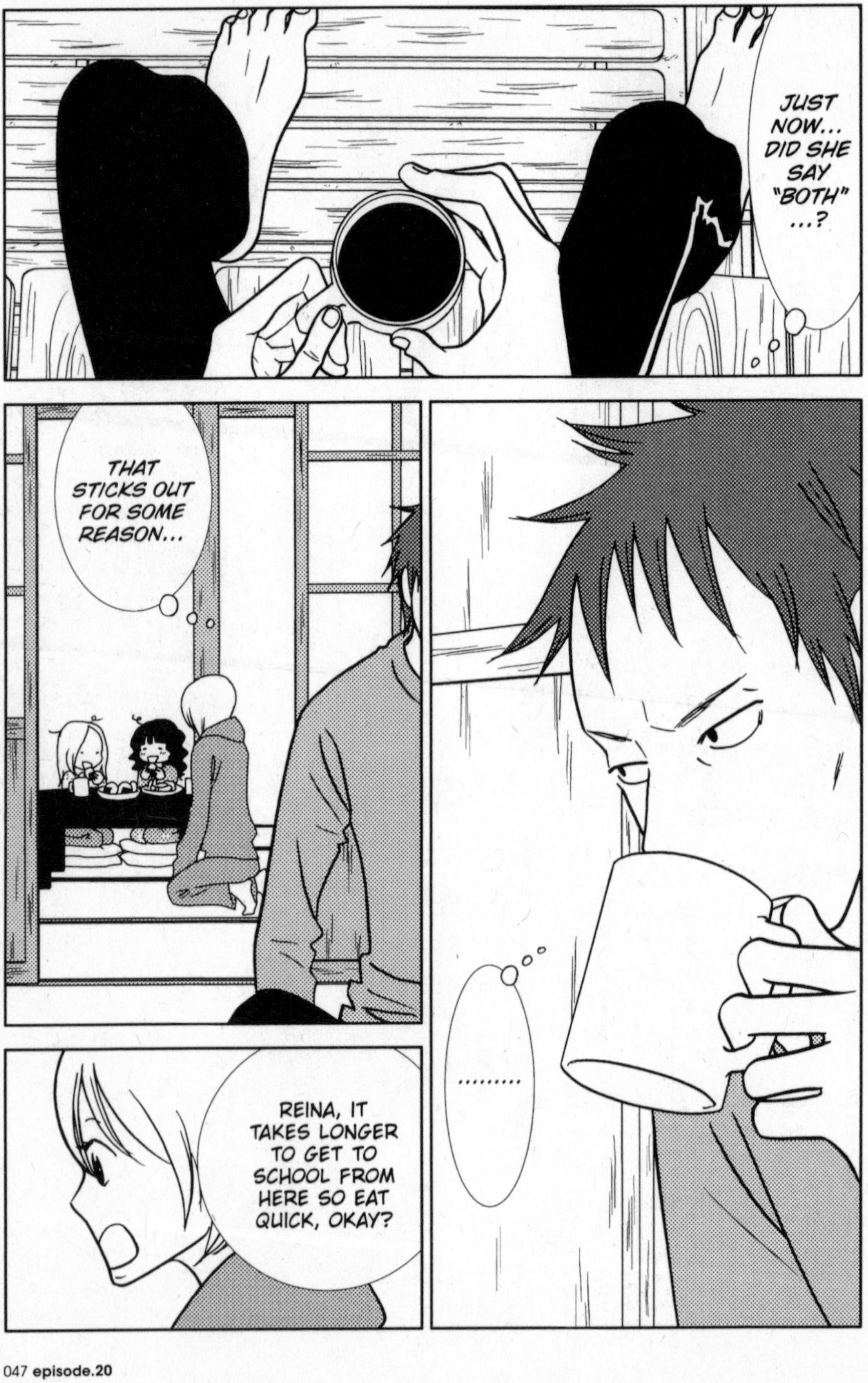
JUST NOW... DID SHE SAY "BOTH" ...?
....
THAT STICKS OUT FOR SOME REASON...
REINA, IT TAKES LONGER TO GET TO SCHOOL FROM HERE SO EAT QUICK, OKAY?

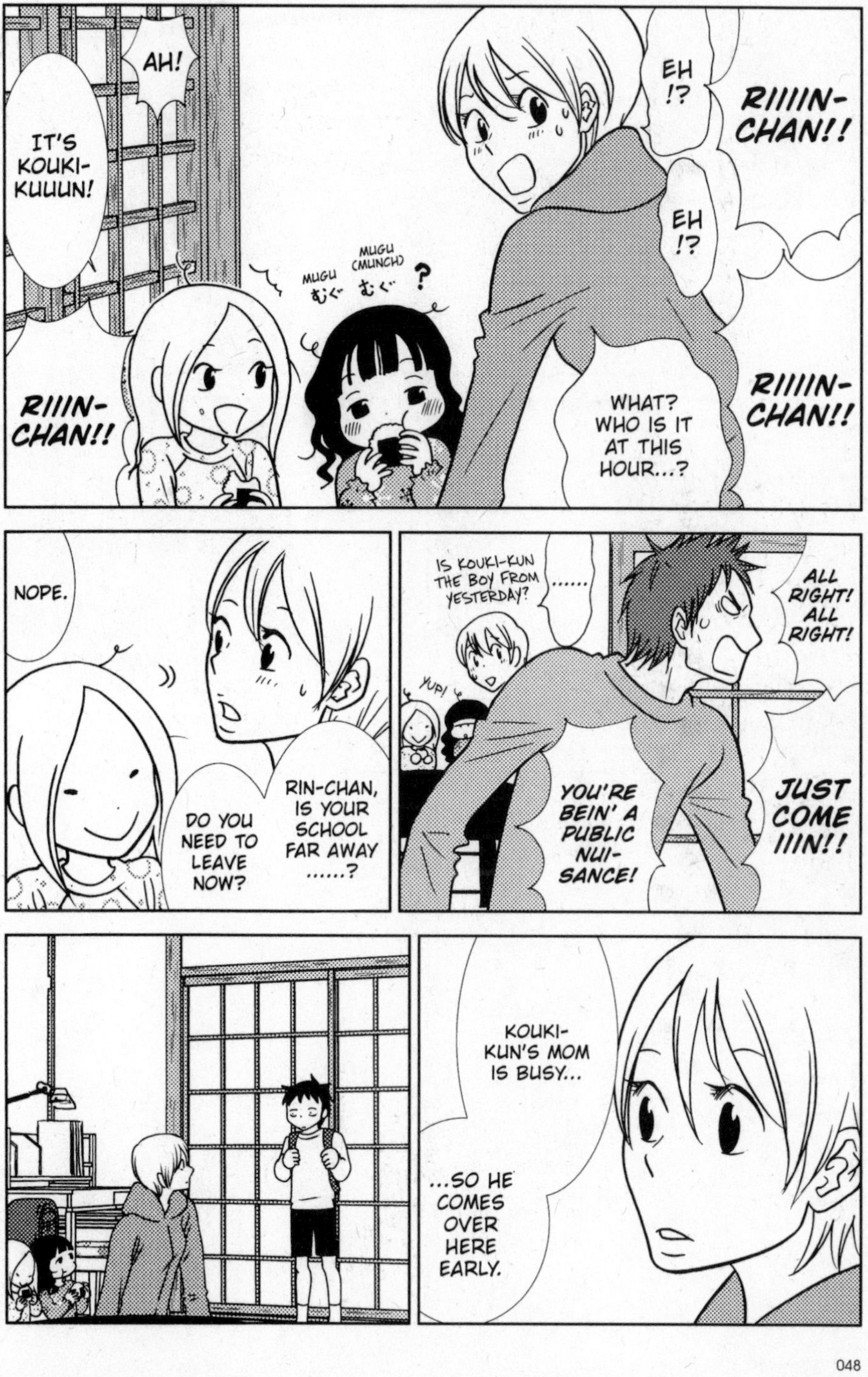
RIIIIN-CHAN!!
EH!?
EH!?
RIIIIN-CHAN!!
WHAT? WHO IS IT AT THIS HOUR...?
AH!
IT'S KOUKI-KUUUN!
MUGU (MUNCH) むぐ
MUGU むぐ
?
RIIIN-CHAN!!
ALL RIGHT! ALL RIGHT!
......
IS KOUKI-KUN THE BOY FROM YESTERDAY?
JUST COME IIIN!!
YUP!
YOU'RE BEIN' A PUBLIC NUI-SANCE!
RIN-CHAN, IS YOUR SCHOOL FAR AWAY ......?
DO YOU NEED TO LEAVE NOW?
NOPE.
KOUKI-KUN'S MOM IS BUSY...
...SO HE COMES OVER HERE EARLY.

DAIKICHI, YOU GOT MARRIED!?
NO!!
SHE'S MY COUSIN!!
SHE SURE IS A TINY COUSIN!!
SHE'S A COUSIN ON MY MA'S SIDE!!
WHAT THE HELL ARE YOU TALKIN' ABOUT!?
!
DAIKICHI, CAN I HAVE AN ONIGIRI?
DIDN'T YOU EAT ALREADY?
DIIIIID.
YOU BRUSHED YOUR TEETH TOO, RIGHT?
YUPPP.
BUT TODAY'S MONDAY SO I BROUGHT MY TOOTHBRUSH WITH ME!!
HUH! ONCE IN A WHILE, YOU REALLY DO HAVE IT TO-GETHER...
FINE, EAT.
BUT JUST SO YOU KNOW, THAT'S MINE!!
ALL RIGHT!!

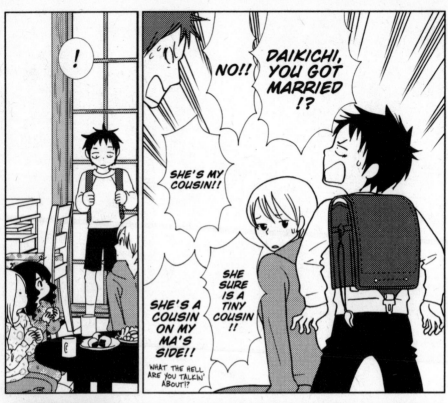

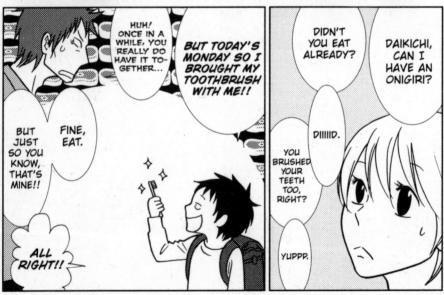

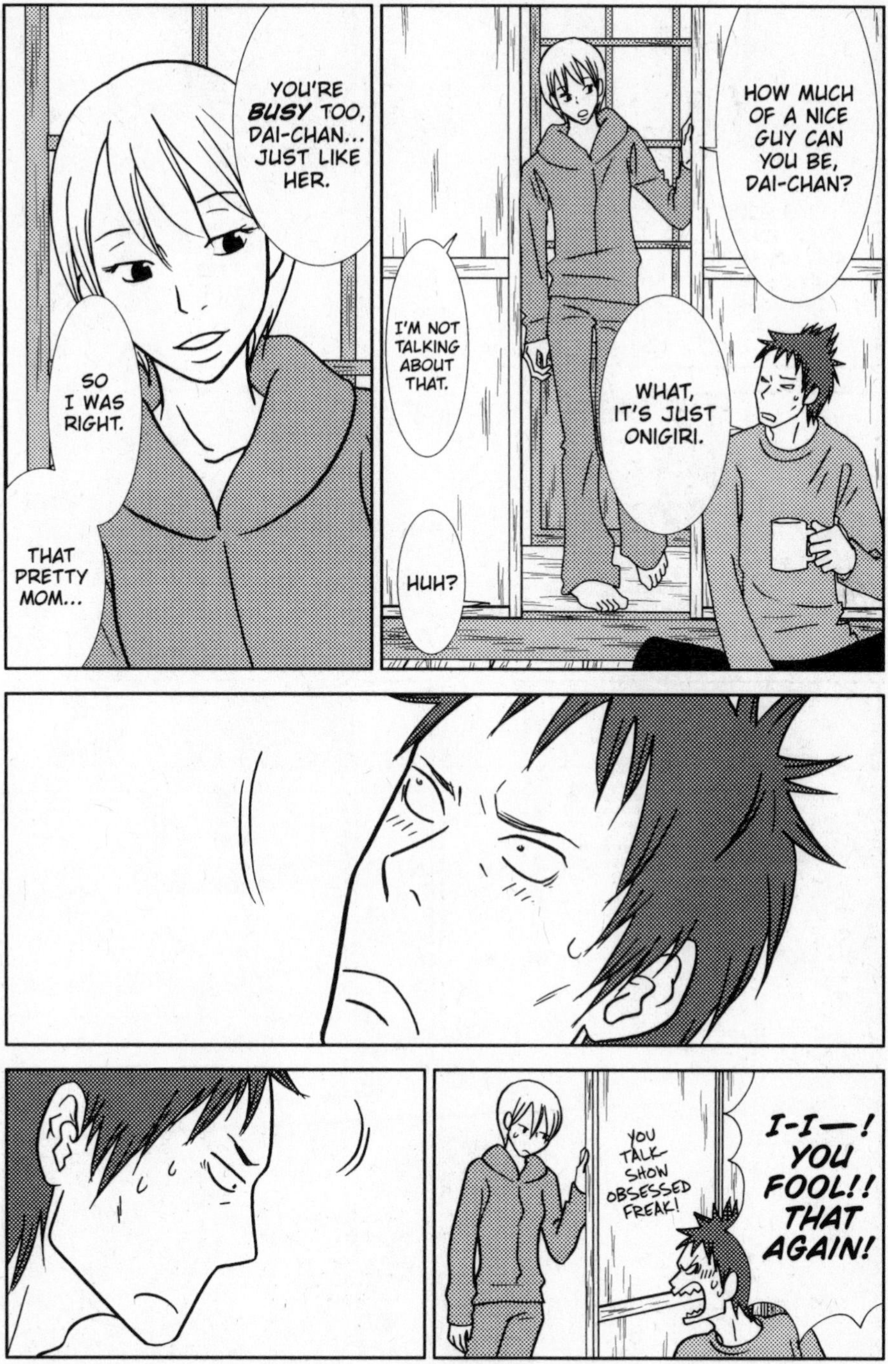
HOW MUCH OF A NICE GUY CAN YOU BE, DAI-CHAN?
WHAT, IT'S JUST ONIGIRI.
I'M NOT TALKING ABOUT THAT.
HUH?
YOU'RE BUSY TOO, DAI-CHAN... JUST LIKE HER.
SO I WAS RIGHT.
THAT PRETTY MOM...
I-I—! YOU FOOL!! THAT AGAIN!
YOU TALK SHOW OBSESSED FREAK!

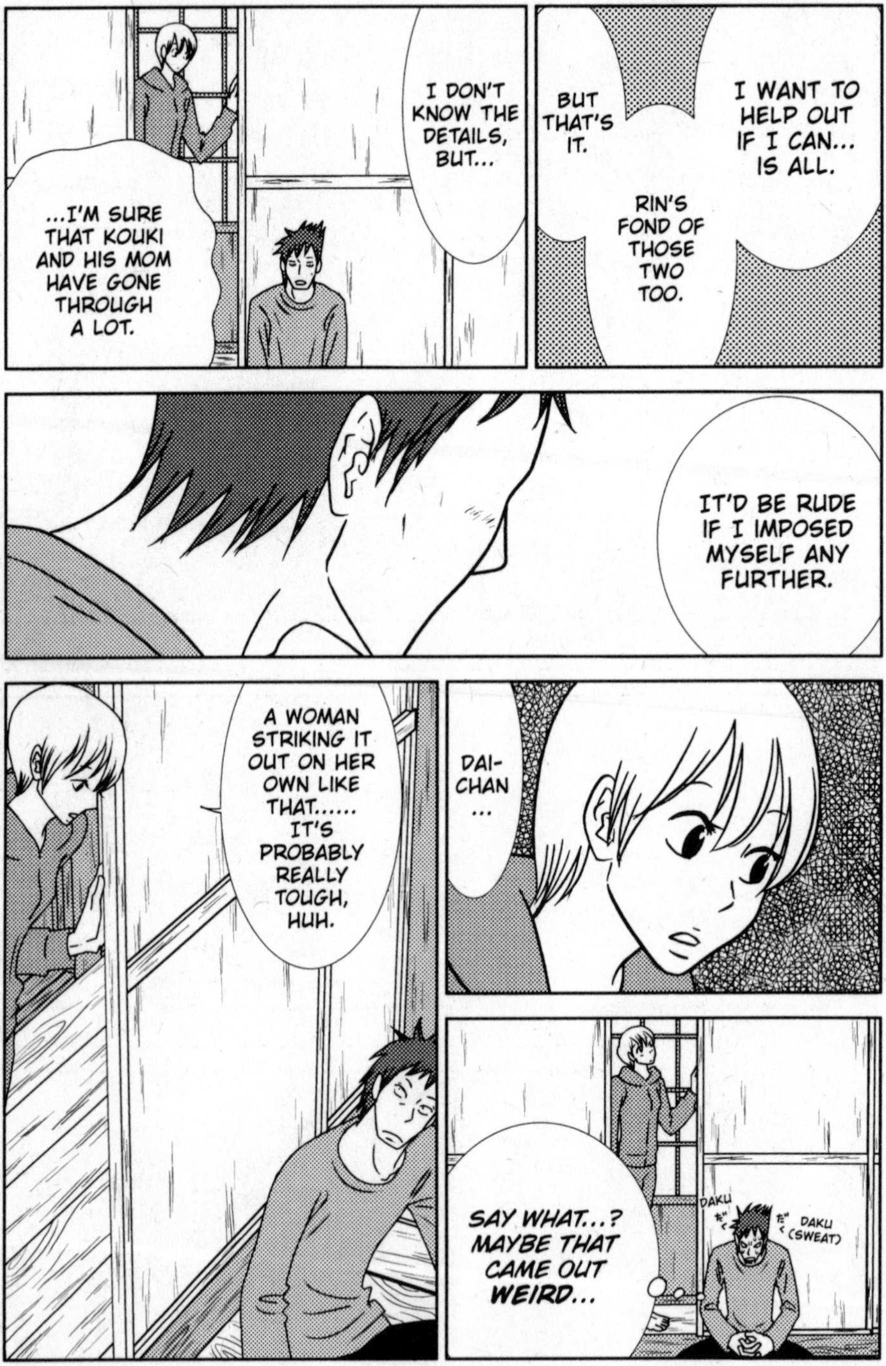
I WANT TO HELP OUT IF I CAN... IS ALL.
BUT THAT'S IT.
RIN'S FOND OF THOSE TWO TOO.
I DON'T KNOW THE DETAILS, BUT...
...I'M SURE THAT KOUKI AND HIS MOM HAVE GONE THROUGH A LOT.
IT'D BE RUDE IF I IMPOSED MYSELF ANY FURTHER.
DAI-CHAN ...
DAKU (SWEAT)
DAKU
SAY WHAT...? MAYBE THAT CAME OUT WEIRD...
A WOMAN STRIKING IT OUT ON HER OWN LIKE THAT...... IT'S PROBABLY REALLY TOUGH, HUH.

EH?
HARU-KO?
SU (TURN)
EH?
REINAAA! DIDN'T MOMMY TELL YOU THAT WE'LL BE LATE IF YOU DON'T HURRY?
EH?
BUT MOMMY, YOU HAVEN'T PUT ON YOUR MAKEUP YET!
WHA-WHAT? WHAT DID THAT MEAN?
MOMMY CAN BE READY IN A FLASH!
YOU TAKE LONGER THAN I DO, MOMMY!
OF COURSE WE DIDN'T HAVE TIME TO TALK PRIVATELY ANYMORE AFTER THAT...

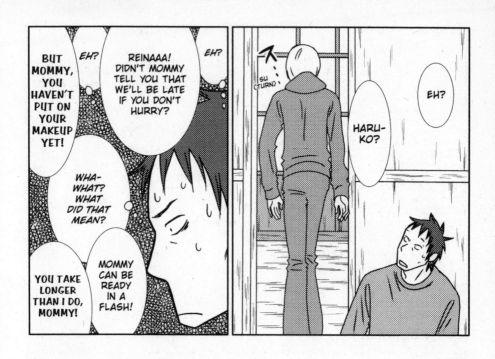

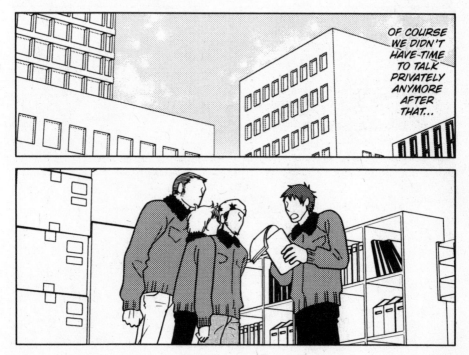

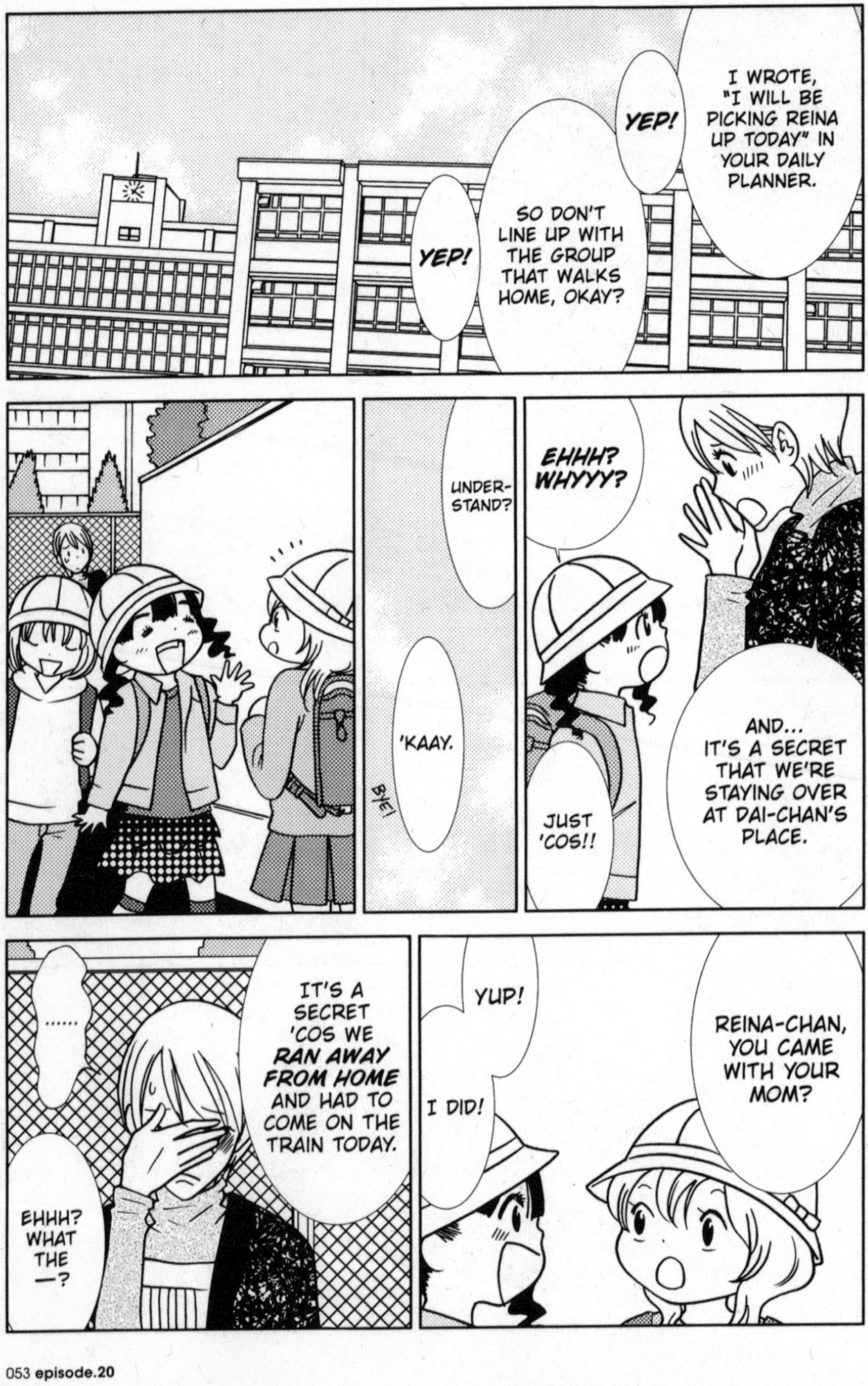

I WROTE, "I WILL BE PICKING REINA UP TODAY" IN YOUR DAILY PLANNER.
YEP!
SO DON'T LINE UP WITH THE GROUP THAT WALKS HOME, OKAY?
YEP!
AND... IT'S A SECRET THAT WE'RE STAYING OVER AT DAI-CHAN'S PLACE.
EHHH? WHYYY?
JUST 'COS!!
UNDER-STAND?
'KAAY.
BYE!
REINA-CHAN, YOU CAME WITH YOUR MOM?
YUP!
I DID!
IT'S A SECRET 'COS WE ***RAN AWAY FROM HOME*** AND HAD TO COME ON THE TRAIN TODAY.
......
EHHH? WHAT THE—?

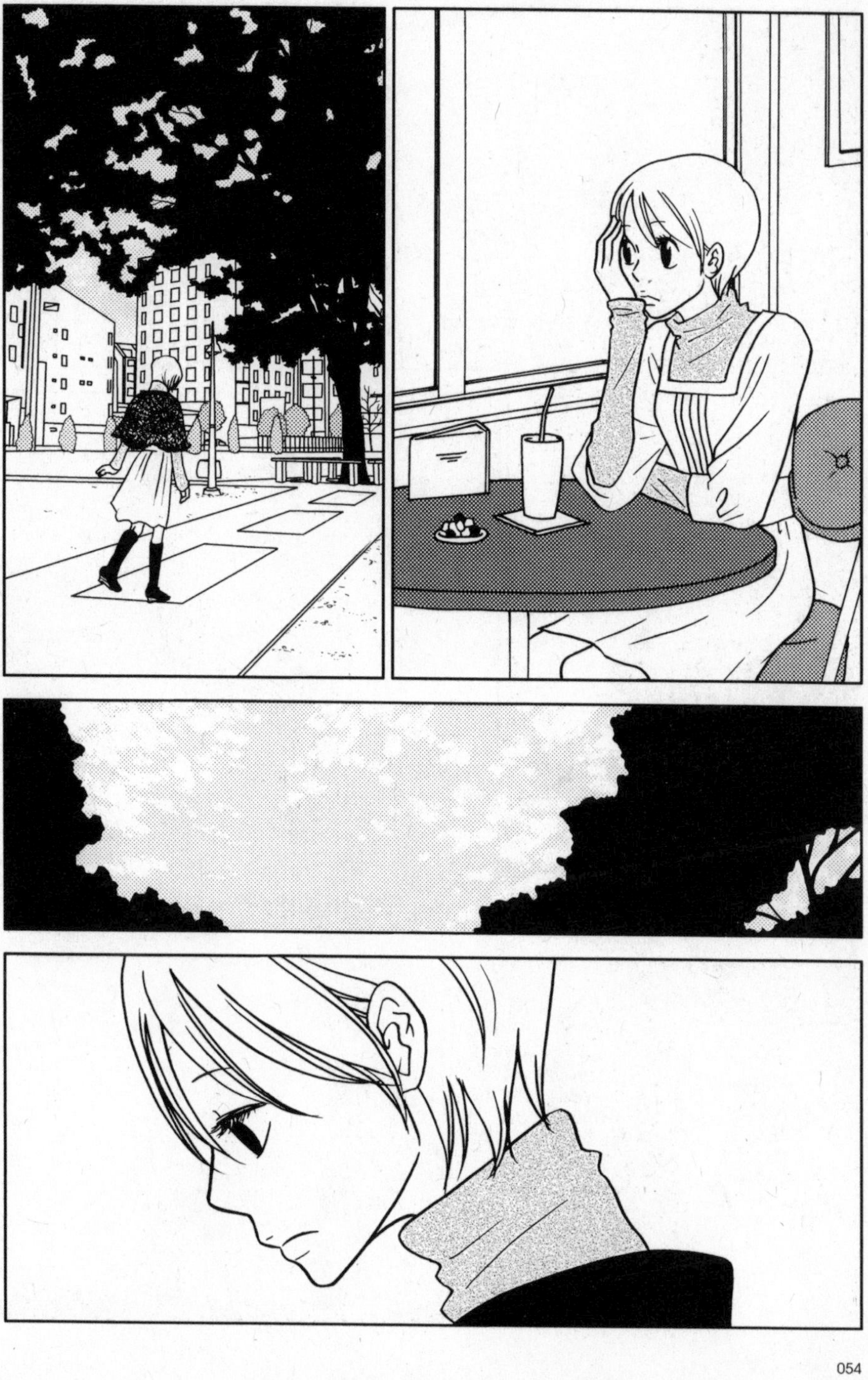

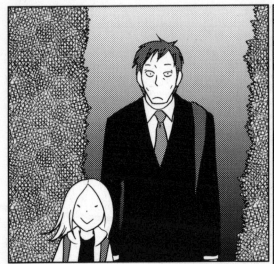

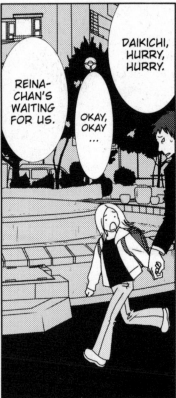

DAIKICHI, HURRY, HURRY.

REINA-CHAN'S WAITING FOR US.

OKAY, OKAY...

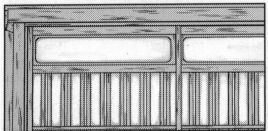

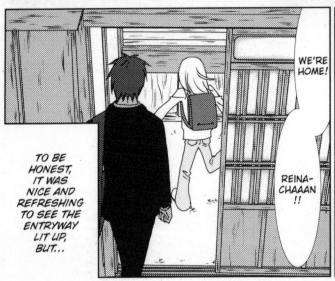

WE'RE HOME!

REINA-CHAAAN!!

TO BE HONEST, IT WAS NICE AND REFRESHING TO SEE THE ENTRYWAY LIT UP, BUT...

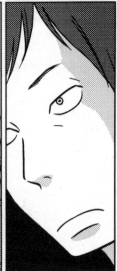

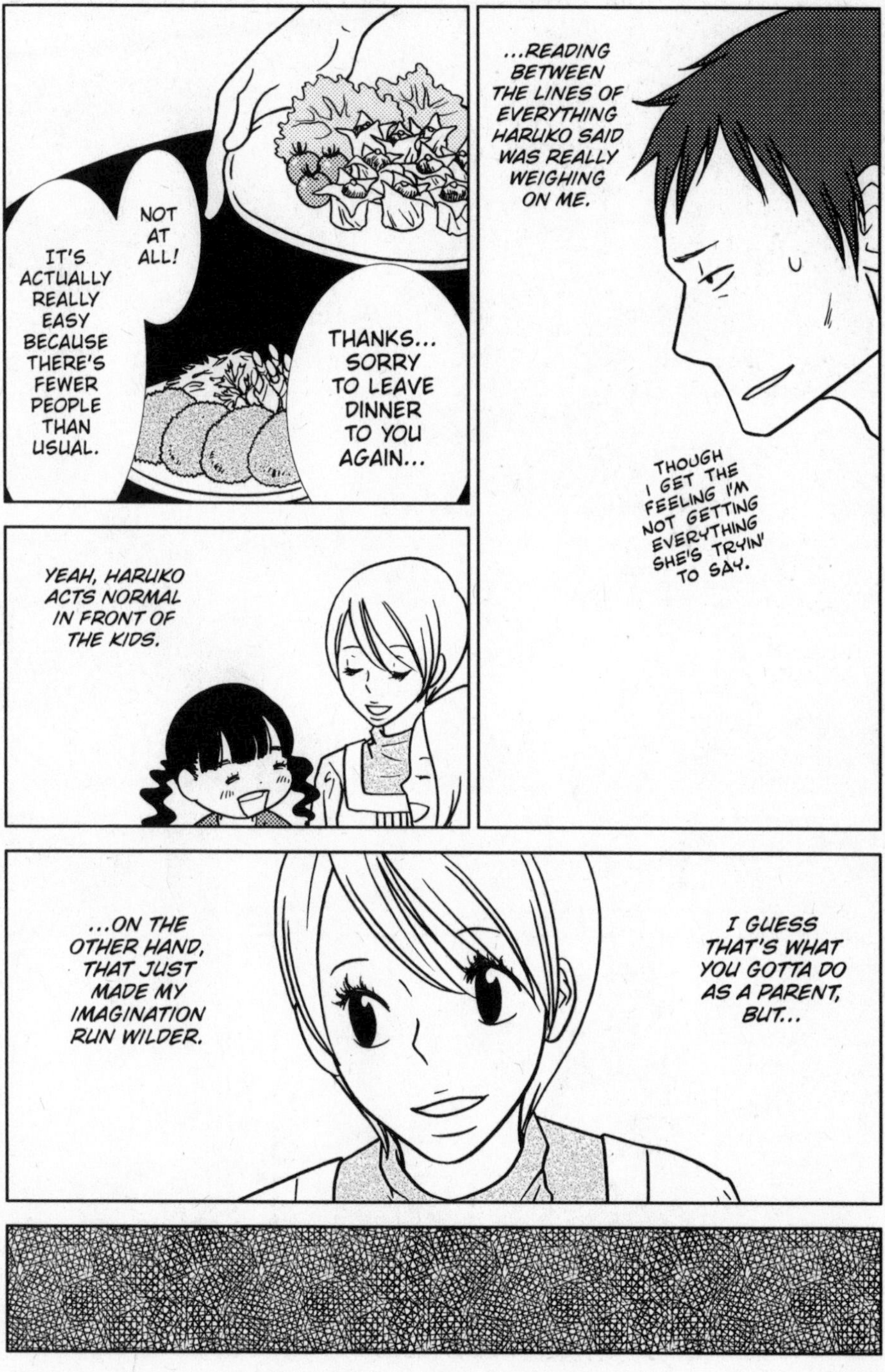
...READING BETWEEN THE LINES OF EVERYTHING HARUKO SAID WAS REALLY WEIGHING ON ME.
THOUGH I GET THE FEELING I'M NOT GETTING EVERYTHING SHE'S TRYIN' TO SAY.
THANKS... SORRY TO LEAVE DINNER TO YOU AGAIN...
NOT AT ALL!
IT'S ACTUALLY REALLY EASY BECAUSE THERE'S FEWER PEOPLE THAN USUAL.
YEAH, HARUKO ACTS NORMAL IN FRONT OF THE KIDS.
I GUESS THAT'S WHAT YOU GOTTA DO AS A PARENT, BUT...
...ON THE OTHER HAND, THAT JUST MADE MY IMAGINATION RUN WILDER.

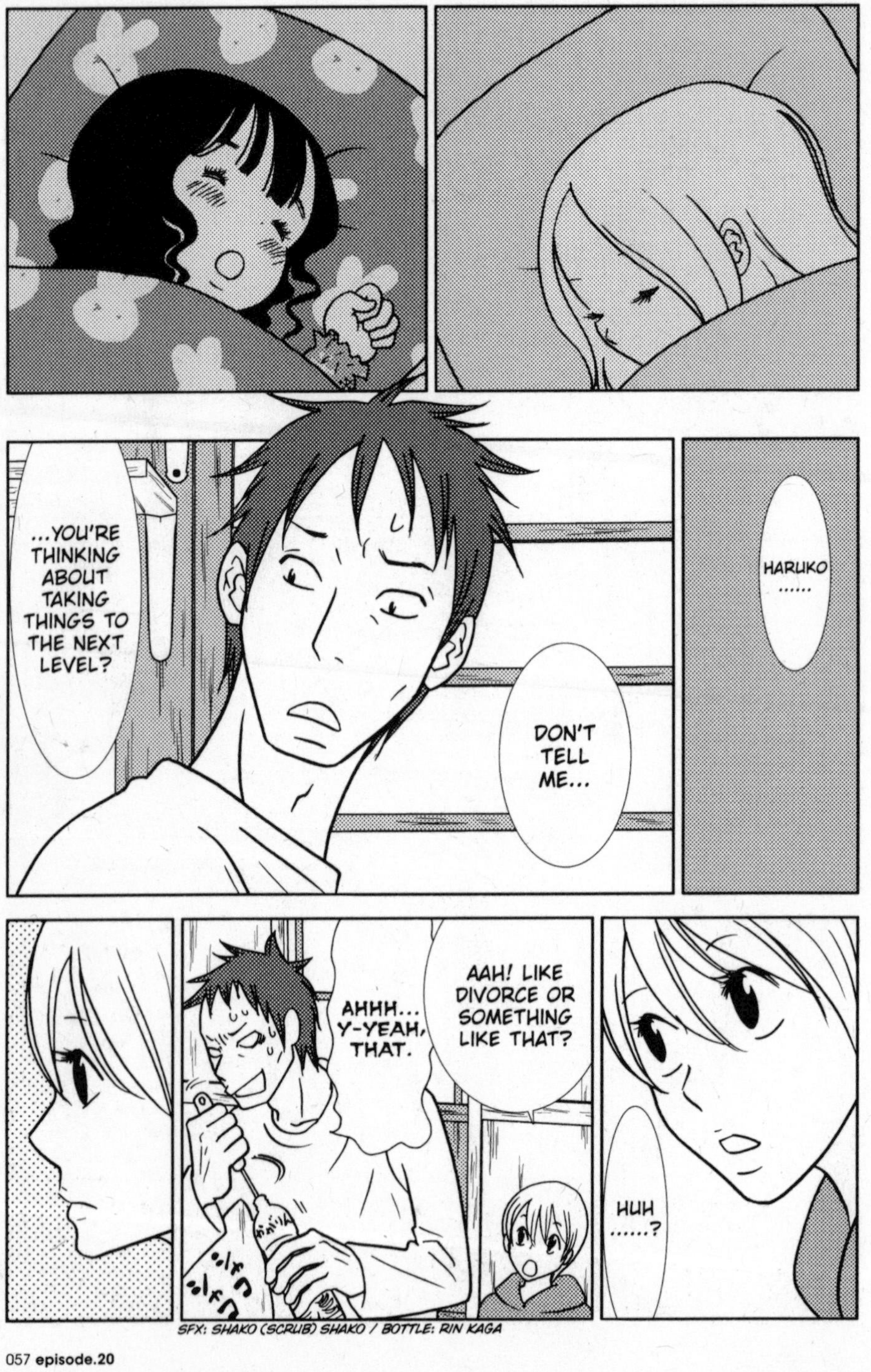
HARUKO ......
DON'T TELL ME...
...YOU'RE THINKING ABOUT TAKING THINGS TO THE NEXT LEVEL?
HUH ......?
AAH! LIKE DIVORCE OR SOMETHING LIKE THAT?
AHHH... Y-YEAH, THAT.

SFX: SHAKO (SCRUB) SHAKO / BOTTLE: RIN KAGA

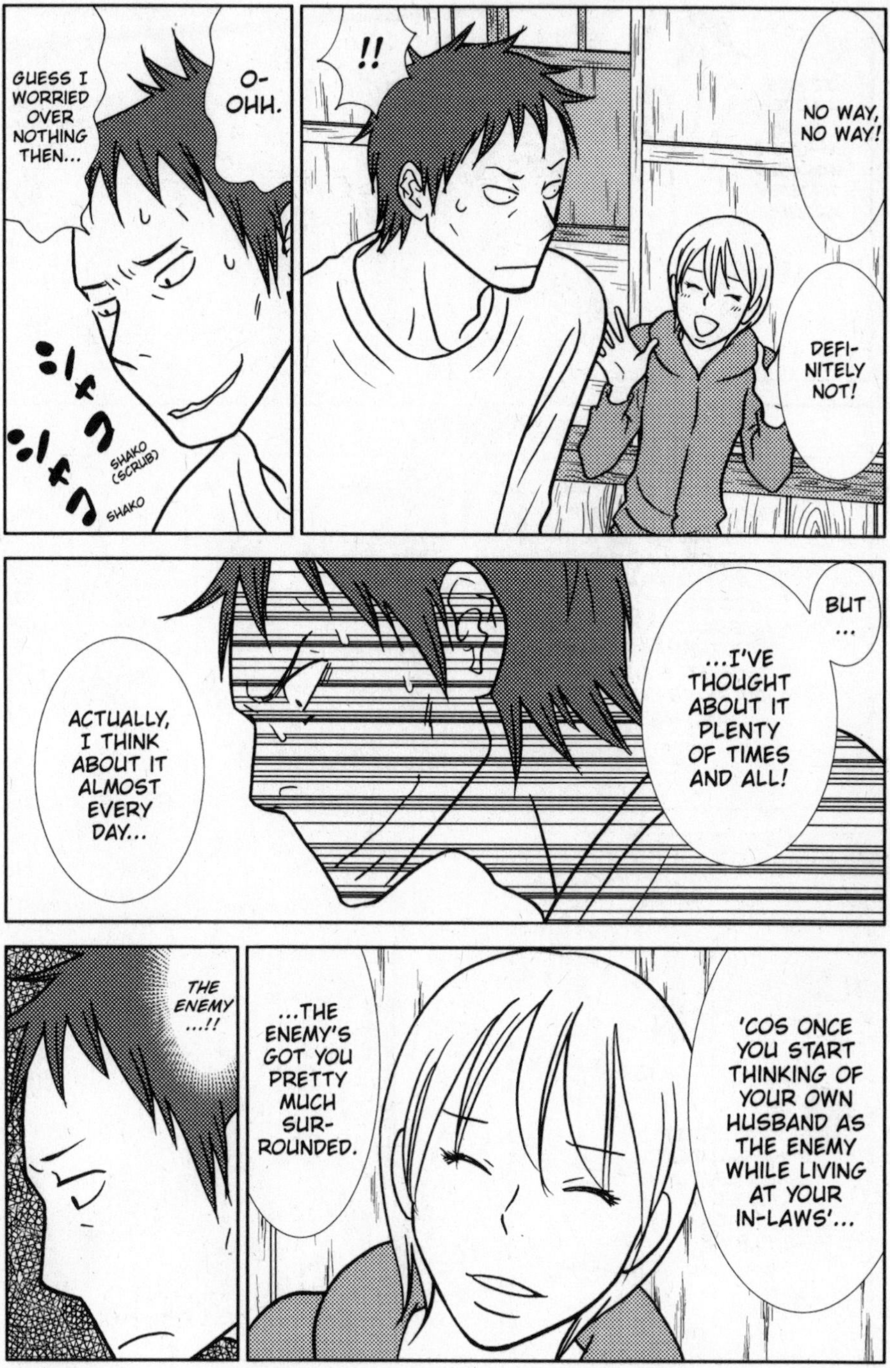
NO WAY, NO WAY!
DEFI-NITELY NOT!
!!
O-OHH.
GUESS I WORRIED OVER NOTHING THEN...
SHAKO (SCRUB)
SHAKO
BUT...
...I'VE THOUGHT ABOUT IT PLENTY OF TIMES AND ALL!
ACTUALLY, I THINK ABOUT IT ALMOST EVERY DAY...
'COS ONCE YOU START THINKING OF YOUR OWN HUSBAND AS THE ENEMY WHILE LIVING AT YOUR IN-LAWS'...
...THE ENEMY'S GOT YOU PRETTY MUCH SUR-ROUNDED.
THE ENEMY...!!

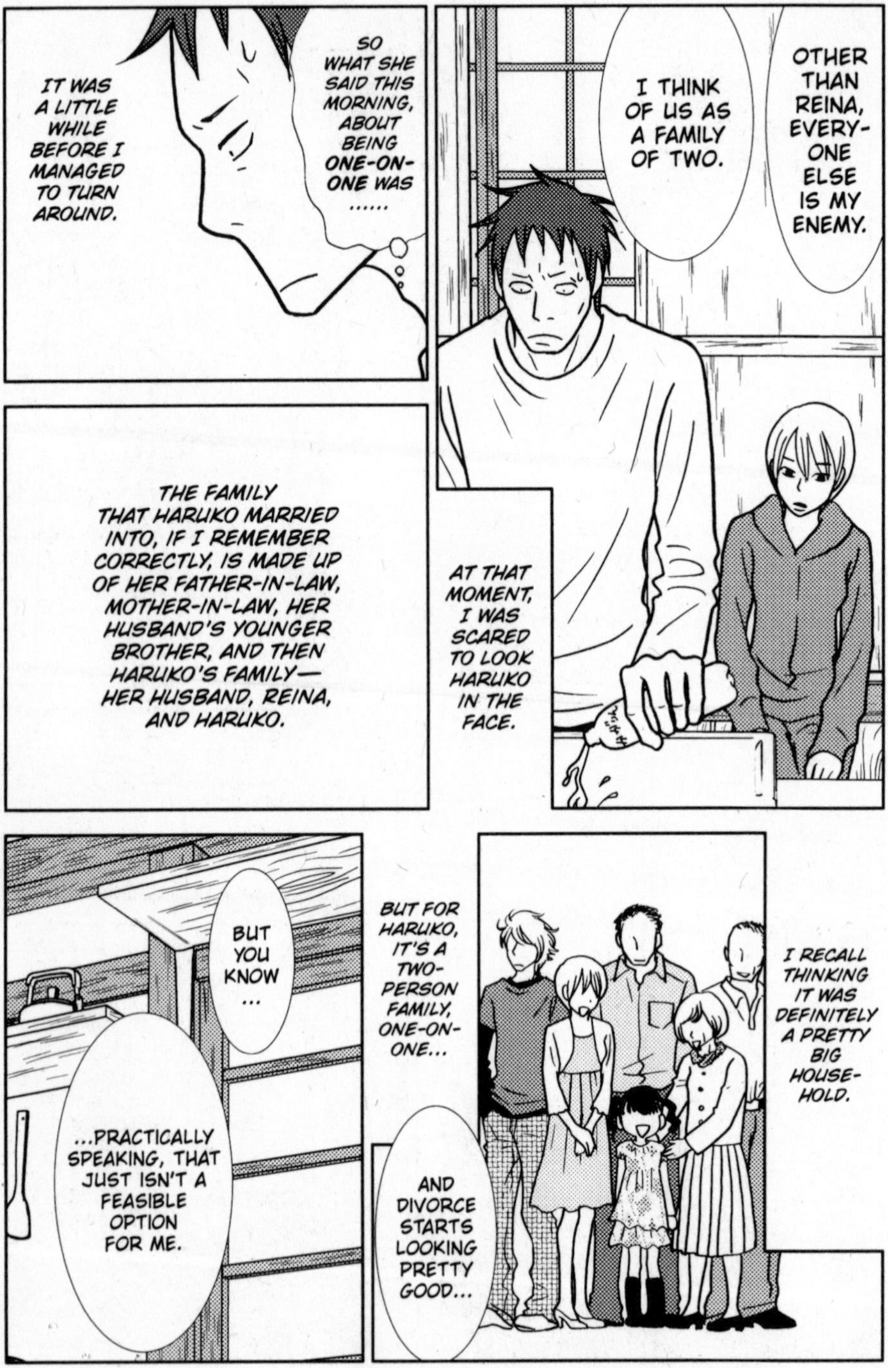
OTHER THAN REINA, EVERYONE ELSE IS MY ENEMY.
I THINK OF US AS A FAMILY OF TWO.
AT THAT MOMENT, I WAS SCARED TO LOOK HARUKO IN THE FACE.
SO WHAT SHE SAID THIS MORNING, ABOUT BEING ONE-ON-ONE WAS ......
IT WAS A LITTLE WHILE BEFORE I MANAGED TO TURN AROUND.
THE FAMILY THAT HARUKO MARRIED INTO, IF I REMEMBER CORRECTLY, IS MADE UP OF HER FATHER-IN-LAW, MOTHER-IN-LAW, HER HUSBAND'S YOUNGER BROTHER, AND THEN HARUKO'S FAMILY—HER HUSBAND, REINA, AND HARUKO.
I RECALL THINKING IT WAS DEFINITELY A PRETTY BIG HOUSEHOLD.
BUT FOR HARUKO, IT'S A TWO-PERSON FAMILY, ONE-ON-ONE...
AND DIVORCE STARTS LOOKING PRETTY GOOD...
BUT YOU KNOW...
...PRACTICALLY SPEAKING, THAT JUST ISN'T A FEASIBLE OPTION FOR ME.

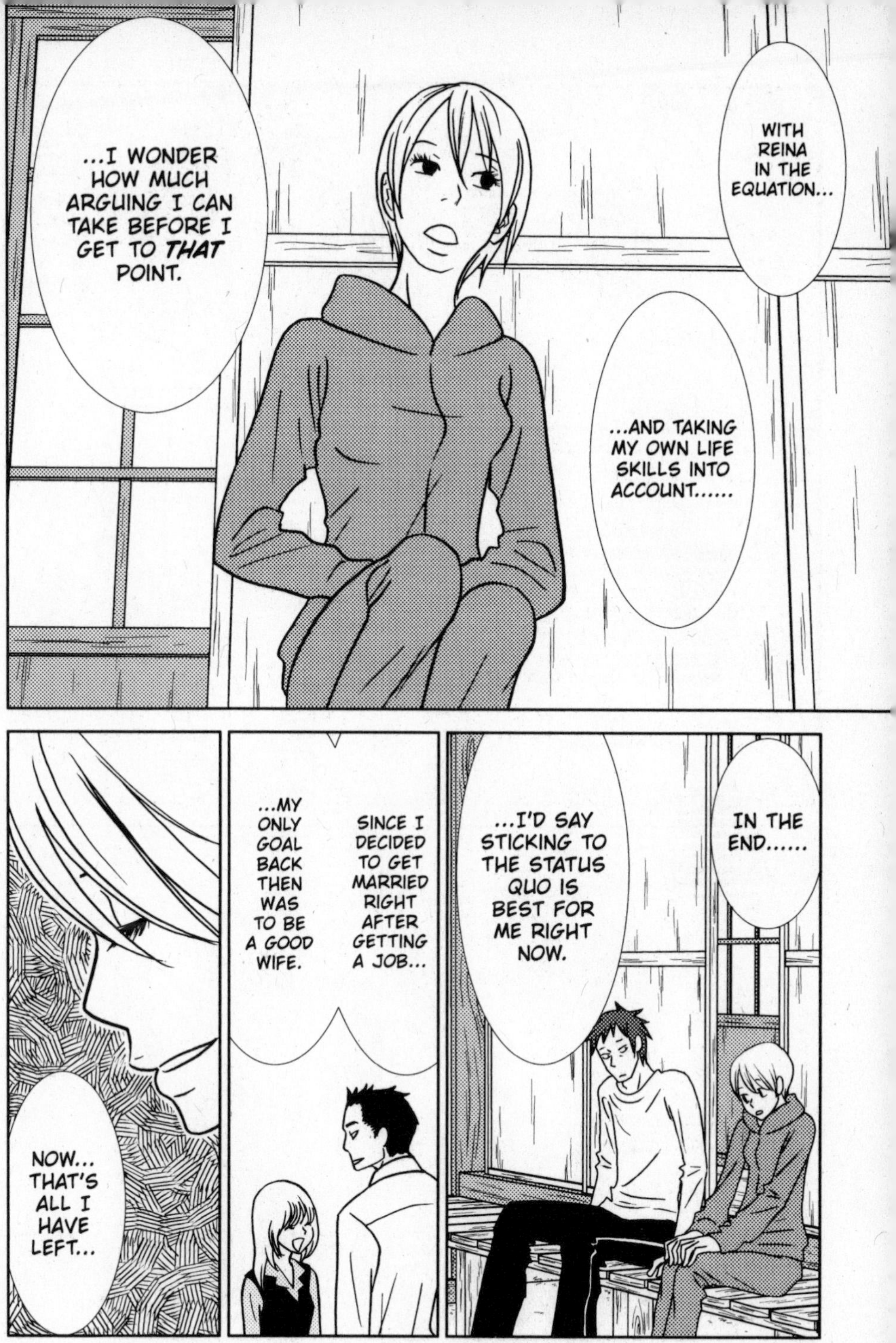
WITH REINA IN THE EQUATION...
...AND TAKING MY OWN LIFE SKILLS INTO ACCOUNT......
...I WONDER HOW MUCH ARGUING I CAN TAKE BEFORE I GET TO *THAT* POINT.
IN THE END......
...I'D SAY STICKING TO THE STATUS QUO IS BEST FOR ME RIGHT NOW.
SINCE I DECIDED TO GET MARRIED RIGHT AFTER GETTING A JOB...
...MY ONLY GOAL BACK THEN WAS TO BE A GOOD WIFE.
NOW... THAT'S ALL I HAVE LEFT...

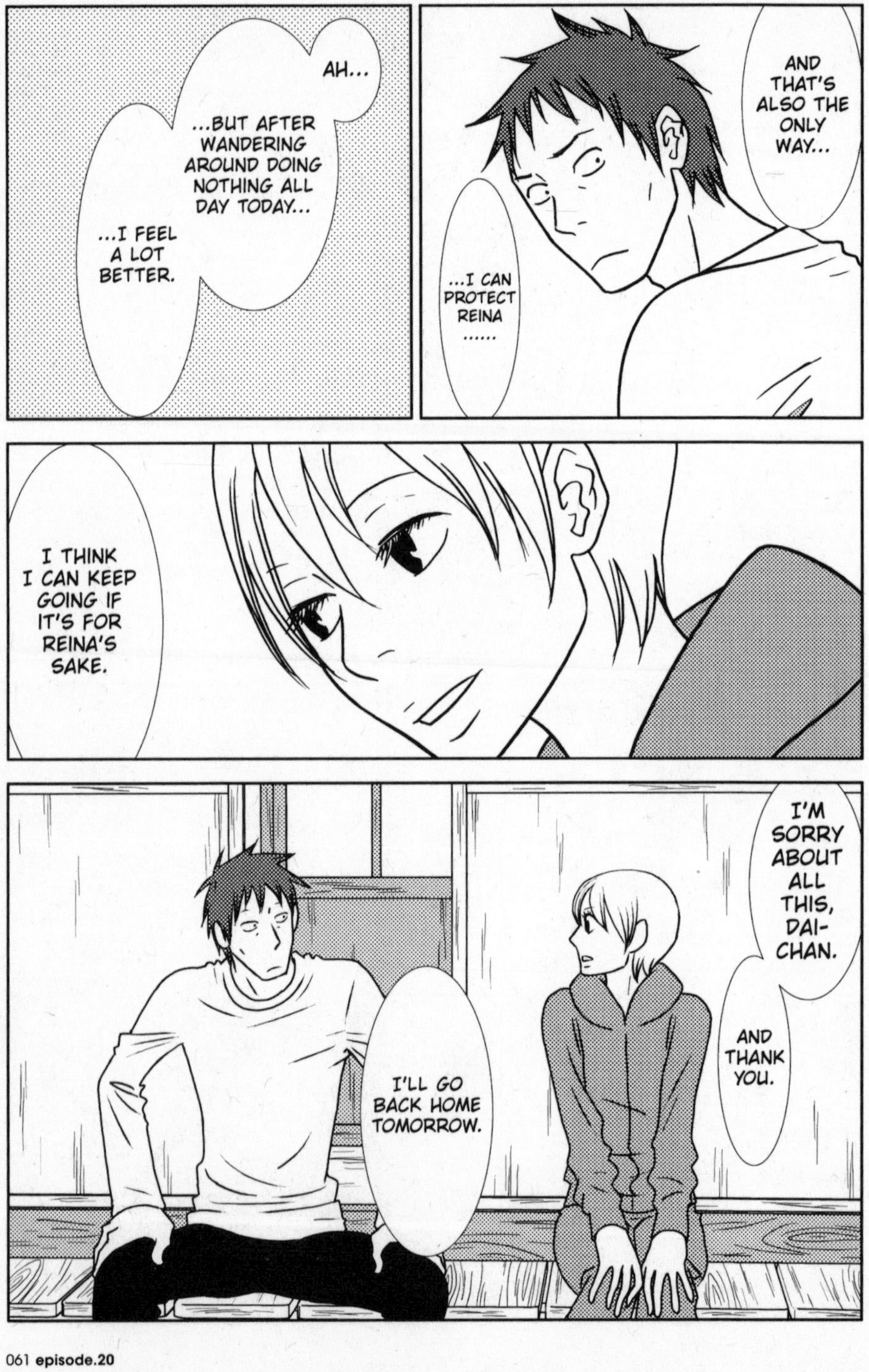
AND THAT'S ALSO THE ONLY WAY...
...I CAN PROTECT REINA ......
AH...
...BUT AFTER WANDERING AROUND DOING NOTHING ALL DAY TODAY...
...I FEEL A LOT BETTER.
I THINK I CAN KEEP GOING IF IT'S FOR REINA'S SAKE.
I'M SORRY ABOUT ALL THIS, DAI-CHAN.
AND THANK YOU.
I'LL GO BACK HOME TOMORROW.

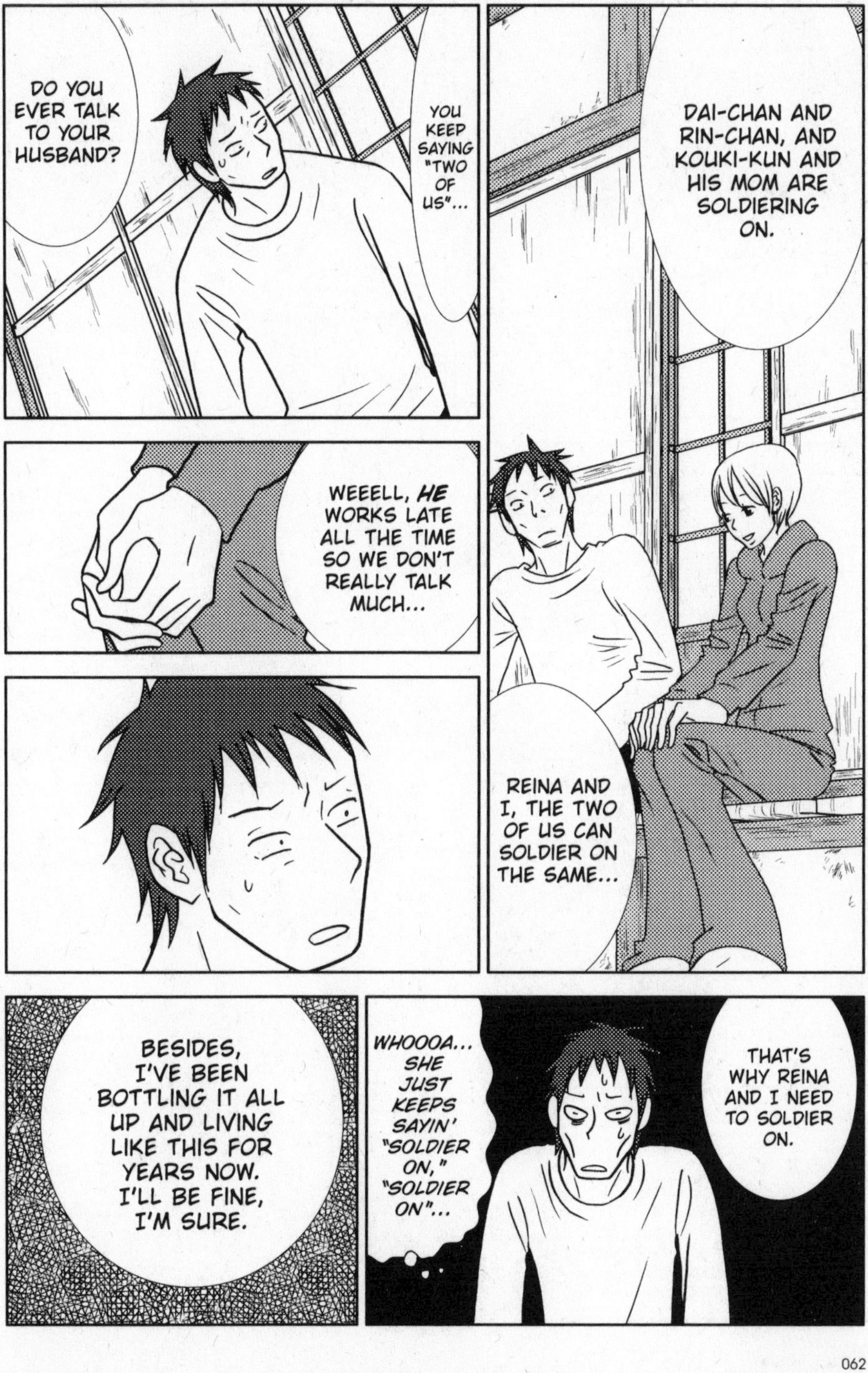
DAI-CHAN AND RIN-CHAN, AND KOUKI-KUN AND HIS MOM ARE SOLDIERING ON.
REINA AND I, THE TWO OF US CAN SOLDIER ON THE SAME...
YOU KEEP SAYING "TWO OF US"...
DO YOU EVER TALK TO YOUR HUSBAND?
WEEELL, *HE* WORKS LATE ALL THE TIME SO WE DON'T REALLY TALK MUCH...
THAT'S WHY REINA AND I NEED TO SOLDIER ON.
WHOOOA... SHE JUST KEEPS SAYIN' "SOLDIER ON," "SOLDIER ON"...
BESIDES, I'VE BEEN BOTTLING IT ALL UP AND LIVING LIKE THIS FOR YEARS NOW. I'LL BE FINE, I'M SURE.

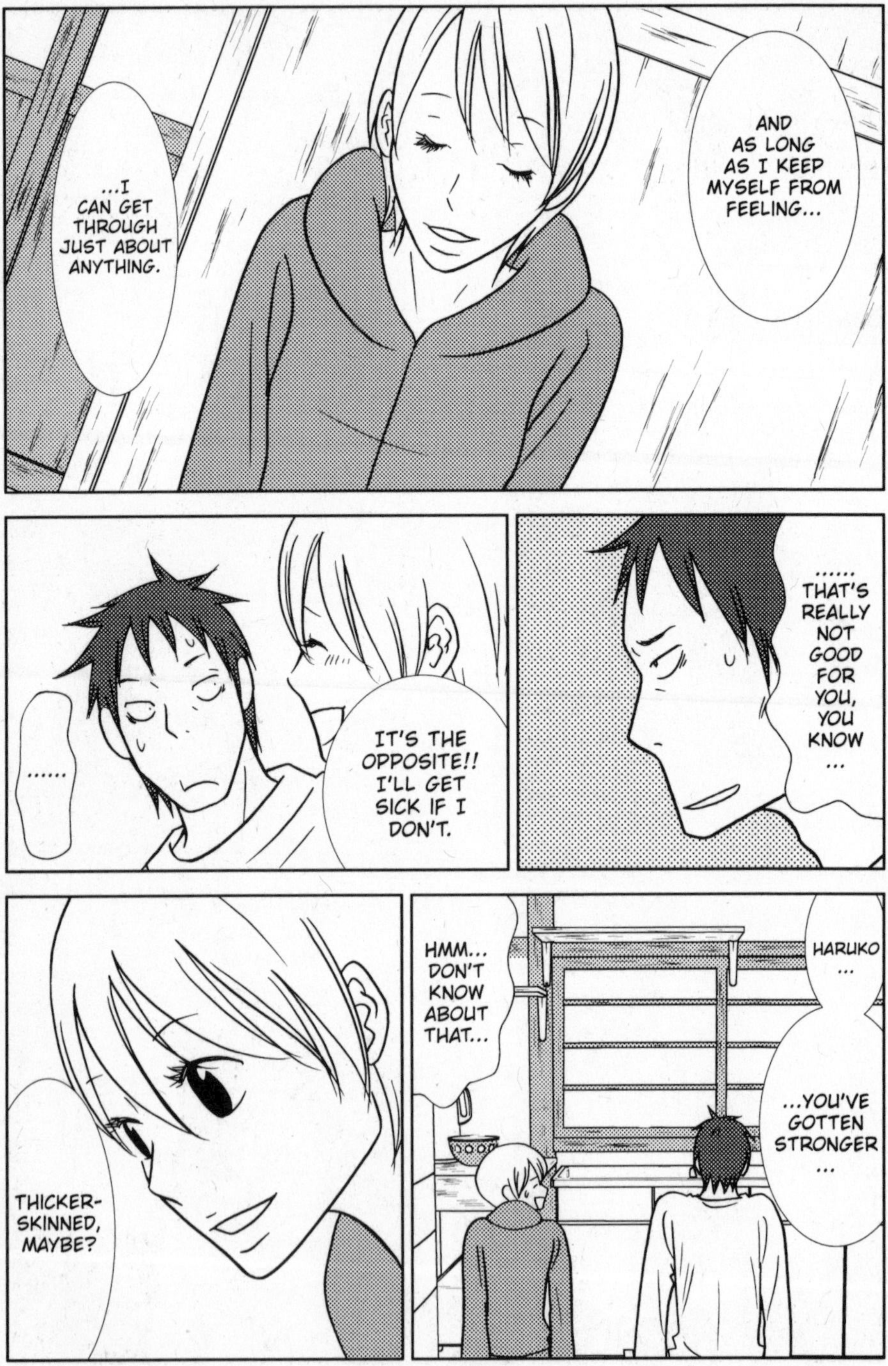
AND AS LONG AS I KEEP MYSELF FROM FEELING...
...I CAN GET THROUGH JUST ABOUT ANYTHING.
......THAT'S REALLY NOT GOOD FOR YOU, YOU KNOW...
IT'S THE OPPOSITE!! I'LL GET SICK IF I DON'T.
......
HARUKO...
...YOU'VE GOTTEN STRONGER...
HMM... DON'T KNOW ABOUT THAT...
THICKER-SKINNED, MAYBE?

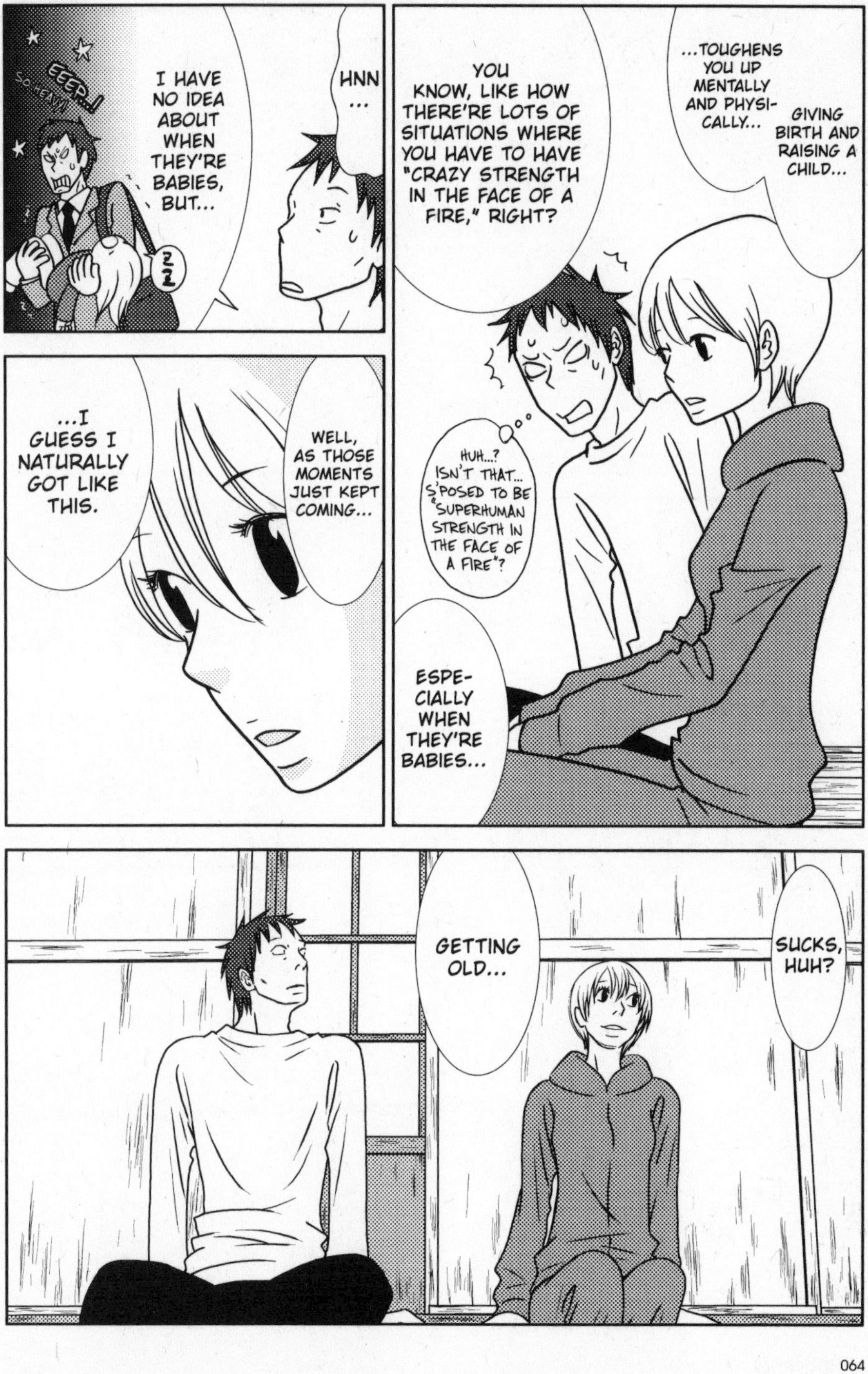

GIVING BIRTH AND RAISING A CHILD...
...TOUGHENS YOU UP MENTALLY AND PHYSI-CALLY...
YOU KNOW, LIKE HOW THERE'RE LOTS OF SITUATIONS WHERE YOU HAVE TO HAVE "CRAZY STRENGTH IN THE FACE OF A FIRE," RIGHT?
HUH...? ISN'T THAT... S'POSED TO BE "SUPERHUMAN STRENGTH IN THE FACE OF A FIRE"?
ESPE-CIALLY WHEN THEY'RE BABIES...
HNN ...
I HAVE NO IDEA ABOUT WHEN THEY'RE BABIES, BUT...
EEEP...!
SO HEAVY
WELL, AS THOSE MOMENTS JUST KEPT COMING...
...I GUESS I NATURALLY GOT LIKE THIS.
SUCKS, HUH?
GETTING OLD...

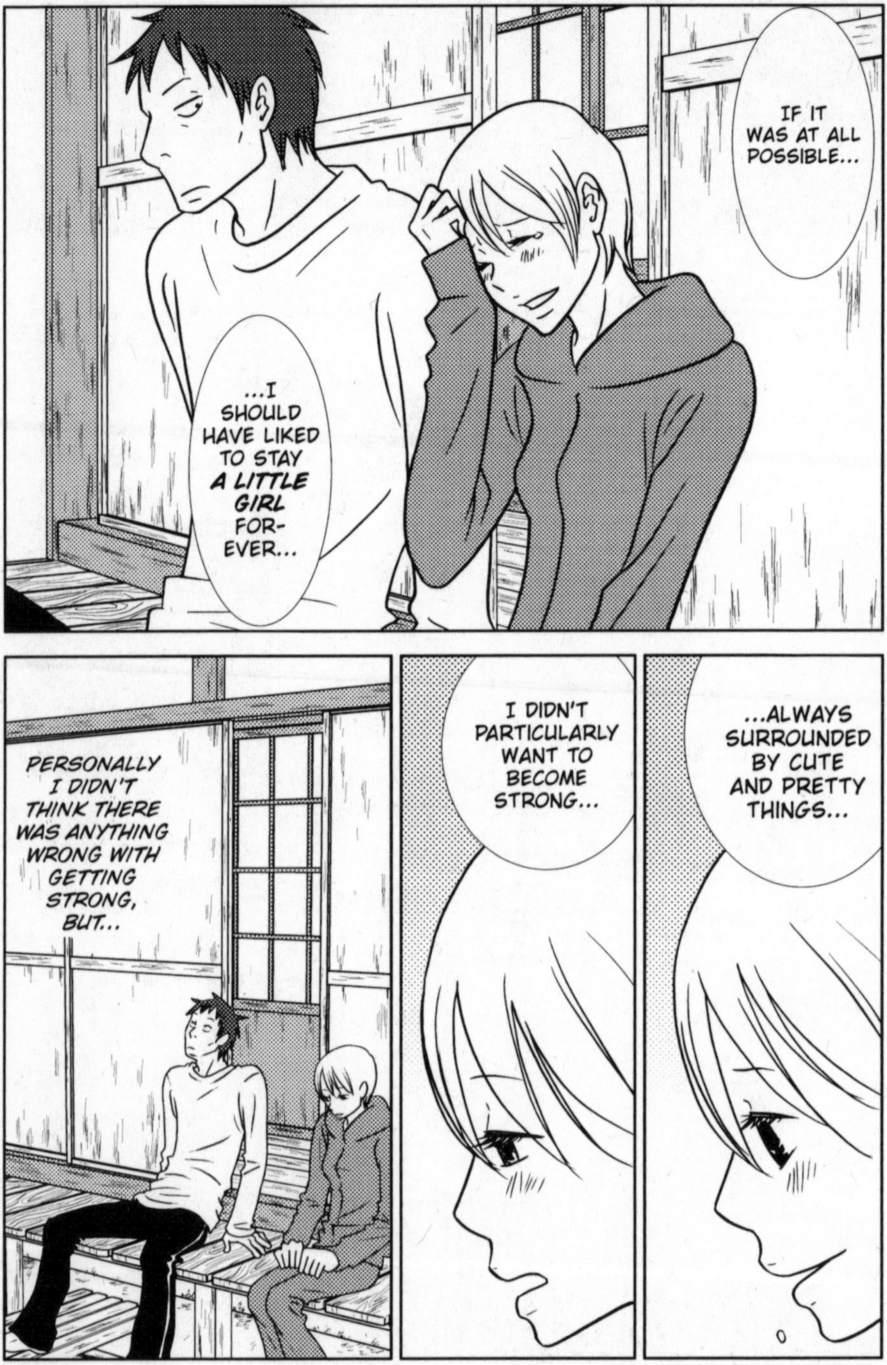
IF IT WAS AT ALL POSSIBLE...
...I SHOULD HAVE LIKED TO STAY *A LITTLE GIRL* FOR-EVER...
...ALWAYS SURROUNDED BY CUTE AND PRETTY THINGS...
I DIDN'T PARTICULARLY WANT TO BECOME STRONG...
PERSONALLY I DIDN'T THINK THERE WAS ANYTHING WRONG WITH GETTING STRONG, BUT...

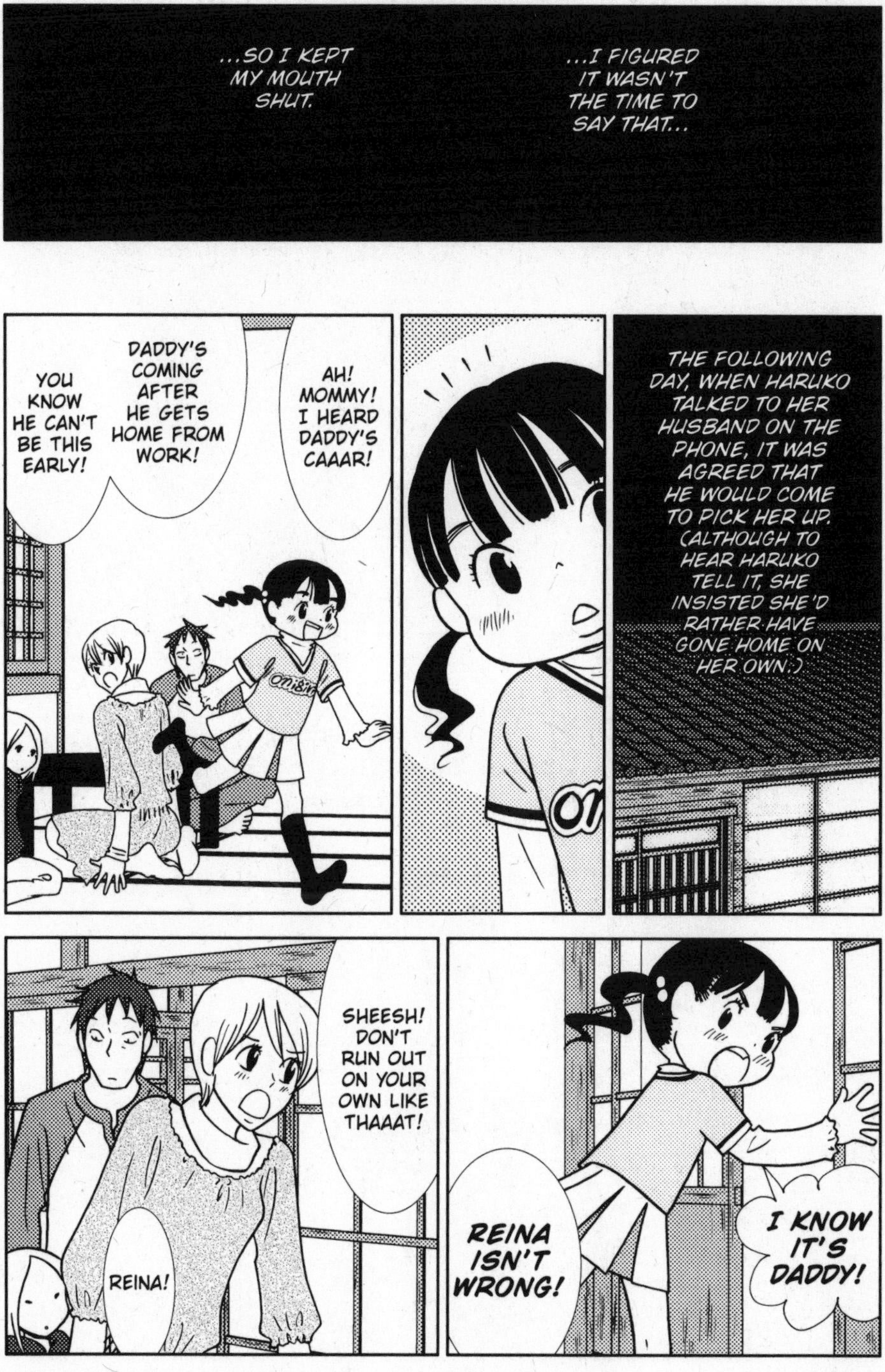
...I FIGURED IT WASN'T THE TIME TO SAY THAT...
...SO I KEPT MY MOUTH SHUT.
THE FOLLOWING DAY, WHEN HARUKO TALKED TO HER HUSBAND ON THE PHONE, IT WAS AGREED THAT HE WOULD COME TO PICK HER UP. (ALTHOUGH TO HEAR HARUKO TELL IT, SHE INSISTED SHE'D RATHER HAVE GONE HOME ON HER OWN.)
AH! MOMMY! I HEARD DADDY'S CAAAR!
DADDY'S COMING AFTER HE GETS HOME FROM WORK!
YOU KNOW HE CAN'T BE THIS EARLY!
I KNOW IT'S DADDY!
REINA ISN'T WRONG!
SHEESH! DON'T RUN OUT ON YOUR OWN LIKE THAAAT!
REINA!

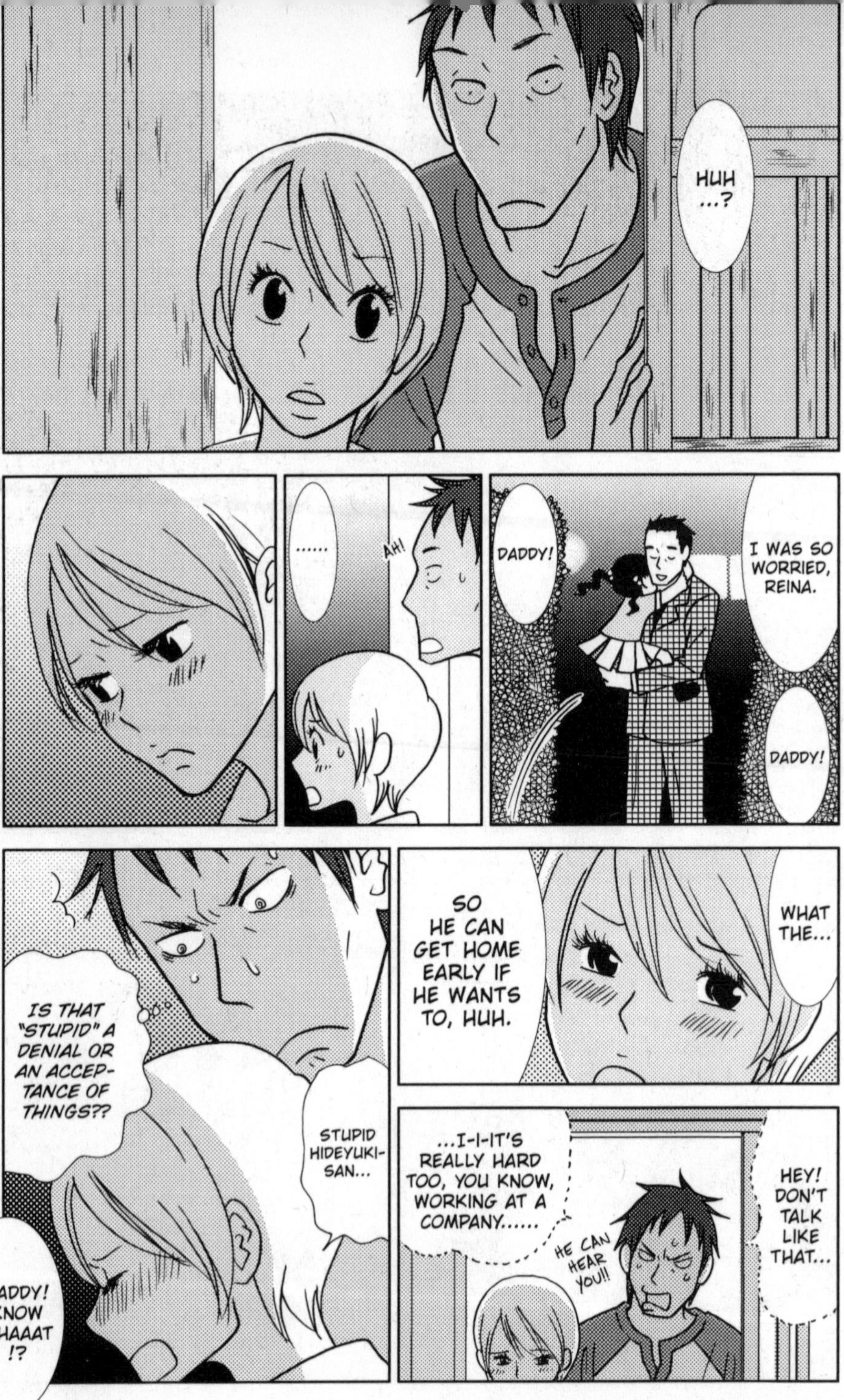
HUH ...?
I WAS SO WORRIED, REINA.
DADDY!
DADDY!
......
AH!
WHAT THE...
SO HE CAN GET HOME EARLY IF HE WANTS TO, HUH.
HEY! DON'T TALK LIKE THAT...
...I-I-IT'S REALLY HARD TOO, YOU KNOW, WORKING AT A COMPANY......
HE CAN HEAR YOU!!
STUPID HIDEYUKI-SAN...
IS THAT "STUPID" A DENIAL OR AN ACCEPTANCE OF THINGS??
DADDY! KNOW WHAAAT !?

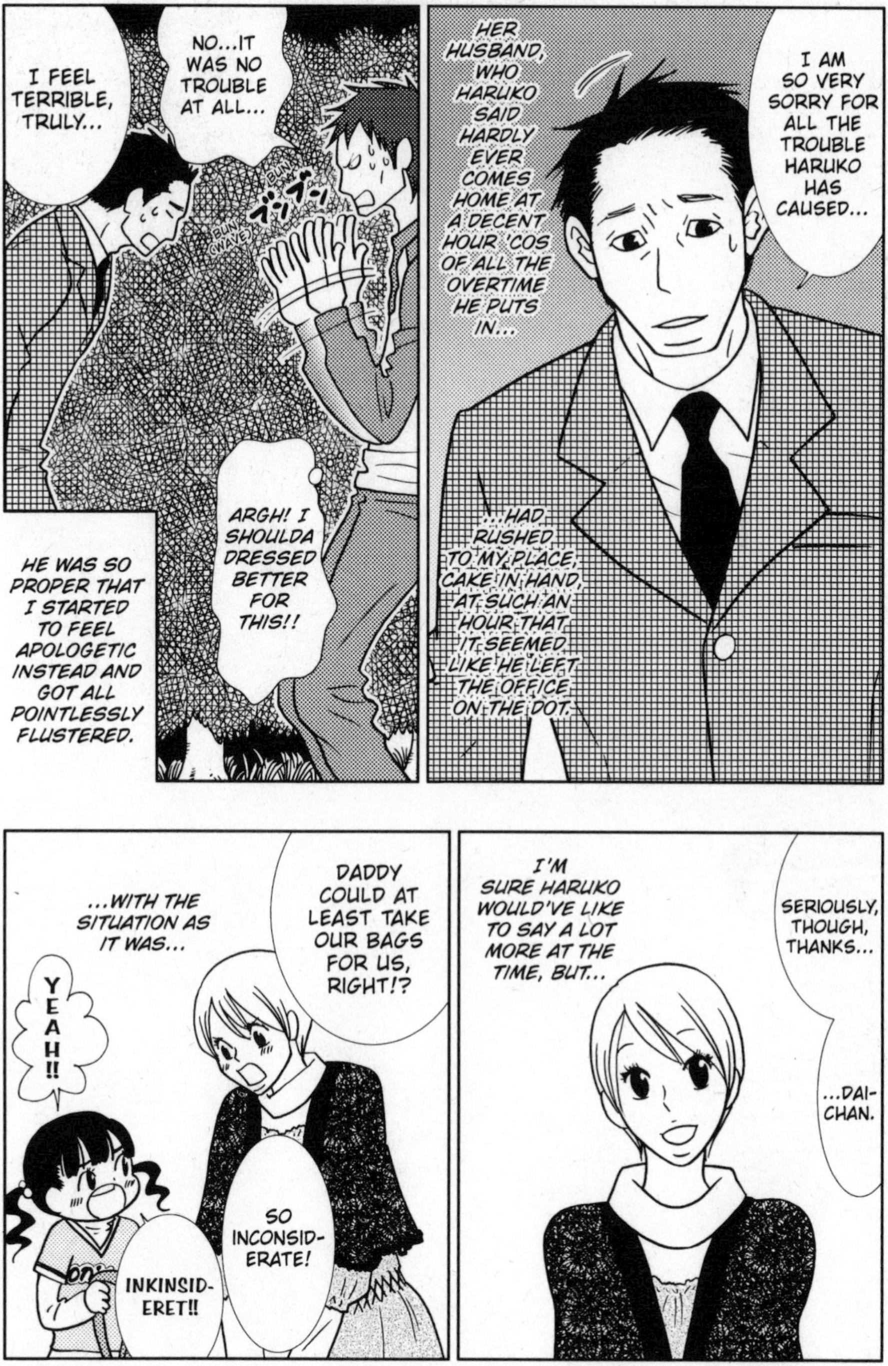
I AM SO VERY SORRY FOR ALL THE TROUBLE HARUKO HAS CAUSED...
HER HUSBAND, WHO HARUKO SAID HARDLY EVER COMES HOME AT A DECENT HOUR 'COS OF ALL THE OVERTIME HE PUTS IN...
...HAD RUSHED TO MY PLACE, CAKE IN HAND, AT SUCH AN HOUR THAT IT SEEMED LIKE HE LEFT THE OFFICE ON THE DOT.
NO...IT WAS NO TROUBLE AT ALL...
I FEEL TERRIBLE, TRULY...
BUN BUN (WAVE)
ARGH! I SHOULDA DRESSED BETTER FOR THIS!!
HE WAS SO PROPER THAT I STARTED TO FEEL APOLOGETIC INSTEAD AND GOT ALL POINTLESSLY FLUSTERED.
SERIOUSLY, THOUGH, THANKS...
I'M SURE HARUKO WOULD'VE LIKE TO SAY A LOT MORE AT THE TIME, BUT...
...DAI-CHAN.
DADDY COULD AT LEAST TAKE OUR BAGS FOR US, RIGHT!?
...WITH THE SITUATION AS IT WAS...
YEAH!!
SO INCONSIDERATE!
INKINSIDERET!!

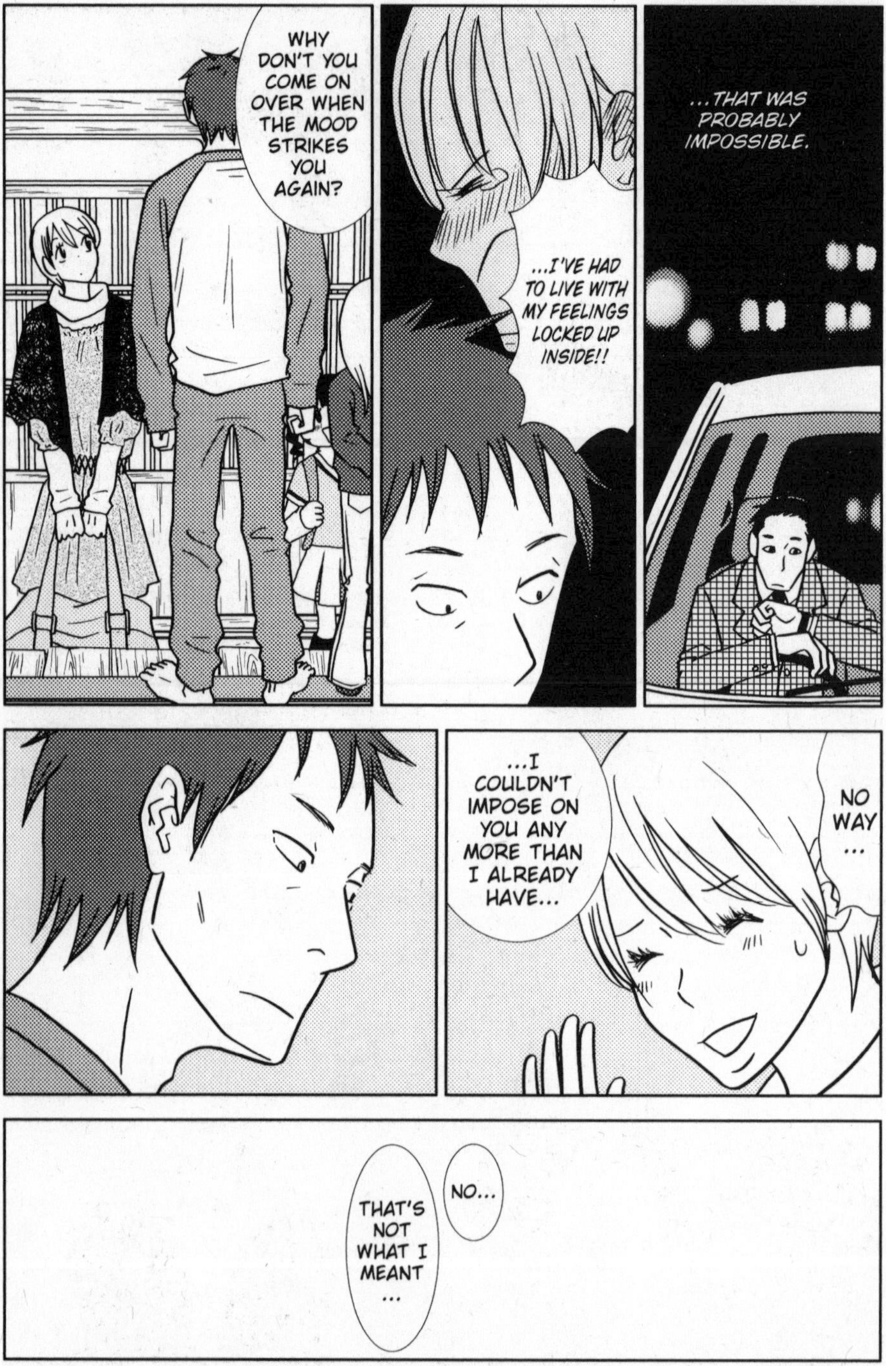
...THAT WAS PROBABLY IMPOSSIBLE.
...I'VE HAD TO LIVE WITH MY FEELINGS LOCKED UP INSIDE!!
WHY DON'T YOU COME ON OVER WHEN THE MOOD STRIKES YOU AGAIN?
NO WAY ...
...I COULDN'T IMPOSE ON YOU ANY MORE THAN I ALREADY HAVE...
NO...
THAT'S NOT WHAT I MEANT ...

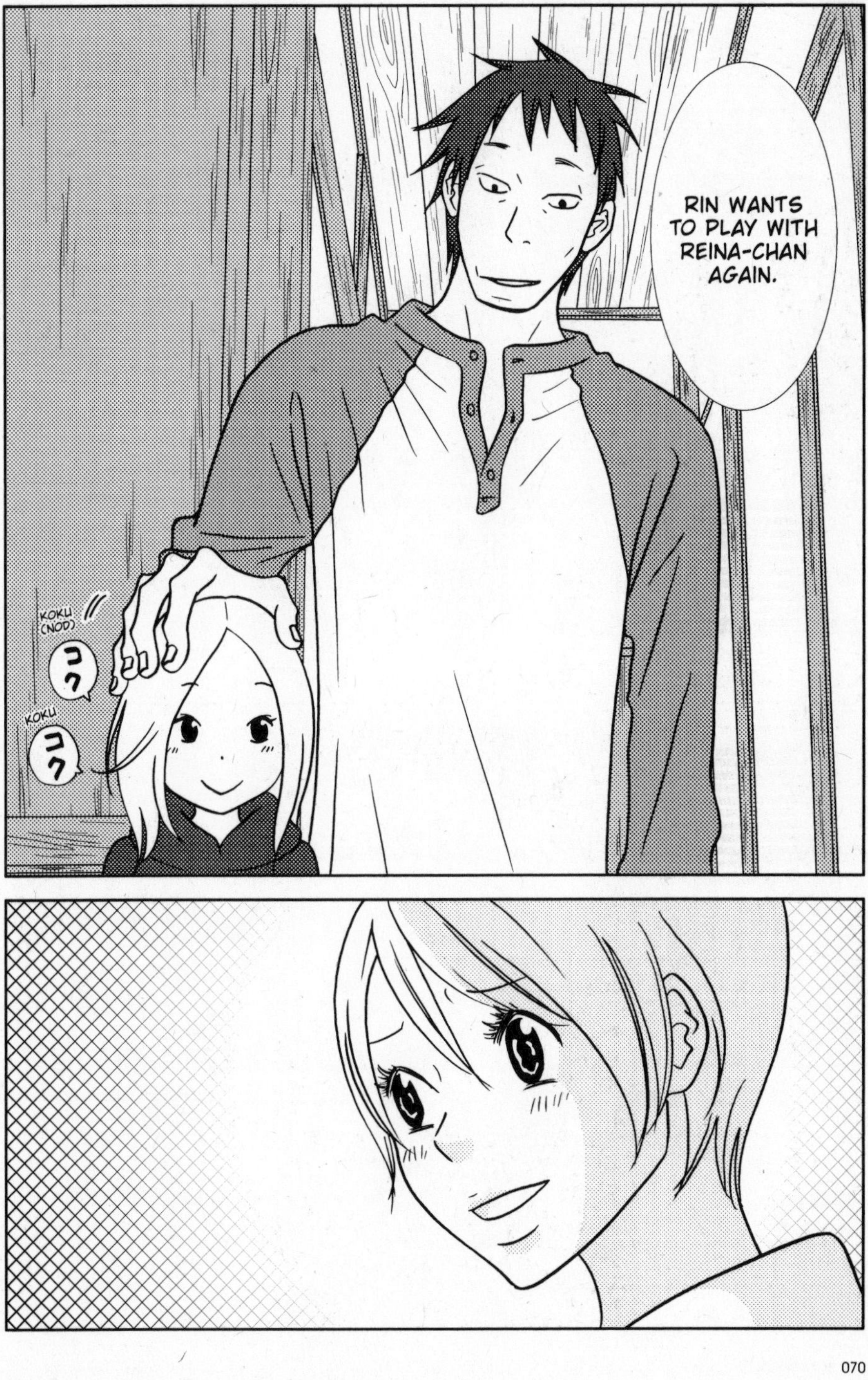
RIN WANTS TO PLAY WITH REINA-CHAN AGAIN.
KOKU (NOD)
コク
KOKU
コク

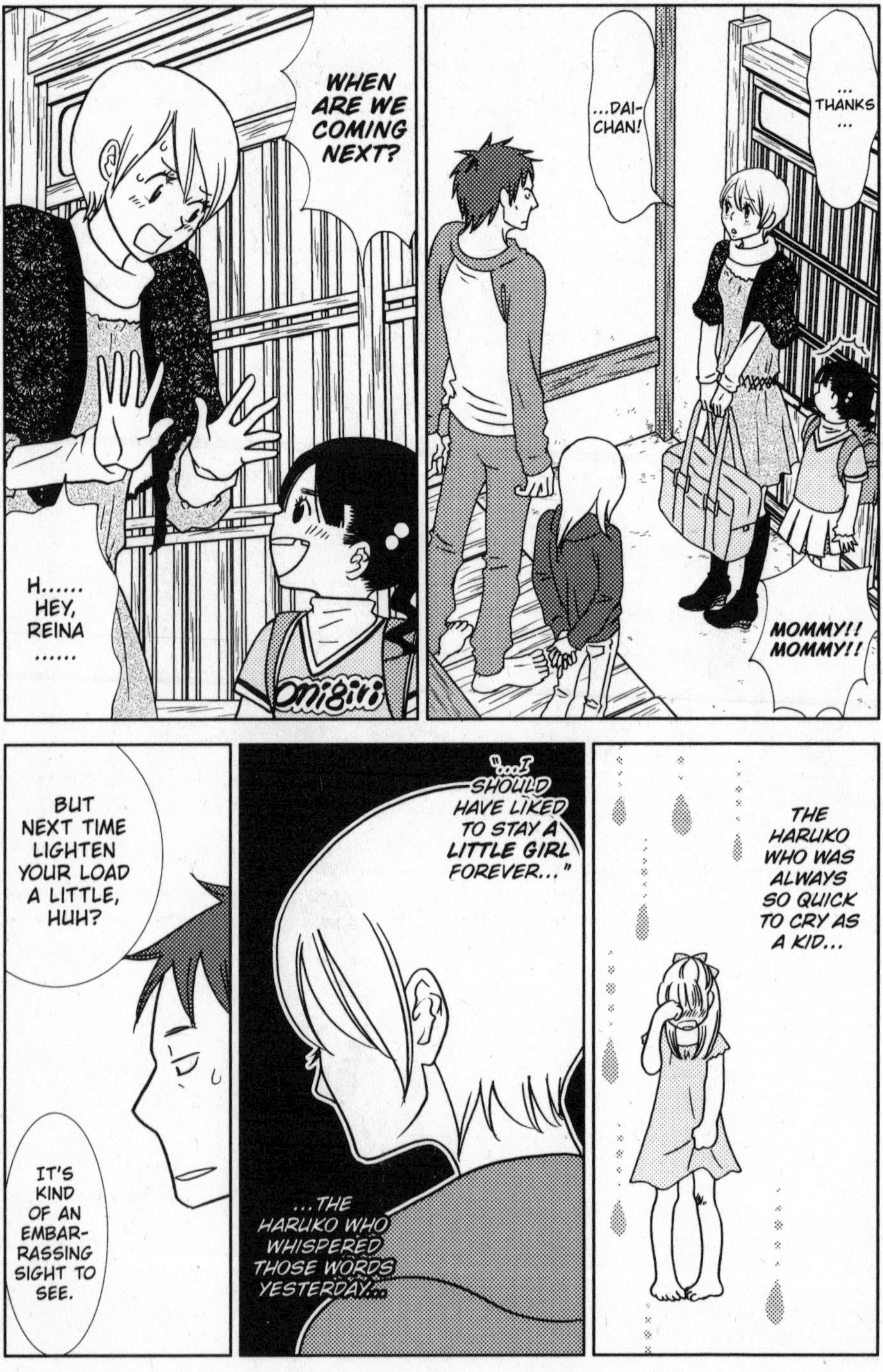

... THANKS ...
...DAI-CHAN!
MOMMY!! MOMMY!!
WHEN ARE WE COMING NEXT?
H...... HEY, REINA ......
THE HARUKO WHO WAS ALWAYS SO QUICK TO CRY AS A KID...
"...I SHOULD HAVE LIKED TO STAY A LITTLE GIRL FOREVER..."
...THE HARUKO WHO WHISPERED THOSE WORDS YESTERDAY...
BUT NEXT TIME LIGHTEN YOUR LOAD A LITTLE, HUH?
IT'S KIND OF AN EMBAR-RASSING SIGHT TO SEE.

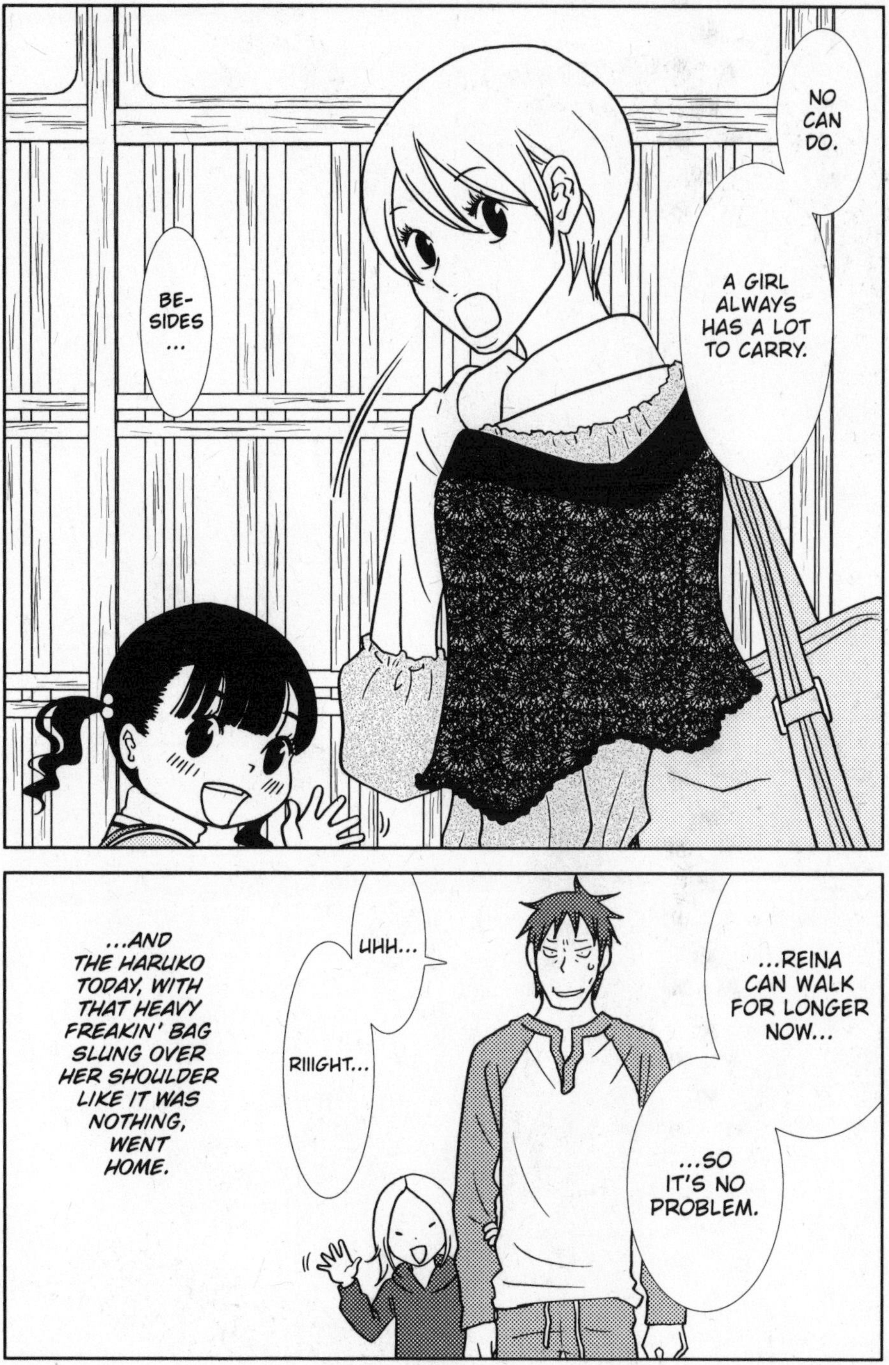
NO CAN DO.
A GIRL ALWAYS HAS A LOT TO CARRY.
BE-SIDES ...
...REINA CAN WALK FOR LONGER NOW...
...SO IT'S NO PROBLEM.
UHH...
RIIIGHT...
...AND THE HARUKO TODAY, WITH THAT HEAVY FREAKIN' BAG SLUNG OVER HER SHOULDER LIKE IT WAS NOTHING, WENT HOME.

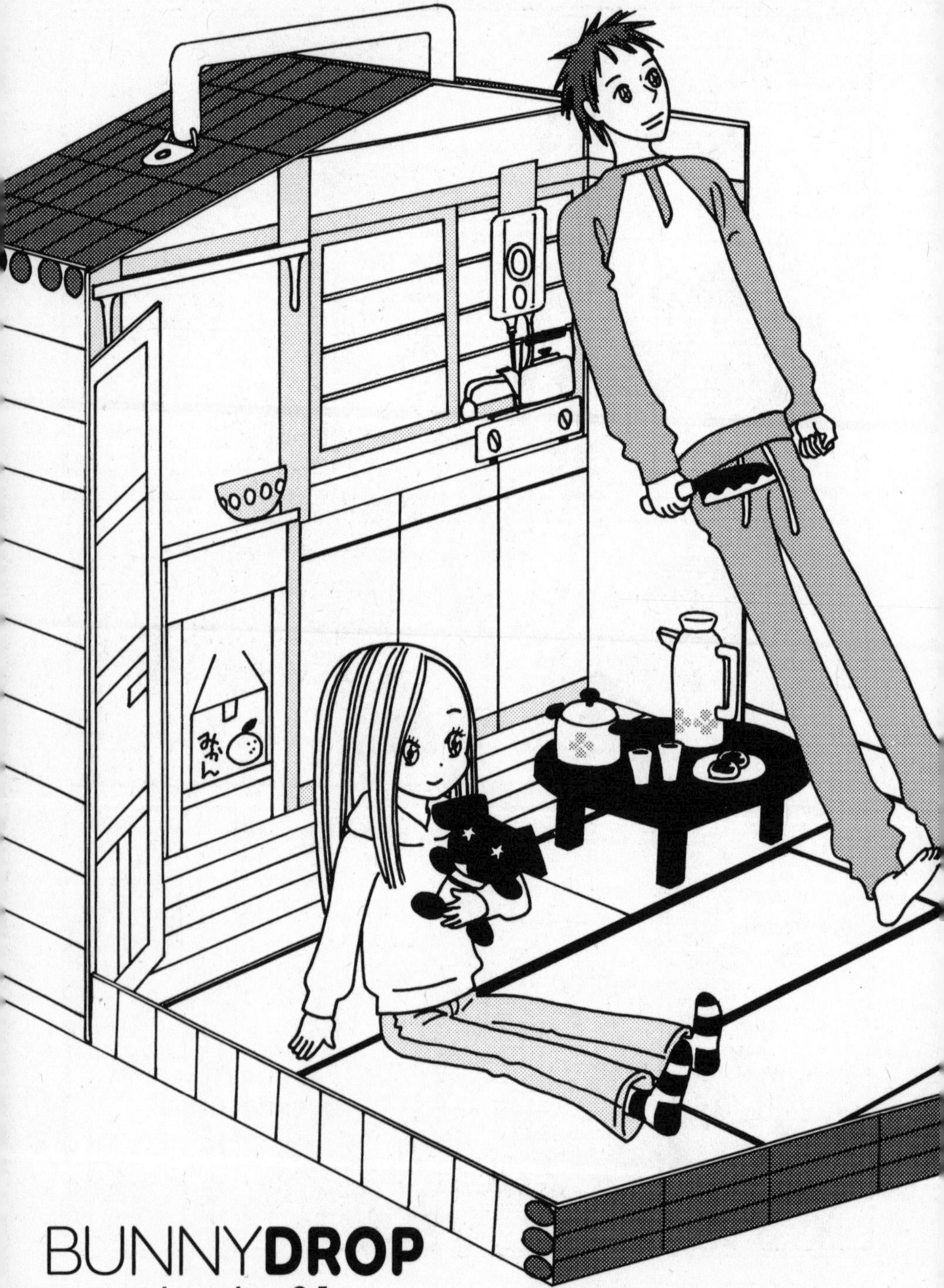
みかん

BUNNY**DROP**

episode.21

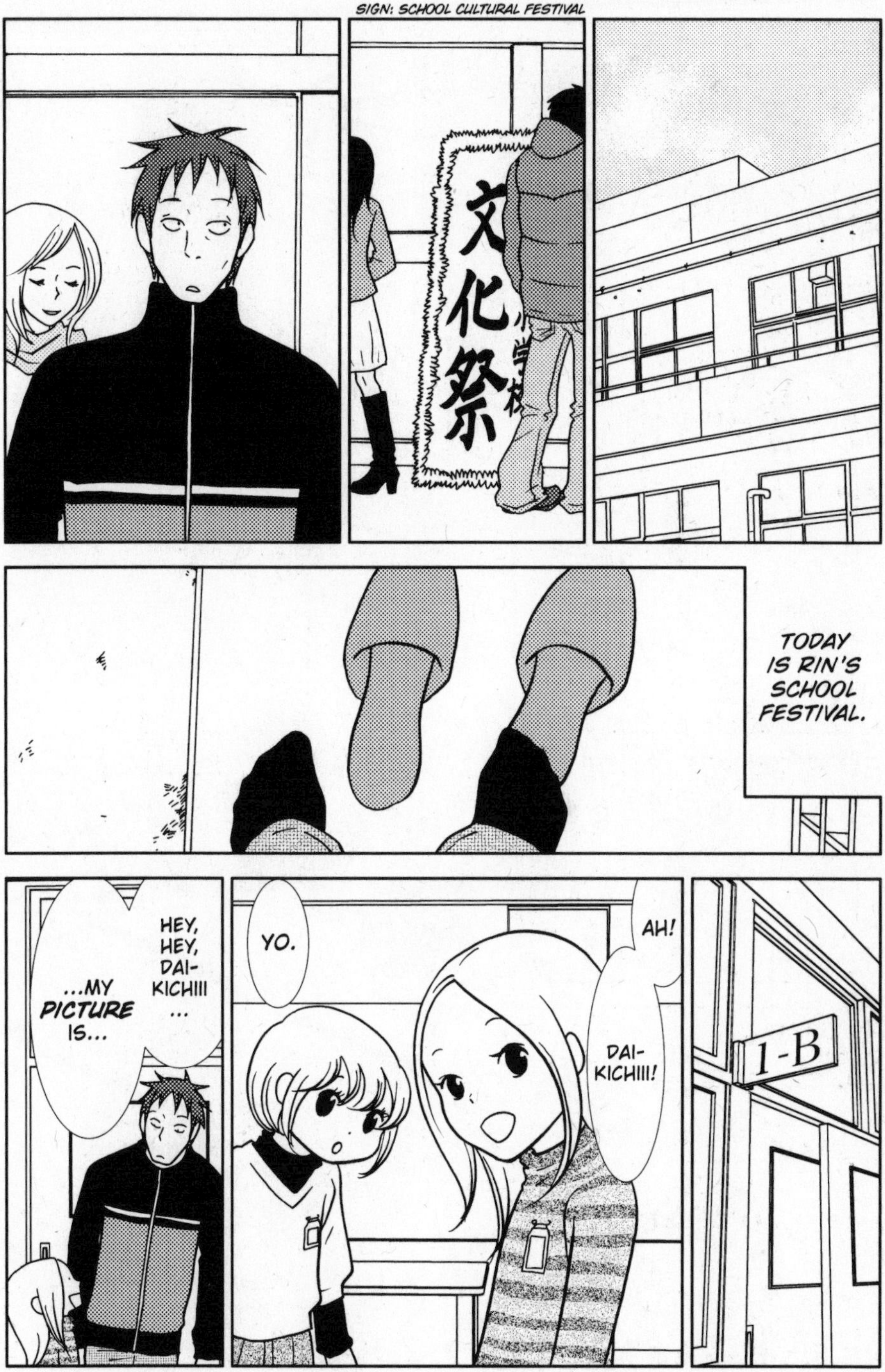
SIGN: SCHOOL CULTURAL FESTIVAL
文化祭
TODAY IS RIN'S SCHOOL FESTIVAL.
1-B
AH!
DAI-KICHIII!
YO.
HEY, HEY, DAI-KICHIII ...
...MY PICTURE IS...

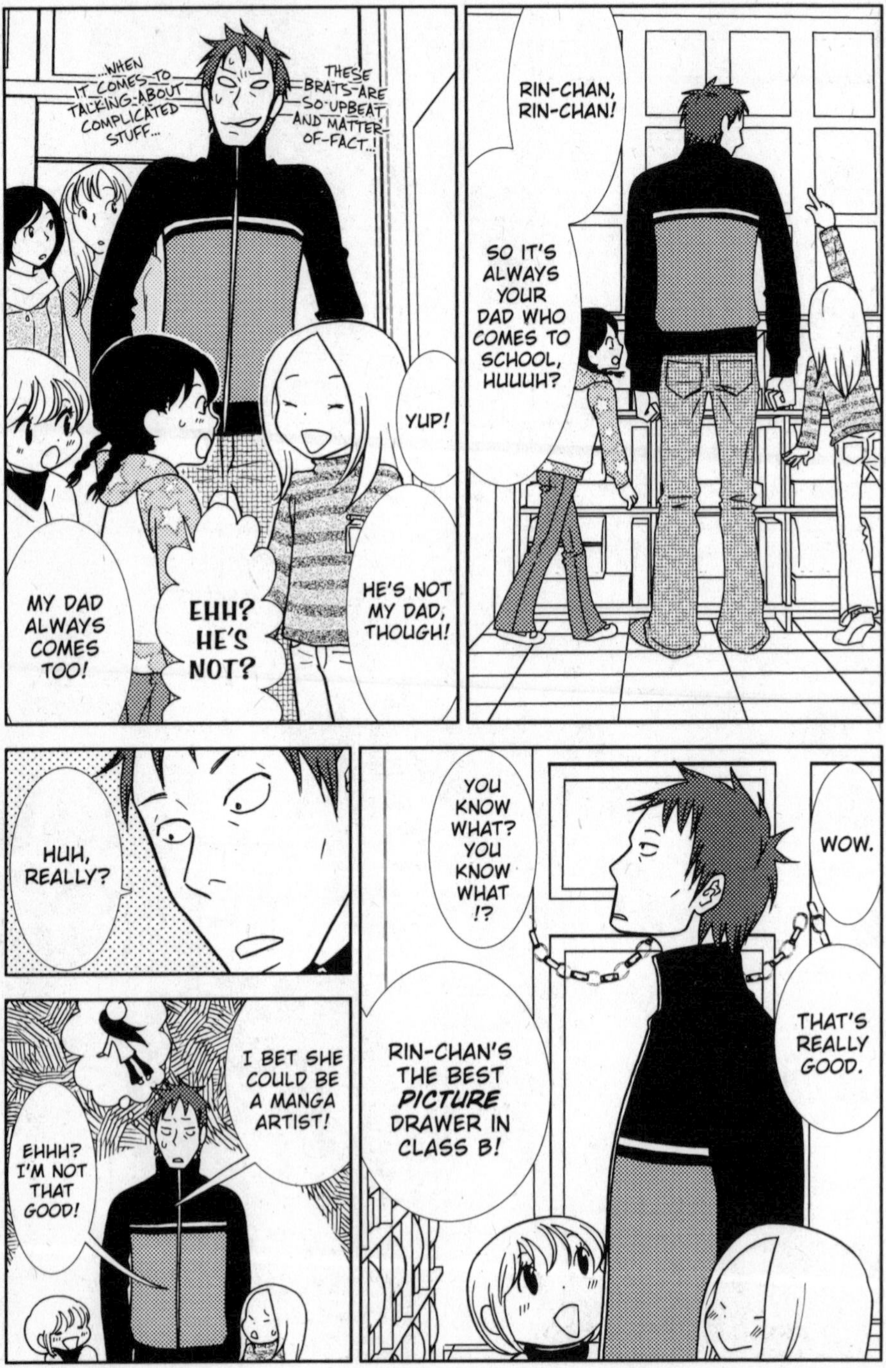
RIN-CHAN, RIN-CHAN!
SO IT'S ALWAYS YOUR DAD WHO COMES TO SCHOOL, HUUUH?
THESE BRATS ARE SO UPBEAT AND MATTER-OF-FACT...
...WHEN IT COMES TO TALKING ABOUT COMPLICATED STUFF...
YUP!
HE'S NOT MY DAD, THOUGH!
EHH? HE'S NOT?
MY DAD ALWAYS COMES TOO!
WOW.
YOU KNOW WHAT? YOU KNOW WHAT!?
THAT'S REALLY GOOD.
RIN-CHAN'S THE BEST *PICTURE* DRAWER IN CLASS B!
HUH, REALLY?
I BET SHE COULD BE A MANGA ARTIST!
EHHH? I'M NOT THAT GOOD!

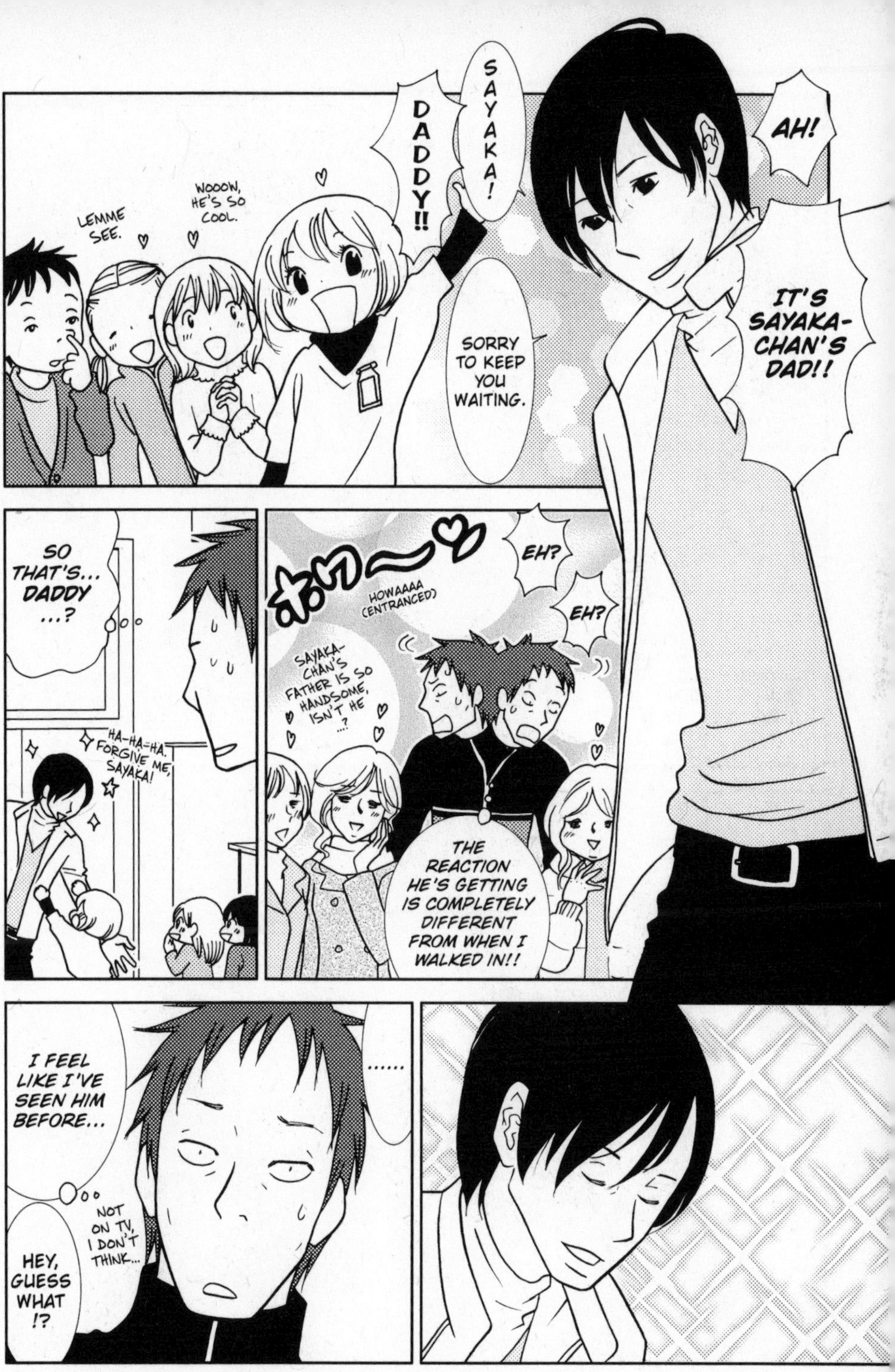
AH!
IT'S SAYAKA-CHAN'S DAD!!
SAYAKA! DADDY!!
SORRY TO KEEP YOU WAITING.
WOOOW, HE'S SO COOL.
LEMME SEE.
EH?
EH?
HOWAAAA (ENTRANCED)
SAYAKA-CHAN'S FATHER IS SO HANDSOME, ISN'T HE ...?
THE REACTION HE'S GETTING IS COMPLETELY DIFFERENT FROM WHEN I WALKED IN!!
SO THAT'S... DADDY ...?
HA-HA-HA. FORGIVE ME, SAYAKA!
......
I FEEL LIKE I'VE SEEN HIM BEFORE...
NOT ON TV, I DON'T THINK...
HEY, GUESS WHAT !?

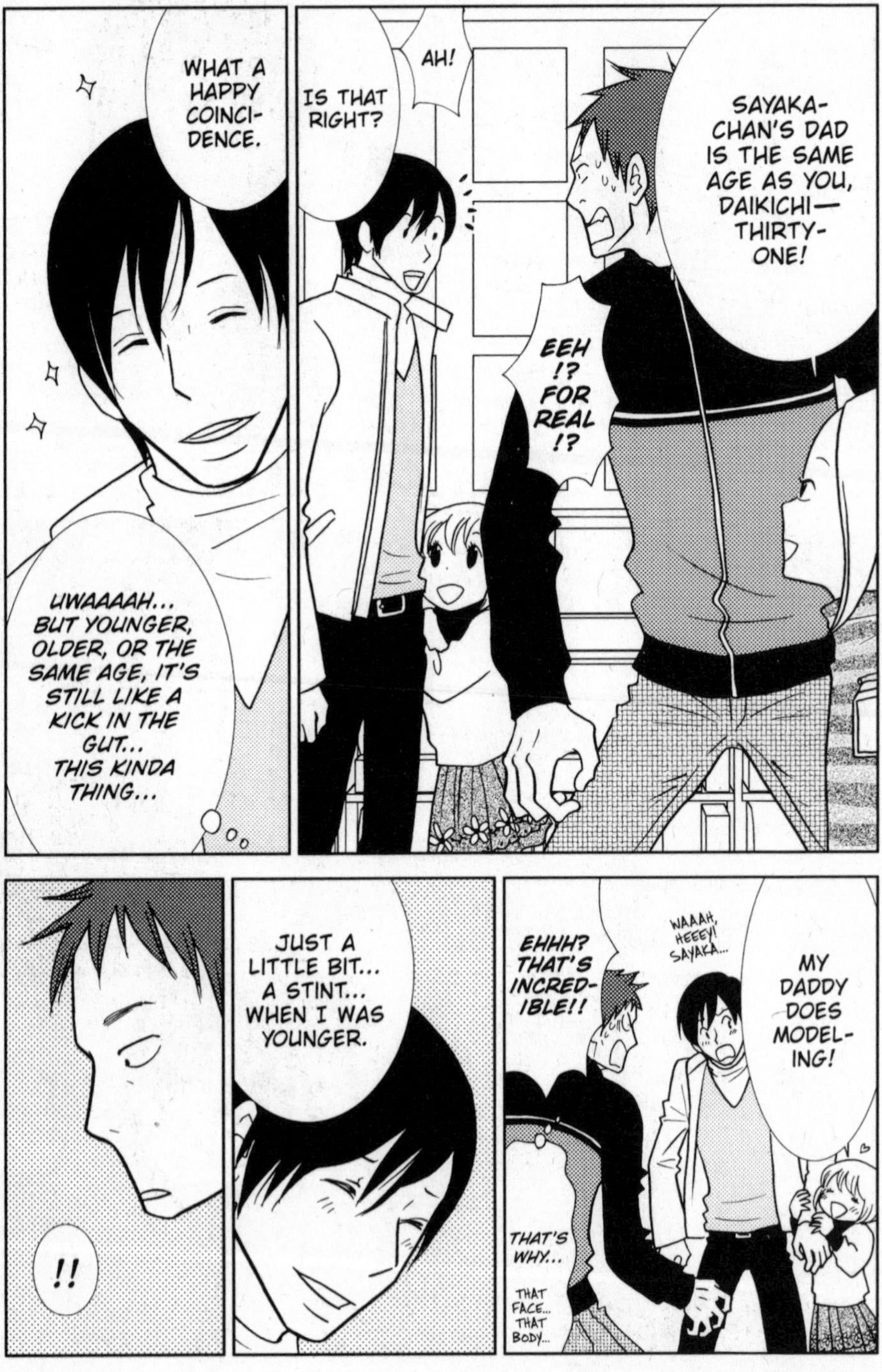
SAYAKA-CHAN'S DAD IS THE SAME AGE AS YOU, DAIKICHI—THIRTY-ONE!
EEH!? FOR REAL!?
AH!
IS THAT RIGHT?
WHAT A HAPPY COINCIDENCE.
UWAAAAH... BUT YOUNGER, OLDER, OR THE SAME AGE, IT'S STILL LIKE A KICK IN THE GUT... THIS KINDA THING...
MY DADDY DOES MODELING!
WAAAH, HEEEY! SAYAKA...
EHHH? THAT'S INCREDIBLE!!
THAT'S WHY...
THAT FACE... THAT BODY...
JUST A LITTLE BIT... A STINT... WHEN I WAS YOUNGER.
!!

CATALOGUE: MEN'S SHIRT

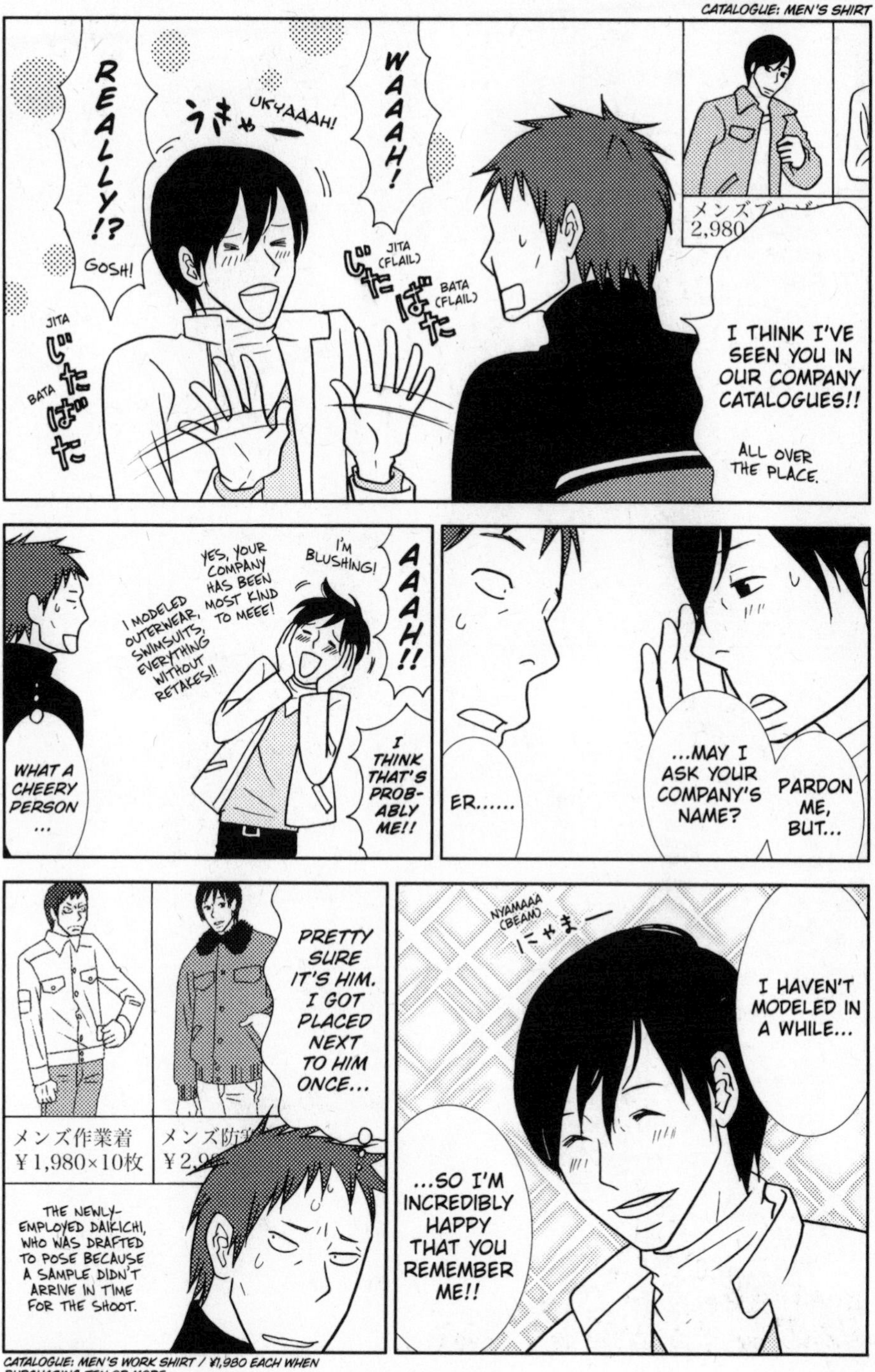
I THINK I'VE SEEN YOU IN OUR COMPANY CATALOGUES!!
ALL OVER THE PLACE.
メンズブ
2,980
WAAAH!
UKYAAAH!
うきゃー
REALLY!?
GOSH!
JITA (FLAIL)
じた
BATA (FLAIL)
ばた
JITA
じた
BATA
ばた
PARDON ME, BUT...
...MAY I ASK YOUR COMPANY'S NAME?
ER......
AAAAH!!
I THINK THAT'S PROBABLY ME!!
I'M BLUSHING!
YES, YOUR COMPANY HAS BEEN MOST KIND TO MEEE!
I MODELED OUTERWEAR, SWIMSUITS, EVERYTHING WITHOUT RETAKES!!
WHAT A CHEERY PERSON...
NYAMAAA (BEAM)
にやまー
I HAVEN'T MODELED IN A WHILE...
...SO I'M INCREDIBLY HAPPY THAT YOU REMEMBER ME!!
PRETTY SURE IT'S HIM. I GOT PLACED NEXT TO HIM ONCE...
メンズ作業着
¥1,980×10枚
メンズ防
THE NEWLY-EMPLOYED DAIKICHI, WHO WAS DRAFTED TO POSE BECAUSE A SAMPLE DIDN'T ARRIVE IN TIME FOR THE SHOOT.

CATALOGUE: MEN'S WORK SHIRT / ¥1,980 EACH WHEN PURCHASING TEN OR MORE

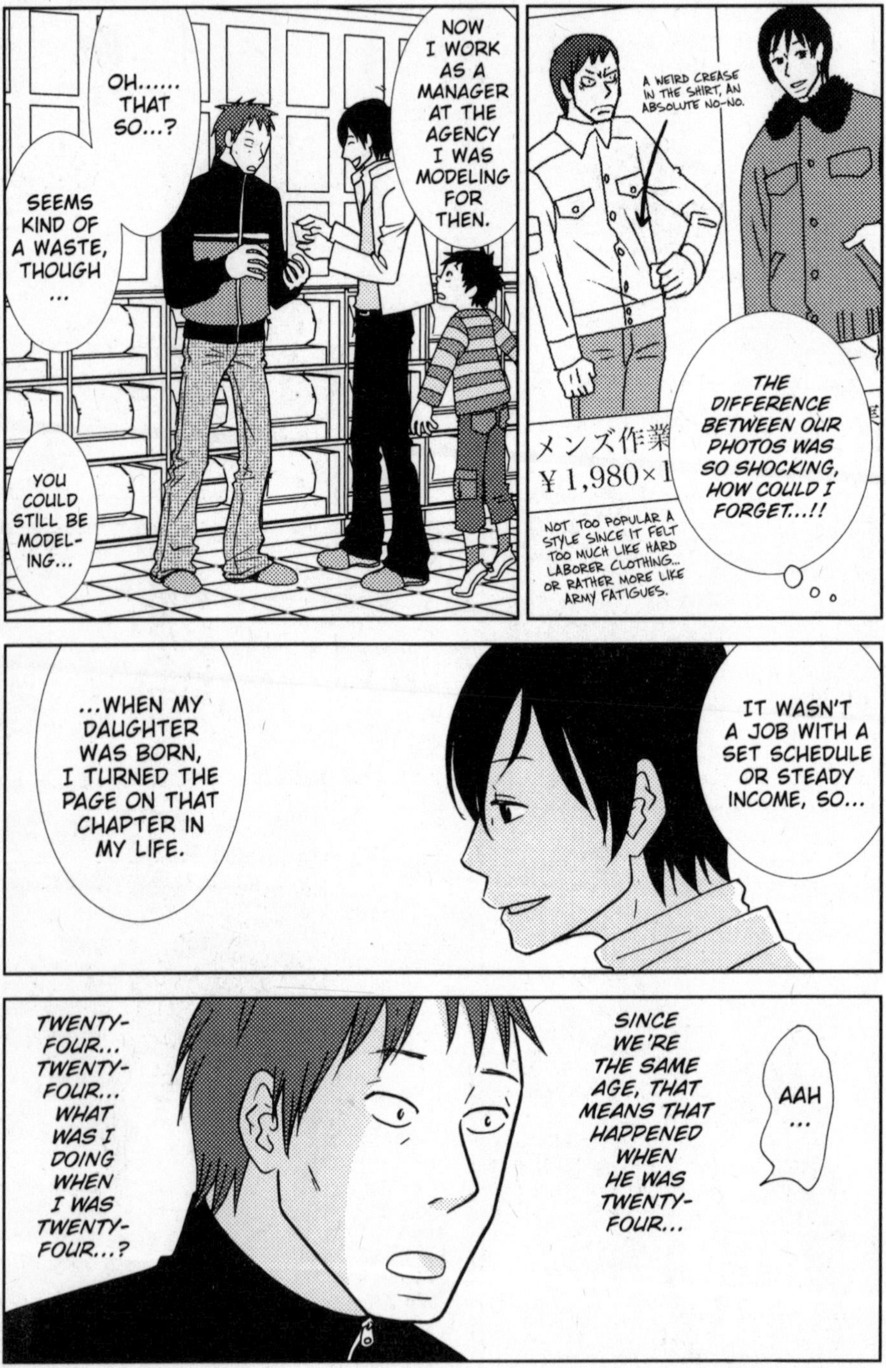
A WEIRD CREASE IN THE SHIRT, AN ABSOLUTE NO-NO.
THE DIFFERENCE BETWEEN OUR PHOTOS WAS SO SHOCKING, HOW COULD I FORGET...!!
メンズ作業
¥1,980×1
NOT TOO POPULAR A STYLE SINCE IT FELT TOO MUCH LIKE HARD LABORER CLOTHING... OR RATHER MORE LIKE ARMY FATIGUES.
NOW I WORK AS A MANAGER AT THE AGENCY I WAS MODELING FOR THEN.
OH...... THAT SO...?
SEEMS KIND OF A WASTE, THOUGH ...
YOU COULD STILL BE MODEL- ING...
IT WASN'T A JOB WITH A SET SCHEDULE OR STEADY INCOME, SO...
...WHEN MY DAUGHTER WAS BORN, I TURNED THE PAGE ON THAT CHAPTER IN MY LIFE.
AAH ...
SINCE WE'RE THE SAME AGE, THAT MEANS THAT HAPPENED WHEN HE WAS TWENTY-FOUR...
TWENTY-FOUR... TWENTY-FOUR... WHAT WAS I DOING WHEN I WAS TWENTY-FOUR...?

HEY! MICCHAN!
HEY! NABE-CHIN.
IT'S BEEN AGES!!
MICCHAN?
NABE-CHIN?
WHEN I WAS TWENTY-FOUR, I KNEW NOTHING ABOUT WORK, I HAD TONS OF FRUSTRATIONS WITH MY COMPANY, AND I DRANK LIKE A FISH.
I ONLY EVER THOUGHT ABOUT MYSELF BACK THEN.
THIS IS OUR HOME-TOWN, AND WE WERE CLASS-MATES TOO.
HIS SON'S IN CLASS A.
CLASS-MATES!
YEAH... THAT'S PROBABLY WHY...
...MY GIRLFRIEND DUMPED ME.
DAIKICHI-SAN'S THE SAME AGE AS US.
OHH!!?
NICE TO MEET YA!!
SAME HERE...
BUT BY THAT TIME, THESE PEOPLE WERE ALREADY PARENTS WATCHING OVER THEIR KIDS...
...HARUKO, MASAKO-SAN, AND NITANI-SAN TOO (THOUGH I DON'T KNOW HER AGE)......

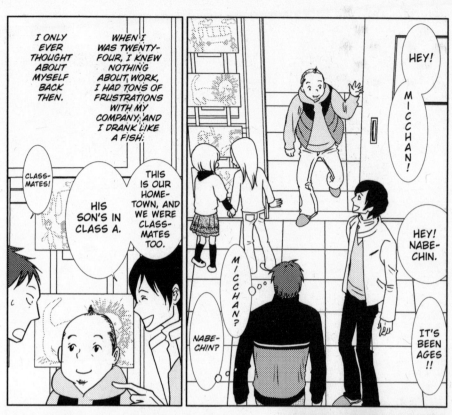

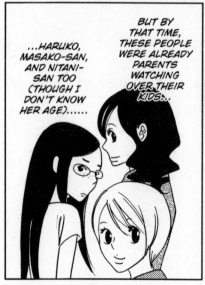

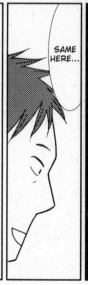

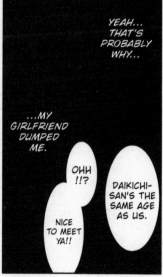

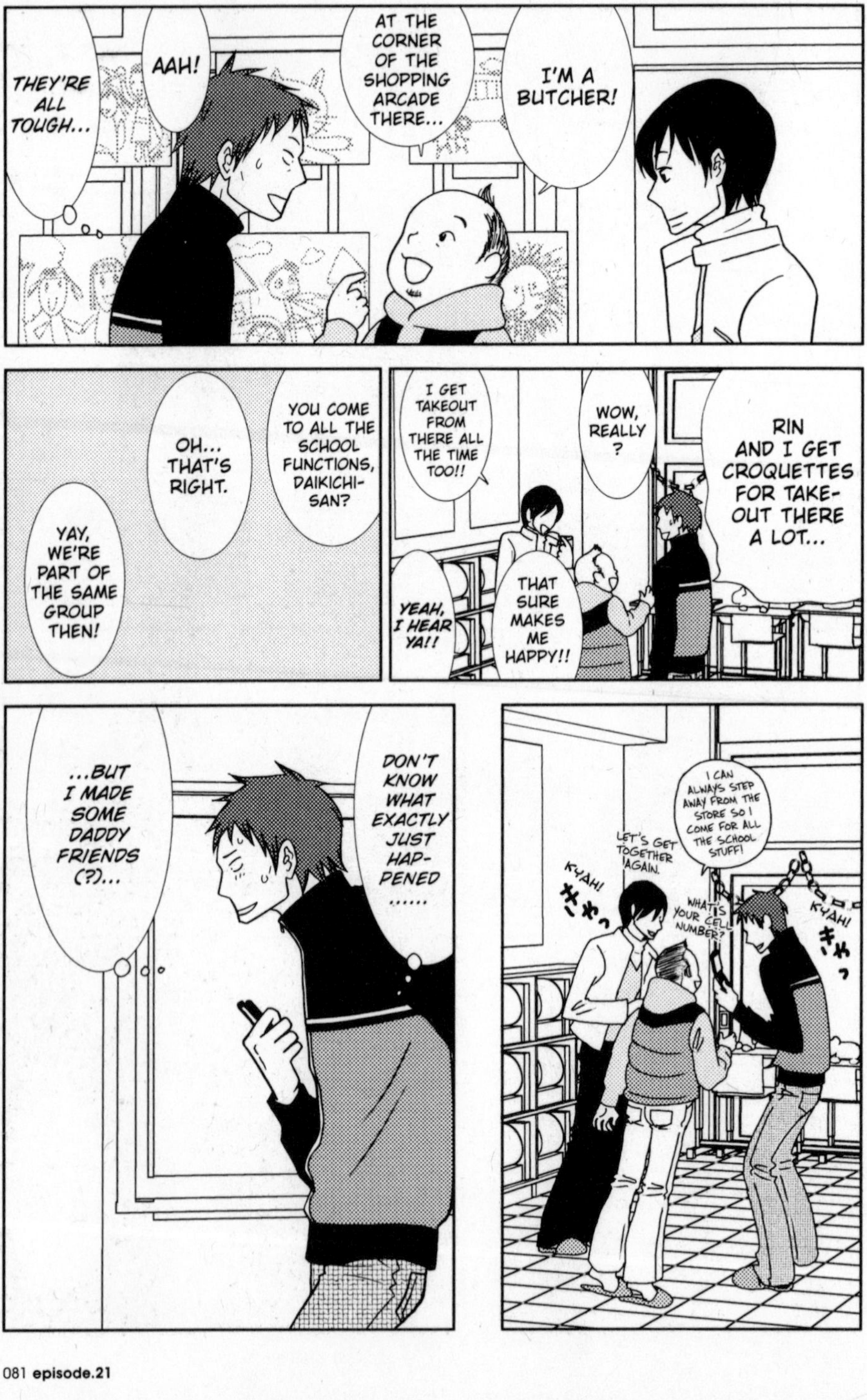
I'M A BUTCHER!
AT THE CORNER OF THE SHOPPING ARCADE THERE...
AAH!
THEY'RE ALL TOUGH...
RIN AND I GET CROQUETTES FOR TAKE-OUT THERE A LOT...
WOW, REALLY?
I GET TAKEOUT FROM THERE ALL THE TIME TOO!!
THAT SURE MAKES ME HAPPY!!
YEAH, I HEAR YA!!
YOU COME TO ALL THE SCHOOL FUNCTIONS, DAIKICHI-SAN?
OH... THAT'S RIGHT.
YAY, WE'RE PART OF THE SAME GROUP THEN!
I CAN ALWAYS STEP AWAY FROM THE STORE SO I COME FOR ALL THE SCHOOL STUFF!
KYAH! きゃっ
WHAT'S YOUR CELL NUMBER?
LET'S GET TOGETHER AGAIN.
KYAH! きゃっ
DON'T KNOW WHAT EXACTLY JUST HAPPENED......
...BUT I MADE SOME DADDY FRIENDS (?)...

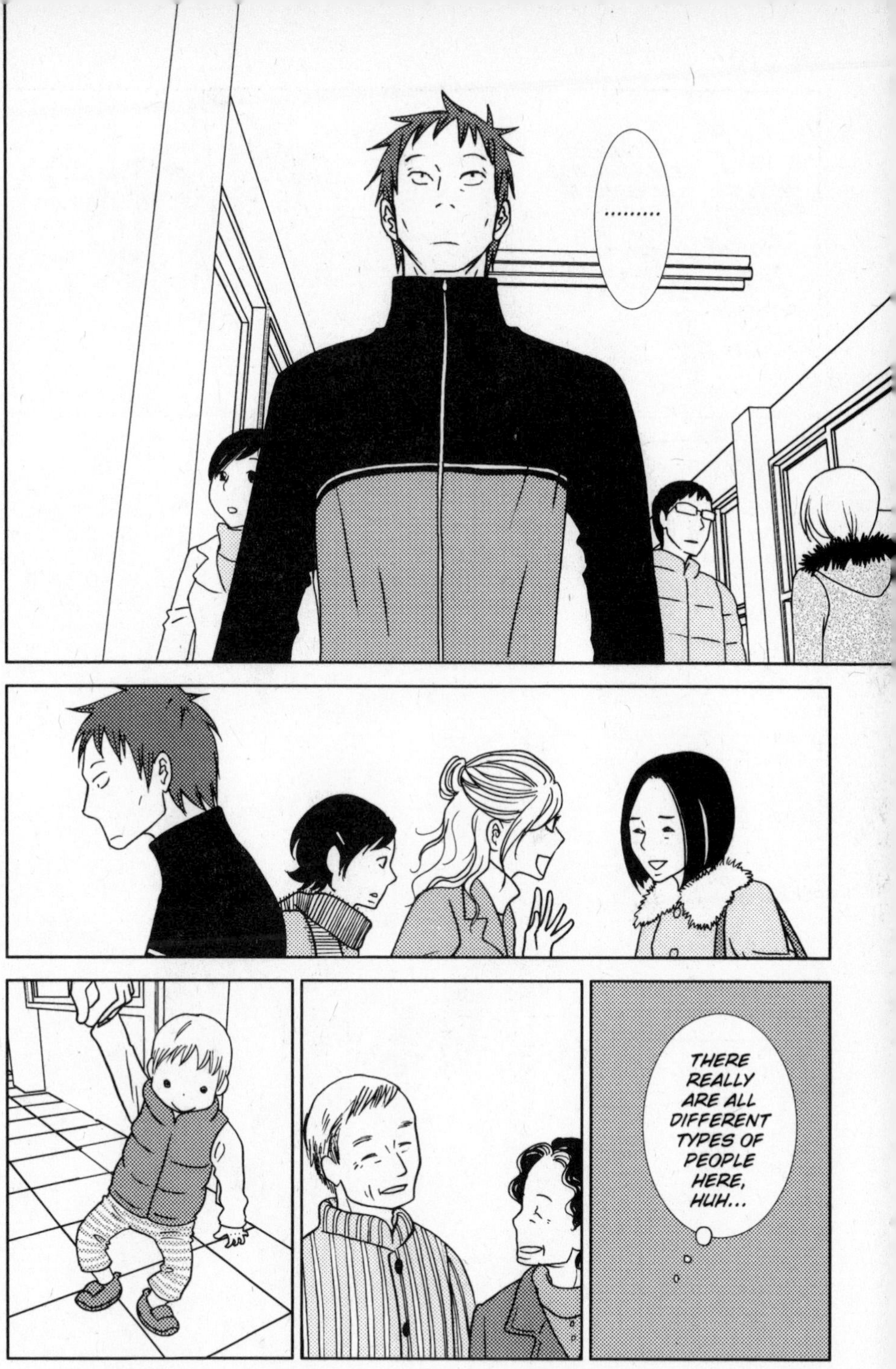
....
THERE REALLY ARE ALL DIFFERENT TYPES OF PEOPLE HERE, HUH...

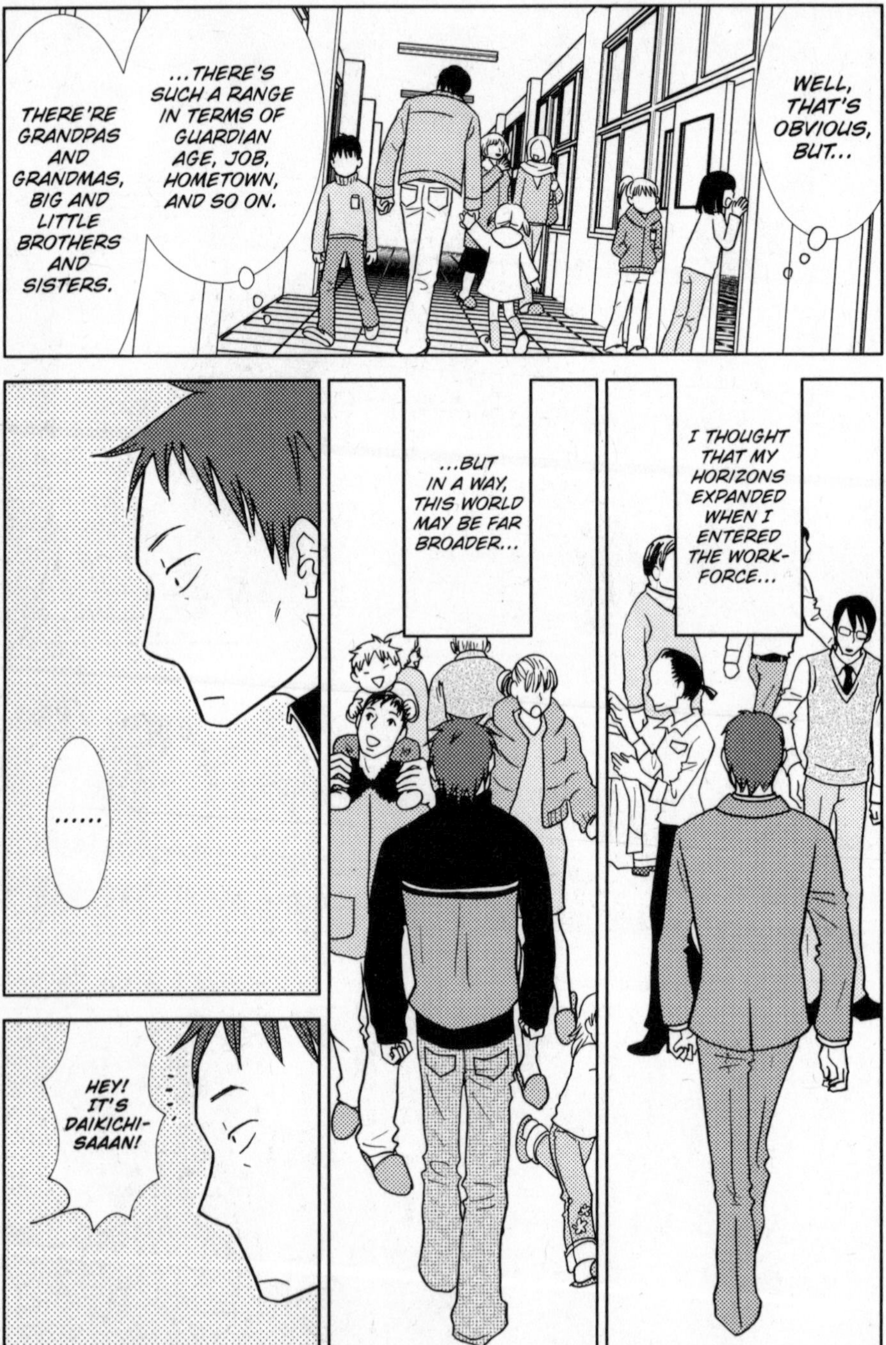
WELL, THAT'S OBVIOUS, BUT...
...THERE'S SUCH A RANGE IN TERMS OF GUARDIAN AGE, JOB, HOMETOWN, AND SO ON.
THERE'RE GRANDPAS AND GRANDMAS, BIG AND LITTLE BROTHERS AND SISTERS.
I THOUGHT THAT MY HORIZONS EXPANDED WHEN I ENTERED THE WORK-FORCE...
...BUT IN A WAY, THIS WORLD MAY BE FAR BROADER...
......
HEY! IT'S DAIKICHI-SAAAN!

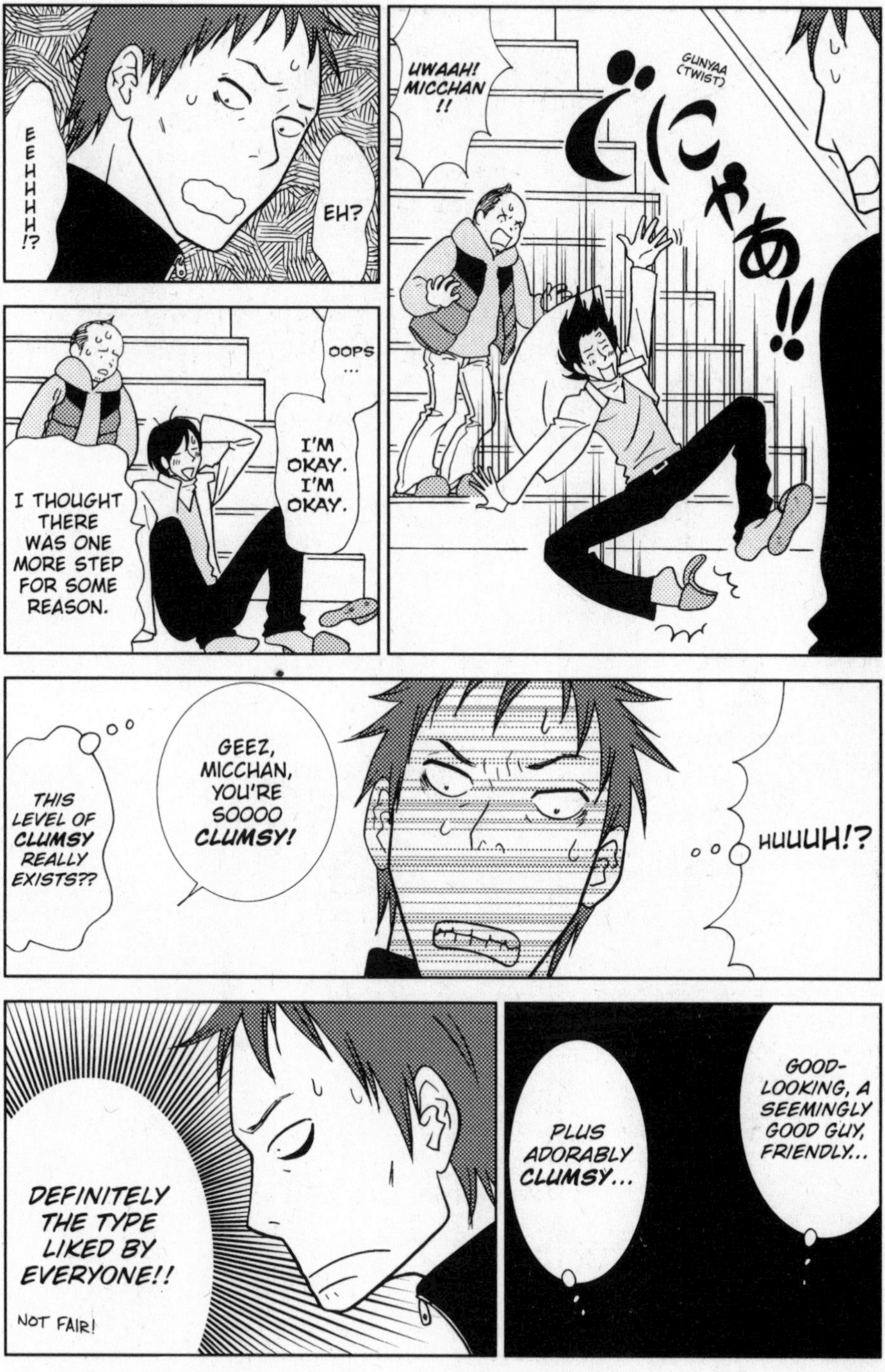
ぐにゃあ!!
GUNYAA (TWIST)
UWAAH! MICCHAN !!
EH?
EEHHHHH!?
OOPS ...
I'M OKAY. I'M OKAY.
I THOUGHT THERE WAS ONE MORE STEP FOR SOME REASON.
HUUUH!?
GEEZ, MICCHAN, YOU'RE SOOOO CLUMSY!
THIS LEVEL OF CLUMSY REALLY EXISTS??
GOOD-LOOKING, A SEEMINGLY GOOD GUY, FRIENDLY...
PLUS ADORABLY CLUMSY...
DEFINITELY THE TYPE LIKED BY EVERYONE!!
NOT FAIR!

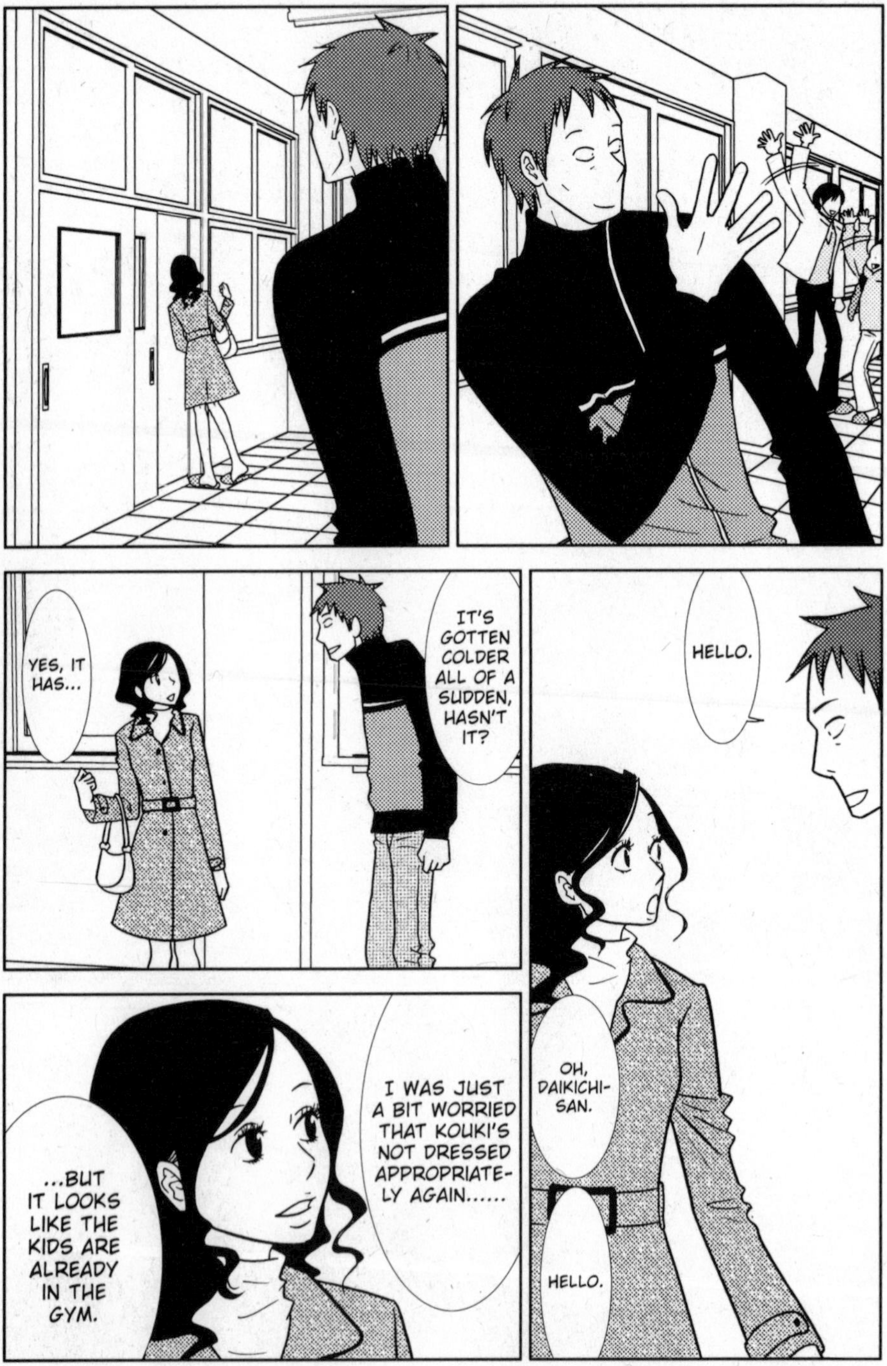
HELLO.
OH, DAIKICHI-SAN.
HELLO.
IT'S GOTTEN COLDER ALL OF A SUDDEN, HASN'T IT?
YES, IT HAS...
I WAS JUST A BIT WORRIED THAT KOUKI'S NOT DRESSED APPROPRIATE-LY AGAIN......
...BUT IT LOOKS LIKE THE KIDS ARE ALREADY IN THE GYM.

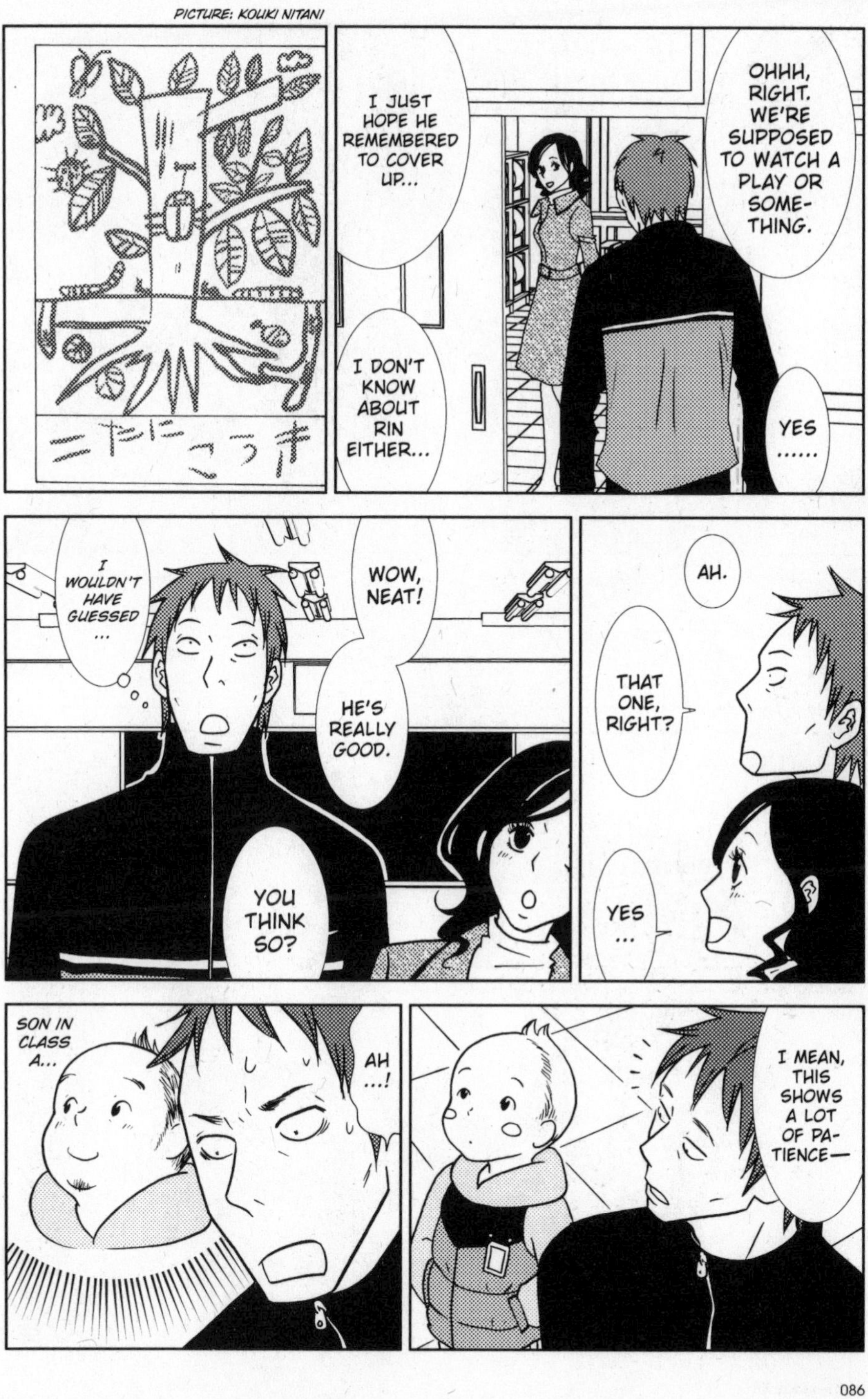
OHHH, RIGHT. WE'RE SUPPOSED TO WATCH A PLAY OR SOMETHING.
YES......
I JUST HOPE HE REMEMBERED TO COVER UP...
I DON'T KNOW ABOUT RIN EITHER...
PICTURE: KOUKI NITANI
AH.
THAT ONE, RIGHT?
YES...
WOW, NEAT!
HE'S REALLY GOOD.
I WOULDN'T HAVE GUESSED...
YOU THINK SO?
I MEAN, THIS SHOWS A LOT OF PATIENCE—
AH...!
SON IN CLASS A...

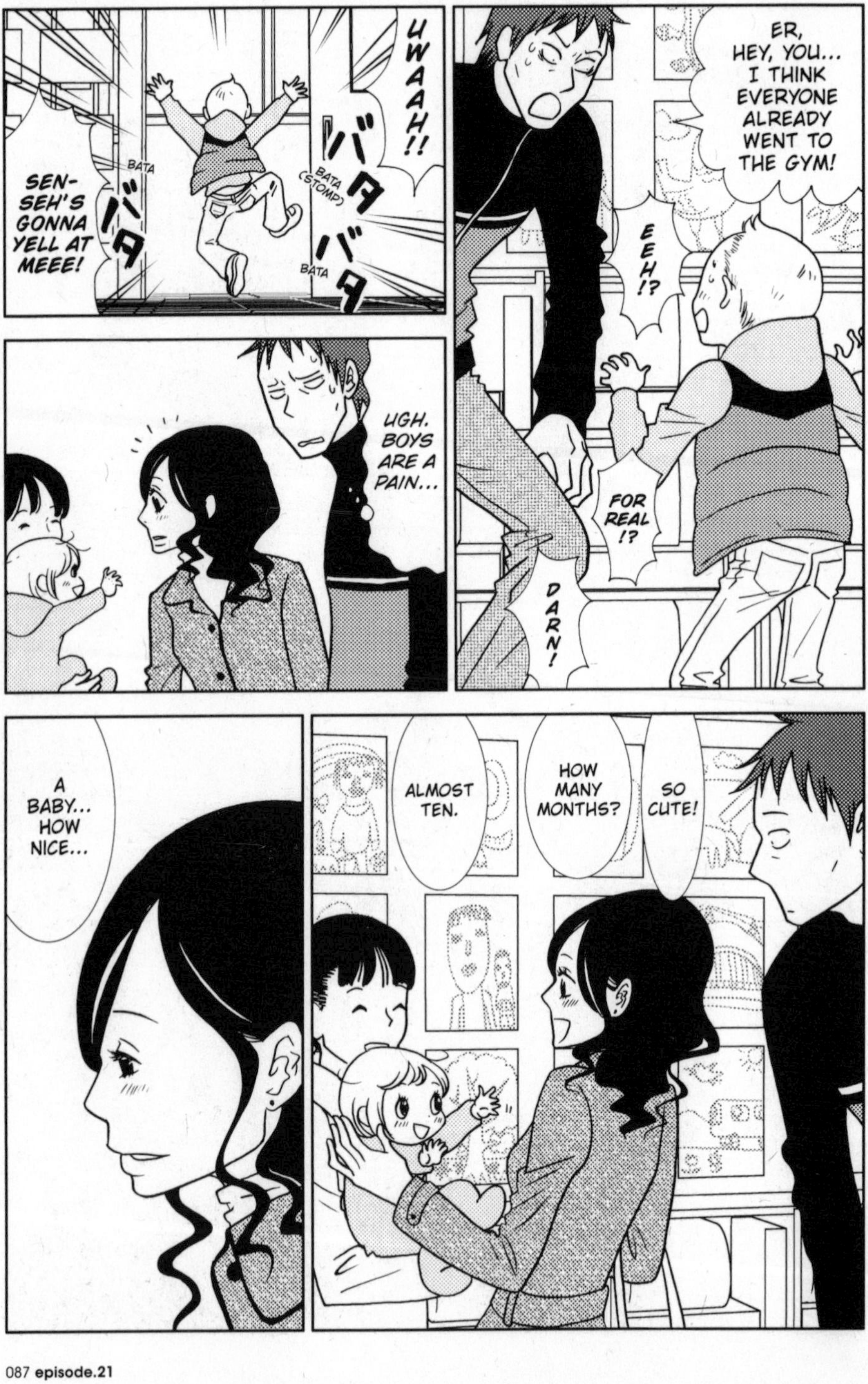
ER, HEY, YOU... I THINK EVERYONE ALREADY WENT TO THE GYM!
EEH!?
FOR REAL!?
DARN!
UWAAAH!!
バタ
BATA (STOMP)
バタ
BATA
SEN-SEH'S GONNA YELL AT MEEE!
バタ
BATA
UGH. BOYS ARE A PAIN...
SO CUTE!
HOW MANY MONTHS?
ALMOST TEN.
A BABY... HOW NICE...

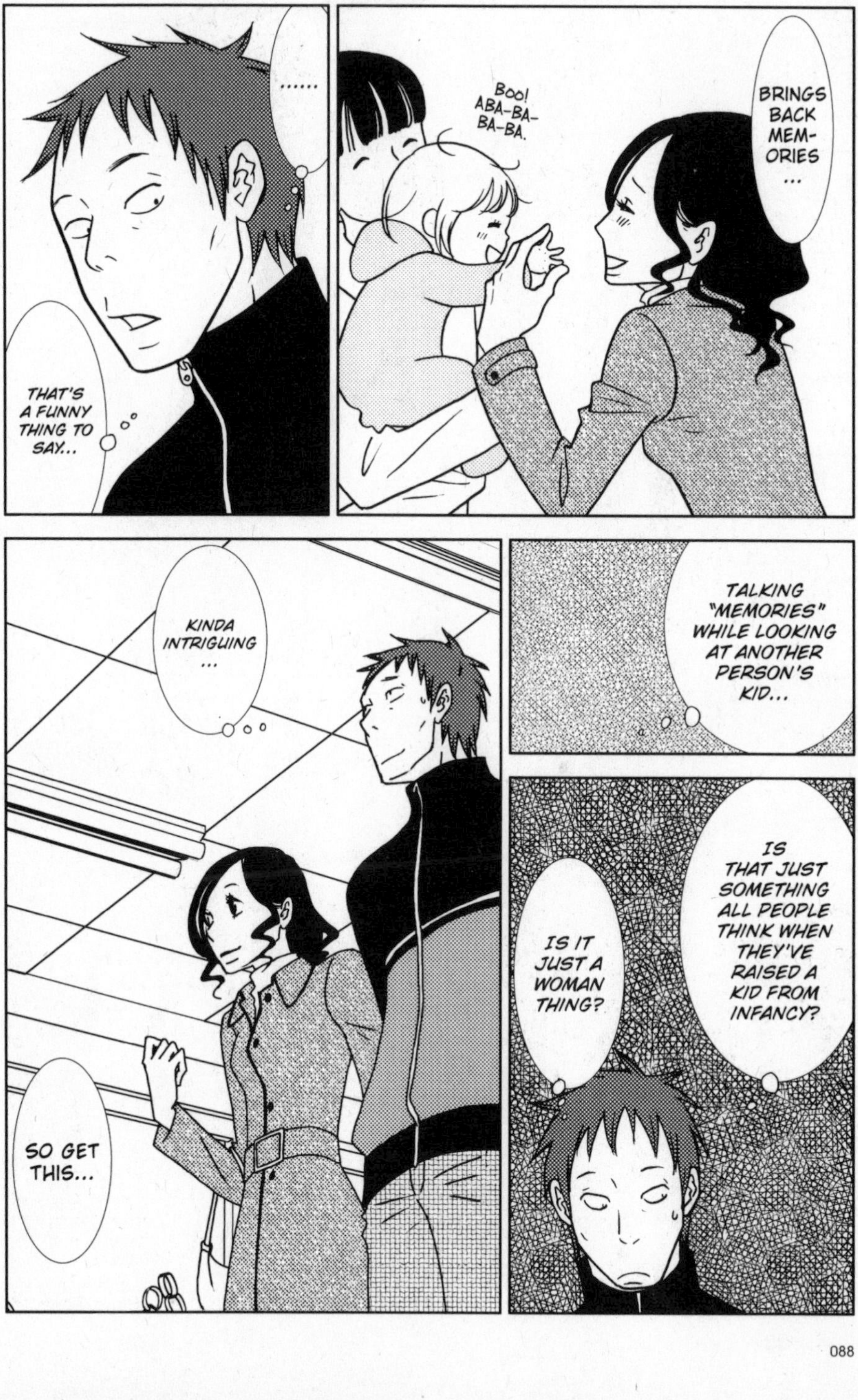
BRINGS BACK MEMORIES...
BOO! ABA-BA-BA-BA.
......
THAT'S A FUNNY THING TO SAY...
TALKING "MEMORIES" WHILE LOOKING AT ANOTHER PERSON'S KID...
IS THAT JUST SOMETHING ALL PEOPLE THINK WHEN THEY'VE RAISED A KID FROM INFANCY?
IS IT JUST A WOMAN THING?
KINDA INTRIGUING...
SO GET THIS...

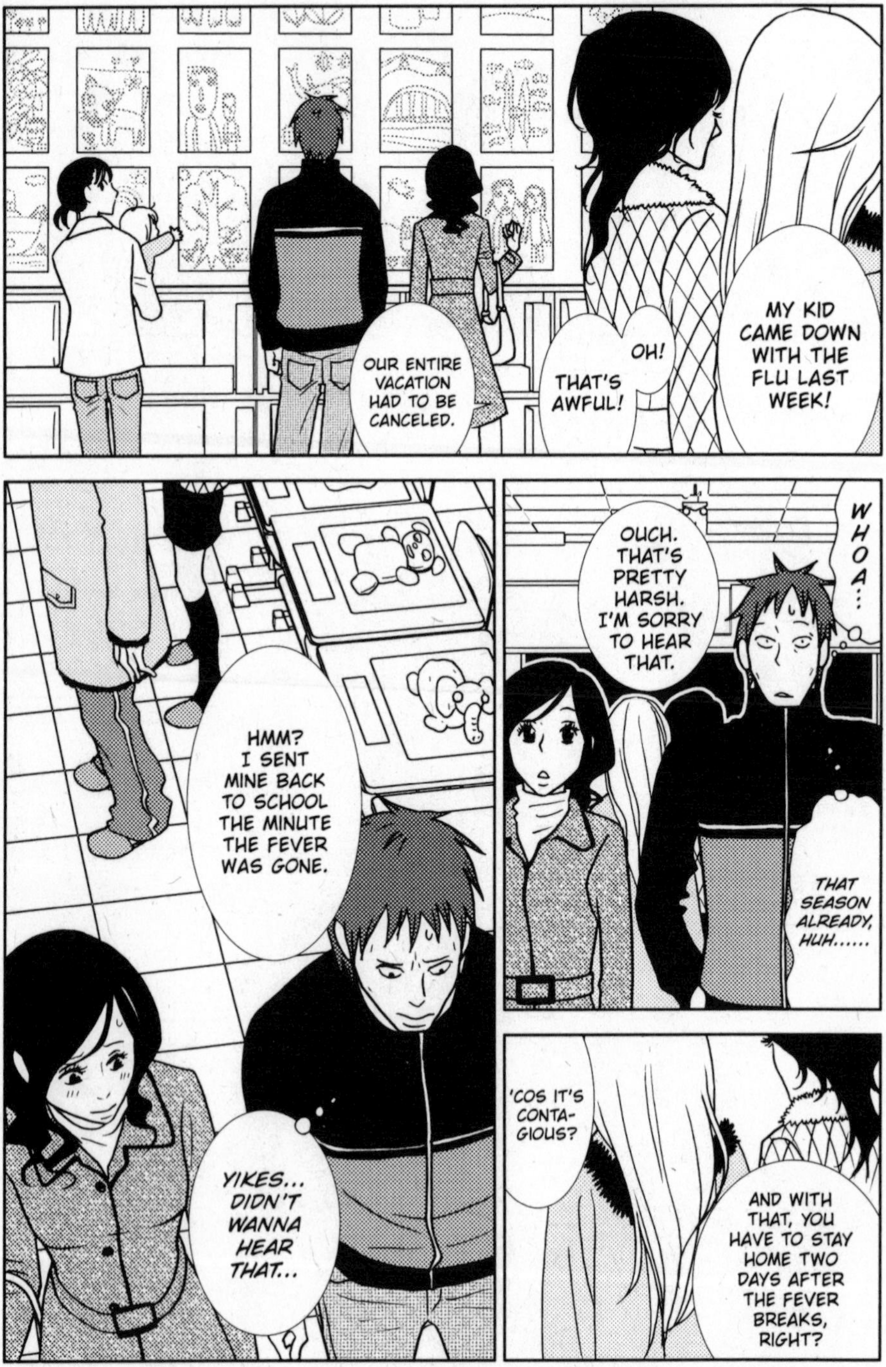
MY KID CAME DOWN WITH THE FLU LAST WEEK!
OH!
THAT'S AWFUL!
OUR ENTIRE VACATION HAD TO BE CANCELED.
WHOA...
OUCH. THAT'S PRETTY HARSH. I'M SORRY TO HEAR THAT.
THAT SEASON ALREADY, HUH......
AND WITH THAT, YOU HAVE TO STAY HOME TWO DAYS AFTER THE FEVER BREAKS, RIGHT?
'COS IT'S CONTA-GIOUS?
HMM? I SENT MINE BACK TO SCHOOL THE MINUTE THE FEVER WAS GONE.
YIKES... DIDN'T WANNA HEAR THAT...

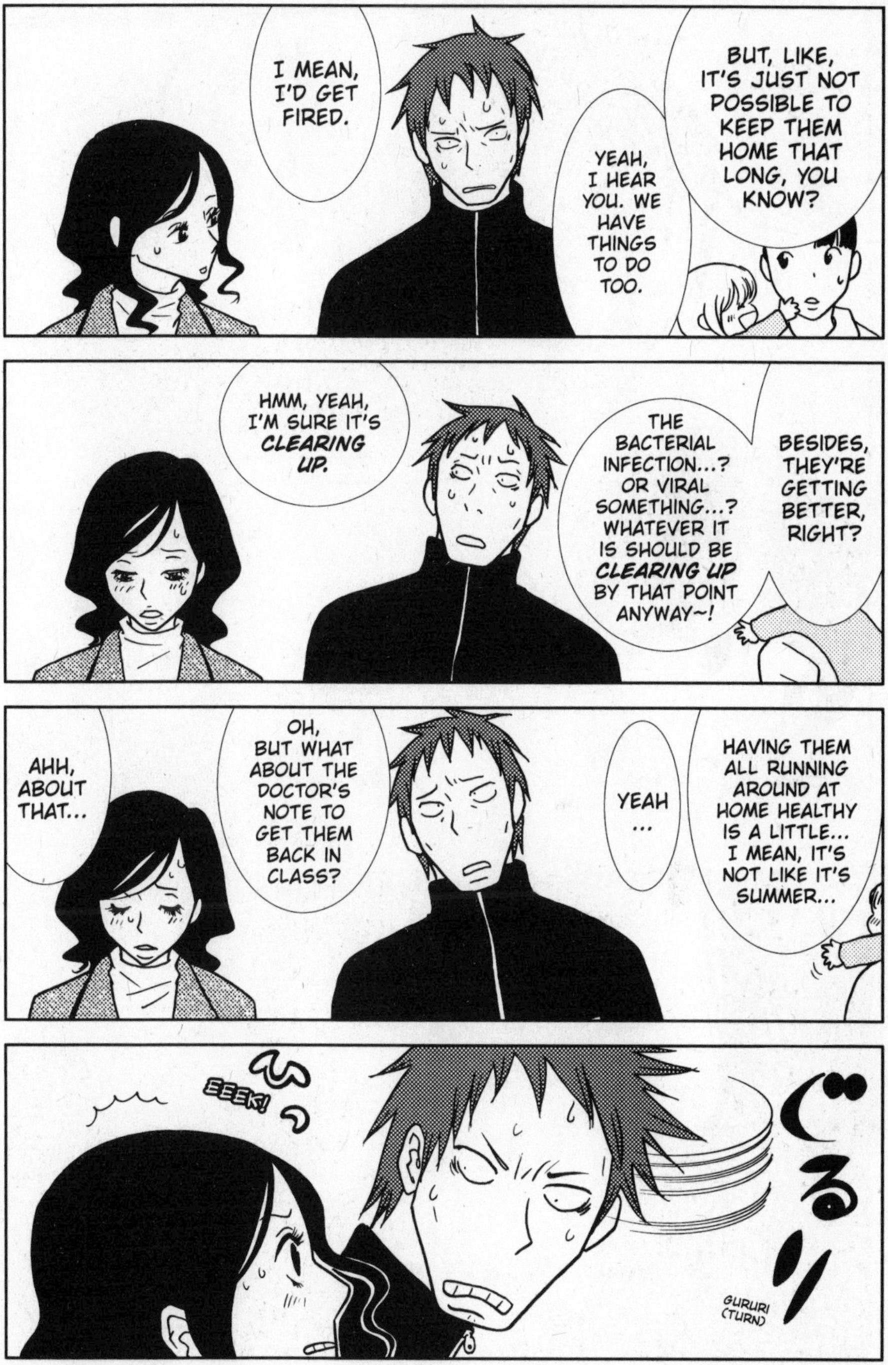
BUT, LIKE, IT'S JUST NOT POSSIBLE TO KEEP THEM HOME THAT LONG, YOU KNOW?
YEAH, I HEAR YOU. WE HAVE THINGS TO DO TOO.
I MEAN, I'D GET FIRED.
BESIDES, THEY'RE GETTING BETTER, RIGHT?
THE BACTERIAL INFECTION...? OR VIRAL SOMETHING...? WHATEVER IT IS SHOULD BE ***CLEARING UP*** BY THAT POINT ANYWAY~!
HMM, YEAH, I'M SURE IT'S ***CLEARING UP.***
HAVING THEM ALL RUNNING AROUND AT HOME HEALTHY IS A LITTLE... I MEAN, IT'S NOT LIKE IT'S SUMMER...
YEAH ...
OH, BUT WHAT ABOUT THE DOCTOR'S NOTE TO GET THEM BACK IN CLASS?
AHH, ABOUT THAT...
ぐるり
GURURI (TURN)
ひっ
EEEK!

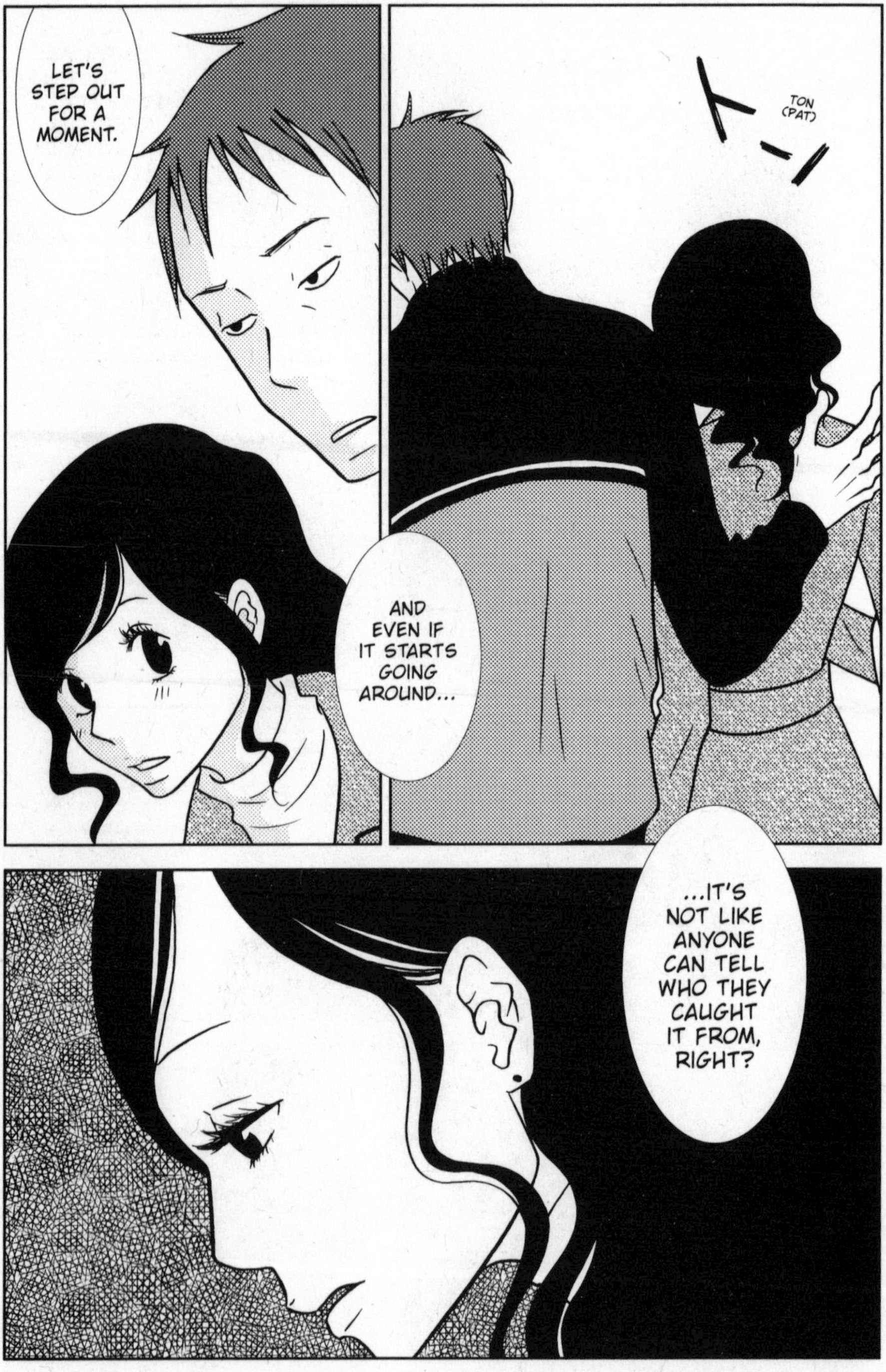
TON (PAT)
LET'S STEP OUT FOR A MOMENT.
AND EVEN IF IT STARTS GOING AROUND...
...IT'S NOT LIKE ANYONE CAN TELL WHO THEY CAUGHT IT FROM, RIGHT?

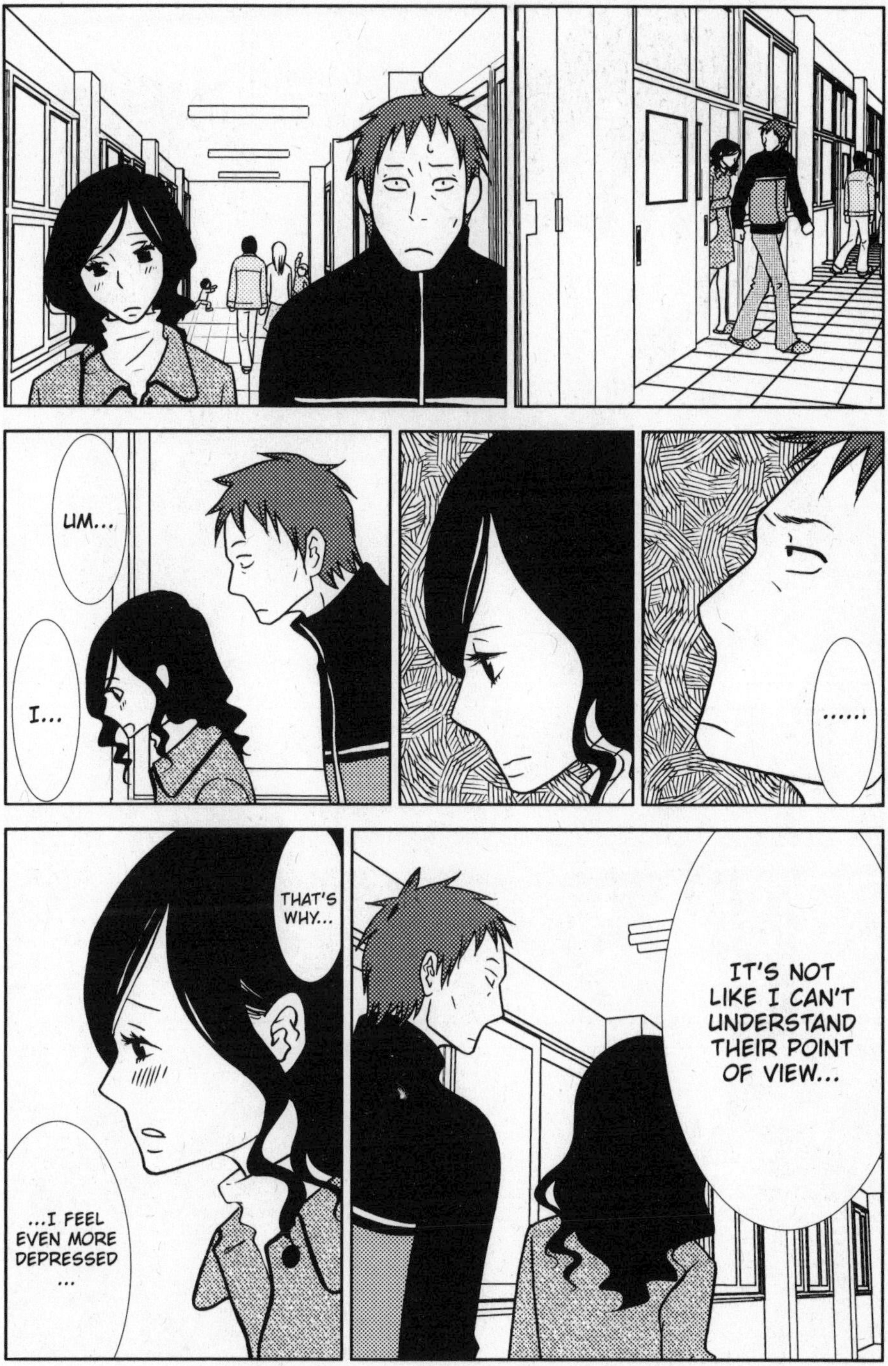
......
UM...
I...
IT'S NOT LIKE I CAN'T UNDERSTAND THEIR POINT OF VIEW...
THAT'S WHY...
...I FEEL EVEN MORE DEPRESSED ...

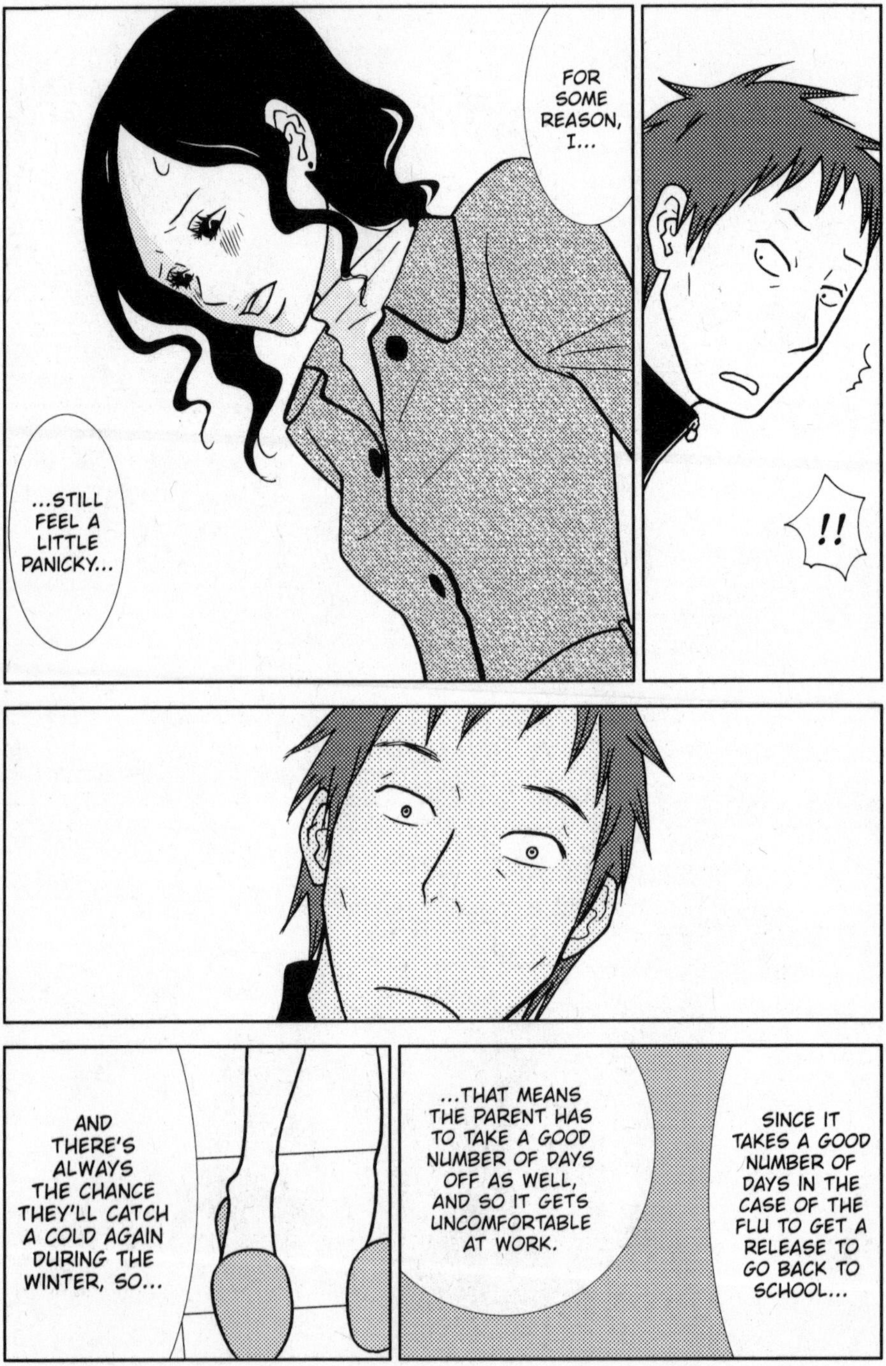
!!
FOR SOME REASON, I...
...STILL FEEL A LITTLE PANICKY...
SINCE IT TAKES A GOOD NUMBER OF DAYS IN THE CASE OF THE FLU TO GET A RELEASE TO GO BACK TO SCHOOL...
...THAT MEANS THE PARENT HAS TO TAKE A GOOD NUMBER OF DAYS OFF AS WELL, AND SO IT GETS UNCOMFORTABLE AT WORK.
AND THERE'S ALWAYS THE CHANCE THEY'LL CATCH A COLD AGAIN DURING THE WINTER, SO...

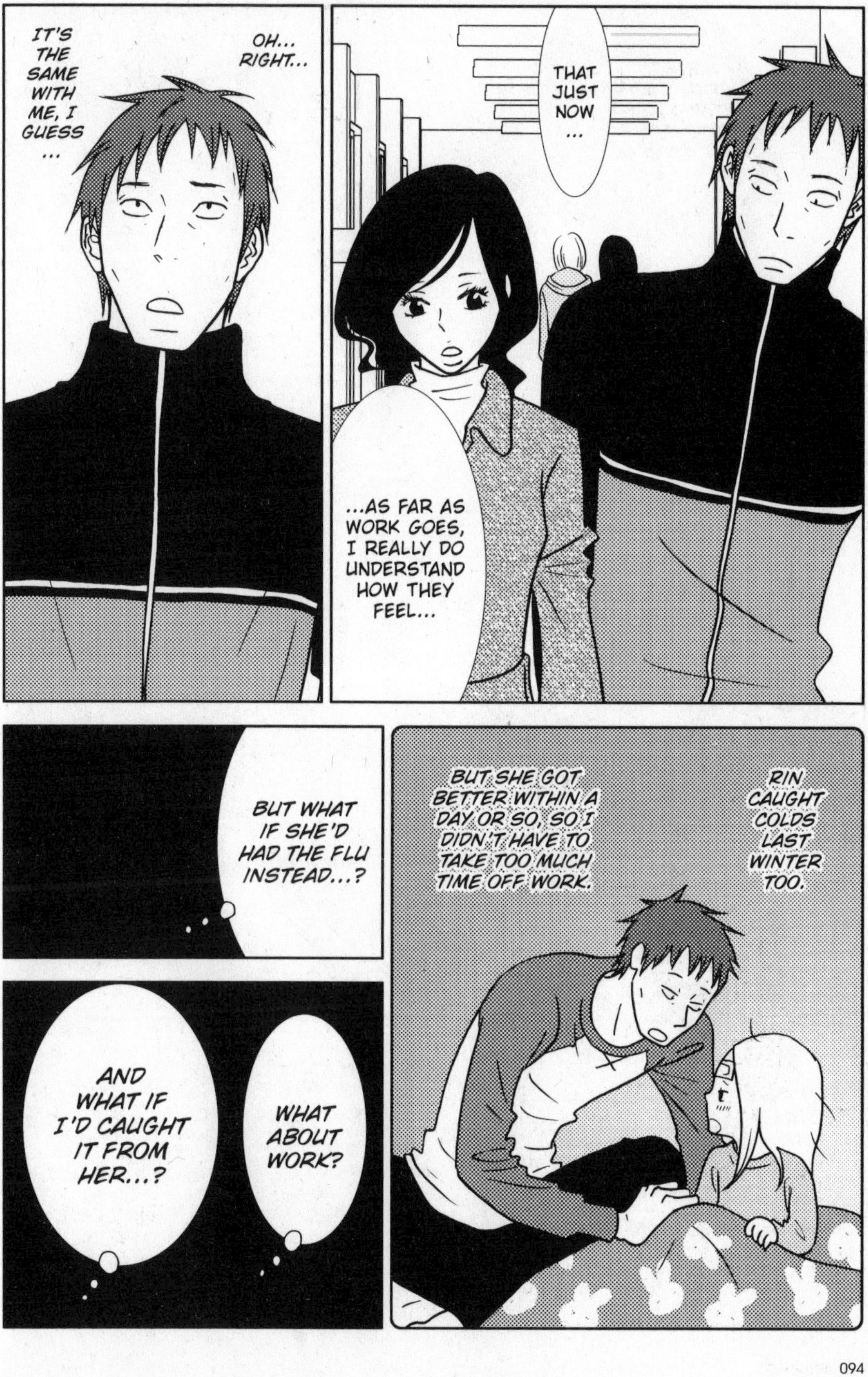
THAT JUST NOW ...
...AS FAR AS WORK GOES, I REALLY DO UNDERSTAND HOW THEY FEEL...
OH... RIGHT...
IT'S THE SAME WITH ME, I GUESS ...
RIN CAUGHT COLDS LAST WINTER TOO.
BUT SHE GOT BETTER WITHIN A DAY OR SO, SO I DIDN'T HAVE TO TAKE TOO MUCH TIME OFF WORK.
BUT WHAT IF SHE'D HAD THE FLU INSTEAD...?
WHAT ABOUT WORK?
AND WHAT IF I'D CAUGHT IT FROM HER...?

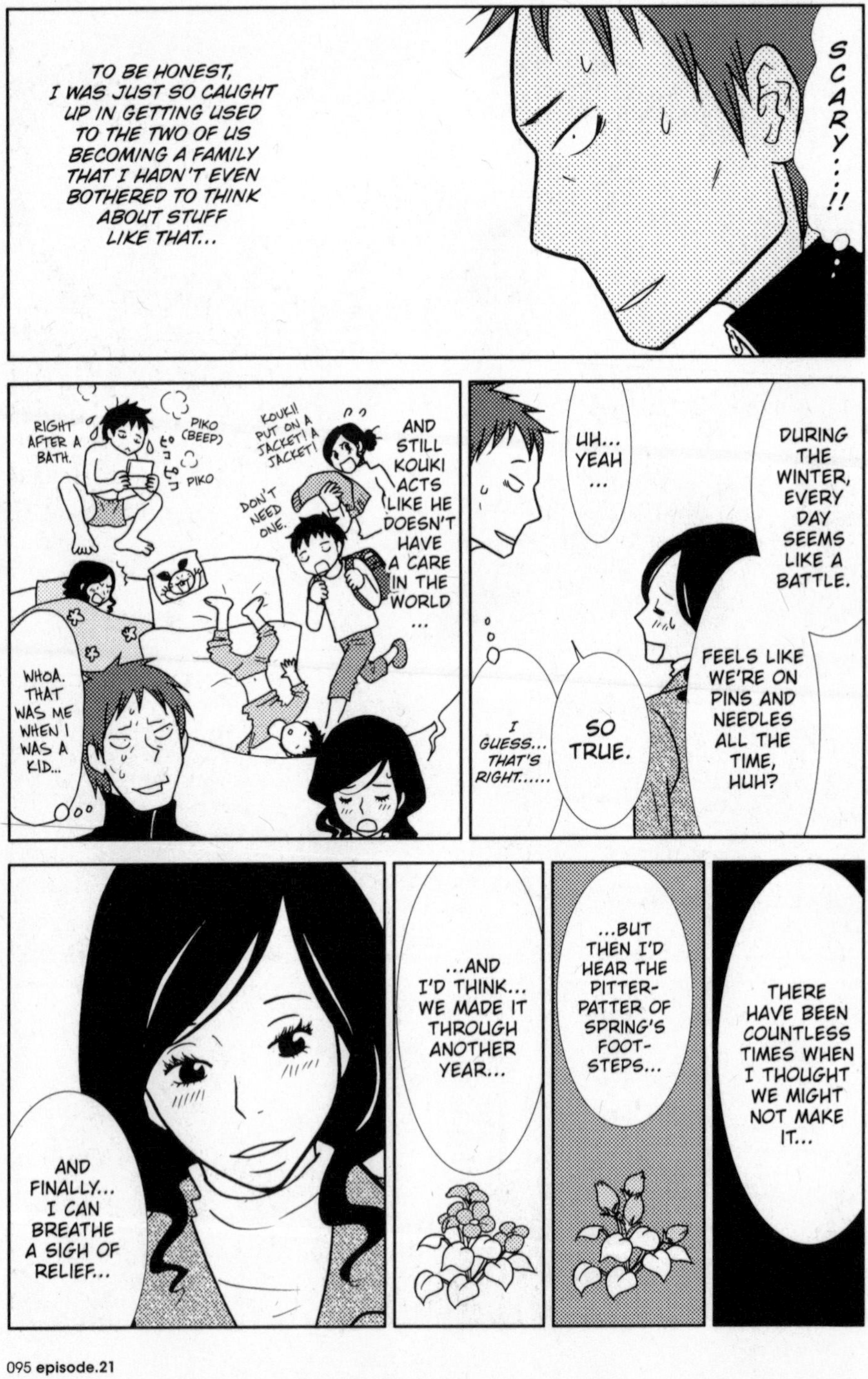
SCARY...!!
TO BE HONEST, I WAS JUST SO CAUGHT UP IN GETTING USED TO THE TWO OF US BECOMING A FAMILY THAT I HADN'T EVEN BOTHERED TO THINK ABOUT STUFF LIKE THAT...
DURING THE WINTER, EVERY DAY SEEMS LIKE A BATTLE.
FEELS LIKE WE'RE ON PINS AND NEEDLES ALL THE TIME, HUH?
UH... YEAH...
SO TRUE.
I GUESS... THAT'S RIGHT......
AND STILL KOUKI ACTS LIKE HE DOESN'T HAVE A CARE IN THE WORLD...
KOUKI! PUT ON A JACKET! A JACKET!
PIKO (BEEP)
PIKO
RIGHT AFTER A BATH.
DON'T NEED ONE.
WHOA. THAT WAS ME WHEN I WAS A KID...
THERE HAVE BEEN COUNTLESS TIMES WHEN I THOUGHT WE MIGHT NOT MAKE IT...
...BUT THEN I'D HEAR THE PITTER-PATTER OF SPRING'S FOOT-STEPS...
...AND I'D THINK... WE MADE IT THROUGH ANOTHER YEAR...
AND FINALLY... I CAN BREATHE A SIGH OF RELIEF...

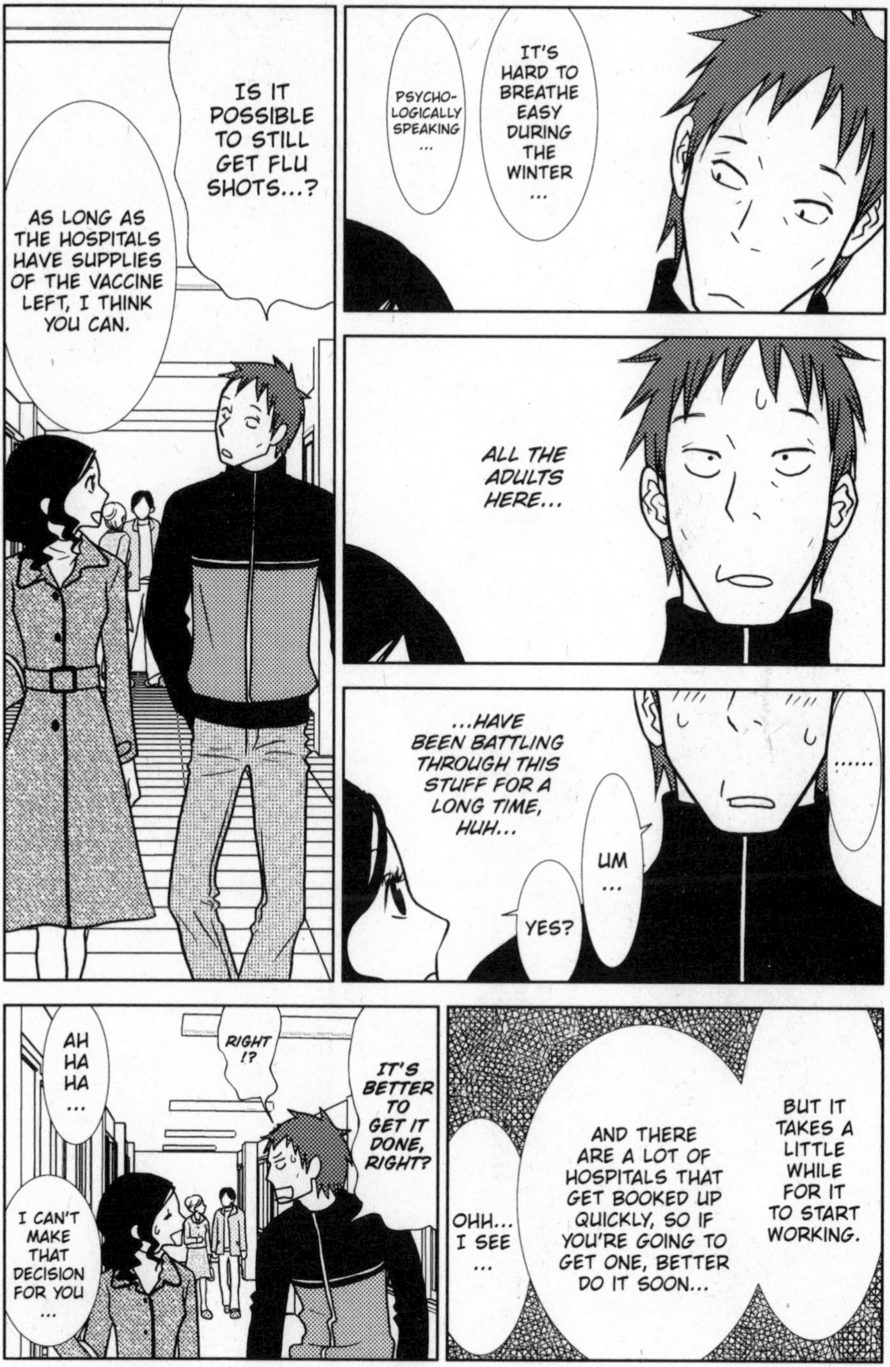
IT'S HARD TO BREATHE EASY DURING THE WINTER...
PSYCHOLOGICALLY SPEAKING...
ALL THE ADULTS HERE...
...HAVE BEEN BATTLING THROUGH THIS STUFF FOR A LONG TIME, HUH...
......
UM...
YES?
IS IT POSSIBLE TO STILL GET FLU SHOTS...?
AS LONG AS THE HOSPITALS HAVE SUPPLIES OF THE VACCINE LEFT, I THINK YOU CAN.
BUT IT TAKES A LITTLE WHILE FOR IT TO START WORKING.
AND THERE ARE A LOT OF HOSPITALS THAT GET BOOKED UP QUICKLY, SO IF YOU'RE GOING TO GET ONE, BETTER DO IT SOON...
OHH... I SEE...
IT'S BETTER TO GET IT DONE, RIGHT?
RIGHT!?
AH HA HA...
I CAN'T MAKE THAT DECISION FOR YOU...

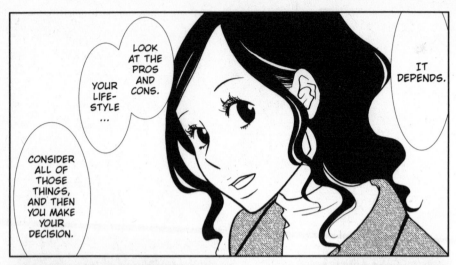

IT DEPENDS.
LOOK AT THE PROS AND CONS.
YOUR LIFE-STYLE ...
CONSIDER ALL OF THOSE THINGS, AND THEN YOU MAKE YOUR DECISION.
UWAAAAH. THAT JUST SEEMS SO COMPLICATED —!!
OR RATHER I JUST HADN'T THOUGHT ENOUGH ABOUT THIS KINDA THING...
IN OUR CASE, THE SICK-CHILD DAY CARE REQUIRES FLU VACCINATIONS...
...SO WE GET IT DONE EVERY YEAR.
SICK-CHILD DAY CARE ......??
I SEE ...
I'M COMPLETELY UNPREPARED FOR THIS...
DAI-KICHI!
DAI-KICHI!

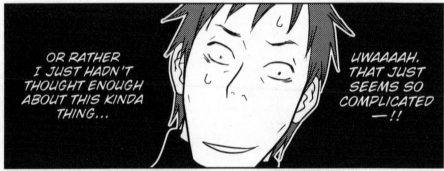

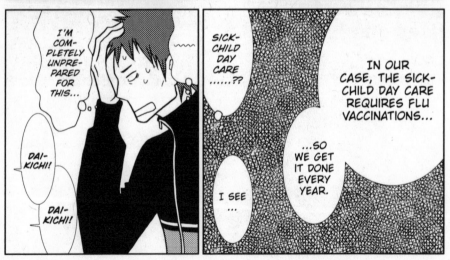

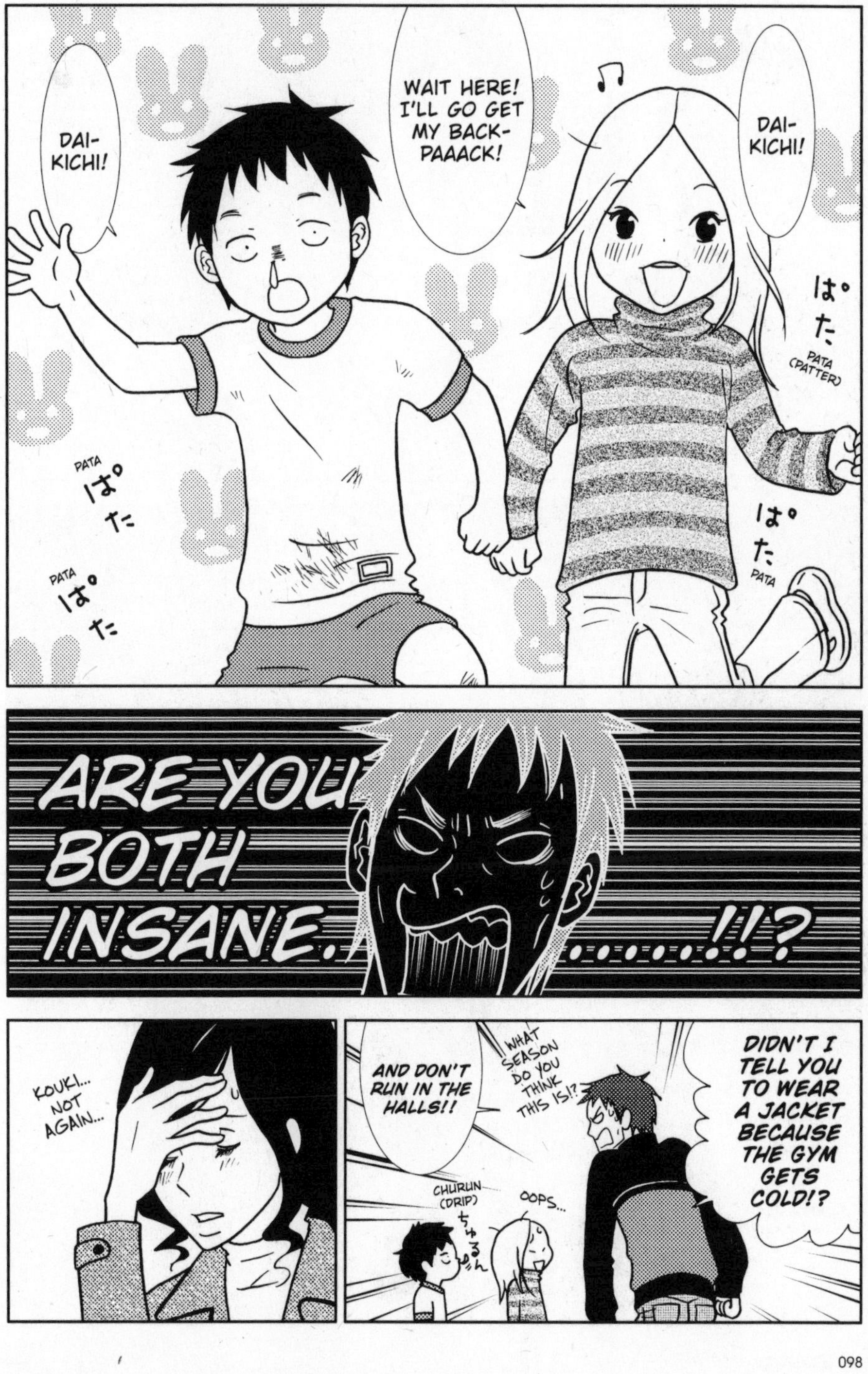
DAI-KICHI!
WAIT HERE! I'LL GO GET MY BACK-PAAACK!
DAI-KICHI!
ぱた
PATA (PATTER)
ぱた
PATA
PATA
ぱた
PATA
ぱた
ARE YOU BOTH INSANE........!!?
DIDN'T I TELL YOU TO WEAR A JACKET BECAUSE THE GYM GETS COLD!?
WHAT SEASON DO YOU THINK THIS IS!?
AND DON'T RUN IN THE HALLS!!
OOPS...
CHURUN (DRIP)
ちゅるん
KOUKI... NOT AGAIN...

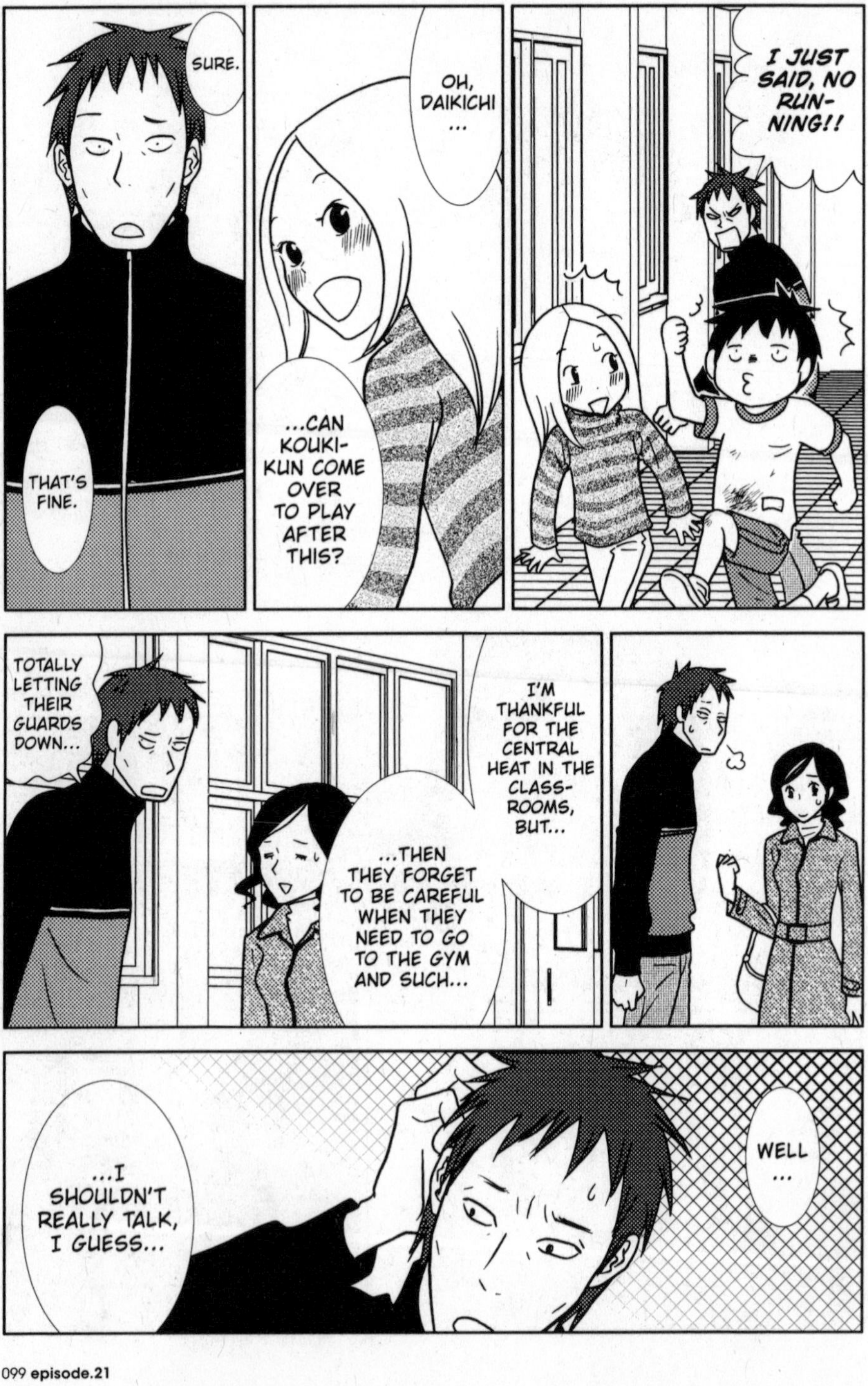
I JUST SAID, NO RUN-NING!!
OH, DAIKICHI ...
...CAN KOUKI-KUN COME OVER TO PLAY AFTER THIS?
SURE.
THAT'S FINE.
I'M THANKFUL FOR THE CENTRAL HEAT IN THE CLASS-ROOMS, BUT...
...THEN THEY FORGET TO BE CAREFUL WHEN THEY NEED TO GO TO THE GYM AND SUCH...
TOTALLY LETTING THEIR GUARDS DOWN...
WELL ...
...I SHOULDN'T REALLY TALK, I GUESS...

SIGNS: CAUTION!! NO SKIPPING STEPS! NO RUNNING IN THE HALLWAYS!

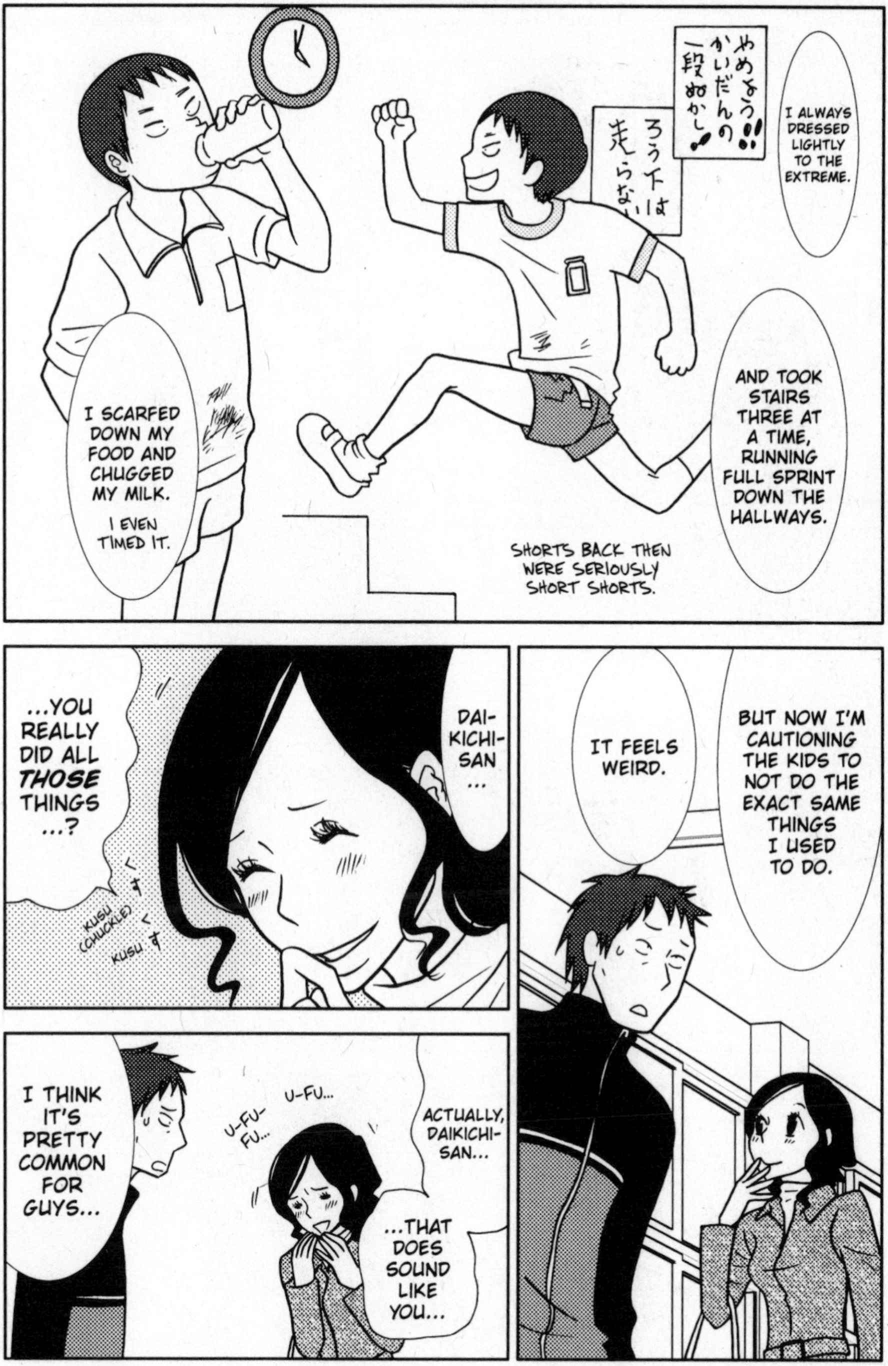
やめよう!! かいだんの 一段ぬかし
ろう下は 走らない
I ALWAYS DRESSED LIGHTLY TO THE EXTREME.
AND TOOK STAIRS THREE AT A TIME, RUNNING FULL SPRINT DOWN THE HALLWAYS.
SHORTS BACK THEN WERE SERIOUSLY SHORT SHORTS.
I SCARFED DOWN MY FOOD AND CHUGGED MY MILK.
I EVEN TIMED IT.
BUT NOW I'M CAUTIONING THE KIDS TO NOT DO THE EXACT SAME THINGS I USED TO DO.
IT FEELS WEIRD.
DAI-KICHI-SAN...
...YOU REALLY DID ALL ***THOSE*** THINGS...?
くすくす
KUSU (CHUCKLE) KUSU
ACTUALLY, DAIKICHI-SAN...
...THAT DOES SOUND LIKE YOU...
U-FU...
U-FU-FU...
I THINK IT'S PRETTY COMMON FOR GUYS...

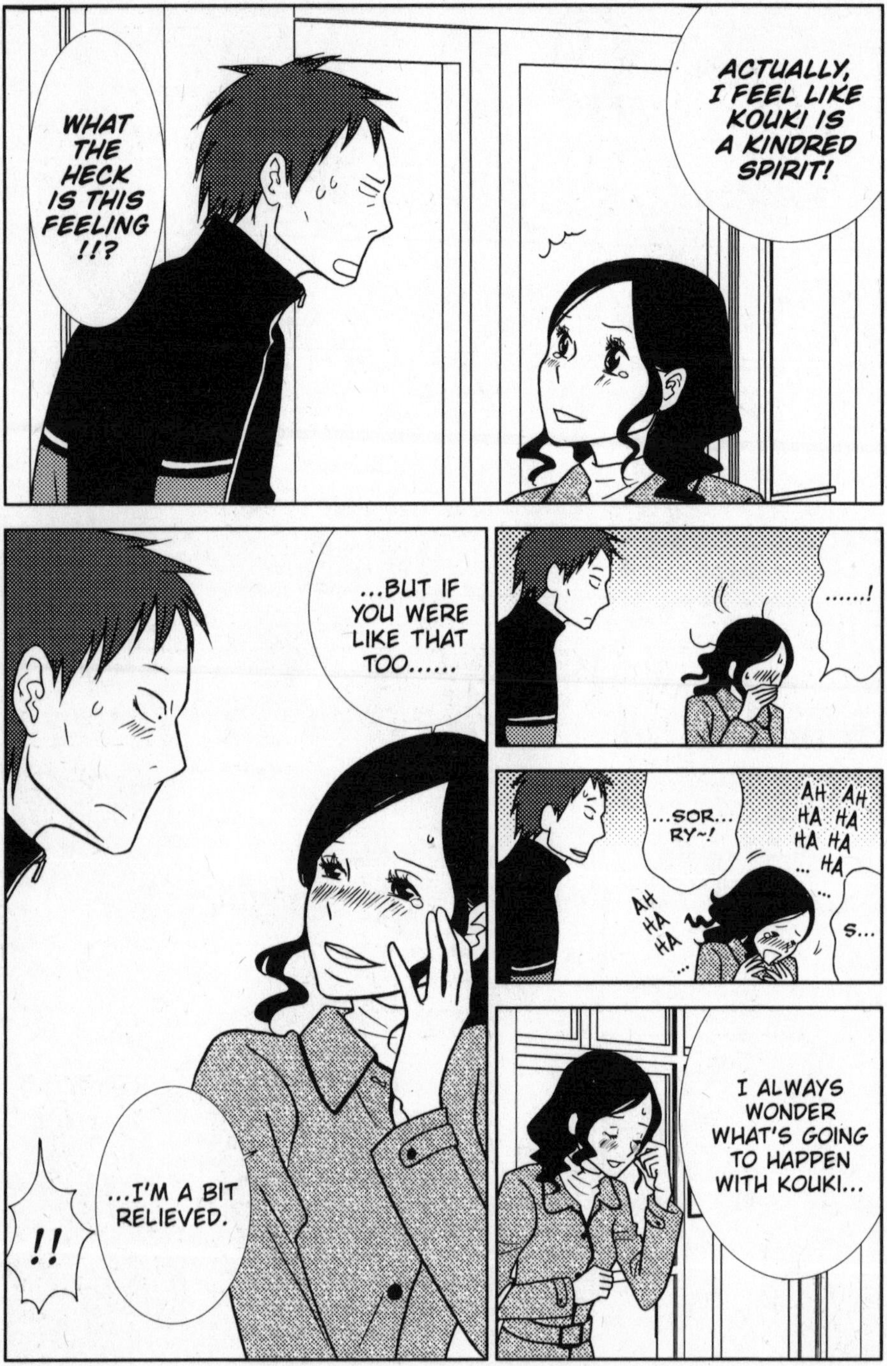
ACTUALLY, I FEEL LIKE KOUKI IS A KINDRED SPIRIT!
WHAT THE HECK IS THIS FEELING !!?
......!
AH AH HA HA HA HA ... HA ...
...SOR... RY~!
S...
AH HA HA ...
I ALWAYS WONDER WHAT'S GOING TO HAPPEN WITH KOUKI...
...BUT IF YOU WERE LIKE THAT TOO......
...I'M A BIT RELIEVED.
!!

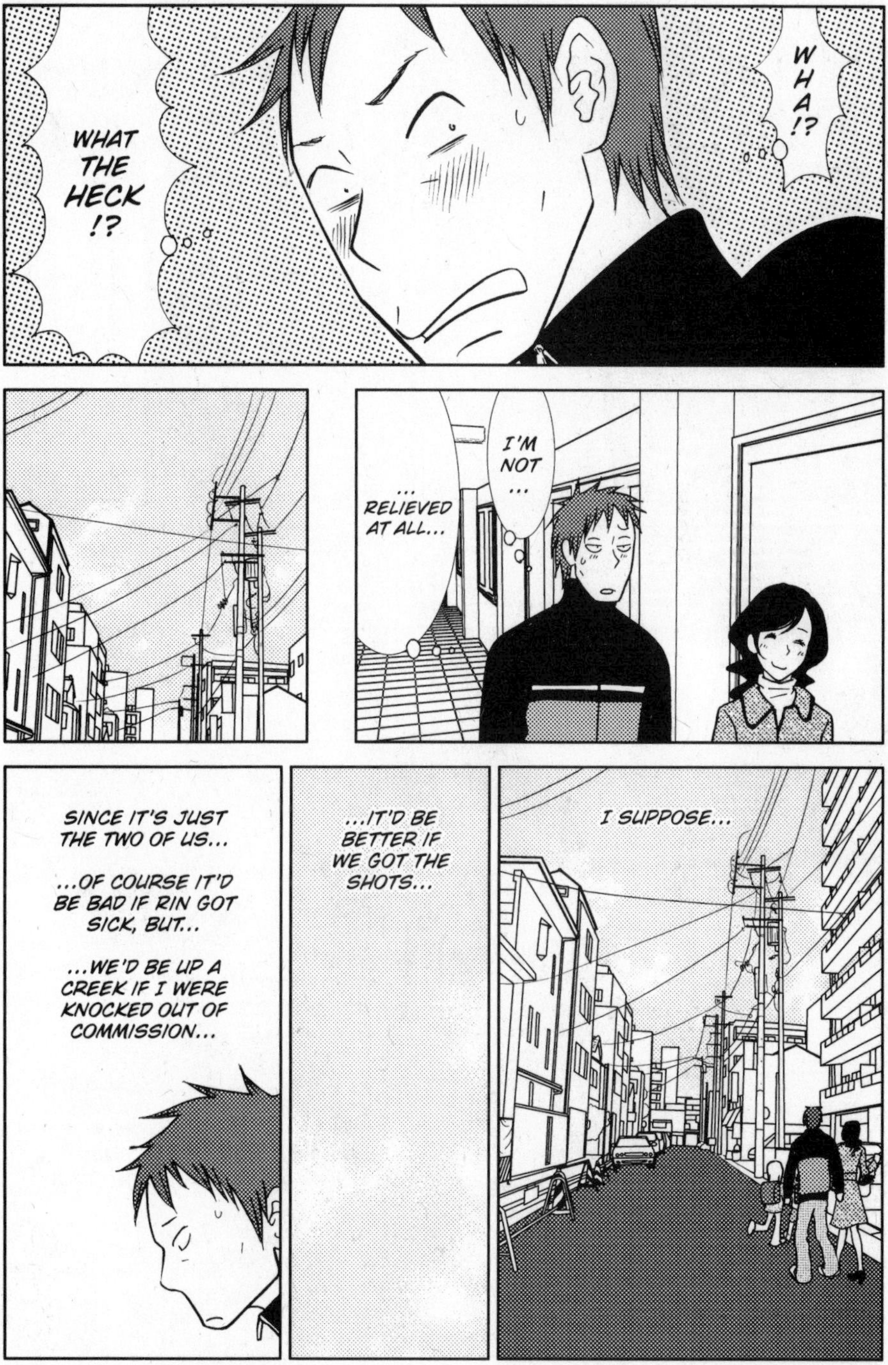
WHA!?
WHAT THE HECK !?
I'M NOT ...
... RELIEVED AT ALL...
I SUPPOSE...
...IT'D BE BETTER IF WE GOT THE SHOTS...
SINCE IT'S JUST THE TWO OF US...
...OF COURSE IT'D BE BAD IF RIN GOT SICK, BUT...
...WE'D BE UP A CREEK IF I WERE KNOCKED OUT OF COMMISSION...

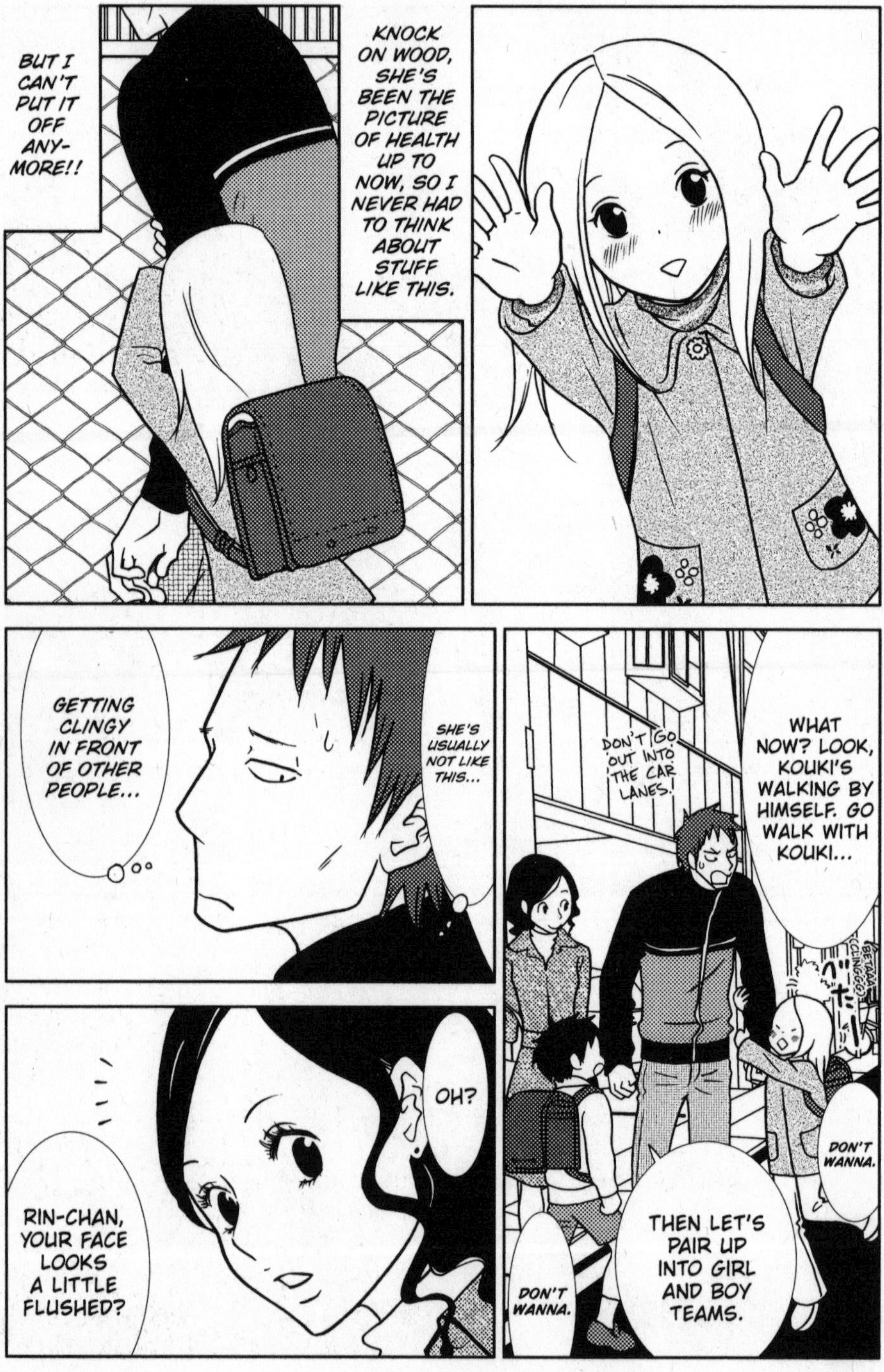
KNOCK ON WOOD, SHE'S BEEN THE PICTURE OF HEALTH UP TO NOW, SO I NEVER HAD TO THINK ABOUT STUFF LIKE THIS.
BUT I CAN'T PUT IT OFF ANY-MORE!!
WHAT NOW? LOOK, KOUKI'S WALKING BY HIMSELF. GO WALK WITH KOUKI...
DON'T GO OUT INTO THE CAR LANES!
BETAAA (CLINGGG)
DON'T WANNA.
THEN LET'S PAIR UP INTO GIRL AND BOY TEAMS.
DON'T WANNA.
SHE'S USUALLY NOT LIKE THIS...
GETTING CLINGY IN FRONT OF OTHER PEOPLE...
OH?
RIN-CHAN, YOUR FACE LOOKS A LITTLE FLUSHED?

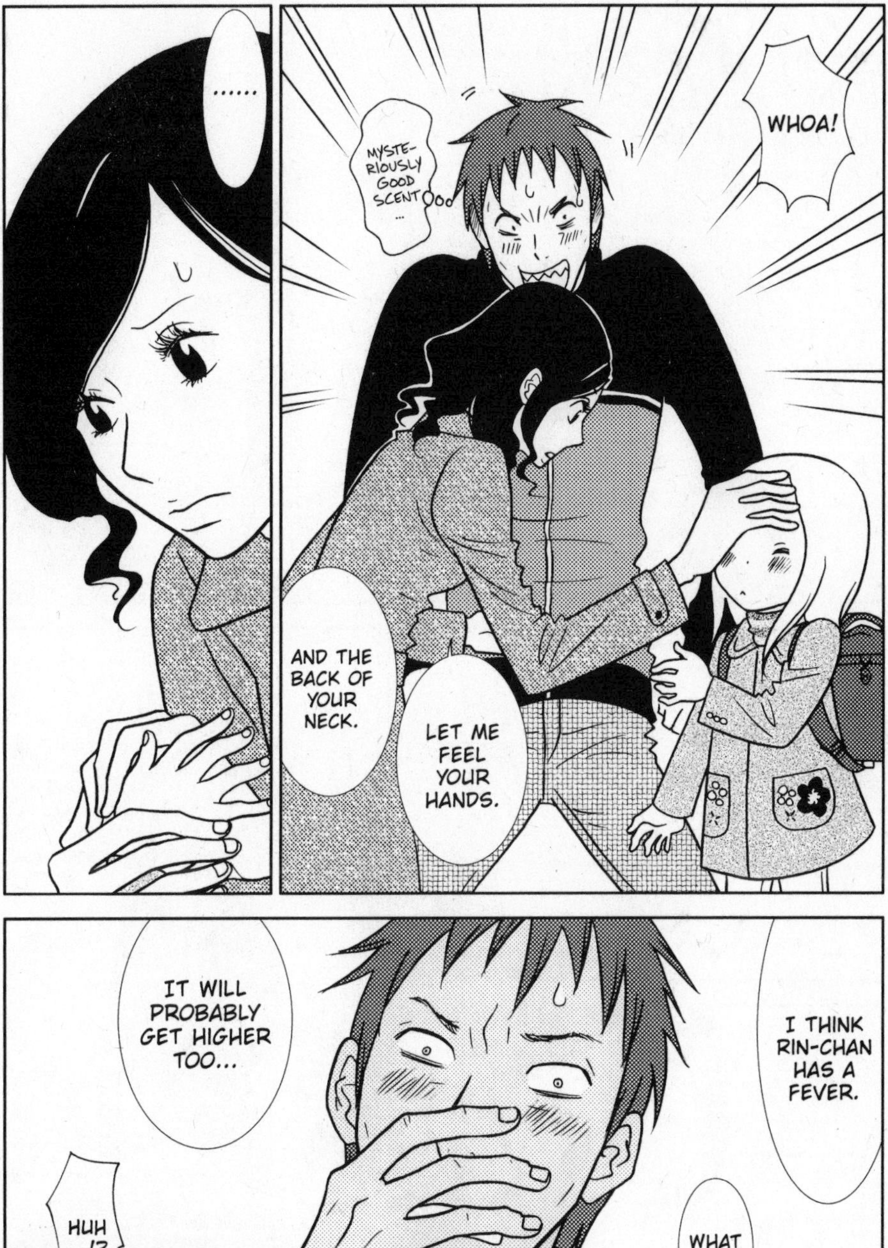
WHOA!
MYSTERIOUSLY GOOD SCENT ...
LET ME FEEL YOUR HANDS.
AND THE BACK OF YOUR NECK.
......
I THINK RIN-CHAN HAS A FEVER.
IT WILL PROBABLY GET HIGHER TOO...
WHAT ...?
HUH ...!?

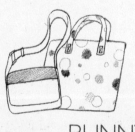

BUNNY**DROP**

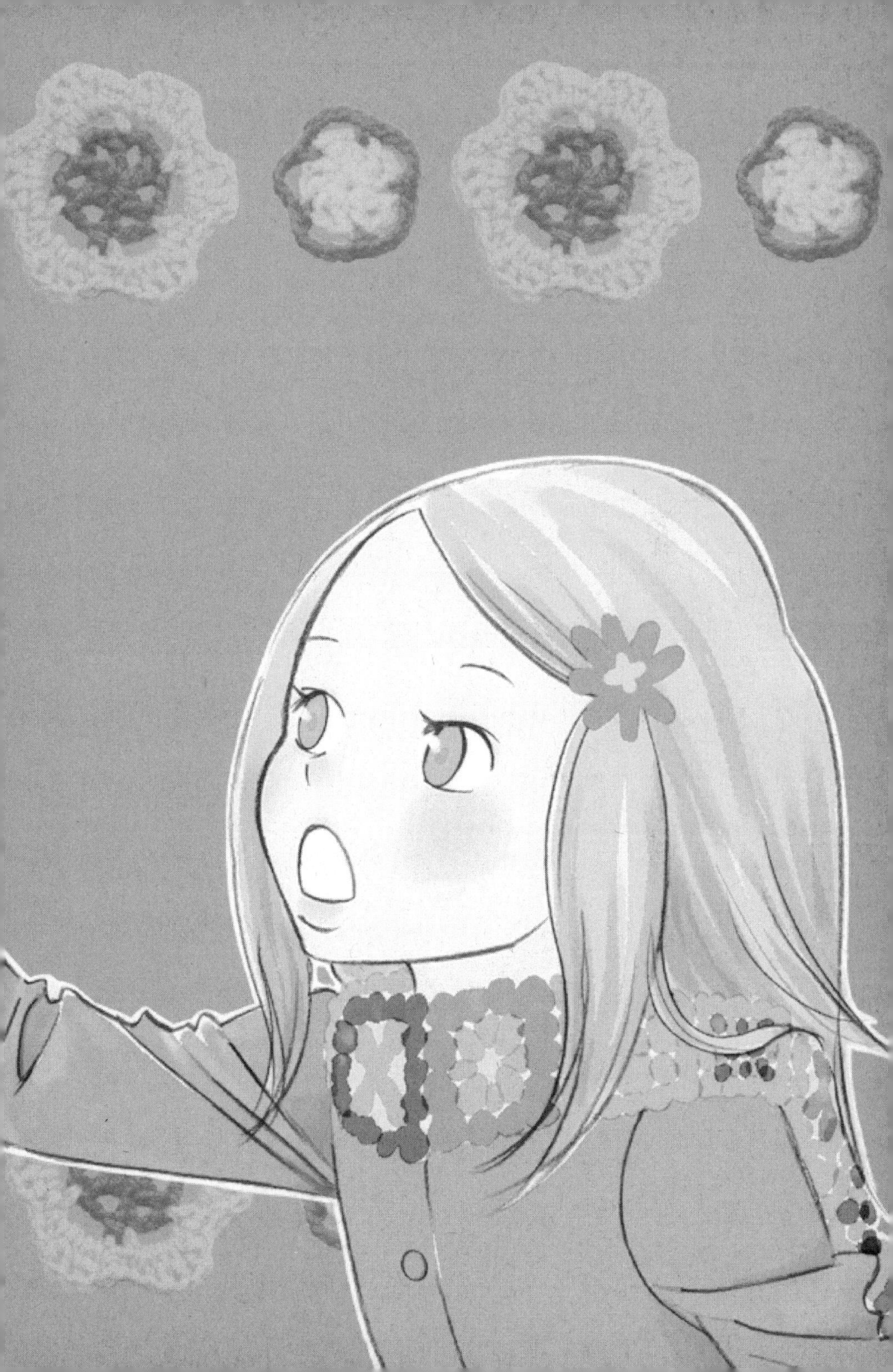

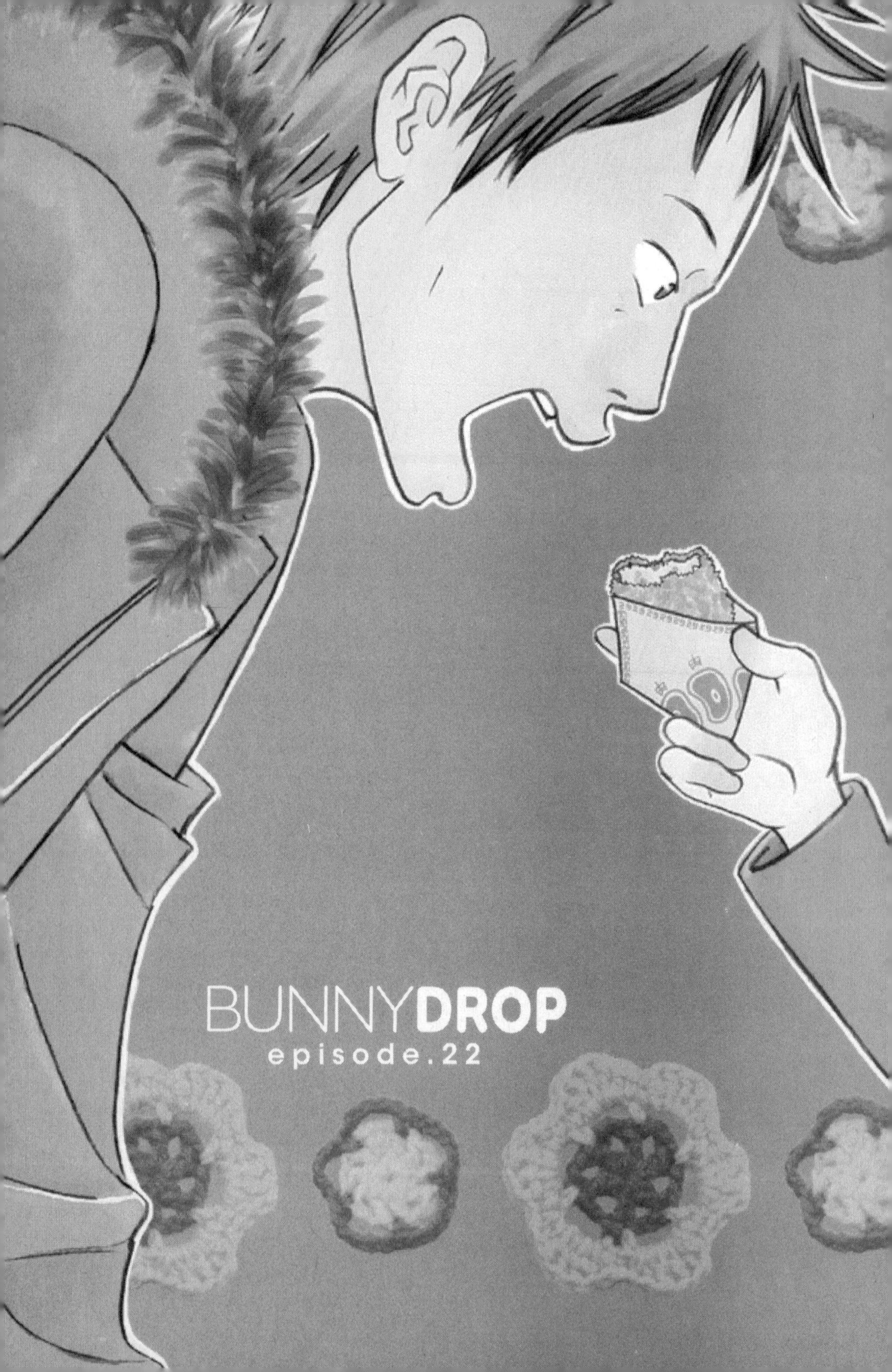
BUNNYDROP
episode.22

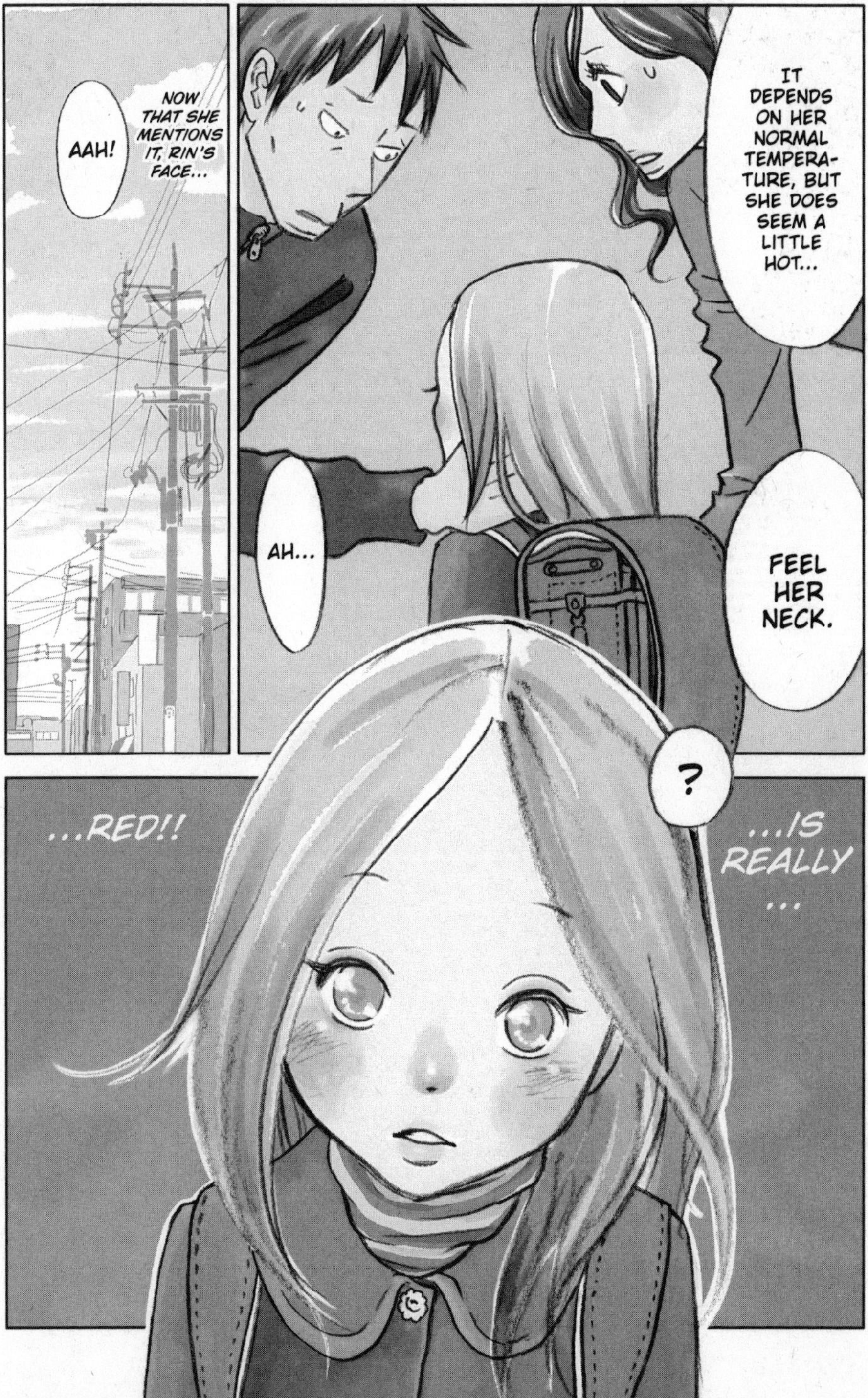
IT DEPENDS ON HER NORMAL TEMPERATURE, BUT SHE DOES SEEM A LITTLE HOT...
FEEL HER NECK.
AH...
NOW THAT SHE MENTIONS IT, RIN'S FACE...
AAH!
?
...IS REALLY ...
...RED!!

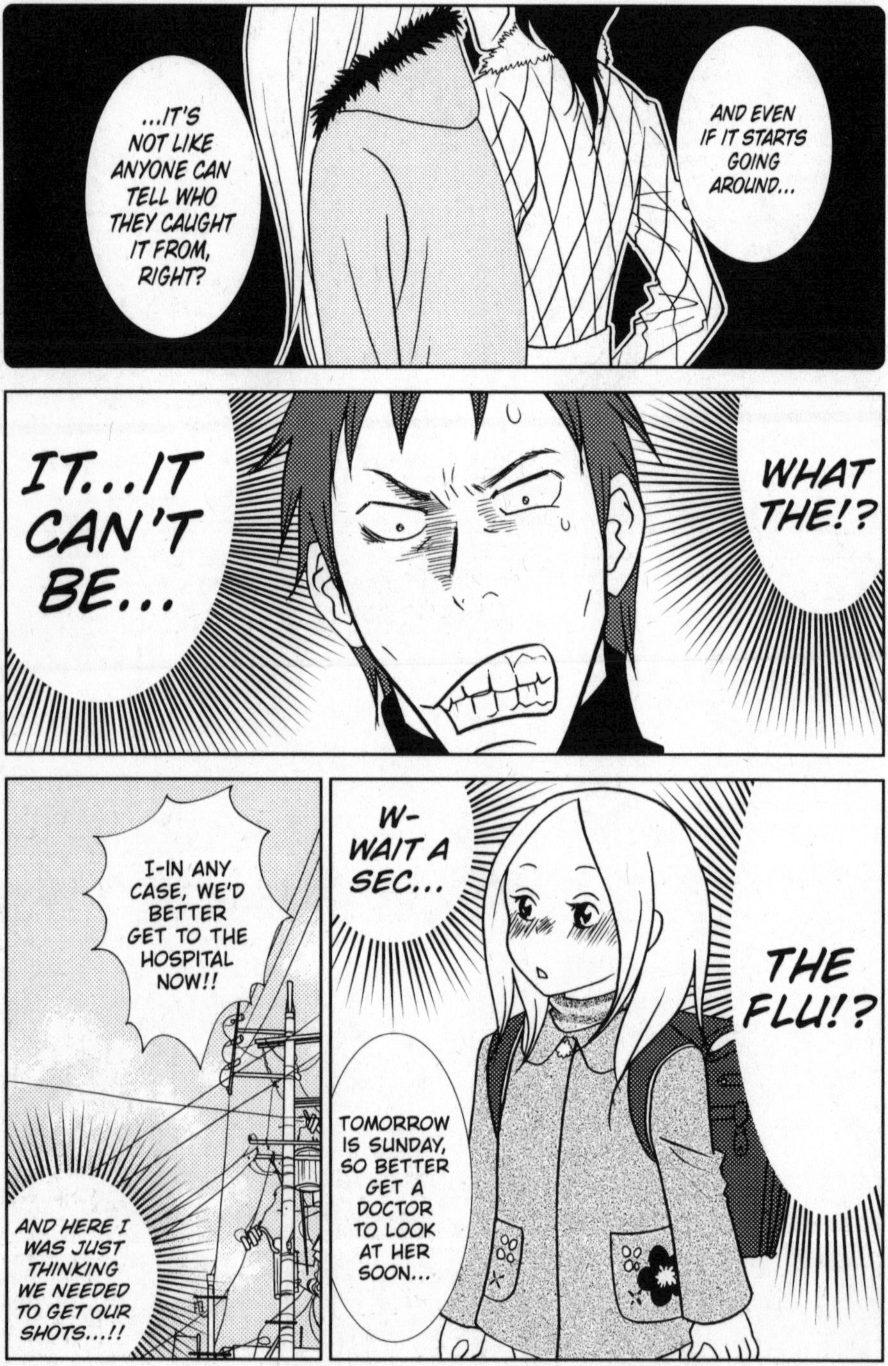
AND EVEN IF IT STARTS GOING AROUND...
...IT'S NOT LIKE ANYONE CAN TELL WHO THEY CAUGHT IT FROM, RIGHT?
WHAT THE!?
IT...IT CAN'T BE...
THE FLU!?
W-WAIT A SEC...
TOMORROW IS SUNDAY, SO BETTER GET A DOCTOR TO LOOK AT HER SOON...
I-IN ANY CASE, WE'D BETTER GET TO THE HOSPITAL NOW!!
AND HERE I WAS JUST THINKING WE NEEDED TO GET OUR SHOTS...!!

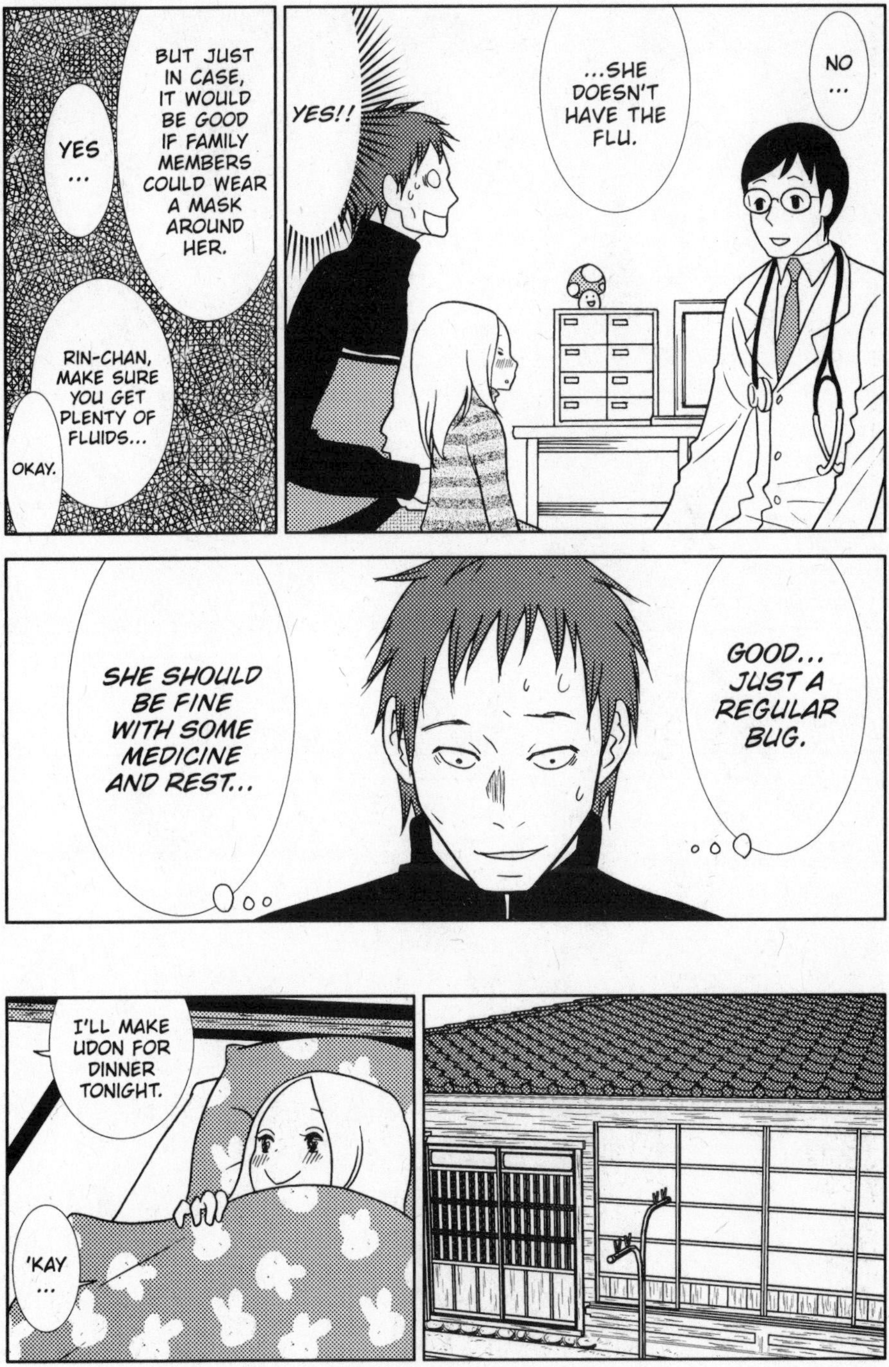
NO ...
...SHE DOESN'T HAVE THE FLU.
YES!!
BUT JUST IN CASE, IT WOULD BE GOOD IF FAMILY MEMBERS COULD WEAR A MASK AROUND HER.
YES ...
RIN-CHAN, MAKE SURE YOU GET PLENTY OF FLUIDS...
OKAY.
GOOD... JUST A REGULAR BUG.
SHE SHOULD BE FINE WITH SOME MEDICINE AND REST...
I'LL MAKE UDON FOR DINNER TONIGHT.
'KAY ...

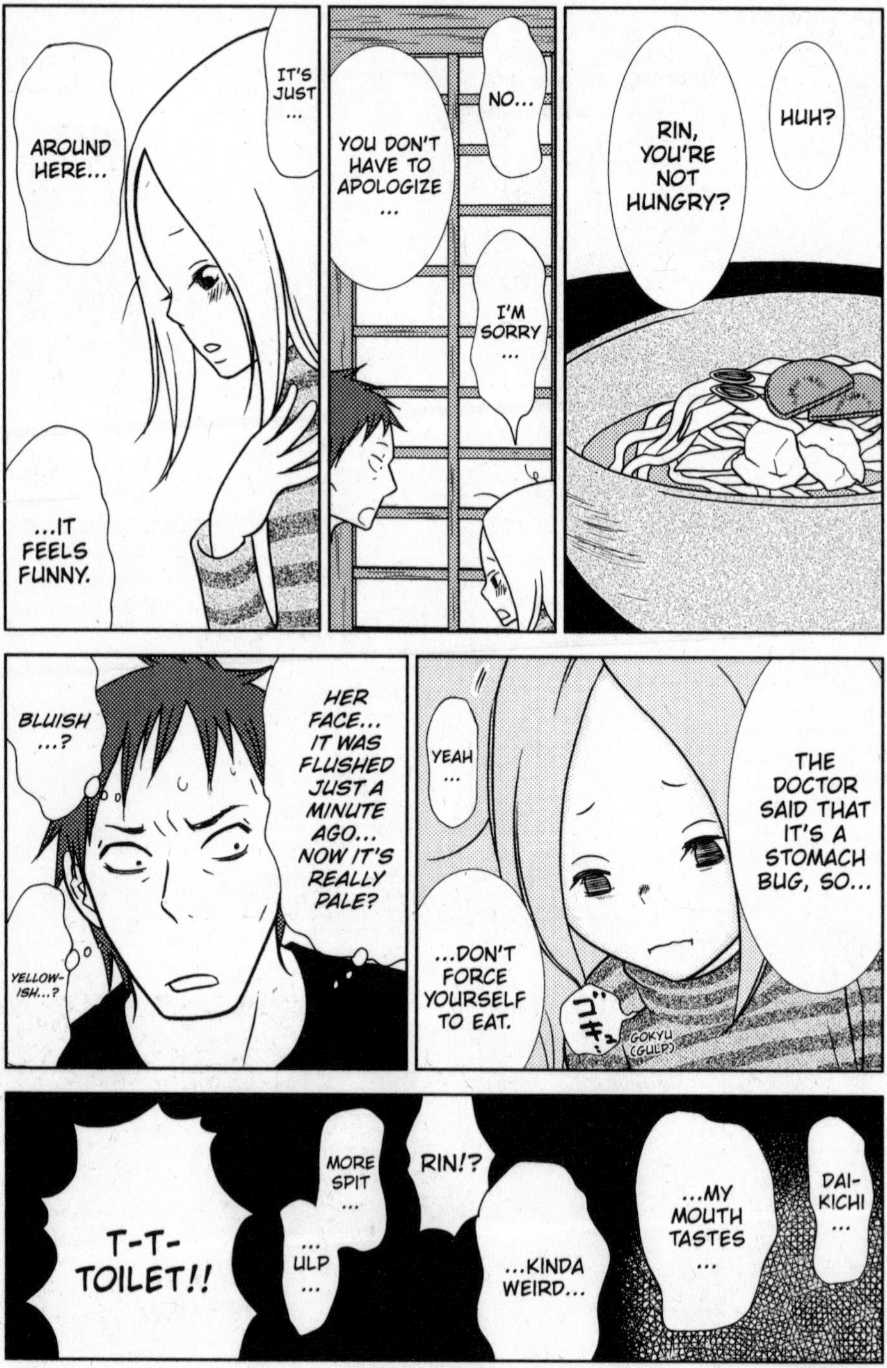
HUH?
RIN, YOU'RE NOT HUNGRY?
I'M SORRY ...
NO...
YOU DON'T HAVE TO APOLOGIZE ...
IT'S JUST ...
AROUND HERE...
...IT FEELS FUNNY.
THE DOCTOR SAID THAT IT'S A STOMACH BUG, SO...
YEAH ...
...DON'T FORCE YOURSELF TO EAT.
ゴキュ
GOKYU (GULP)
HER FACE... IT WAS FLUSHED JUST A MINUTE AGO... NOW IT'S REALLY PALE?
BLUISH ...?
YELLOW-ISH...?
DAI-KICHI ...
...MY MOUTH TASTES ...
...KINDA WEIRD...
RIN!?
MORE SPIT ...
... ULP ...
T-T-TOILET!!

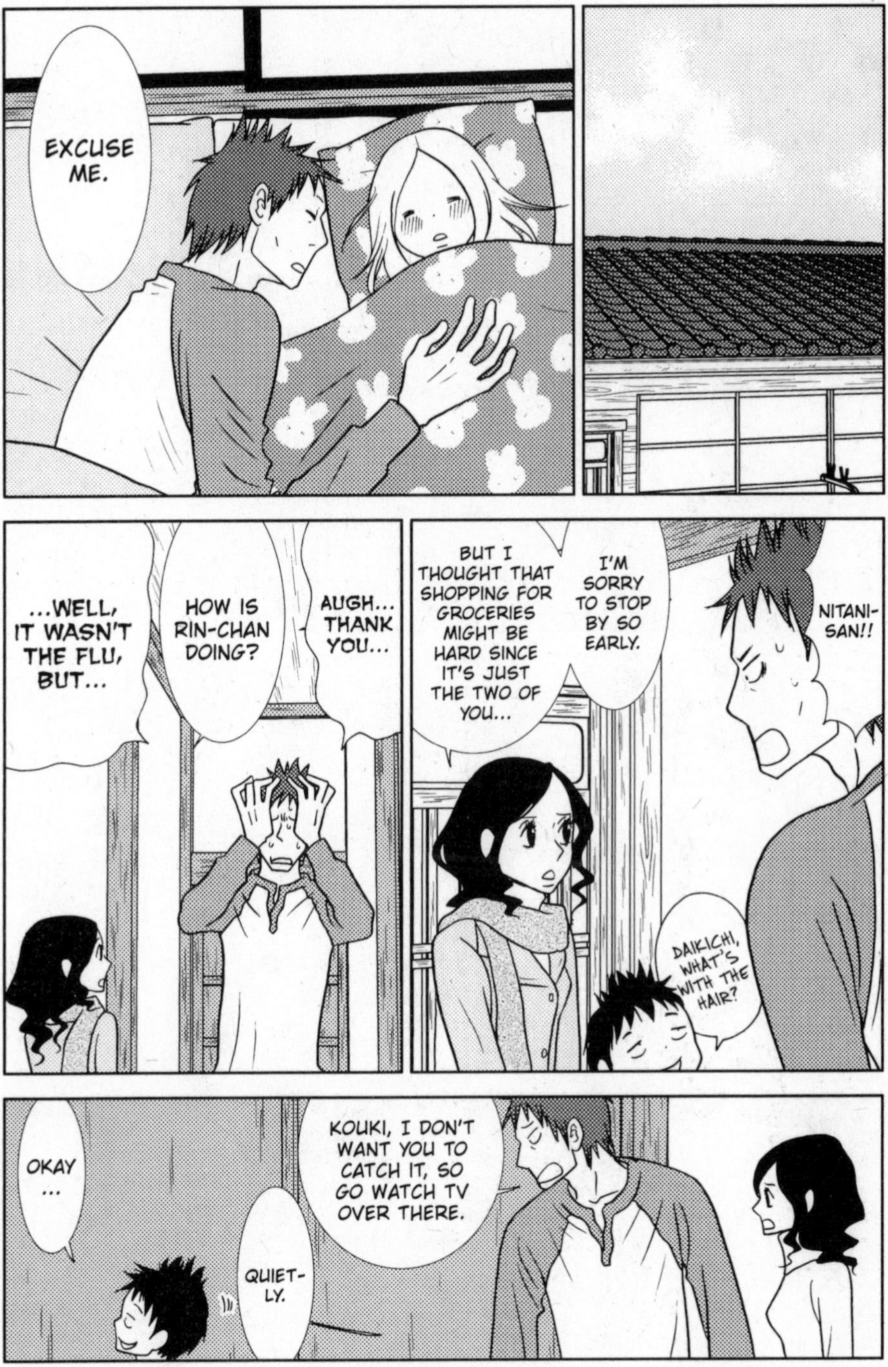
EXCUSE ME.
NITANI-SAN!!
I'M SORRY TO STOP BY SO EARLY.
BUT I THOUGHT THAT SHOPPING FOR GROCERIES MIGHT BE HARD SINCE IT'S JUST THE TWO OF YOU...
DAIKICHI, WHAT'S WITH THE HAIR?
AUGH... THANK YOU...
HOW IS RIN-CHAN DOING?
...WELL, IT WASN'T THE FLU, BUT...
KOUKI, I DON'T WANT YOU TO CATCH IT, SO GO WATCH TV OVER THERE.
QUIET-LY.
OKAY ...

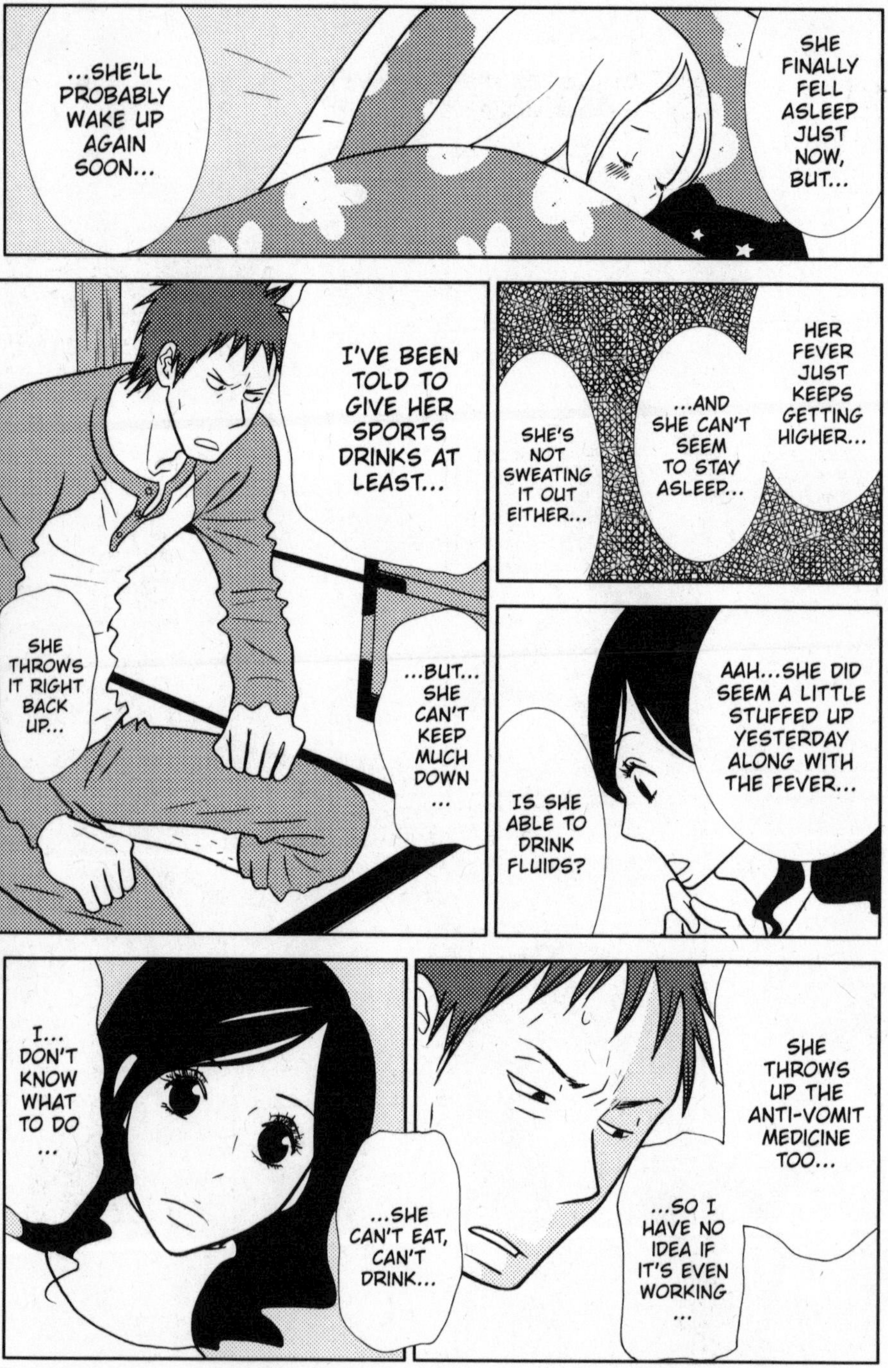
SHE FINALLY FELL ASLEEP JUST NOW, BUT...
...SHE'LL PROBABLY WAKE UP AGAIN SOON...
HER FEVER JUST KEEPS GETTING HIGHER...
...AND SHE CAN'T SEEM TO STAY ASLEEP...
SHE'S NOT SWEATING IT OUT EITHER...
AAH...SHE DID SEEM A LITTLE STUFFED UP YESTERDAY ALONG WITH THE FEVER...
IS SHE ABLE TO DRINK FLUIDS?
I'VE BEEN TOLD TO GIVE HER SPORTS DRINKS AT LEAST...
...BUT... SHE CAN'T KEEP MUCH DOWN...
SHE THROWS IT RIGHT BACK UP...
SHE THROWS UP THE ANTI-VOMIT MEDICINE TOO...
...SO I HAVE NO IDEA IF IT'S EVEN WORKING...
...SHE CAN'T EAT, CAN'T DRINK...
I... DON'T KNOW WHAT TO DO...

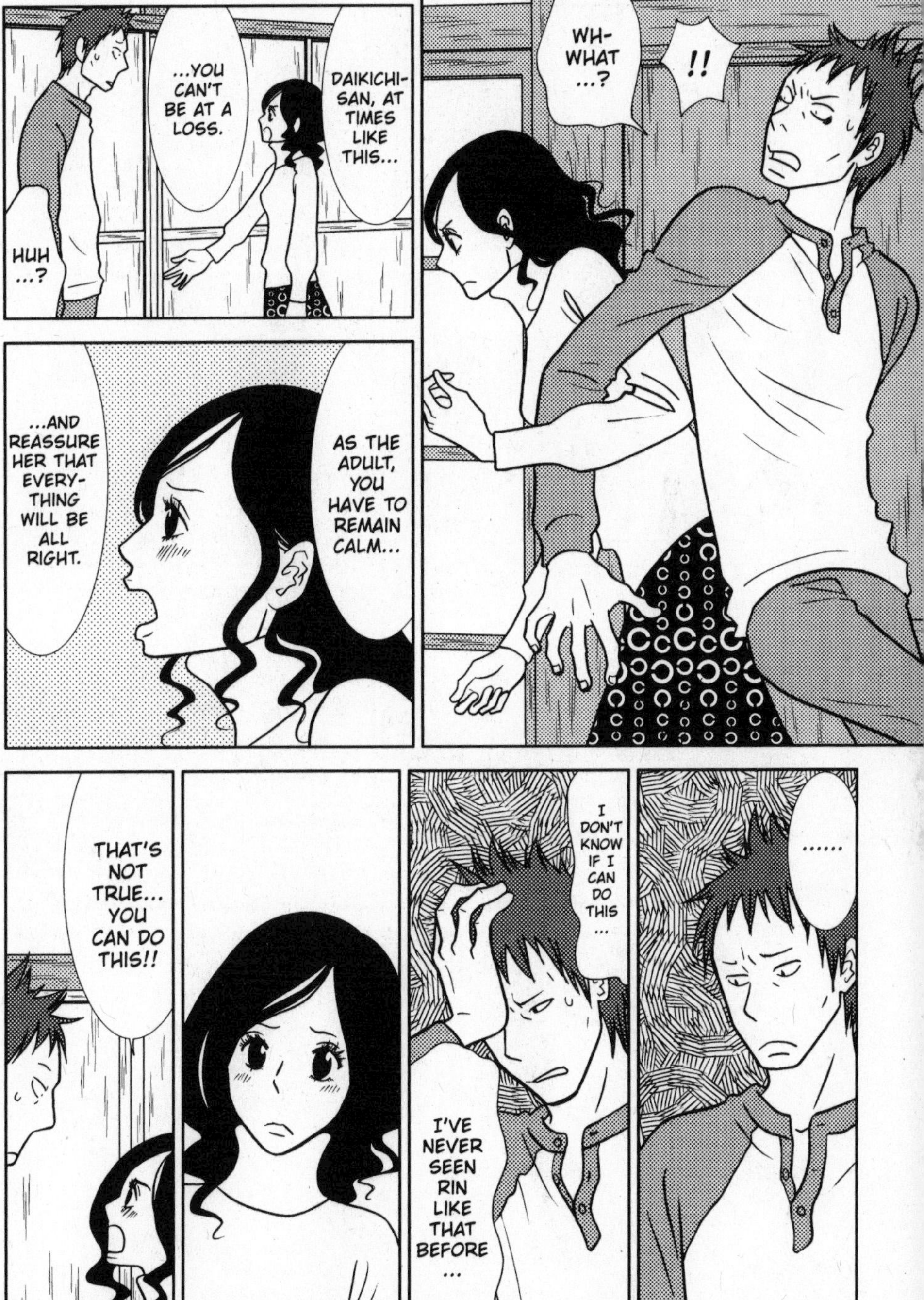

!!
WH- WHAT ...?
DAIKICHI-SAN, AT TIMES LIKE THIS...
...YOU CAN'T BE AT A LOSS.
HUH ...?
AS THE ADULT, YOU HAVE TO REMAIN CALM...
...AND REASSURE HER THAT EVERY-THING WILL BE ALL RIGHT.
......
I DON'T KNOW IF I CAN DO THIS ...
I'VE NEVER SEEN RIN LIKE THAT BEFORE ...
THAT'S NOT TRUE... YOU CAN DO THIS!!

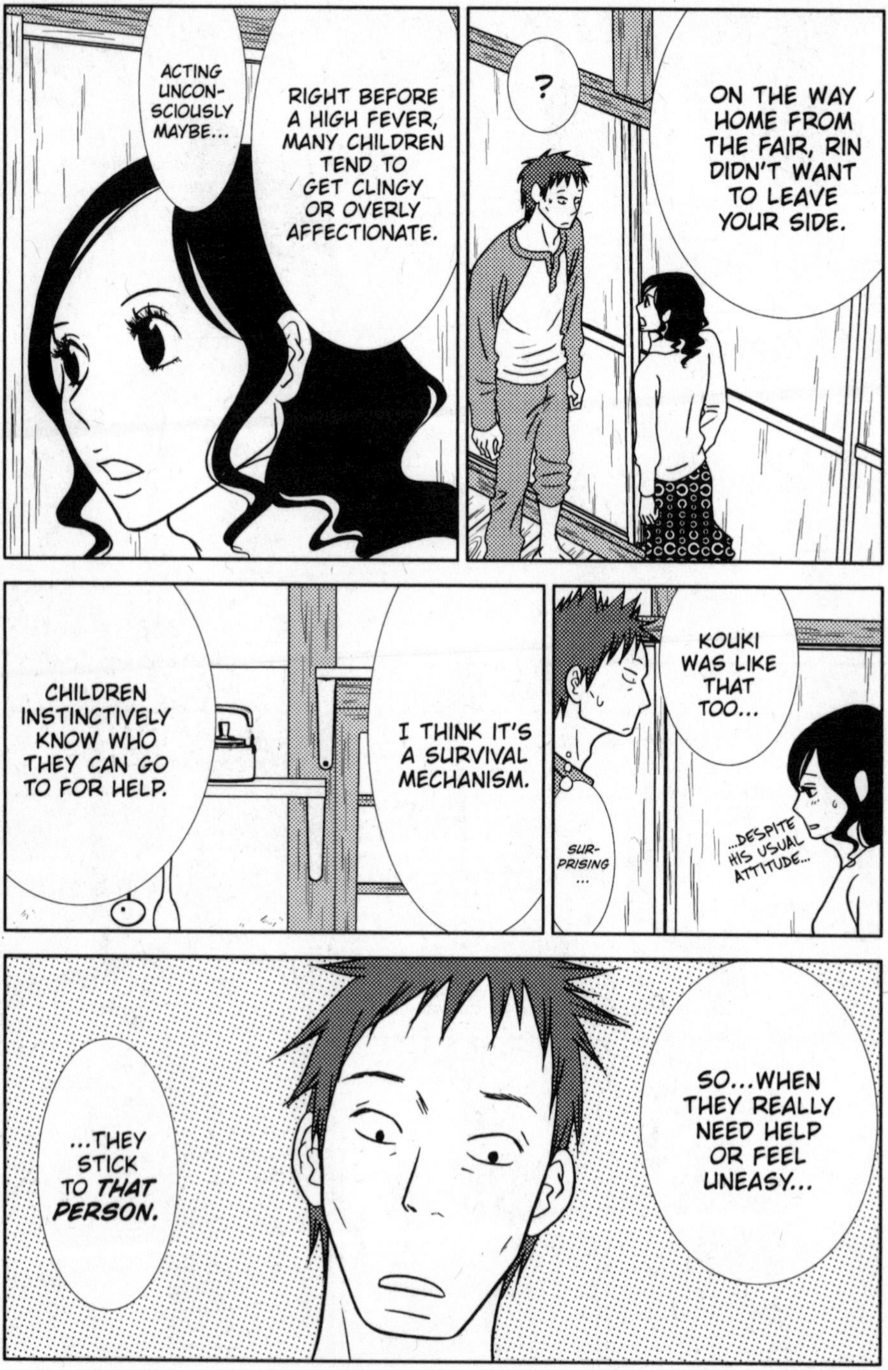
ON THE WAY HOME FROM THE FAIR, RIN DIDN'T WANT TO LEAVE YOUR SIDE.
?
RIGHT BEFORE A HIGH FEVER, MANY CHILDREN TEND TO GET CLINGY OR OVERLY AFFECTIONATE.
ACTING UNCON-SCIOUSLY MAYBE...
KOUKI WAS LIKE THAT TOO...
...DESPITE HIS USUAL ATTITUDE...
SUR-PRISING...
I THINK IT'S A SURVIVAL MECHANISM.
CHILDREN INSTINCTIVELY KNOW WHO THEY CAN GO TO FOR HELP.
SO...WHEN THEY REALLY NEED HELP OR FEEL UNEASY...
...THEY STICK TO *THAT PERSON.*

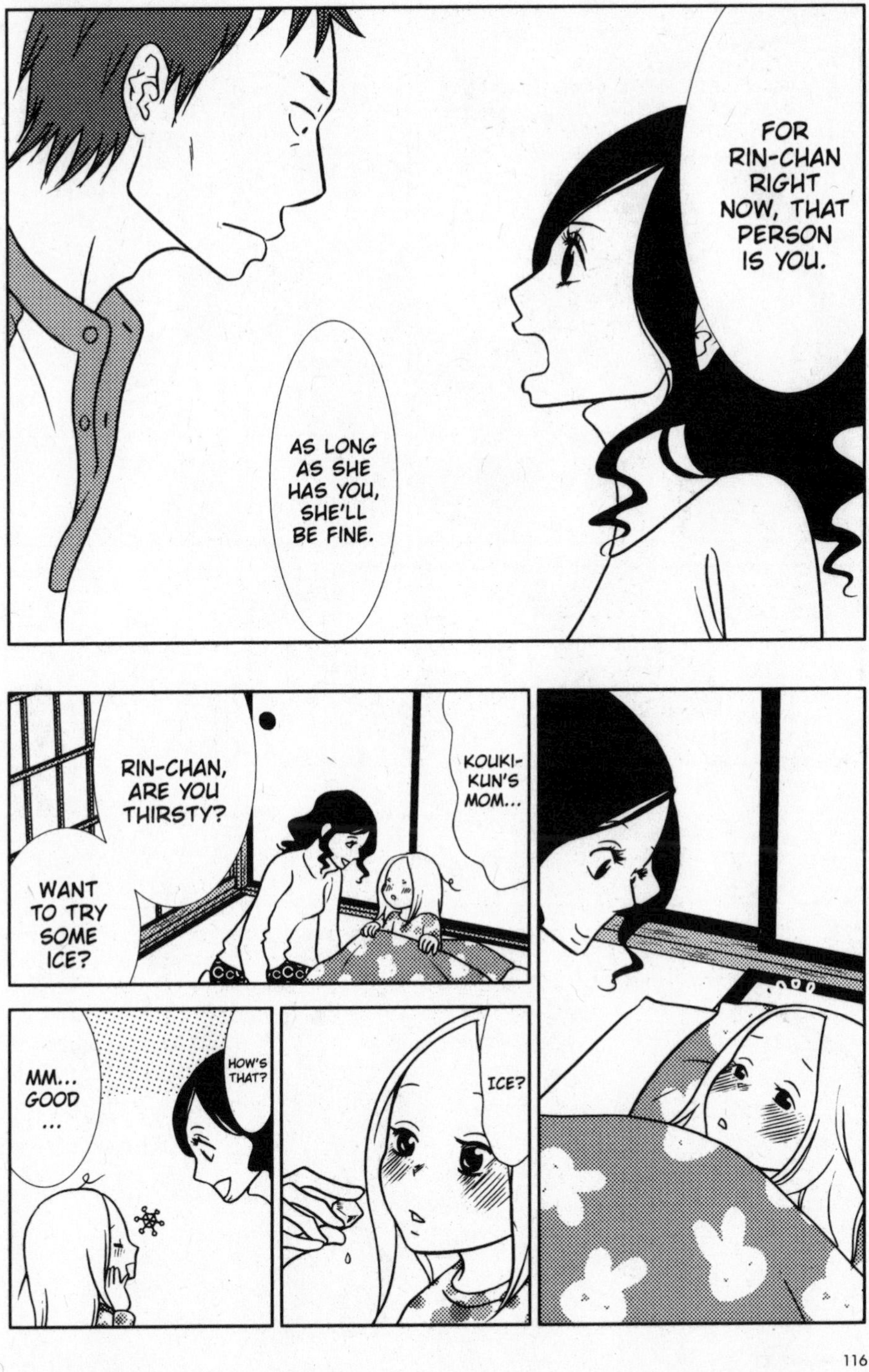
FOR RIN-CHAN RIGHT NOW, THAT PERSON IS YOU.
AS LONG AS SHE HAS YOU, SHE'LL BE FINE.
KOUKI-KUN'S MOM...
RIN-CHAN, ARE YOU THIRSTY?
WANT TO TRY SOME ICE?
ICE?
HOW'S THAT?
MM... GOOD ...

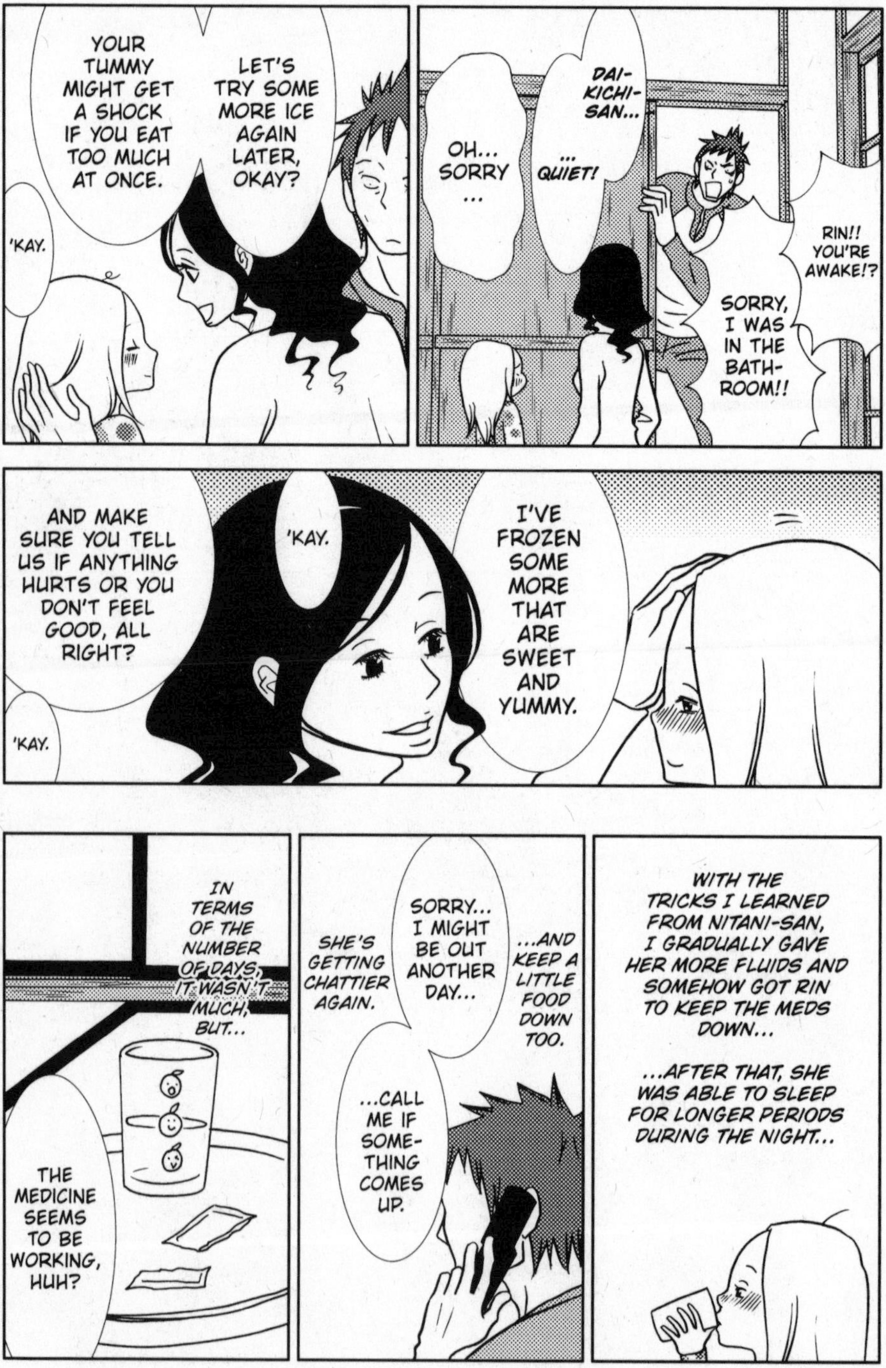
RIN!! YOU'RE AWAKE!?
SORRY, I WAS IN THE BATHROOM!!
DAI-KICHI-SAN...
...QUIET!
OH... SORRY...
LET'S TRY SOME MORE ICE AGAIN LATER, OKAY?
YOUR TUMMY MIGHT GET A SHOCK IF YOU EAT TOO MUCH AT ONCE.
'KAY.
I'VE FROZEN SOME MORE THAT ARE SWEET AND YUMMY.
'KAY.
AND MAKE SURE YOU TELL US IF ANYTHING HURTS OR YOU DON'T FEEL GOOD, ALL RIGHT?
'KAY.
WITH THE TRICKS I LEARNED FROM NITANI-SAN, I GRADUALLY GAVE HER MORE FLUIDS AND SOMEHOW GOT RIN TO KEEP THE MEDS DOWN...
...AFTER THAT, SHE WAS ABLE TO SLEEP FOR LONGER PERIODS DURING THE NIGHT...
...AND KEEP A LITTLE FOOD DOWN TOO.
SORRY... I MIGHT BE OUT ANOTHER DAY...
SHE'S GETTING CHATTIER AGAIN.
...CALL ME IF SOMETHING COMES UP.
IN TERMS OF THE NUMBER OF DAYS, IT WASN'T MUCH, BUT...
THE MEDICINE SEEMS TO BE WORKING, HUH?

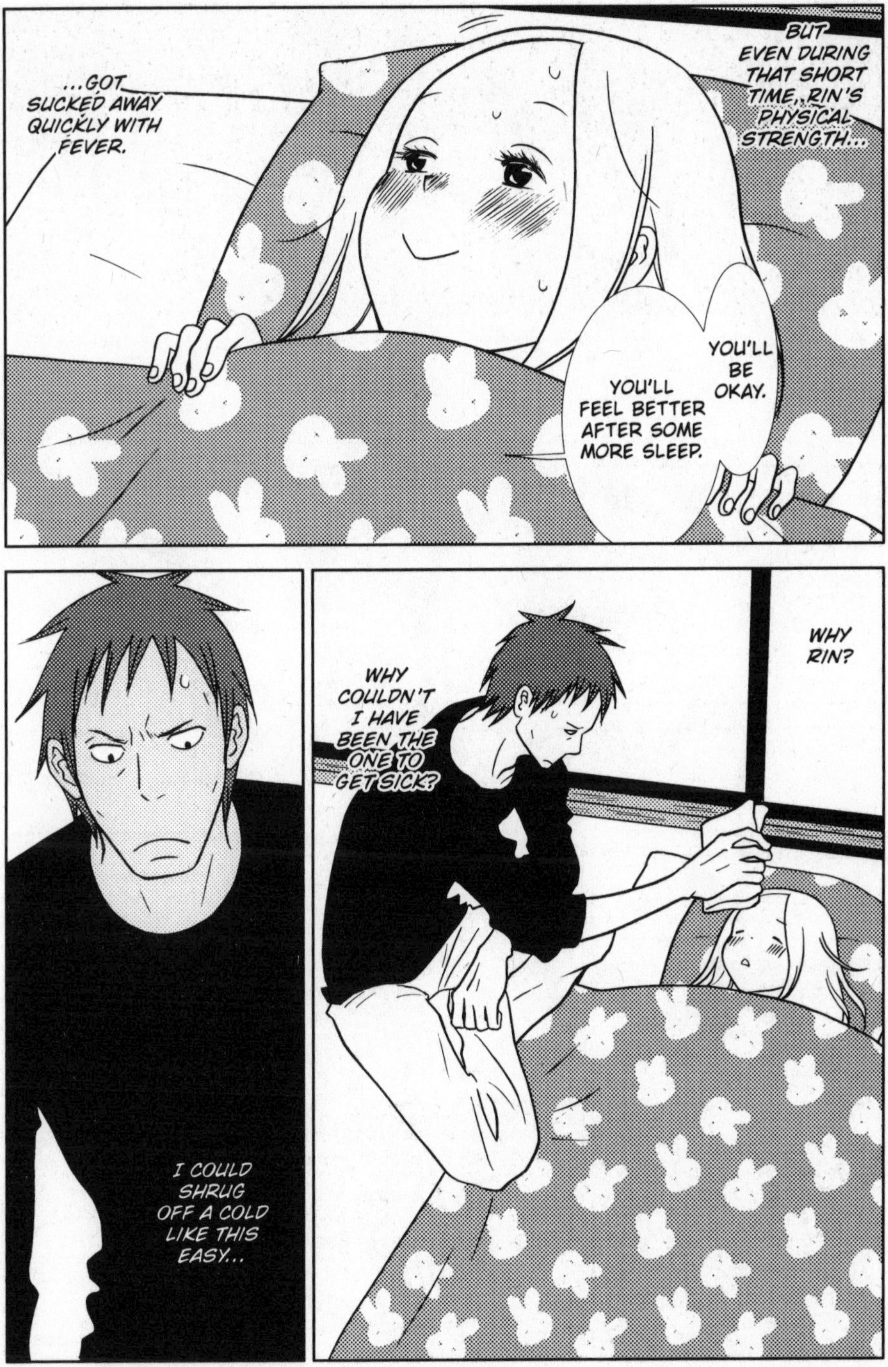
BUT EVEN DURING THAT SHORT TIME, RIN'S PHYSICAL STRENGTH...
...GOT SUCKED AWAY QUICKLY WITH FEVER.
YOU'LL BE OKAY.
YOU'LL FEEL BETTER AFTER SOME MORE SLEEP.
WHY RIN?
WHY COULDN'T I HAVE BEEN THE ONE TO GET SICK?
I COULD SHRUG OFF A COLD LIKE THIS EASY...

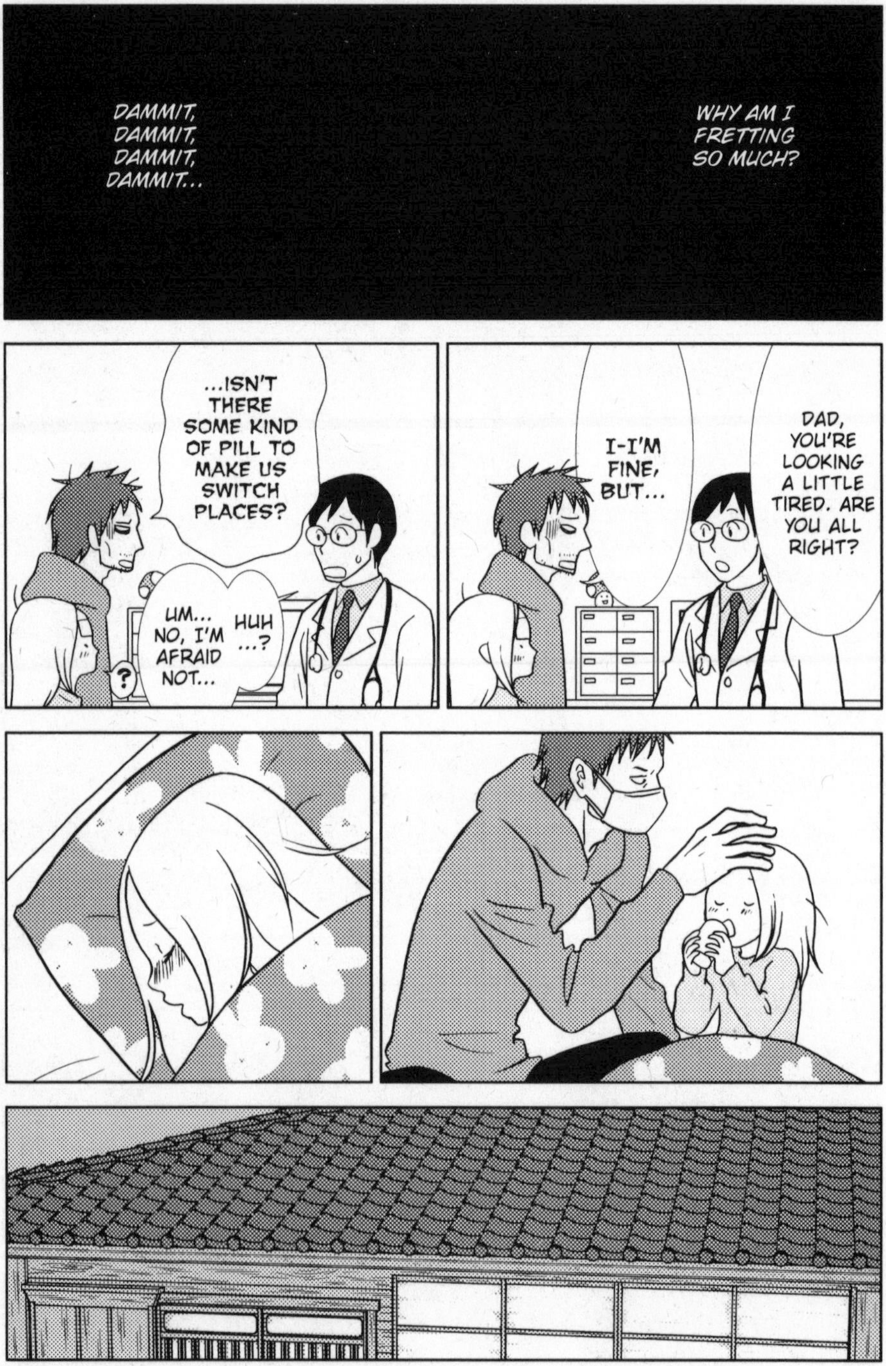
WHY AM I FRETTING SO MUCH?
DAMMIT, DAMMIT, DAMMIT, DAMMIT...
DAD, YOU'RE LOOKING A LITTLE TIRED. ARE YOU ALL RIGHT?
I-I'M FINE, BUT...
...ISN'T THERE SOME KIND OF PILL TO MAKE US SWITCH PLACES?
HUH ...?
UM... NO, I'M AFRAID NOT...
?

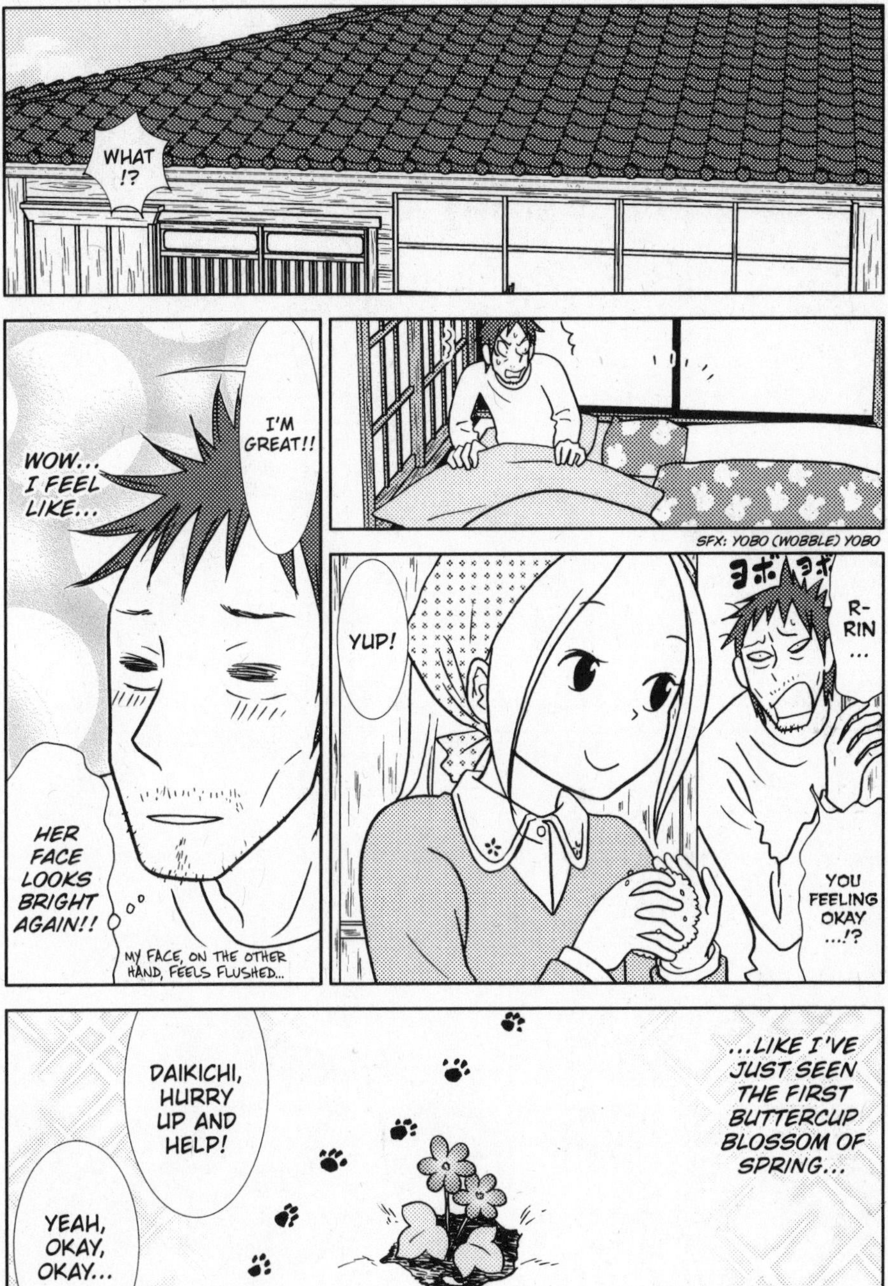
WHAT !?
R-RIN ...
ヨボヨボ
SFX: YOBO (WOBBLE) YOBO
YUP!
YOU FEELING OKAY ...!?
I'M GREAT!!
WOW... I FEEL LIKE...
HER FACE LOOKS BRIGHT AGAIN!!
MY FACE, ON THE OTHER HAND, FEELS FLUSHED...
...LIKE I'VE JUST SEEN THE FIRST BUTTERCUP BLOSSOM OF SPRING...
DAIKICHI, HURRY UP AND HELP!
YEAH, OKAY, OKAY...

SIGN: HAPPY FACE SCHOOL / KIDS' CLUB

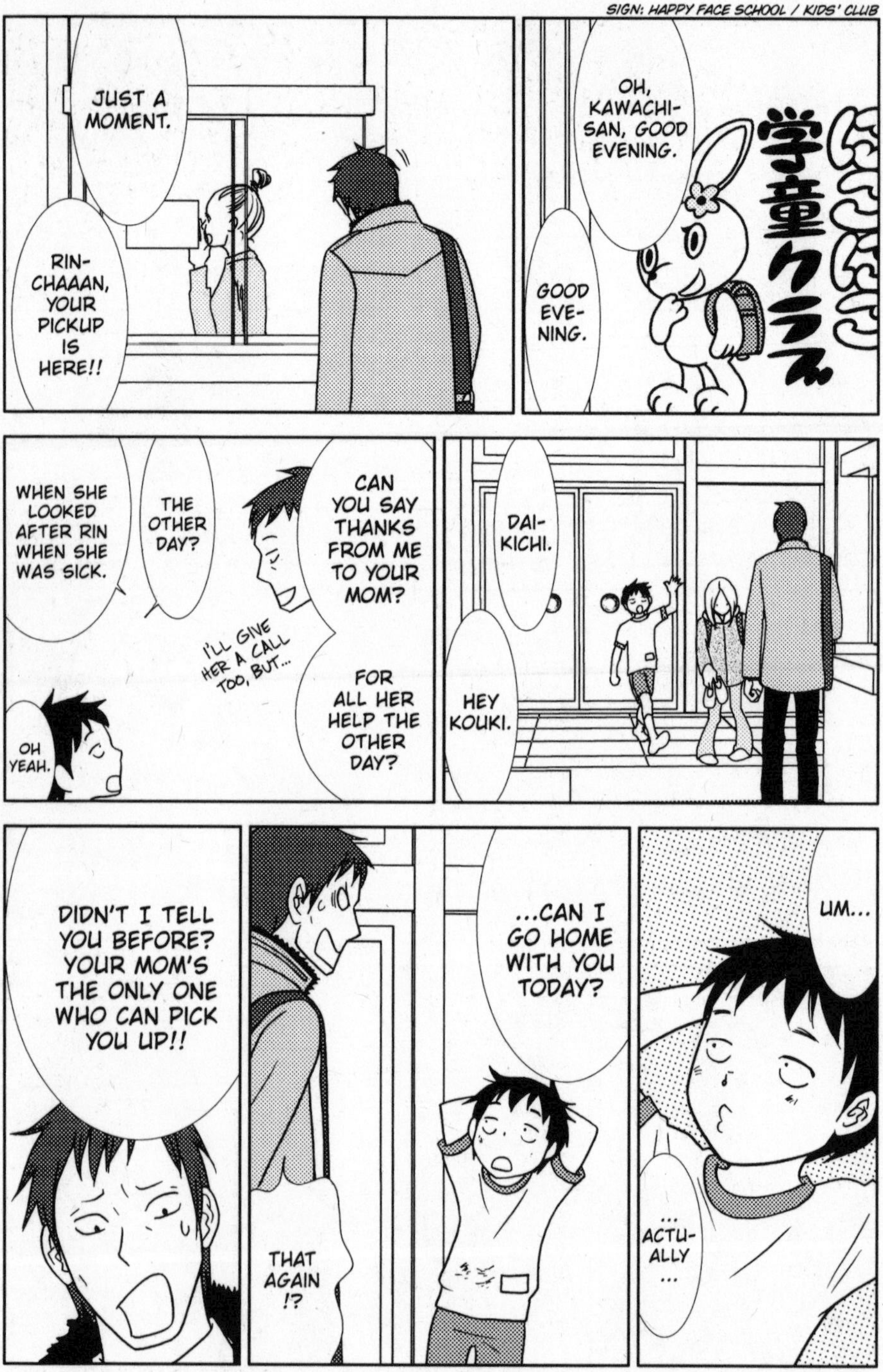
OH, KAWACHI-SAN, GOOD EVENING.
GOOD EVE-NING.
JUST A MOMENT.
RIN-CHAAAN, YOUR PICKUP IS HERE!!
DAI-KICHI.
HEY KOUKI.
CAN YOU SAY THANKS FROM ME TO YOUR MOM?
FOR ALL HER HELP THE OTHER DAY?
I'LL GIVE HER A CALL TOO, BUT...
THE OTHER DAY?
WHEN SHE LOOKED AFTER RIN WHEN SHE WAS SICK.
OH YEAH.
UM...
...ACTU-ALLY...
...CAN I GO HOME WITH YOU TODAY?
THAT AGAIN!?
DIDN'T I TELL YOU BEFORE? YOUR MOM'S THE ONLY ONE WHO CAN PICK YOU UP!!

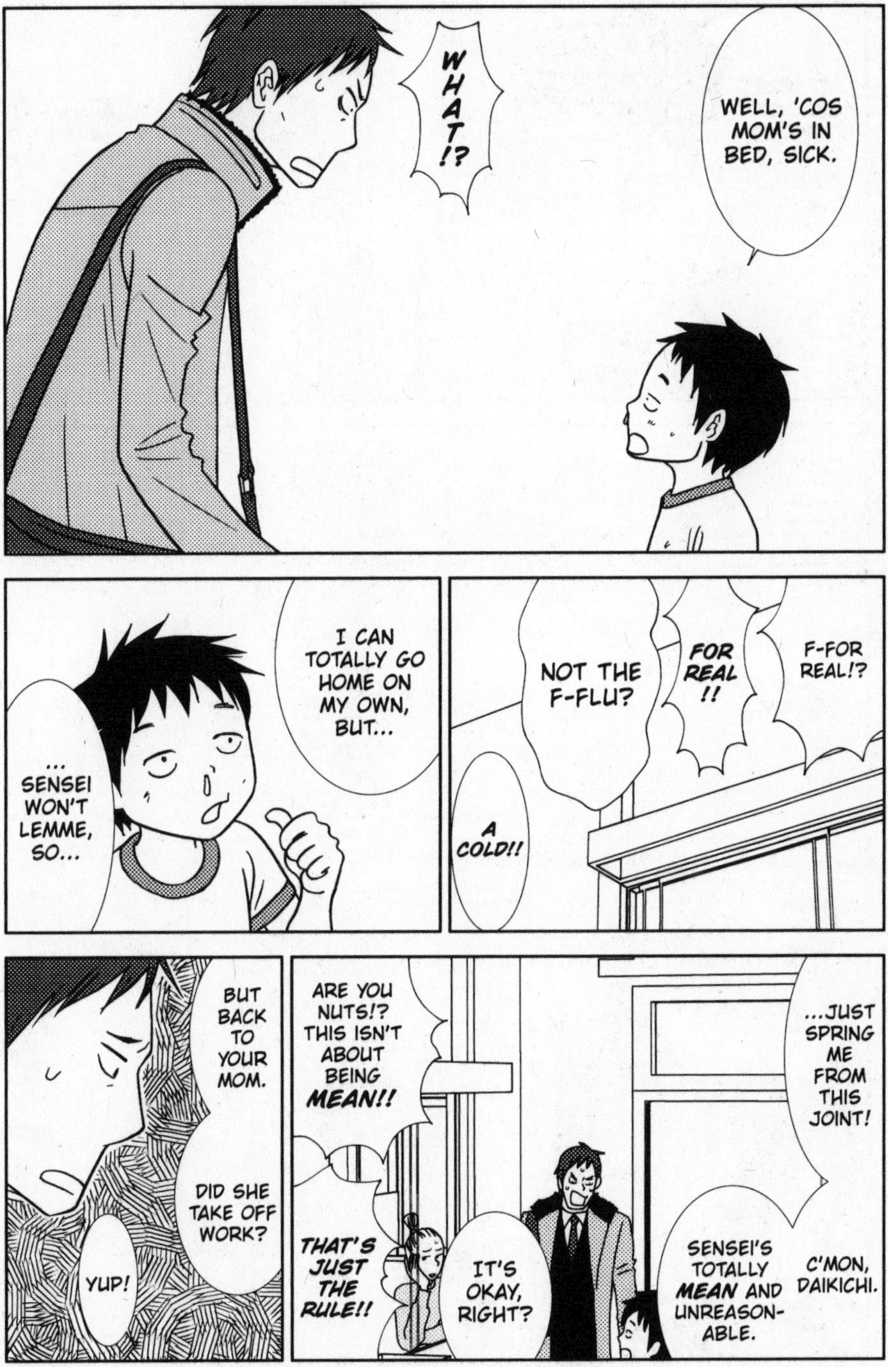
WELL, 'COS MOM'S IN BED, SICK.
WHAT!?
F-FOR REAL!?
FOR REAL!!
NOT THE F-FLU?
A COLD!!
I CAN TOTALLY GO HOME ON MY OWN, BUT...
... SENSEI WON'T LEMME, SO...
...JUST SPRING ME FROM THIS JOINT!
C'MON, DAIKICHI.
SENSEI'S TOTALLY MEAN AND UNREASON-ABLE.
ARE YOU NUTS!? THIS ISN'T ABOUT BEING MEAN!!
IT'S OKAY, RIGHT?
THAT'S JUST THE RULE!!
BUT BACK TO YOUR MOM.
DID SHE TAKE OFF WORK?
YUP!

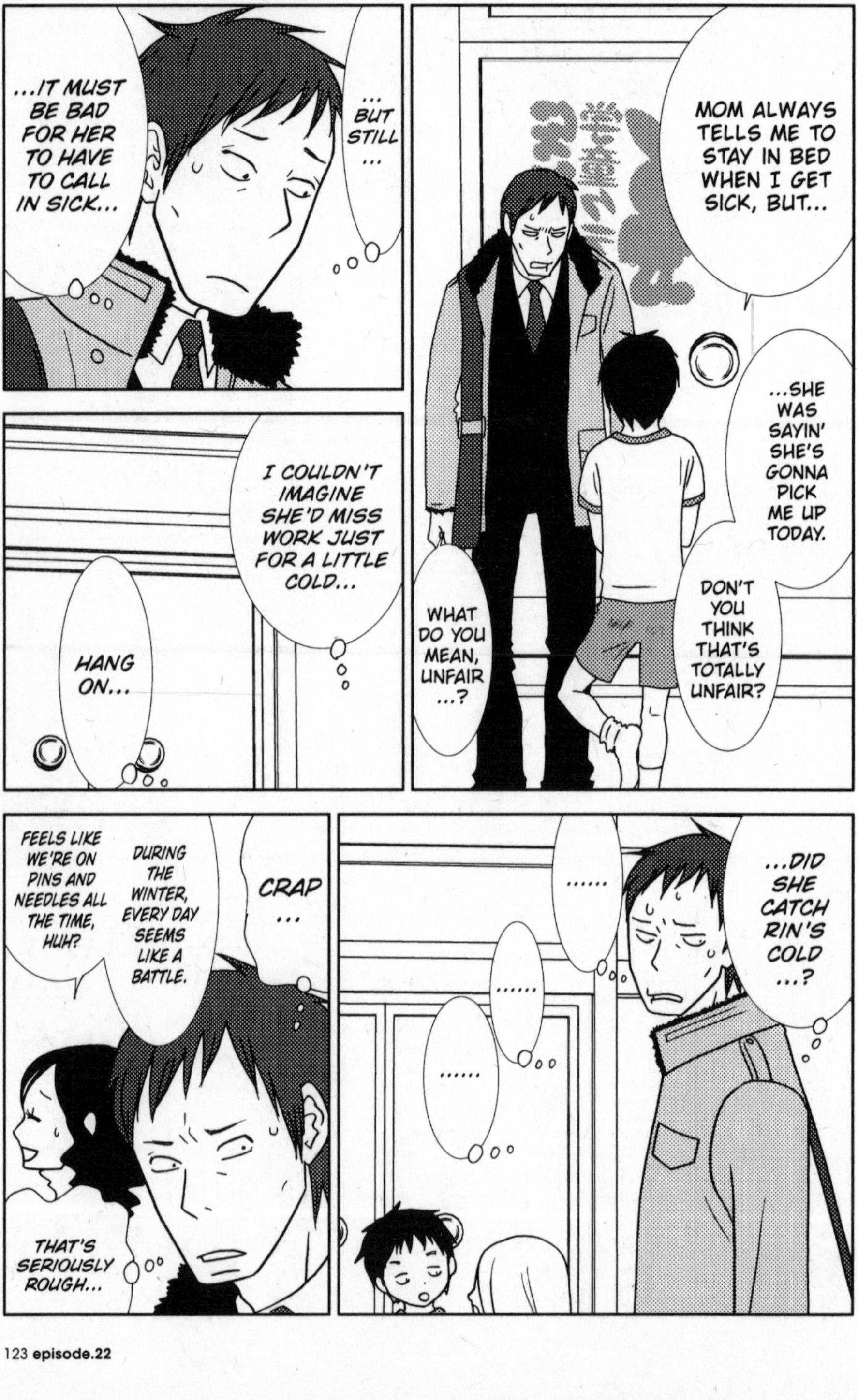
MOM ALWAYS TELLS ME TO STAY IN BED WHEN I GET SICK, BUT...
...SHE WAS SAYIN' SHE'S GONNA PICK ME UP TODAY.
DON'T YOU THINK THAT'S TOTALLY UNFAIR?
WHAT DO YOU MEAN, UNFAIR ...?
... BUT STILL ...
...IT MUST BE BAD FOR HER TO HAVE TO CALL IN SICK...
I COULDN'T IMAGINE SHE'D MISS WORK JUST FOR A LITTLE COLD...
HANG ON...
...DID SHE CATCH RIN'S COLD ...?
......
......
......
CRAP ...
DURING THE WINTER, EVERY DAY SEEMS LIKE A BATTLE.
FEELS LIKE WE'RE ON PINS AND NEEDLES ALL THE TIME, HUH?
THAT'S SERIOUSLY ROUGH...

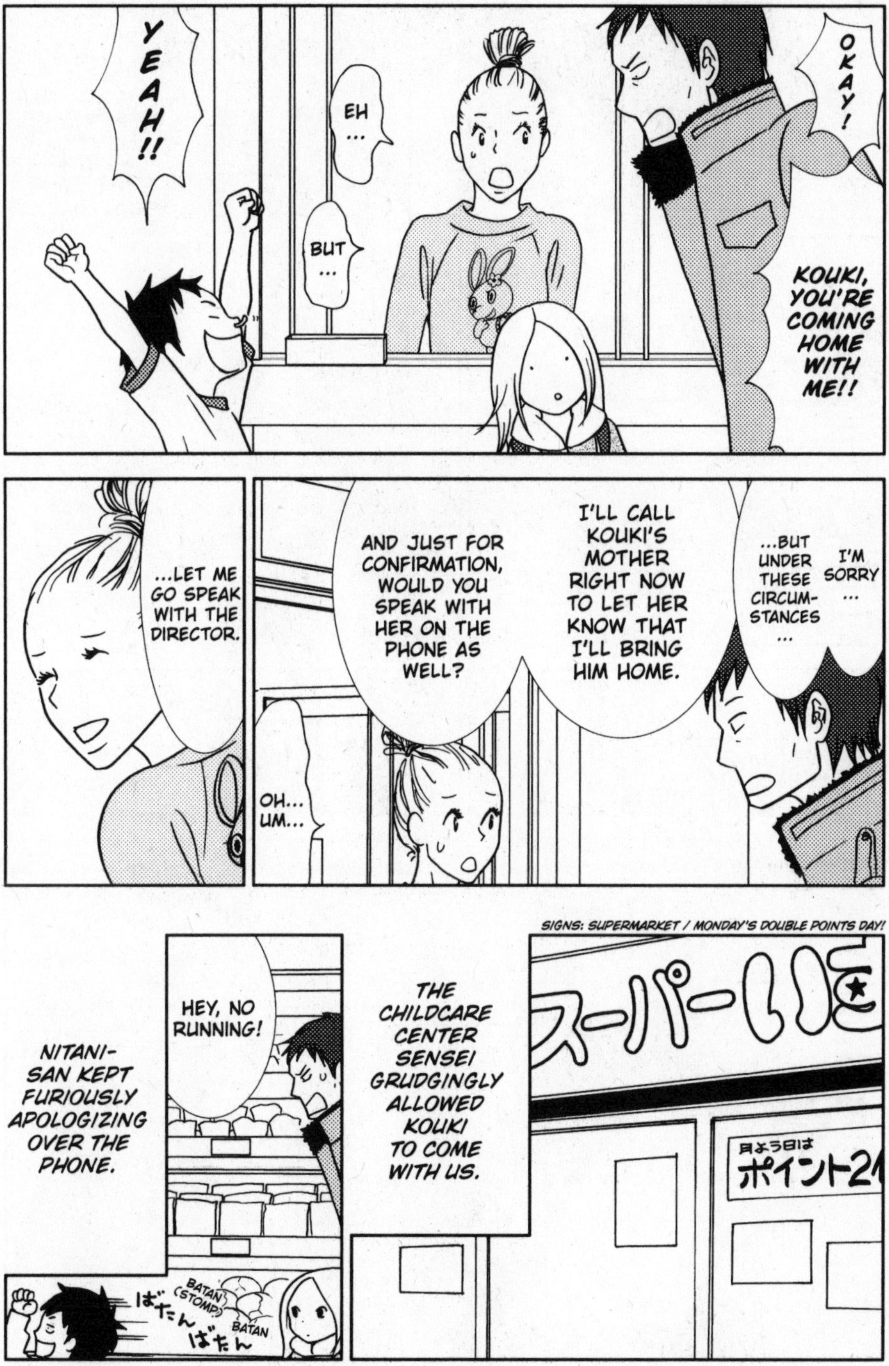
OKAY!
KOUKI, YOU'RE COMING HOME WITH ME!!
EH...
BUT...
YEAH!!
I'M SORRY...
...BUT UNDER THESE CIRCUMSTANCES...
I'LL CALL KOUKI'S MOTHER RIGHT NOW TO LET HER KNOW THAT I'LL BRING HIM HOME.
AND JUST FOR CONFIRMATION, WOULD YOU SPEAK WITH HER ON THE PHONE AS WELL?
OH... UM...
...LET ME GO SPEAK WITH THE DIRECTOR.
SIGNS: SUPERMARKET / MONDAY'S DOUBLE POINTS DAY!
スーパーい★
月よう日は
ポイント2
THE CHILDCARE CENTER SENSEI GRUDGINGLY ALLOWED KOUKI TO COME WITH US.
NITANI-SAN KEPT FURIOUSLY APOLOGIZING OVER THE PHONE.
HEY, NO RUNNING!
ばたん BATAN (STOMP)
ばたん BATAN

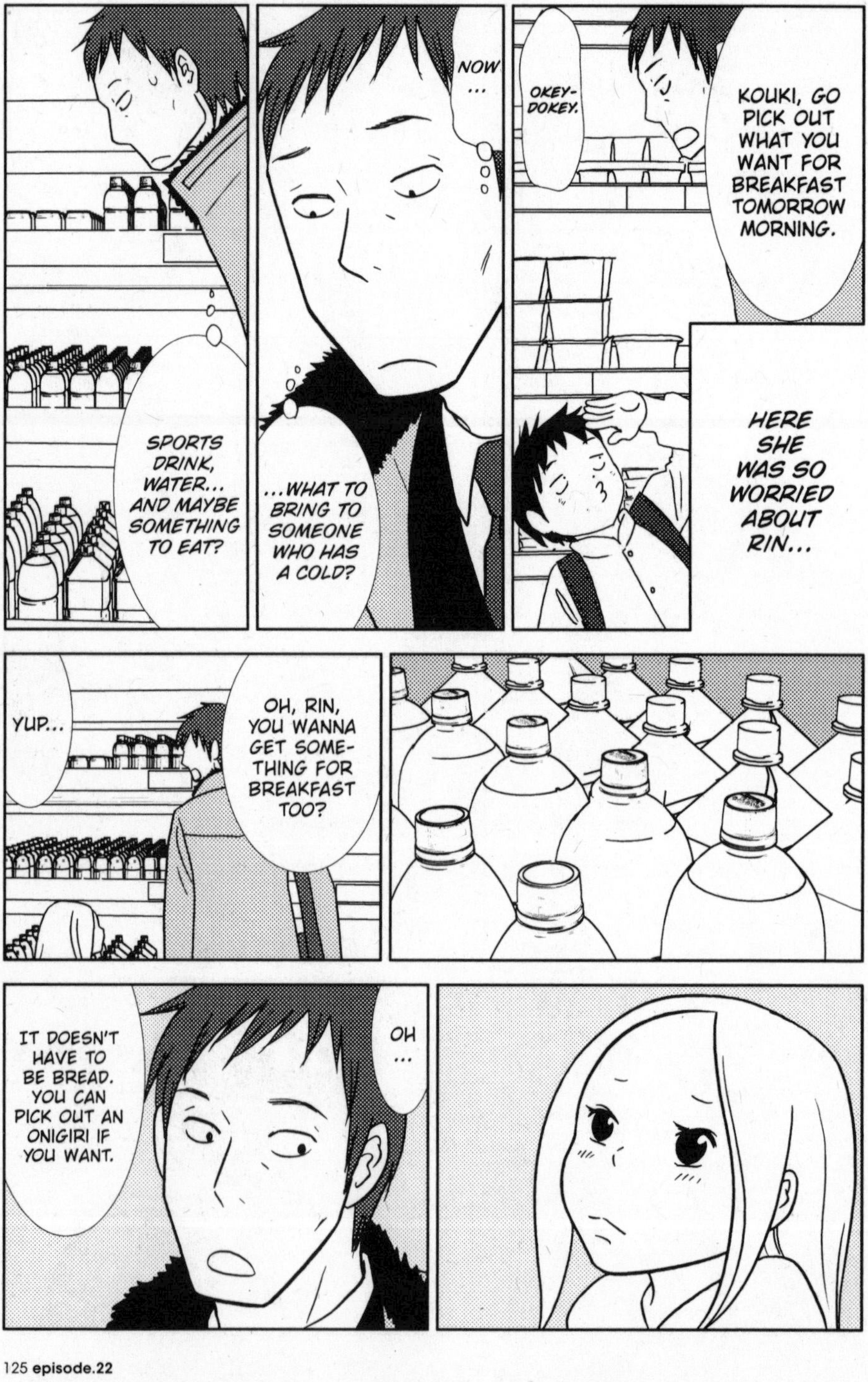
KOUKI, GO PICK OUT WHAT YOU WANT FOR BREAKFAST TOMORROW MORNING.
OKEY-DOKEY.
HERE SHE WAS SO WORRIED ABOUT RIN...
NOW ...
...WHAT TO BRING TO SOMEONE WHO HAS A COLD?
SPORTS DRINK, WATER... AND MAYBE SOMETHING TO EAT?
OH, RIN, YOU WANNA GET SOME-THING FOR BREAKFAST TOO?
YUP...
OH ...
IT DOESN'T HAVE TO BE BREAD. YOU CAN PICK OUT AN ONIGIRI IF YOU WANT.

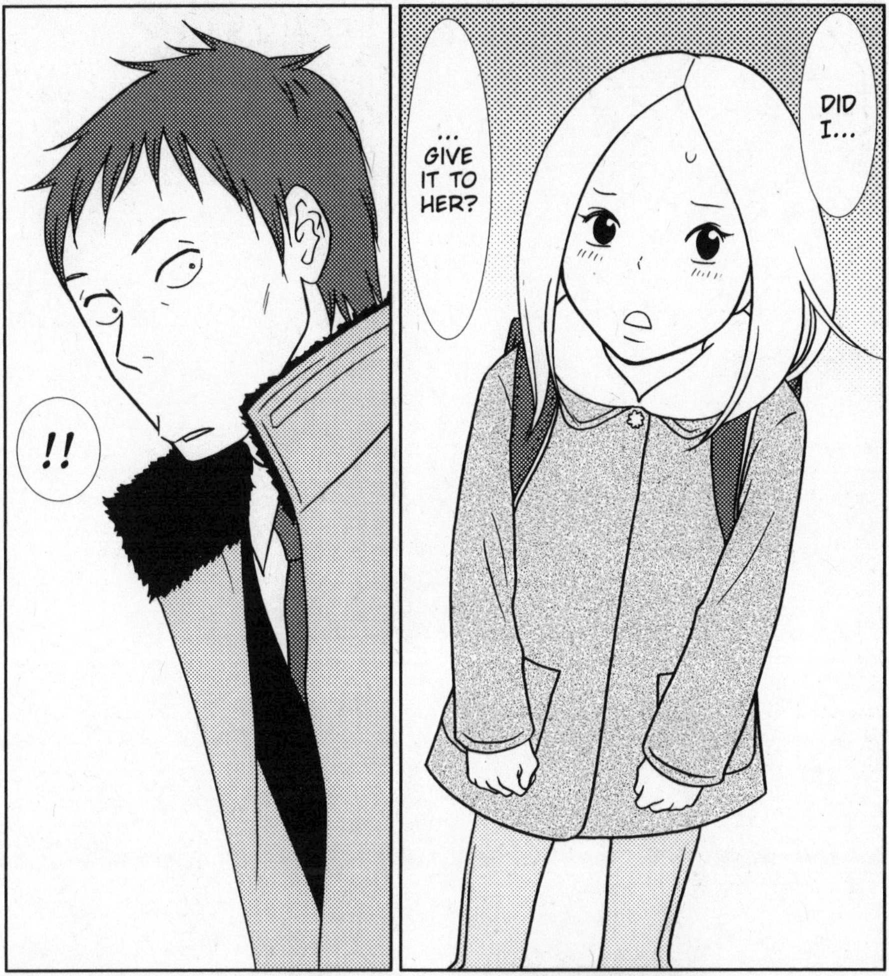
DID I...
...GIVE IT TO HER?
!!

CARD: CHARACTER CARD

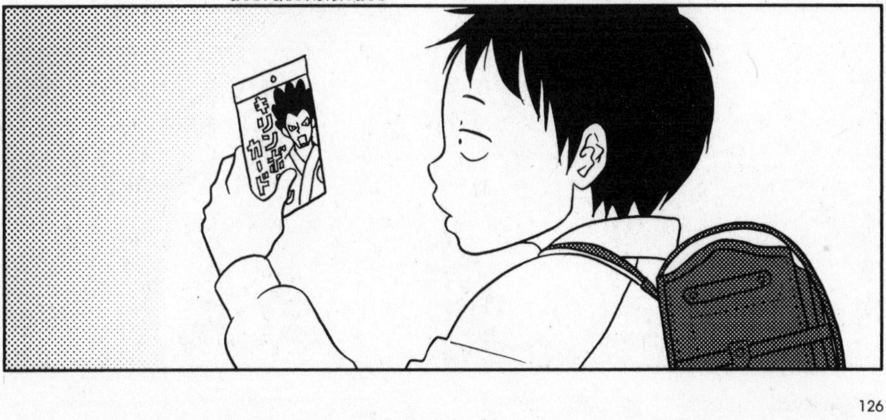
キリンぼカード

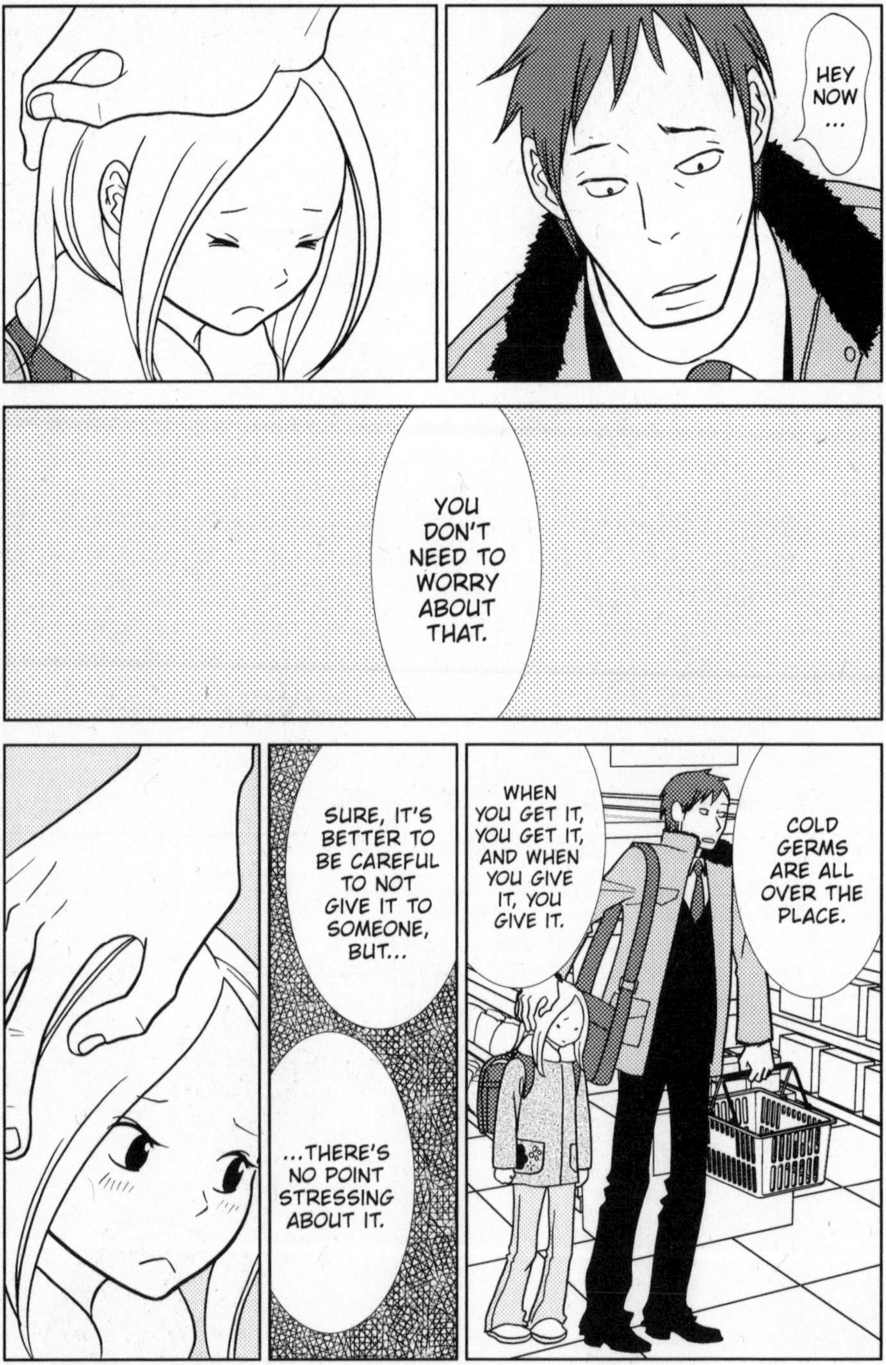
HEY NOW ...
YOU DON'T NEED TO WORRY ABOUT THAT.
COLD GERMS ARE ALL OVER THE PLACE.
WHEN YOU GET IT, YOU GET IT, AND WHEN YOU GIVE IT, YOU GIVE IT.
SURE, IT'S BETTER TO BE CAREFUL TO NOT GIVE IT TO SOMEONE, BUT...
...THERE'S NO POINT STRESSING ABOUT IT.

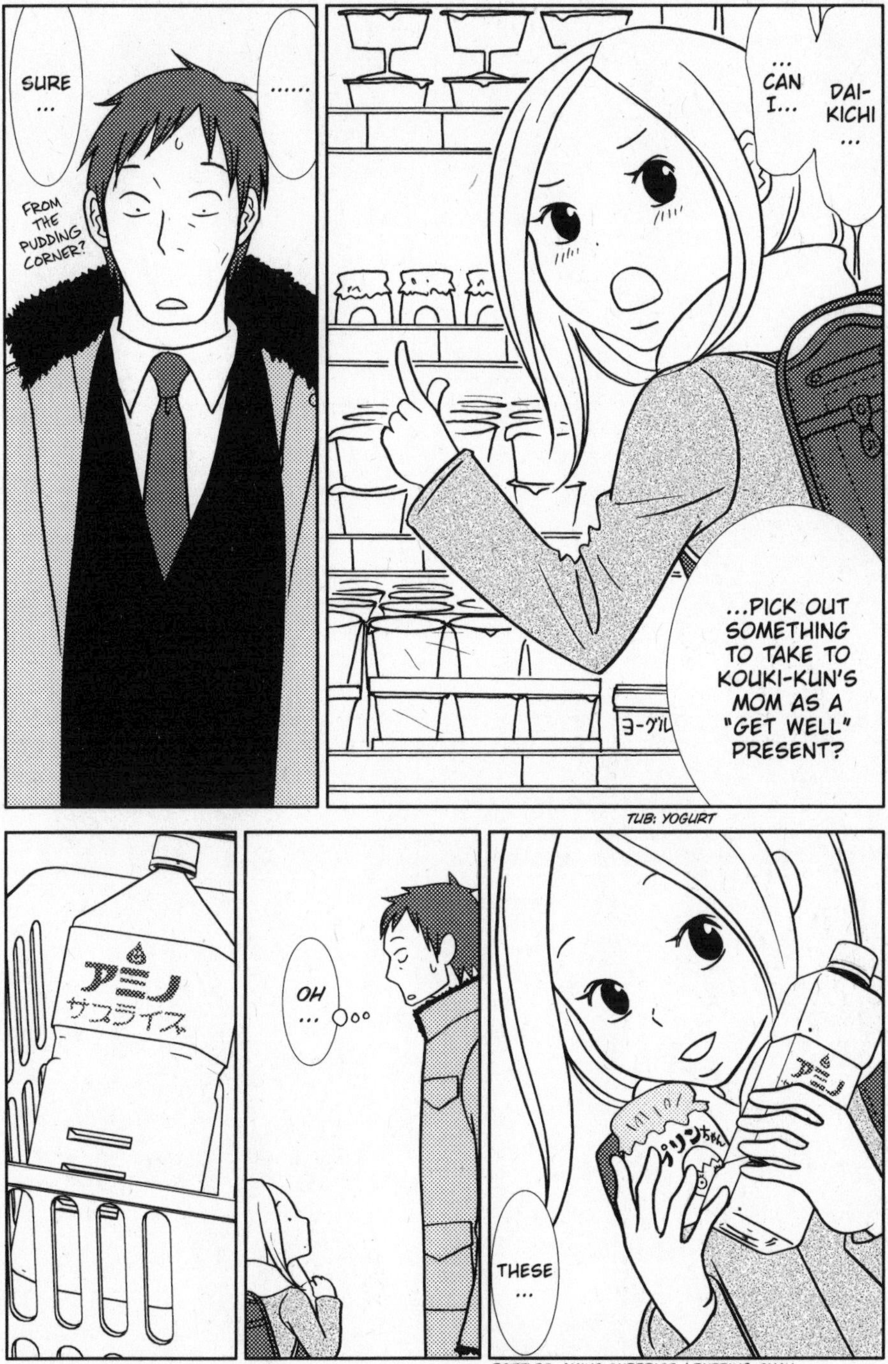
DAI-KICHI ...
... CAN I...
...PICK OUT SOMETHING TO TAKE TO KOUKI-KUN'S MOM AS A "GET WELL" PRESENT?
ヨーグル
......
SURE ...
FROM THE PUDDING CORNER?
THESE ...
プリンちゃん
OH ...
アミノ
サプライズ

TUB: YOGURT

BOTTLES: AMINO SURPRISE / PUDDING-CHAN

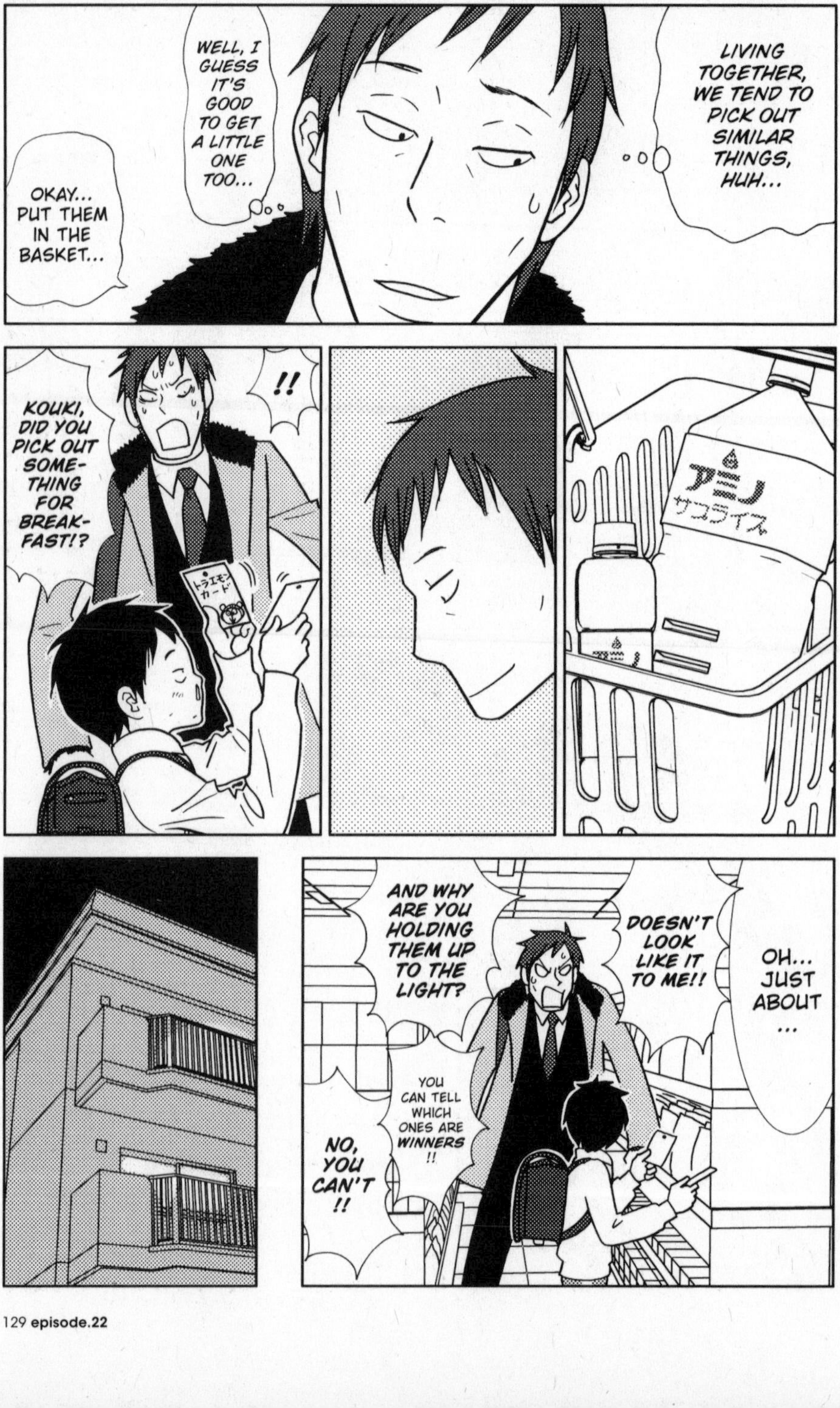
LIVING TOGETHER, WE TEND TO PICK OUT SIMILAR THINGS, HUH...
WELL, I GUESS IT'S GOOD TO GET A LITTLE ONE TOO...
OKAY... PUT THEM IN THE BASKET...
アミノ
!!
KOUKI, DID YOU PICK OUT SOME-THING FOR BREAK-FAST!?
トラエモンカード
OH... JUST ABOUT ...
DOESN'T LOOK LIKE IT TO ME!!
AND WHY ARE YOU HOLDING THEM UP TO THE LIGHT?
YOU CAN TELL WHICH ONES ARE WINNERS !!
NO, YOU CAN'T !!

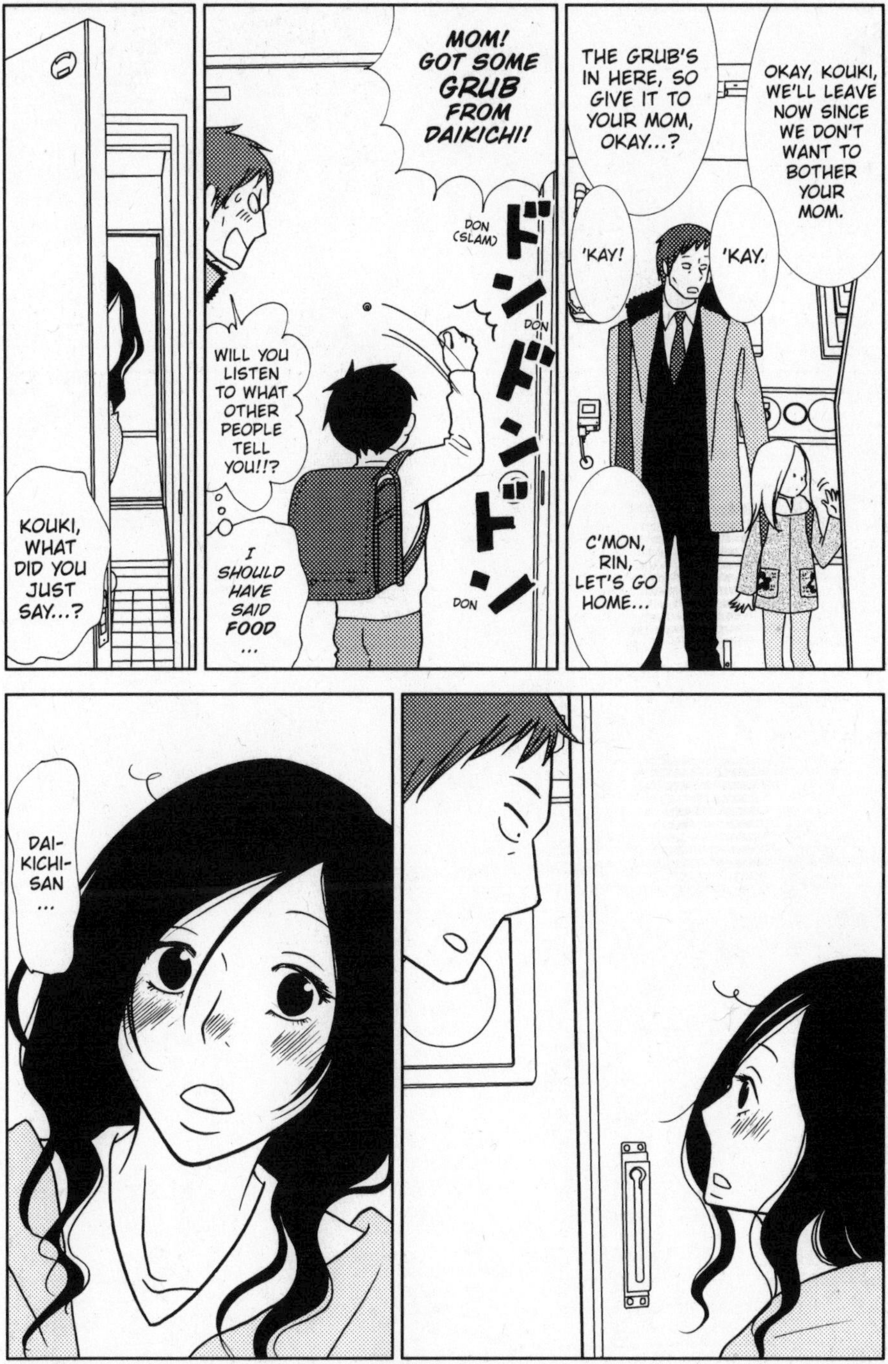
OKAY, KOUKI, WE'LL LEAVE NOW SINCE WE DON'T WANT TO BOTHER YOUR MOM.
THE GRUB'S IN HERE, SO GIVE IT TO YOUR MOM, OKAY...?
'KAY.
'KAY!
C'MON, RIN, LET'S GO HOME...
MOM! GOT SOME GRUB FROM DAIKICHI!
DON (SLAM)
ドン
DON
ドン
DON
ドン
WILL YOU LISTEN TO WHAT OTHER PEOPLE TELL YOU!!?
I SHOULD HAVE SAID FOOD ...
KOUKI, WHAT DID YOU JUST SAY...?
DAI-KICHI-SAN ...

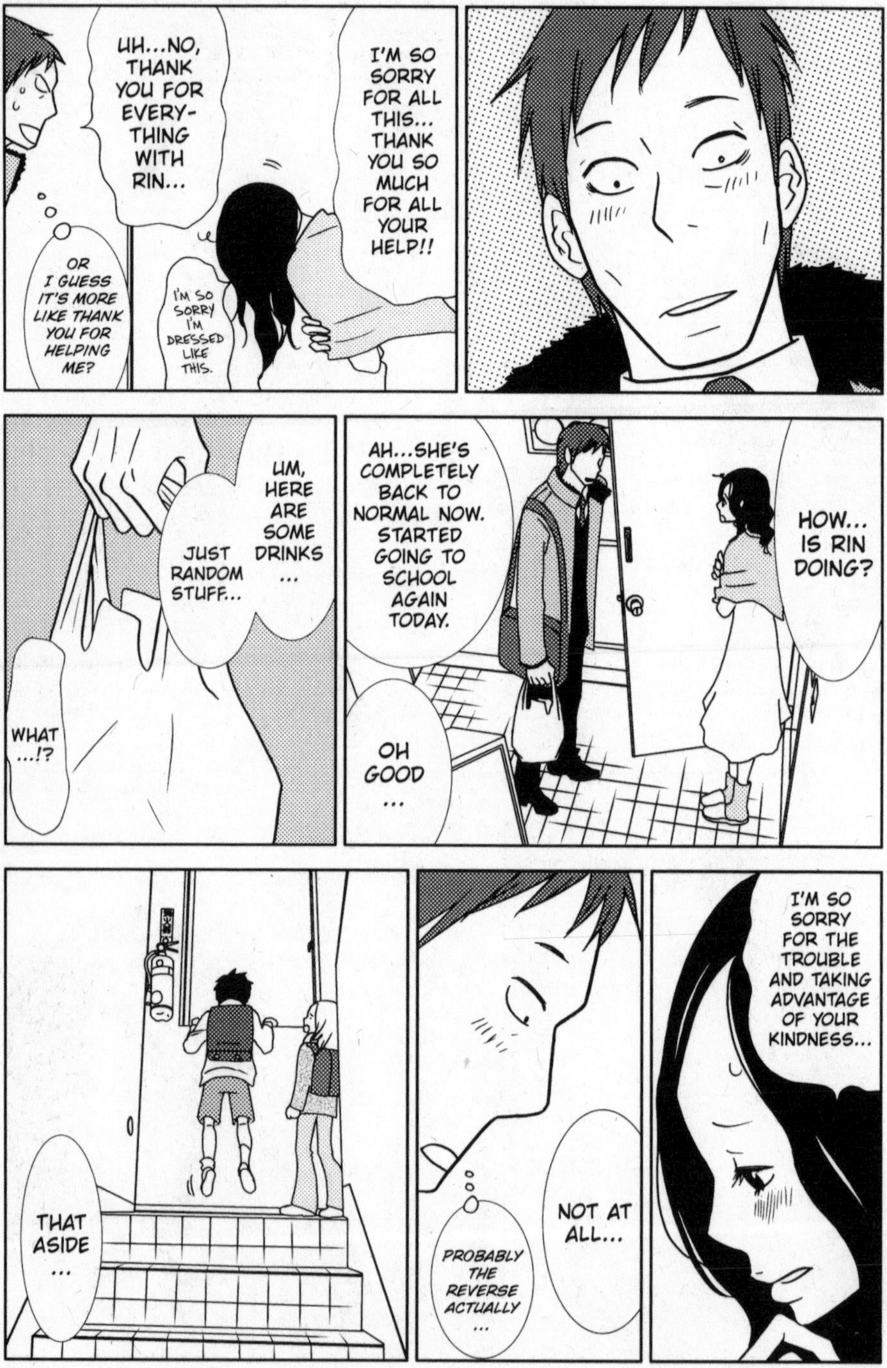
I'M SO SORRY FOR ALL THIS... THANK YOU SO MUCH FOR ALL YOUR HELP!!
UH...NO, THANK YOU FOR EVERYTHING WITH RIN...
I'M SO SORRY I'M DRESSED LIKE THIS.
OR I GUESS IT'S MORE LIKE THANK YOU FOR HELPING ME?
HOW... IS RIN DOING?
AH...SHE'S COMPLETELY BACK TO NORMAL NOW. STARTED GOING TO SCHOOL AGAIN TODAY.
OH GOOD ...
UM, HERE ARE SOME DRINKS ...
JUST RANDOM STUFF...
WHAT ...!?
I'M SO SORRY FOR THE TROUBLE AND TAKING ADVANTAGE OF YOUR KINDNESS...
NOT AT ALL...
PROBABLY THE REVERSE ACTUALLY ...
THAT ASIDE ...

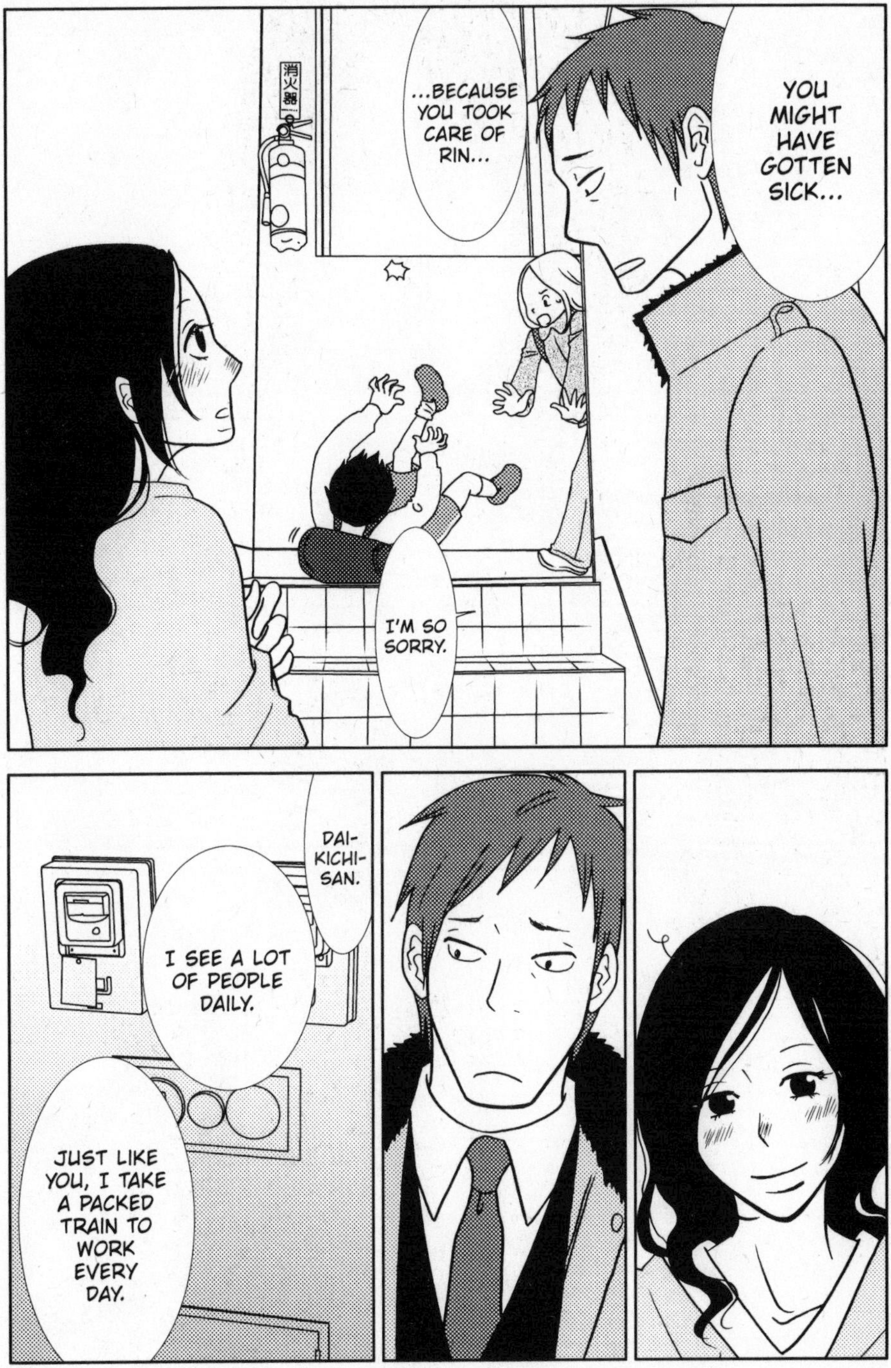
YOU MIGHT HAVE GOTTEN SICK...
...BECAUSE YOU TOOK CARE OF RIN...
消火器
I'M SO SORRY.
DAI-KICHI-SAN.
I SEE A LOT OF PEOPLE DAILY.
JUST LIKE YOU, I TAKE A PACKED TRAIN TO WORK EVERY DAY.

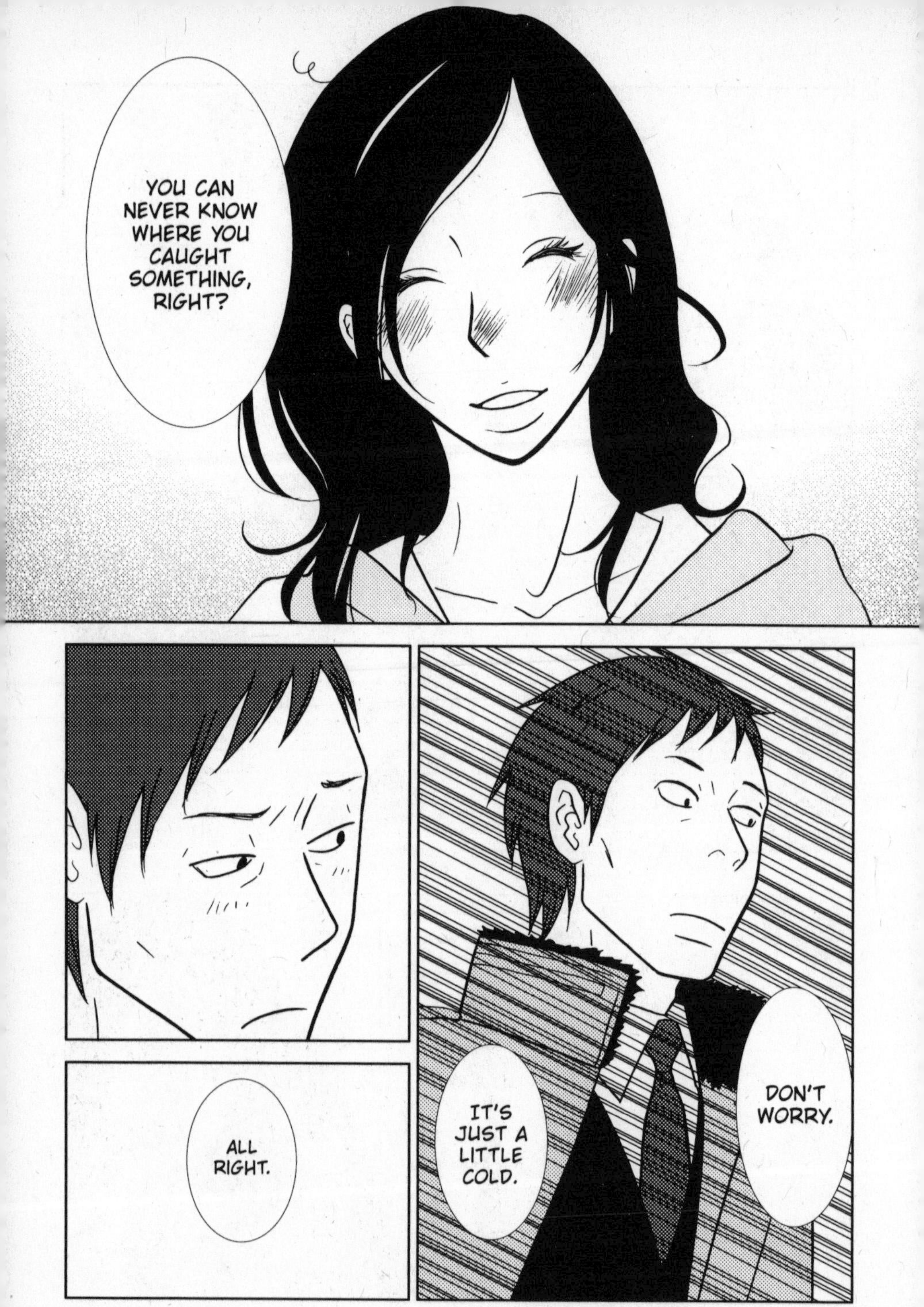
YOU CAN NEVER KNOW WHERE YOU CAUGHT SOMETHING, RIGHT?
DON'T WORRY.
IT'S JUST A LITTLE COLD.
ALL RIGHT.

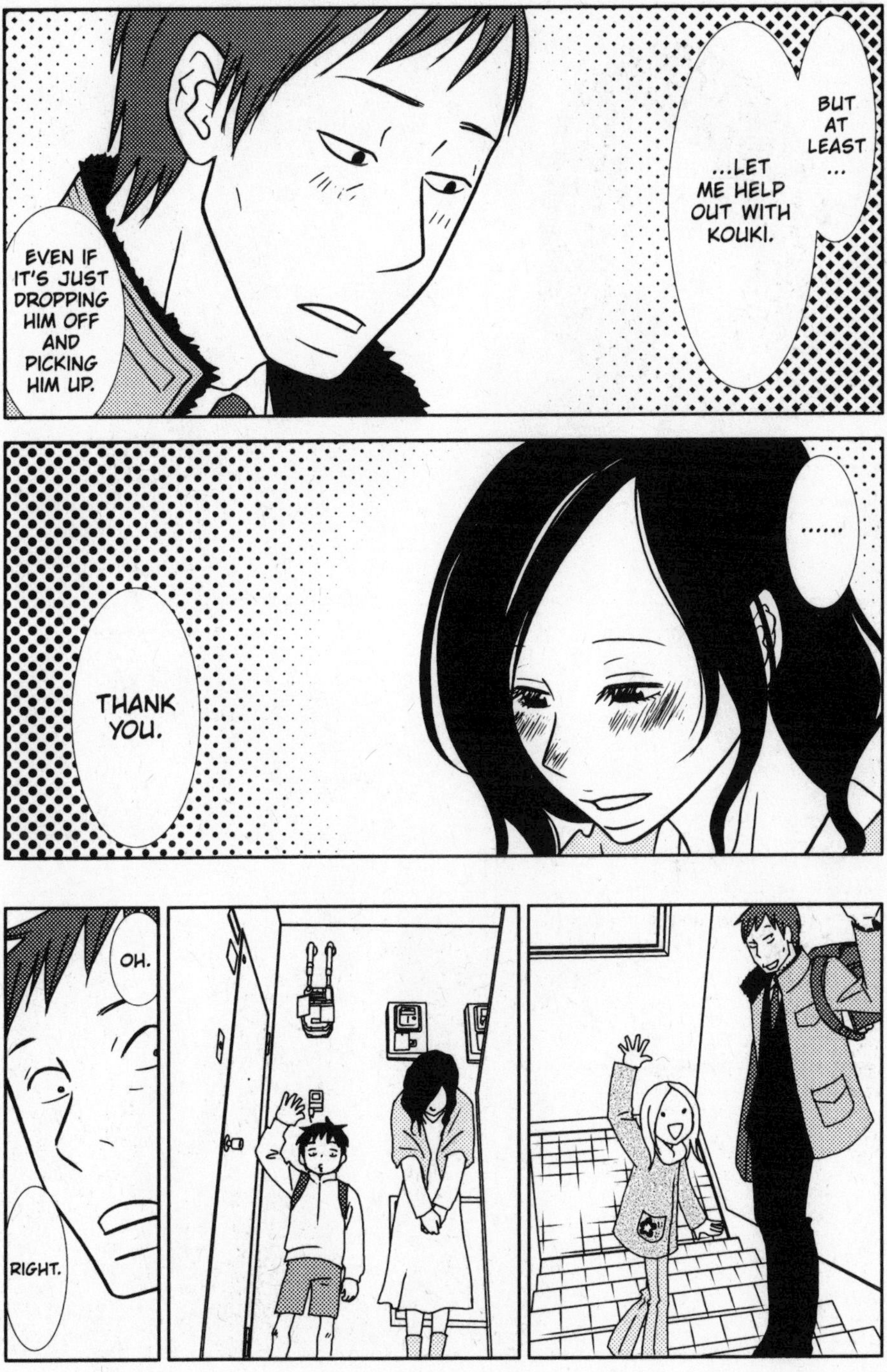
BUT AT LEAST ...
...LET ME HELP OUT WITH KOUKI.
EVEN IF IT'S JUST DROPPING HIM OFF AND PICKING HIM UP.
......
THANK YOU.
OH.
RIGHT.

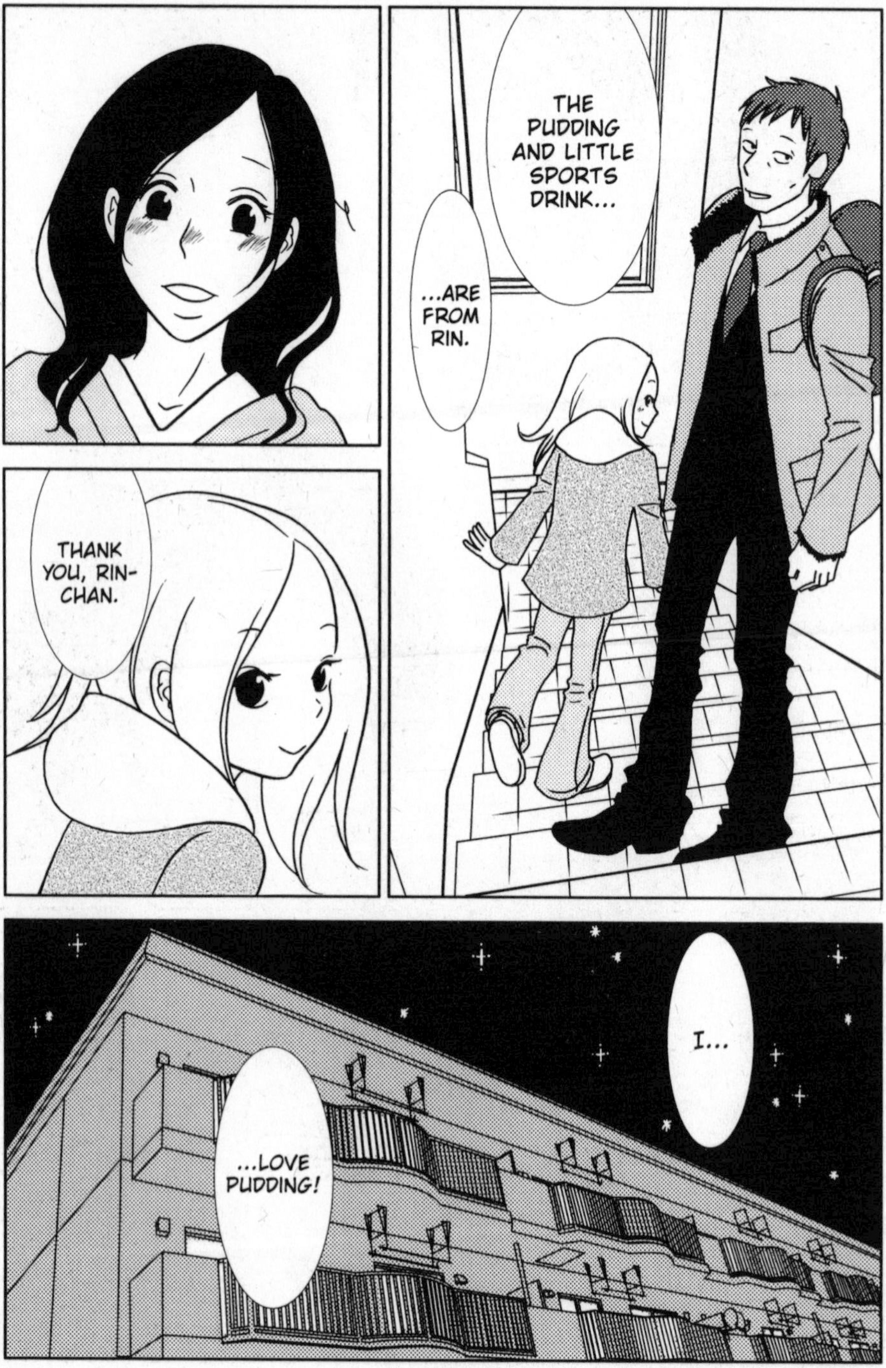
THE PUDDING AND LITTLE SPORTS DRINK...
...ARE FROM RIN.
THANK YOU, RIN-CHAN.
I...
...LOVE PUDDING!

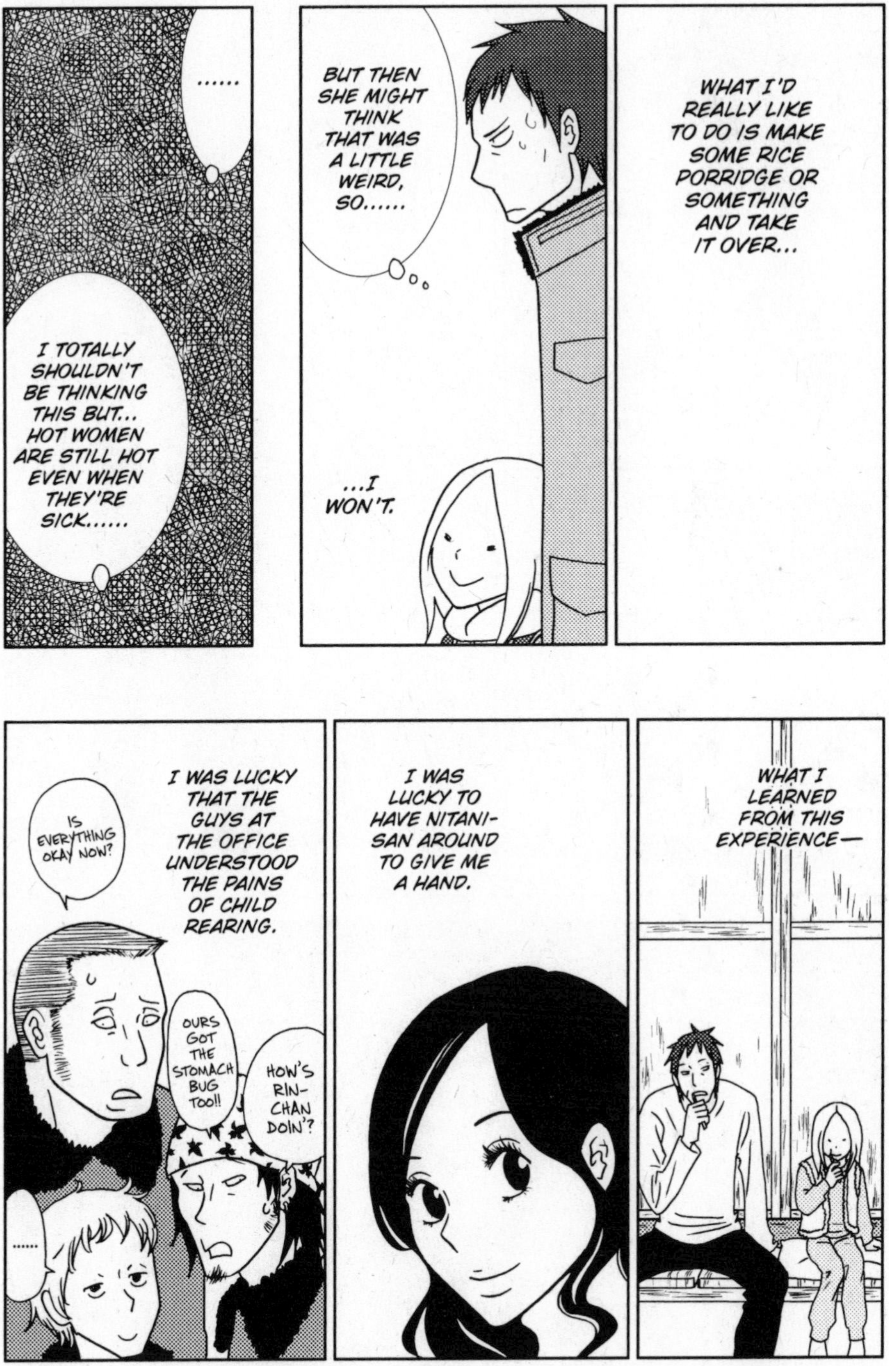
WHAT I'D REALLY LIKE TO DO IS MAKE SOME RICE PORRIDGE OR SOMETHING AND TAKE IT OVER...
BUT THEN SHE MIGHT THINK THAT WAS A LITTLE WEIRD, SO......
...I WON'T.
......
I TOTALLY SHOULDN'T BE THINKING THIS BUT... HOT WOMEN ARE STILL HOT EVEN WHEN THEY'RE SICK......
WHAT I LEARNED FROM THIS EXPERIENCE—
I WAS LUCKY TO HAVE NITANI-SAN AROUND TO GIVE ME A HAND.
I WAS LUCKY THAT THE GUYS AT THE OFFICE UNDERSTOOD THE PAINS OF CHILD REARING.
IS EVERYTHING OKAY NOW?
HOW'S RIN-CHAN DOIN'?
OURS GOT THE STOMACH BUG TOO!!
......

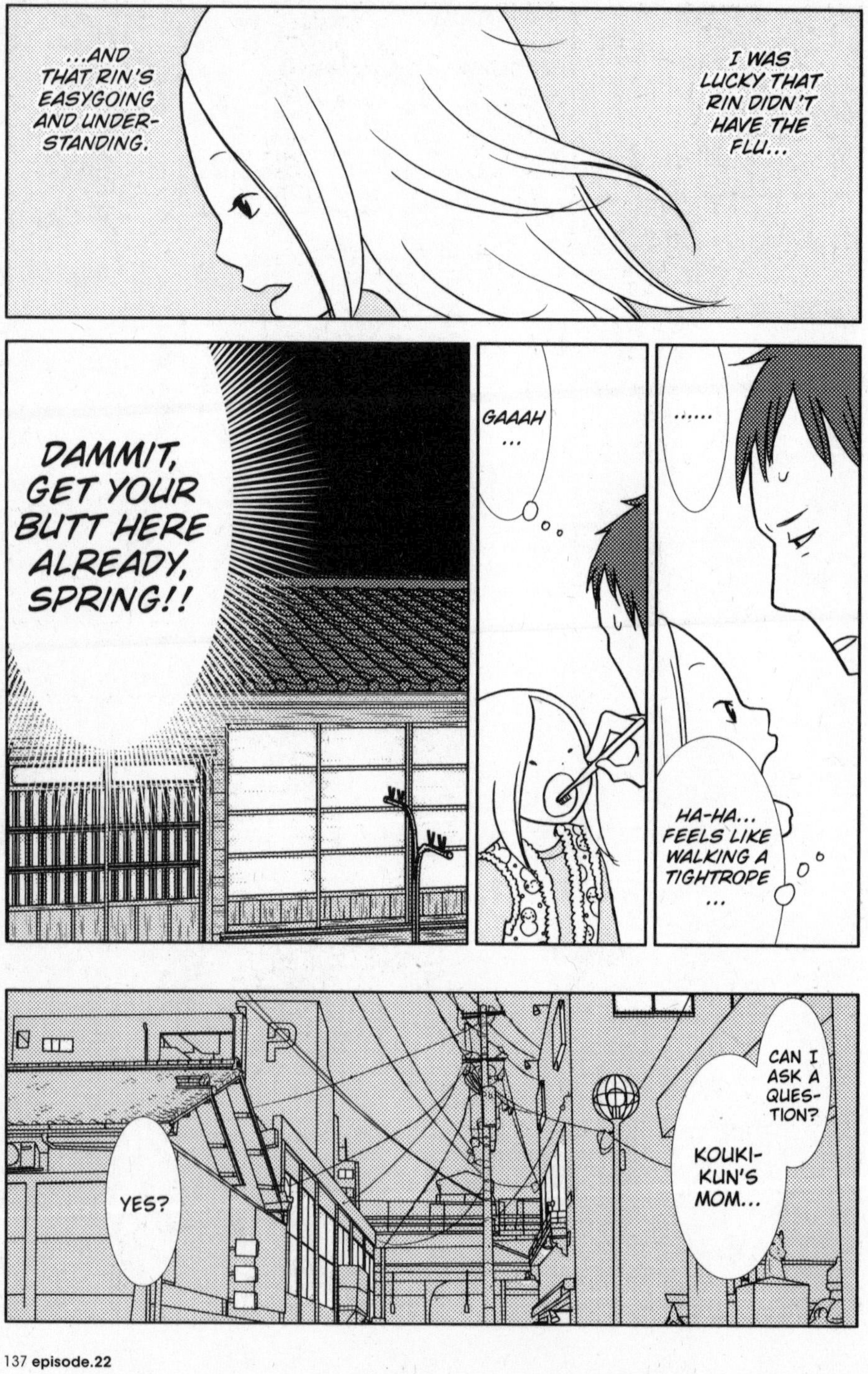
I WAS LUCKY THAT RIN DIDN'T HAVE THE FLU...
...AND THAT RIN'S EASYGOING AND UNDER-STANDING.
......
HA-HA... FEELS LIKE WALKING A TIGHTROPE...
GAAAH...
DAMMIT, GET YOUR BUTT HERE ALREADY, SPRING!!
CAN I ASK A QUES-TION?
KOUKI-KUN'S MOM...
YES?

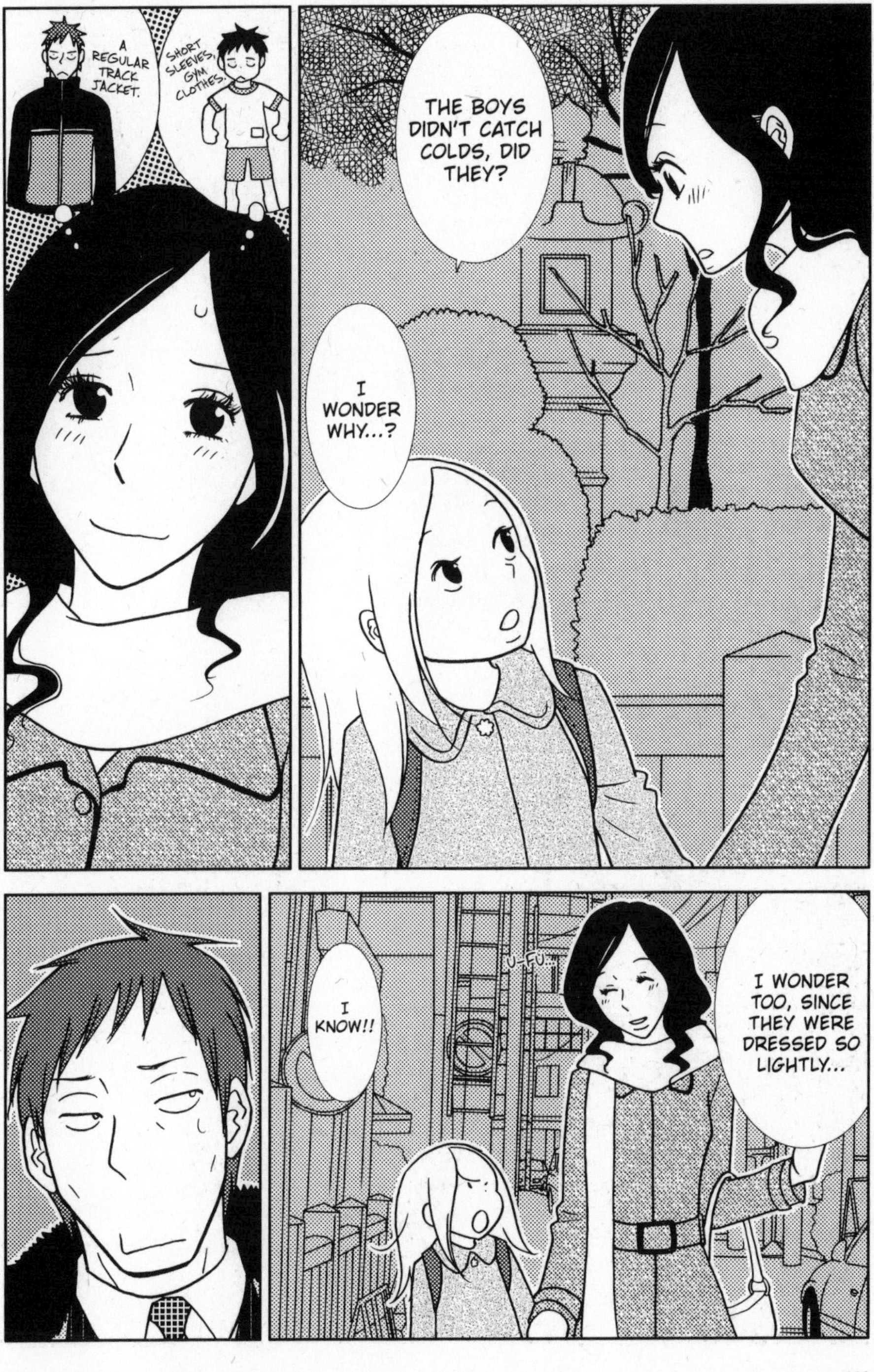
THE BOYS DIDN'T CATCH COLDS, DID THEY?
I WONDER WHY...?
SHORT SLEEVES, GYM CLOTHES.
A REGULAR TRACK JACKET.
I WONDER TOO, SINCE THEY WERE DRESSED SO LIGHTLY...
U-FU...
I KNOW!!

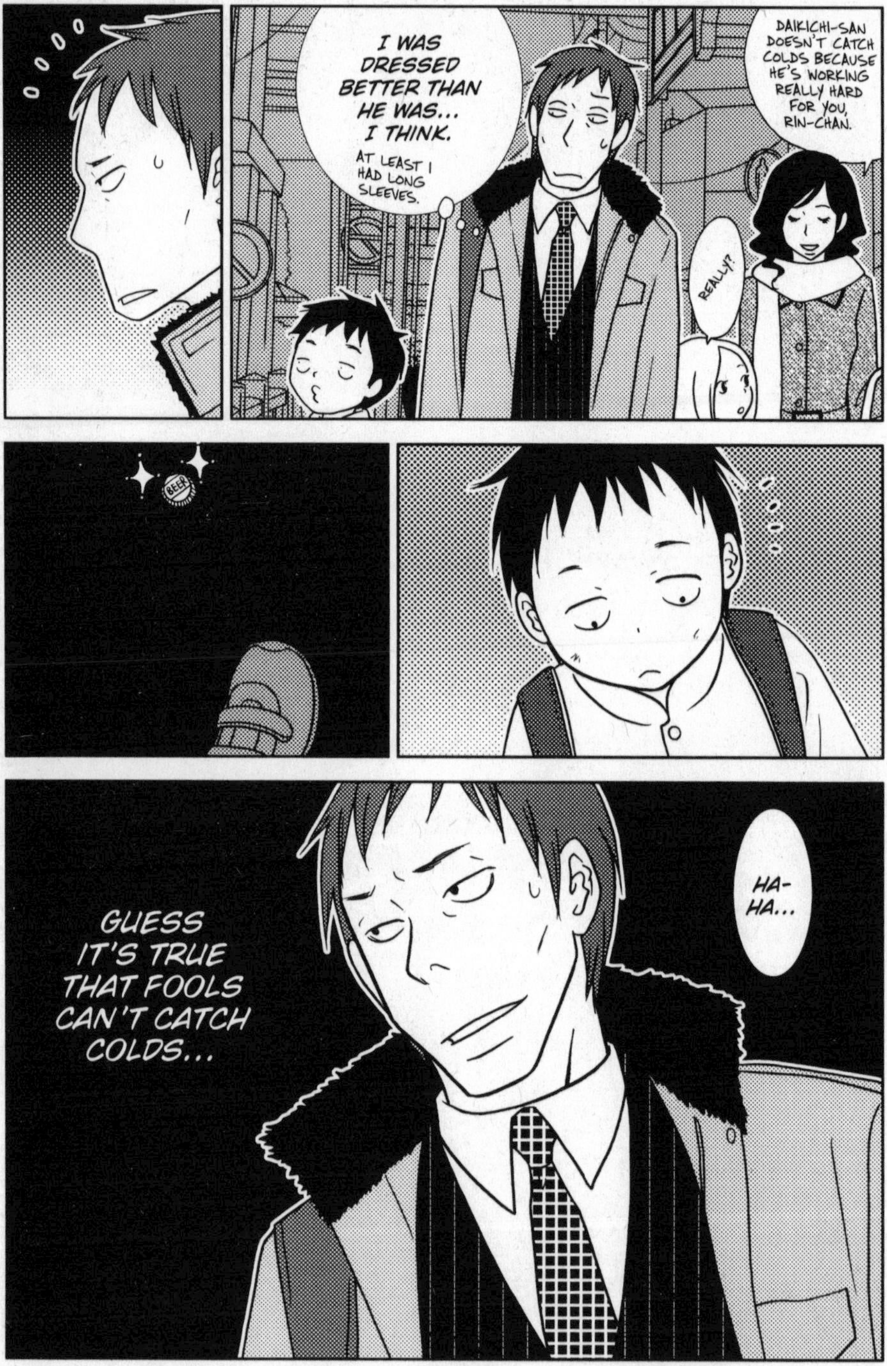
DAIKICHI-SAN DOESN'T CATCH COLDS BECAUSE HE'S WORKING REALLY HARD FOR YOU, RIN-CHAN.
REALLY?
I WAS DRESSED BETTER THAN HE WAS... I THINK.
AT LEAST I HAD LONG SLEEVES.
BEER
HA-HA...
GUESS IT'S TRUE THAT FOOLS CAN'T CATCH COLDS...

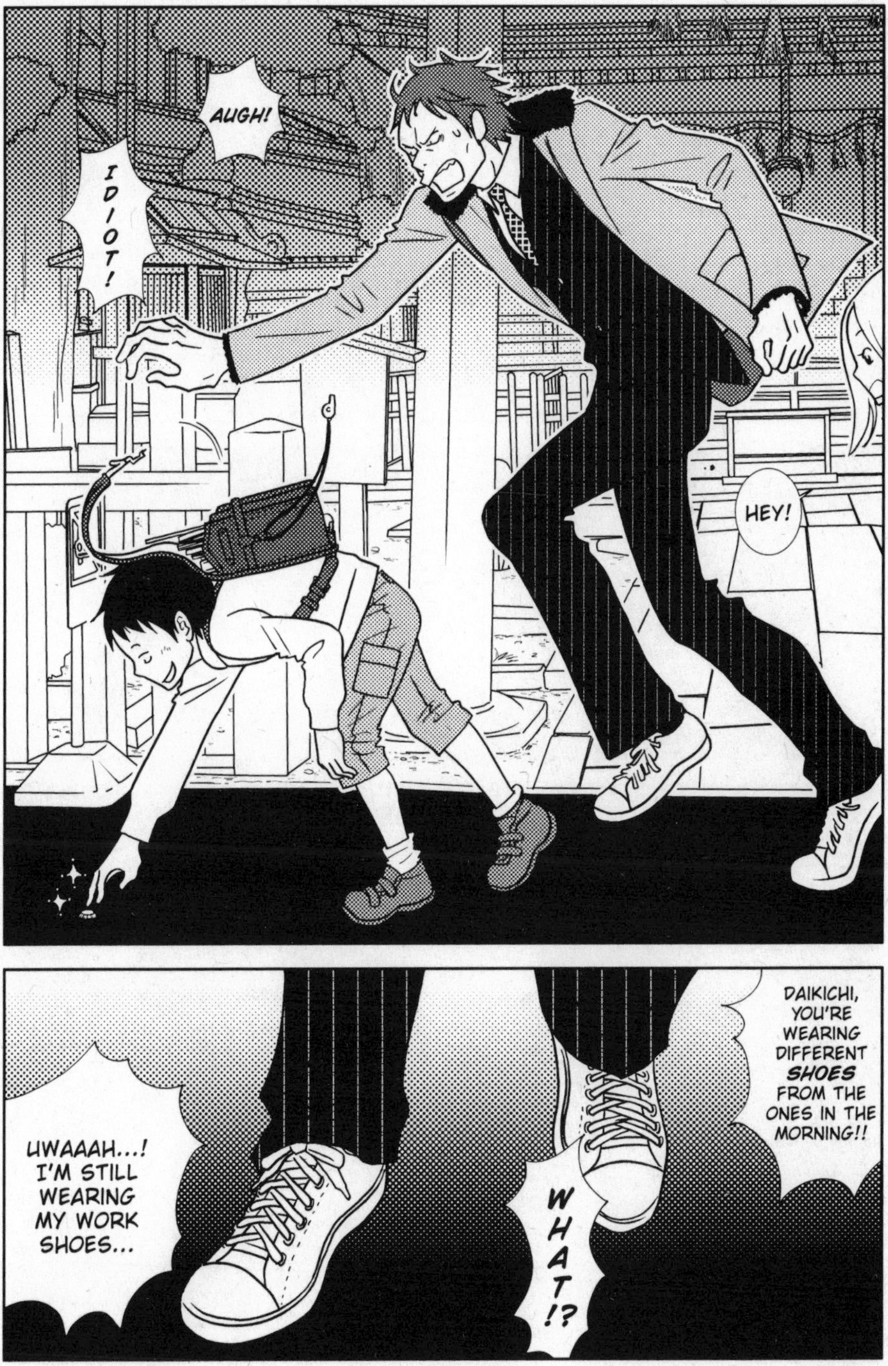
AUGH!
IDIOT!
HEY!
DAIKICHI, YOU'RE WEARING DIFFERENT ***SHOES*** FROM THE ONES IN THE MORNING!!
WHAT!?
UWAAAH...! I'M STILL WEARING MY WORK SHOES...

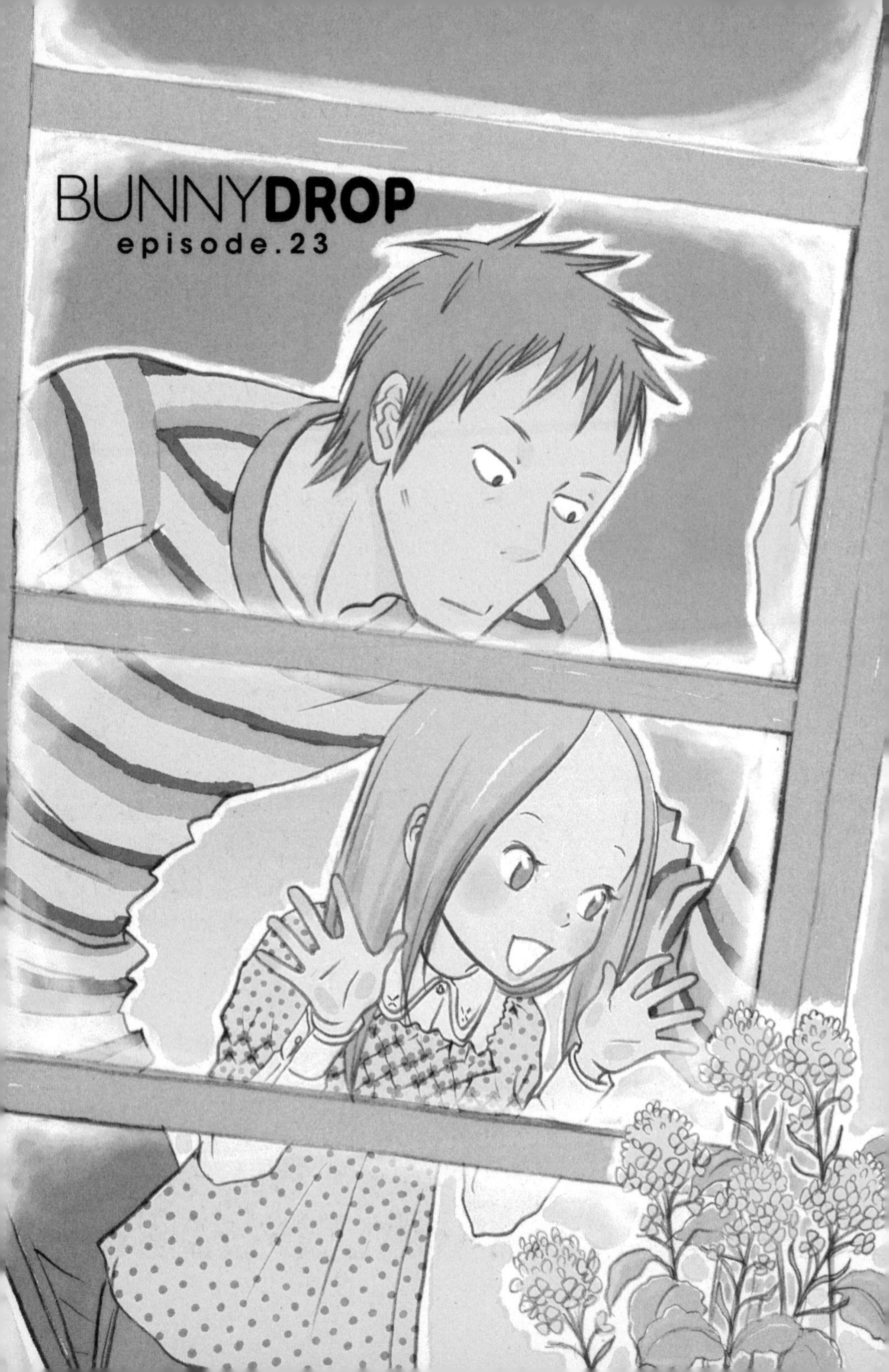
BUNNY**DROP**
episode.23

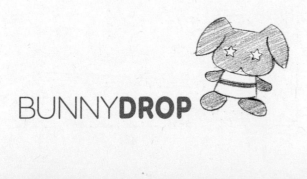

BUNNY**DROP**

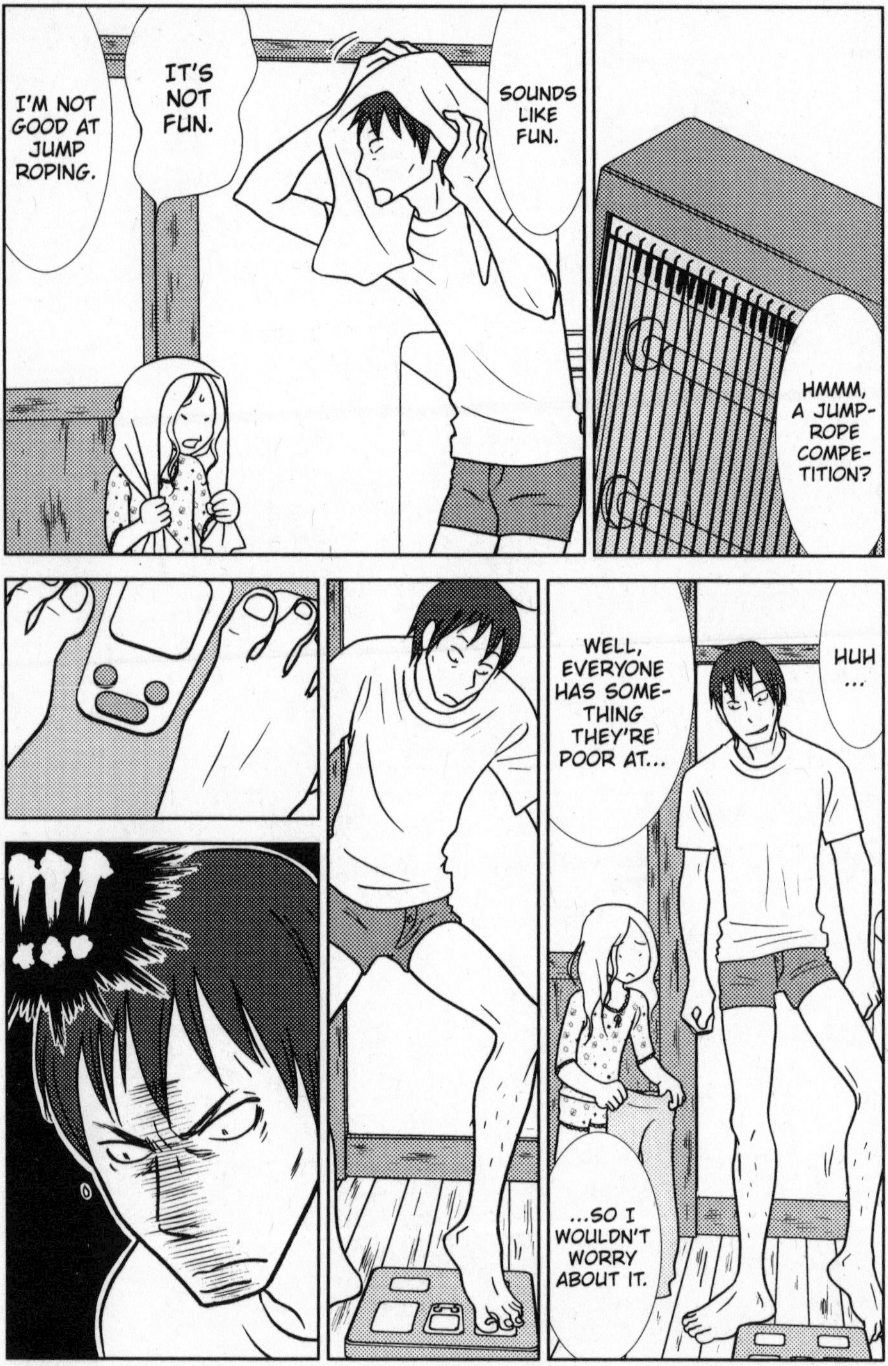
HMMM, A JUMP-ROPE COMPE-TITION?
SOUNDS LIKE FUN.
IT'S NOT FUN.
I'M NOT GOOD AT JUMP ROPING.
HUH ...
WELL, EVERYONE HAS SOME-THING THEY'RE POOR AT...
...SO I WOULDN'T WORRY ABOUT IT.
!!

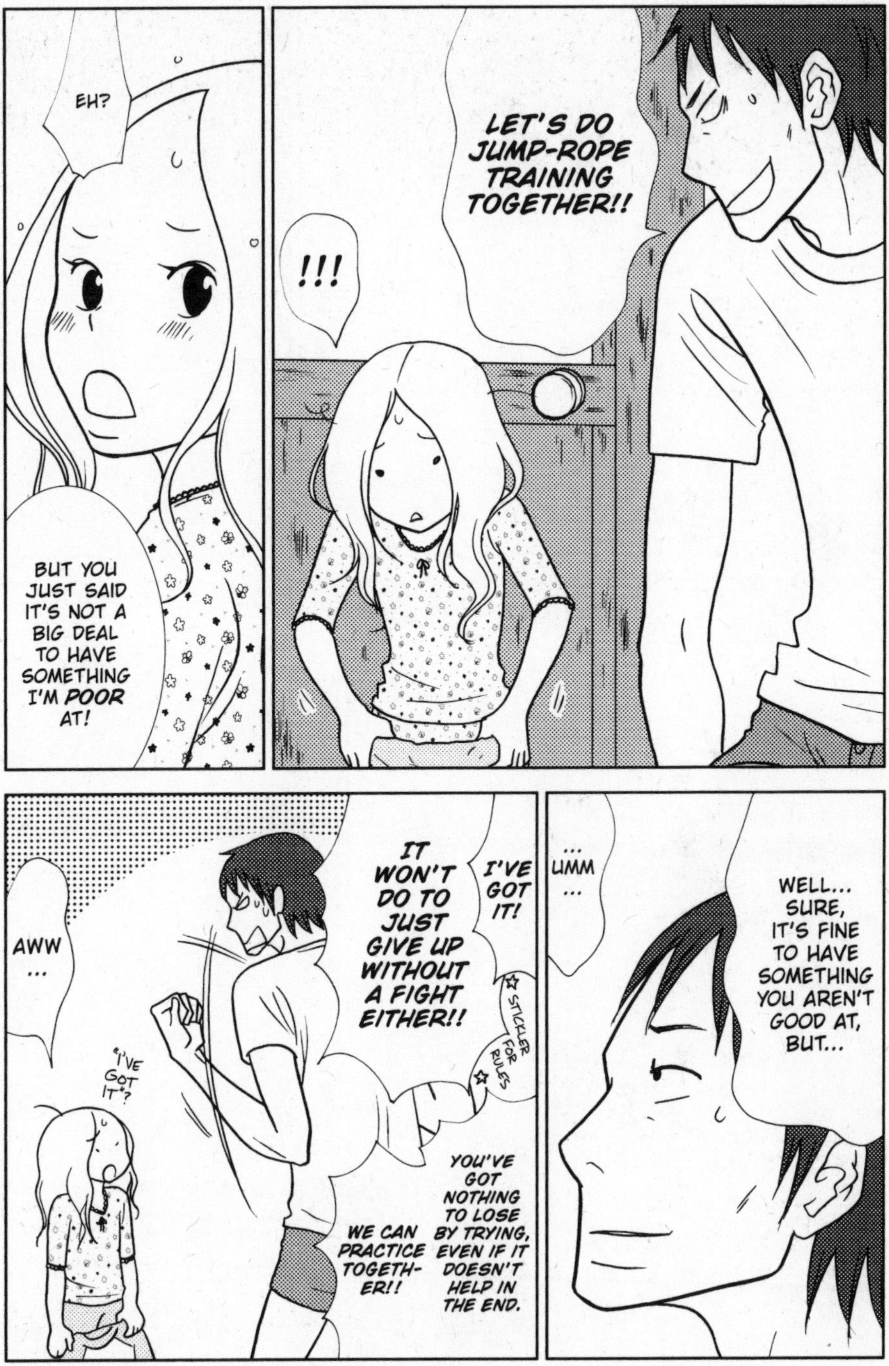
LET'S DO JUMP-ROPE TRAINING TOGETHER!!
!!!
EH?
BUT YOU JUST SAID IT'S NOT A BIG DEAL TO HAVE SOMETHING I'M *POOR* AT!
WELL... SURE, IT'S FINE TO HAVE SOMETHING YOU AREN'T GOOD AT, BUT...
... UMM ...
I'VE GOT IT!
IT WON'T DO TO JUST GIVE UP WITHOUT A FIGHT EITHER!!
STICKLER FOR RULES
AWW ...
YOU'VE GOT NOTHING TO LOSE BY TRYING, EVEN IF IT DOESN'T HELP IN THE END.
WE CAN PRACTICE TOGETHER!!
"I'VE GOT IT"?

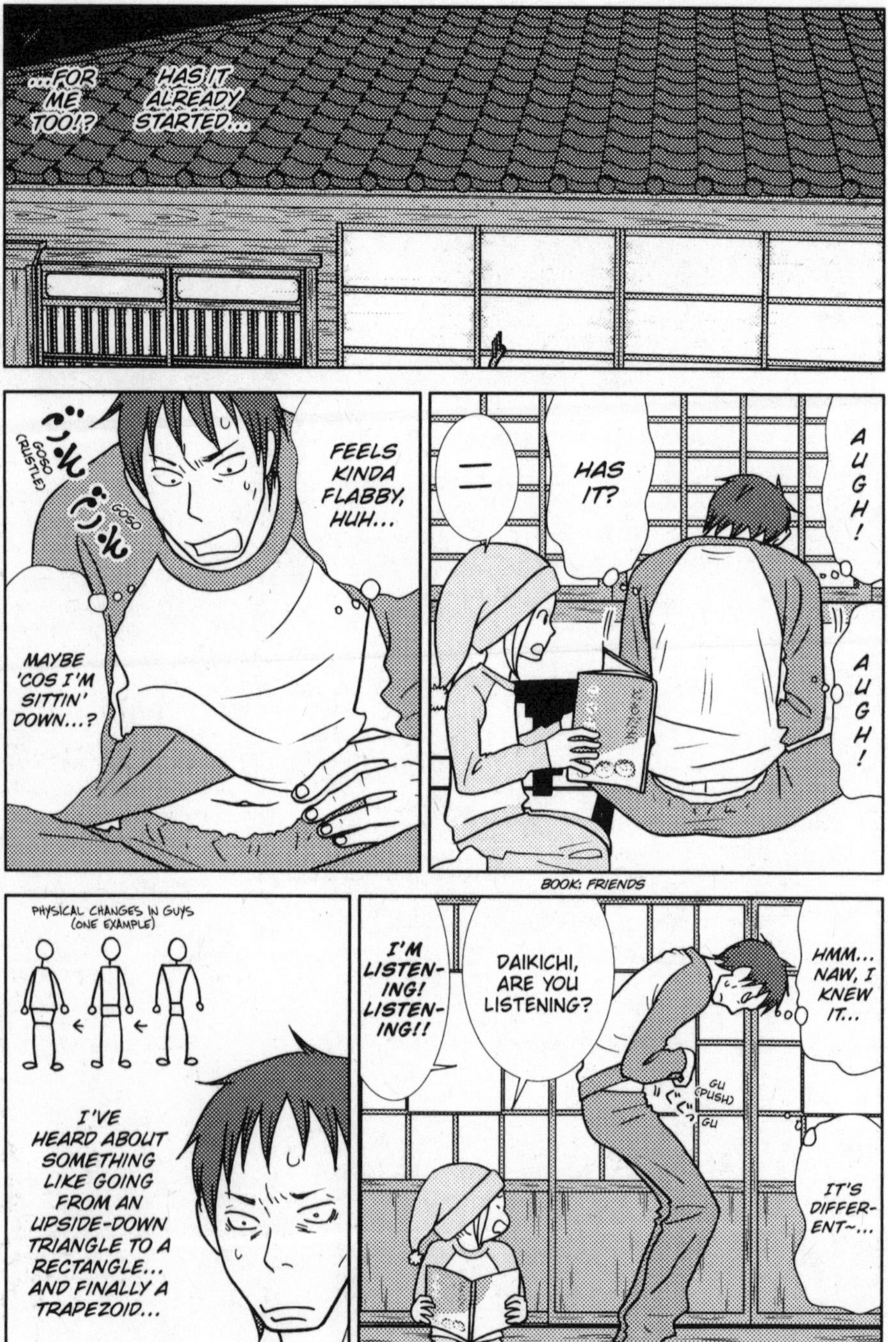
HAS IT ALREADY STARTED...
...FOR ME TOO!?
AUGH!
AUGH!
HAS IT?
BOOK: FRIENDS
FEELS KINDA FLABBY, HUH...
GOSO (RUSTLE)
GOSO
MAYBE 'COS I'M SITTIN' DOWN...?
HMM... NAW, I KNEW IT...
DAIKICHI, ARE YOU LISTENING?
I'M LISTENING! LISTENING!!
GU (PUSH)
GU
IT'S DIFFERENT~...
PHYSICAL CHANGES IN GUYS (ONE EXAMPLE)
I'VE HEARD ABOUT SOMETHING LIKE GOING FROM AN UPSIDE-DOWN TRIANGLE TO A RECTANGLE... AND FINALLY A TRAPEZOID...

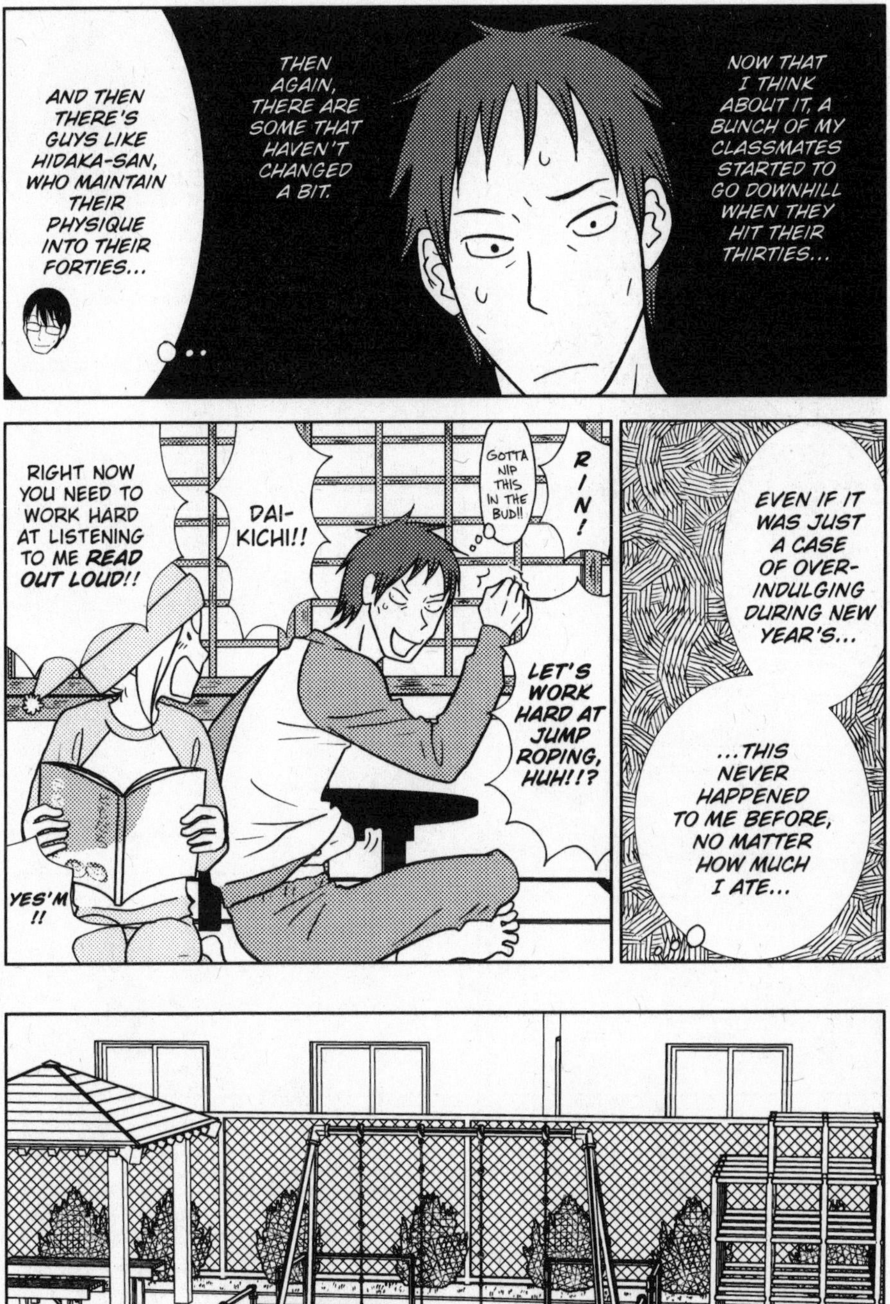
NOW THAT I THINK ABOUT IT, A BUNCH OF MY CLASSMATES STARTED TO GO DOWNHILL WHEN THEY HIT THEIR THIRTIES...
THEN AGAIN, THERE ARE SOME THAT HAVEN'T CHANGED A BIT.
AND THEN THERE'S GUYS LIKE HIDAKA-SAN, WHO MAINTAIN THEIR PHYSIQUE INTO THEIR FORTIES...
EVEN IF IT WAS JUST A CASE OF OVER-INDULGING DURING NEW YEAR'S...
...THIS NEVER HAPPENED TO ME BEFORE, NO MATTER HOW MUCH I ATE...
RIN!
GOTTA NIP THIS IN THE BUD!!
DAI-KICHI!!
RIGHT NOW YOU NEED TO WORK HARD AT LISTENING TO ME **READ OUT LOUD!!**
LET'S WORK HARD AT JUMP ROPING, HUH!!?
YES'M!!

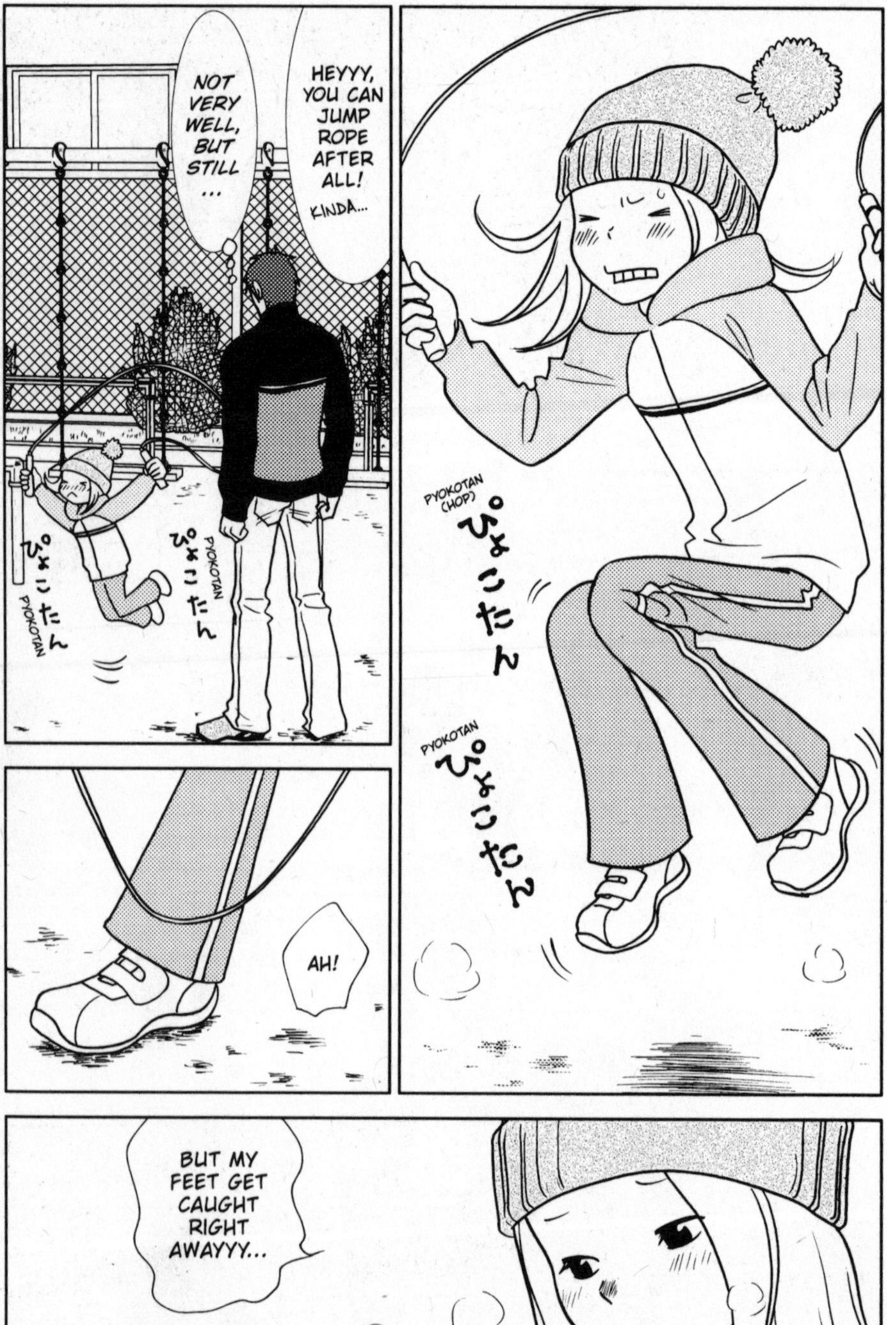
PYOKOTAN (HOP)
ぴょこたん
PYOKOTAN
ぴょこたん
HEYYY, YOU CAN JUMP ROPE AFTER ALL!
KINDA...
NOT VERY WELL, BUT STILL...
PYOKOTAN
ぴょこたん
ぴょこたん
PYOKOTAN
AH!
BUT MY FEET GET CAUGHT RIGHT AWAYYY...

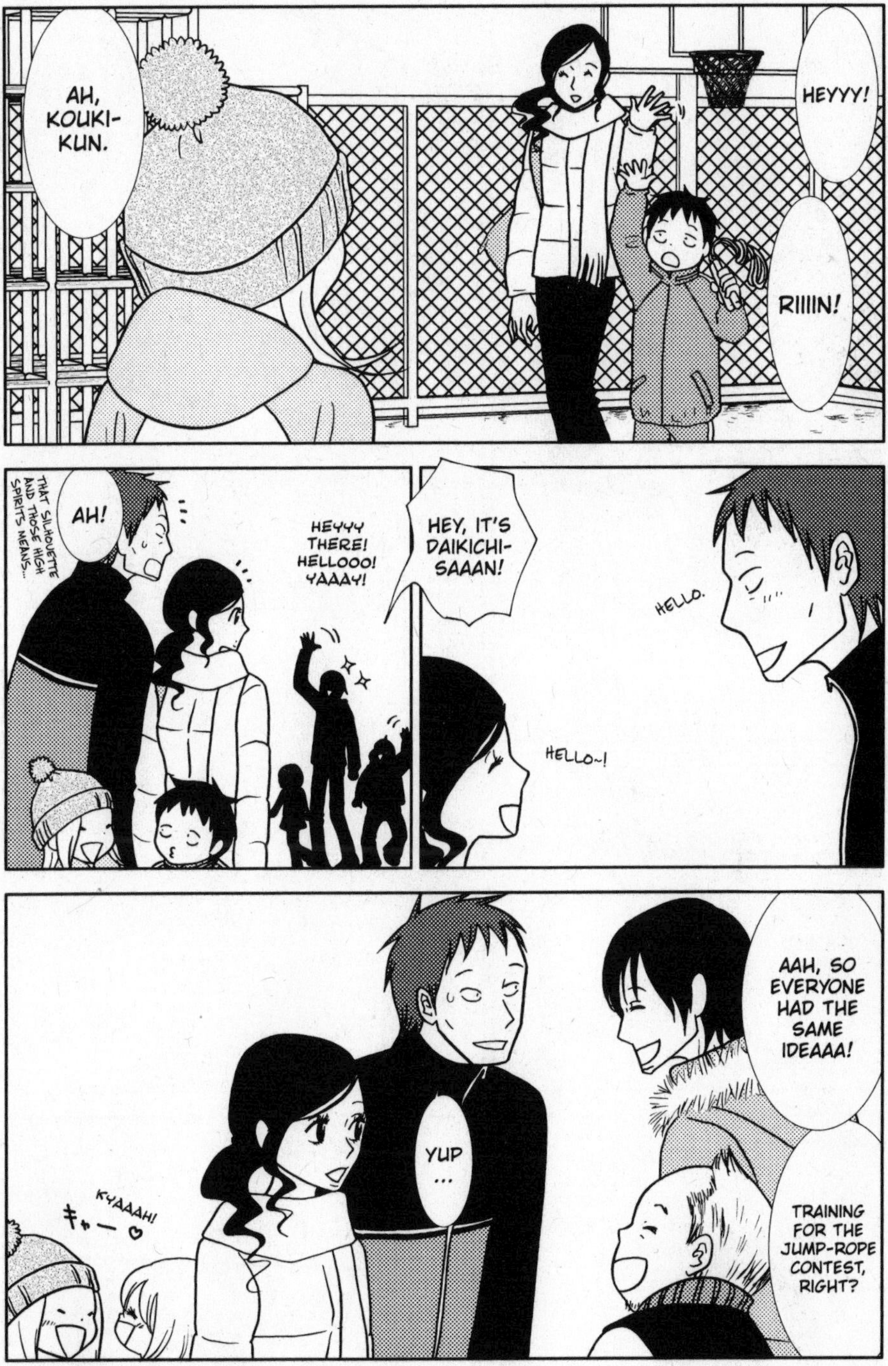
HEYYY!
RIIIIN!
AH, KOUKI-KUN.
HELLO.
HELLO~!
HEY, IT'S DAIKICHI-SAAAN!
HEYYY THERE! HELLOOO! YAAAY!
AH!
THAT SILHOUETTE AND THOSE HIGH SPIRITS MEANS...
AAH, SO EVERYONE HAD THE SAME IDEAAA!
TRAINING FOR THE JUMP-ROPE CONTEST, RIGHT?
YUP ...
KYAAAH!
キャー♡

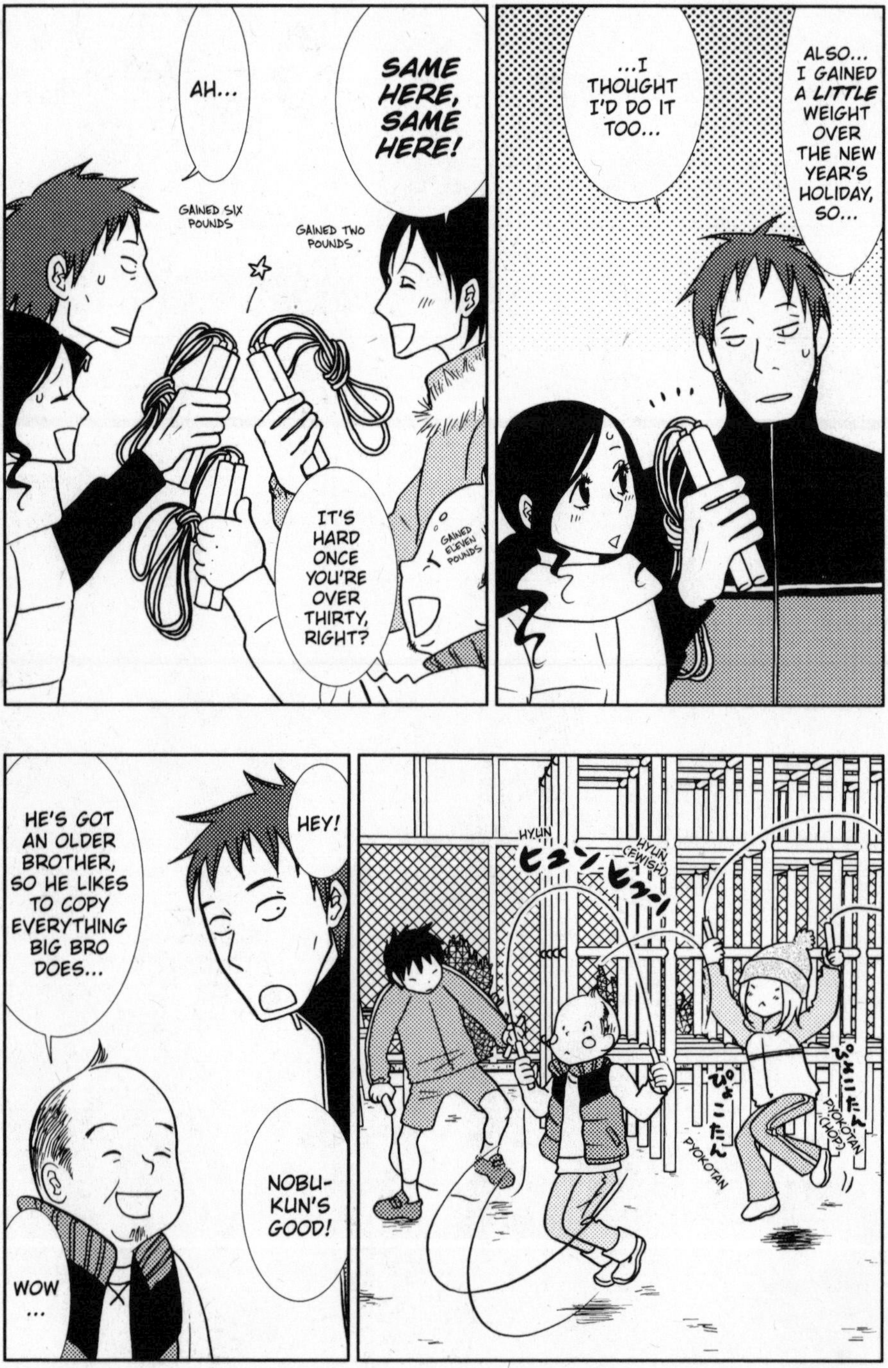
ALSO... I GAINED A *LITTLE* WEIGHT OVER THE NEW YEAR'S HOLIDAY, SO...
...I THOUGHT I'D DO IT TOO...
SAME HERE, SAME HERE!
AH...
GAINED TWO POUNDS
GAINED SIX POUNDS
GAINED ELEVEN POUNDS
IT'S HARD ONCE YOU'RE OVER THIRTY, RIGHT?
HYUN
ヒュン
HYUN (FWISH)
ヒュン
ぴょこたん
PYOKOTAN (CHOP)
ぴょこたん
PYOKOTAN
HEY!
HE'S GOT AN OLDER BROTHER, SO HE LIKES TO COPY EVERYTHING BIG BRO DOES...
NOBU-KUN'S GOOD!
WOW ...

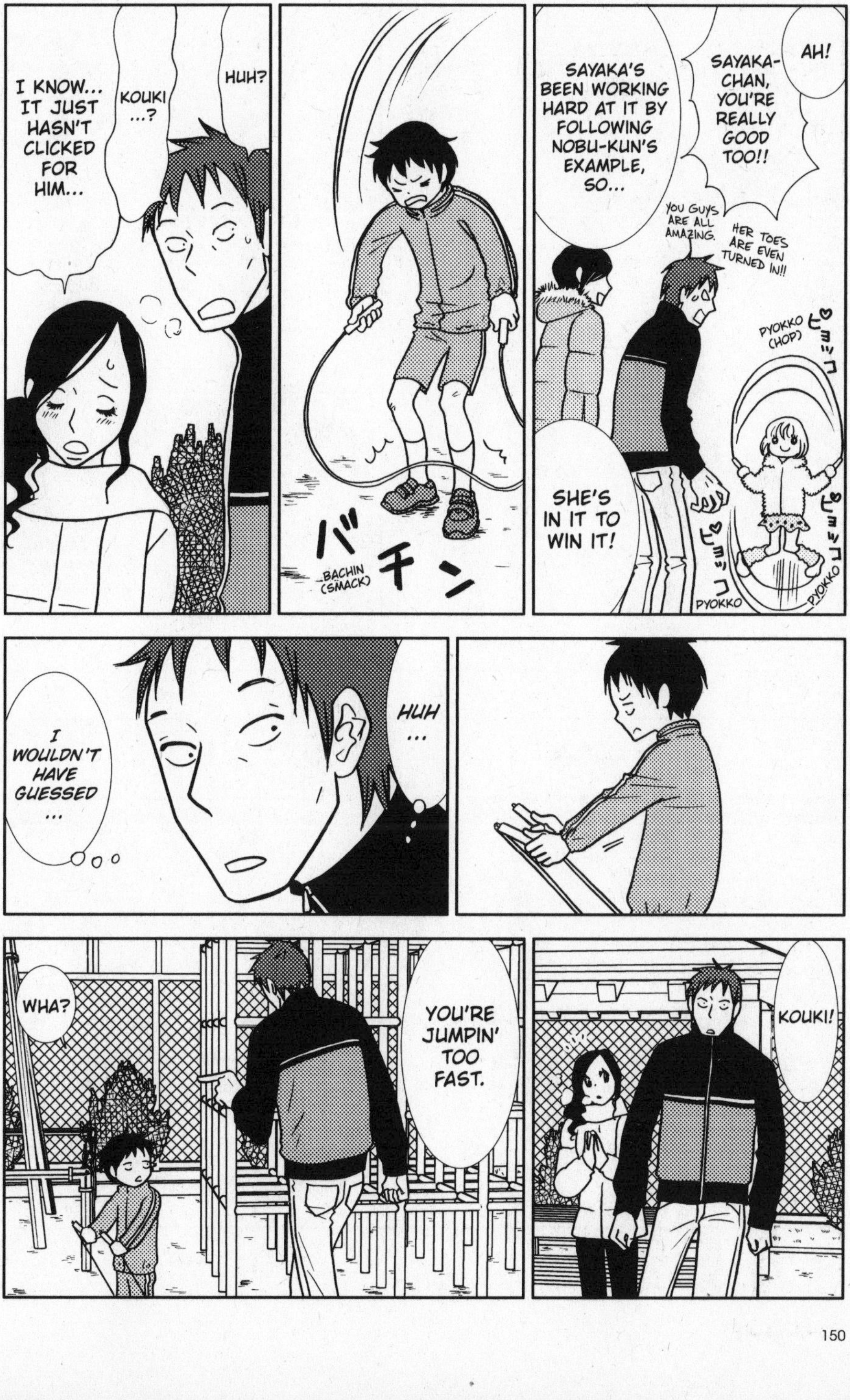
AH!
SAYAKA-CHAN, YOU'RE REALLY GOOD TOO!!
SAYAKA'S BEEN WORKING HARD AT IT BY FOLLOWING NOBU-KUN'S EXAMPLE, SO...
YOU GUYS ARE ALL AMAZING.
HER TOES ARE EVEN TURNED IN!!
ピョッコ
PYOKKO (HOP)
ピョッコ
PYOKKO
ピョッコ
PYOKKO
SHE'S IN IT TO WIN IT!
バチン
BACHIN (SMACK)
HUH?
KOUKI ...?
I KNOW... IT JUST HASN'T CLICKED FOR HIM...
HUH ...
I WOULDN'T HAVE GUESSED ...
KOUKI!
YOU'RE JUMPIN' TOO FAST.
WHA?

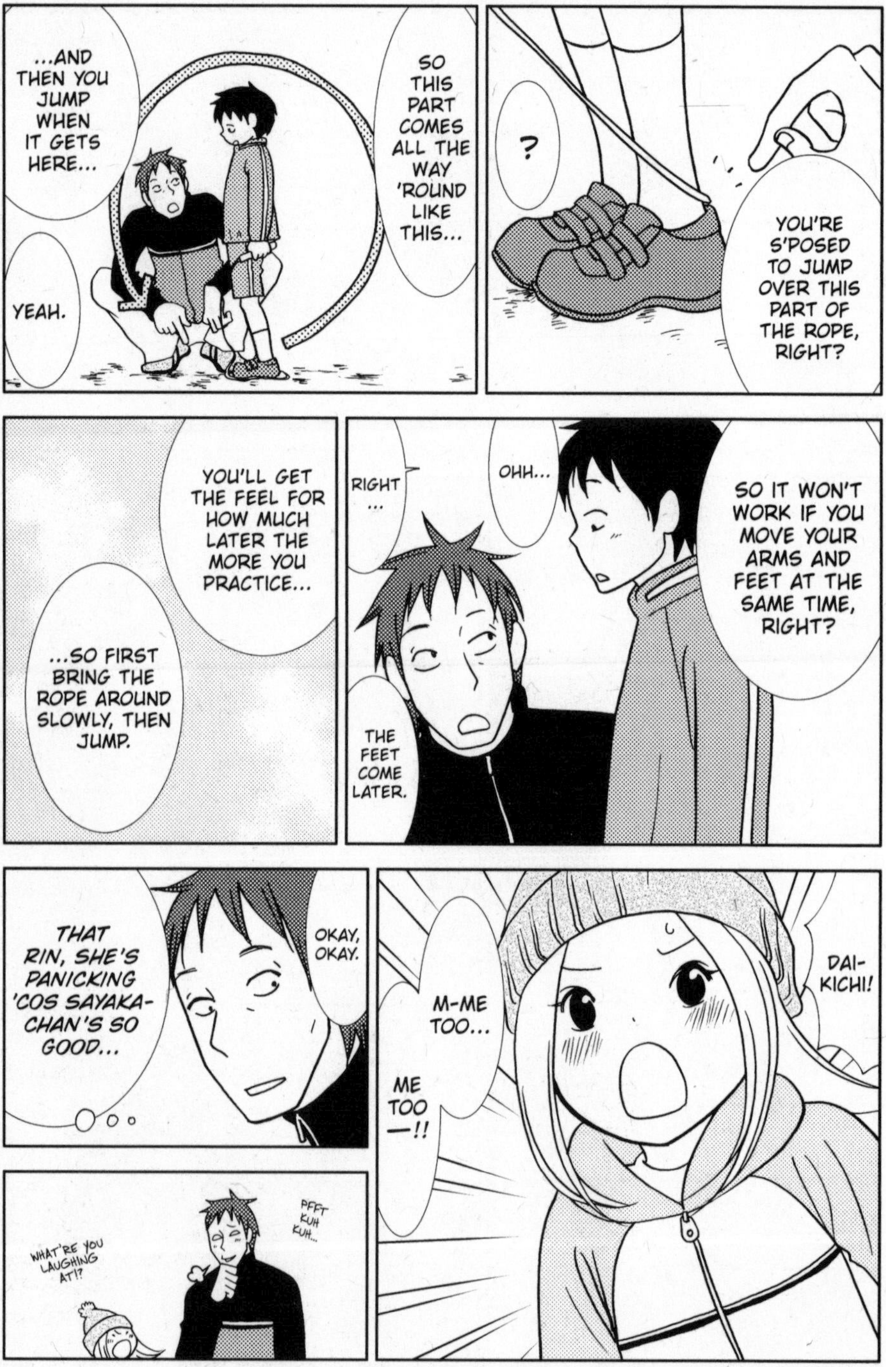

?
YOU'RE S'POSED TO JUMP OVER THIS PART OF THE ROPE, RIGHT?
SO THIS PART COMES ALL THE WAY 'ROUND LIKE THIS...
...AND THEN YOU JUMP WHEN IT GETS HERE...
YEAH.
SO IT WON'T WORK IF YOU MOVE YOUR ARMS AND FEET AT THE SAME TIME, RIGHT?
OHH...
RIGHT...
THE FEET COME LATER.
YOU'LL GET THE FEEL FOR HOW MUCH LATER THE MORE YOU PRACTICE...
...SO FIRST BRING THE ROPE AROUND SLOWLY, THEN JUMP.
DAI-KICHI!
M-ME TOO...
ME TOO—!!
OKAY, OKAY.
THAT RIN, SHE'S PANICKING 'COS SAYAKA-CHAN'S SO GOOD...
PFFT KUH KUH...
WHAT'RE YOU LAUGHING AT!?

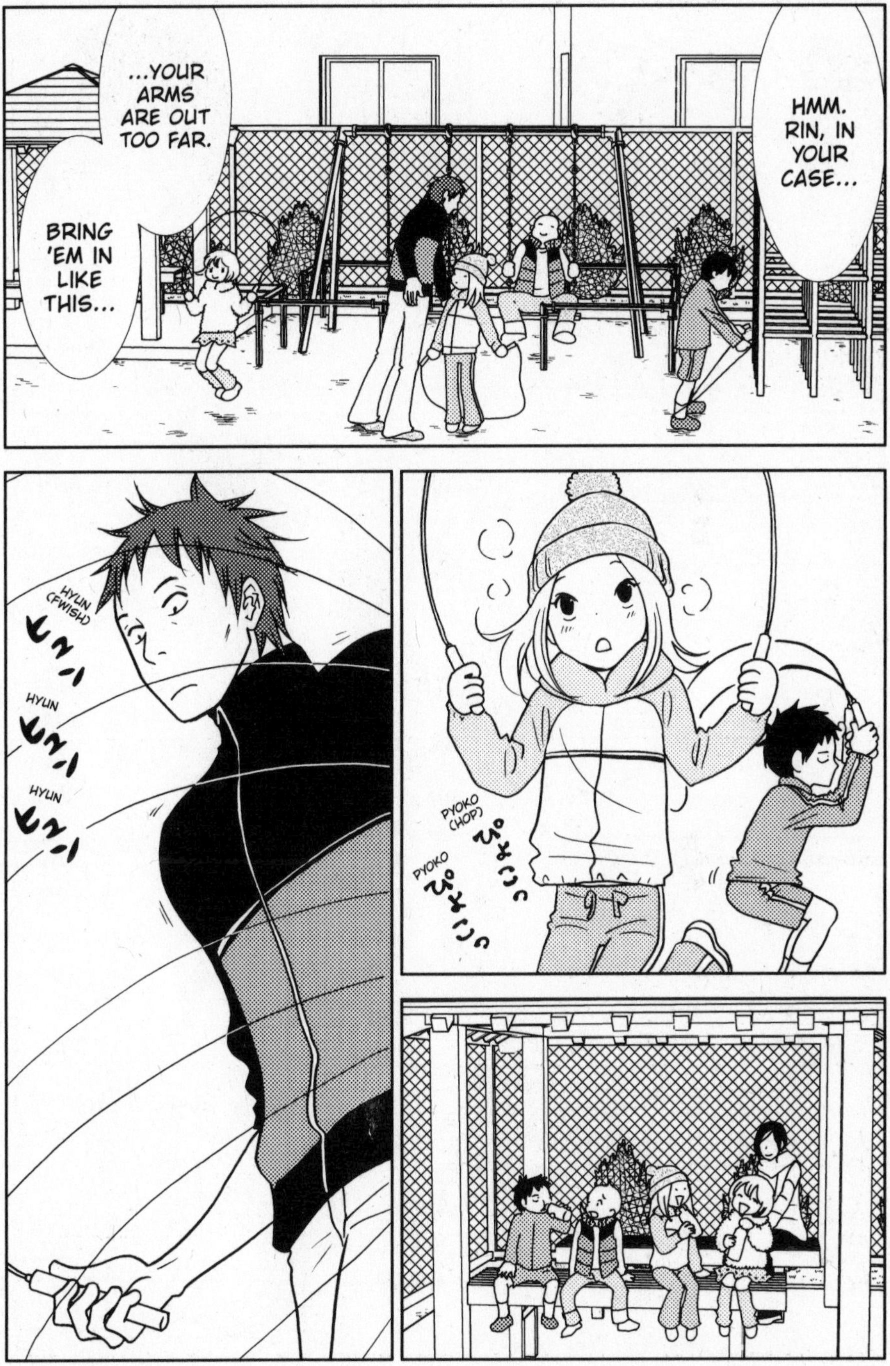
HMM. RIN, IN YOUR CASE...
...YOUR ARMS ARE OUT TOO FAR.
BRING 'EM IN LIKE THIS...
PYOKO (HOP)
ぴょこ
PYOKO
ぴょこ
HYUN (FWISH)
ひゅん
HYUN
ひゅん
HYUN
ひゅん

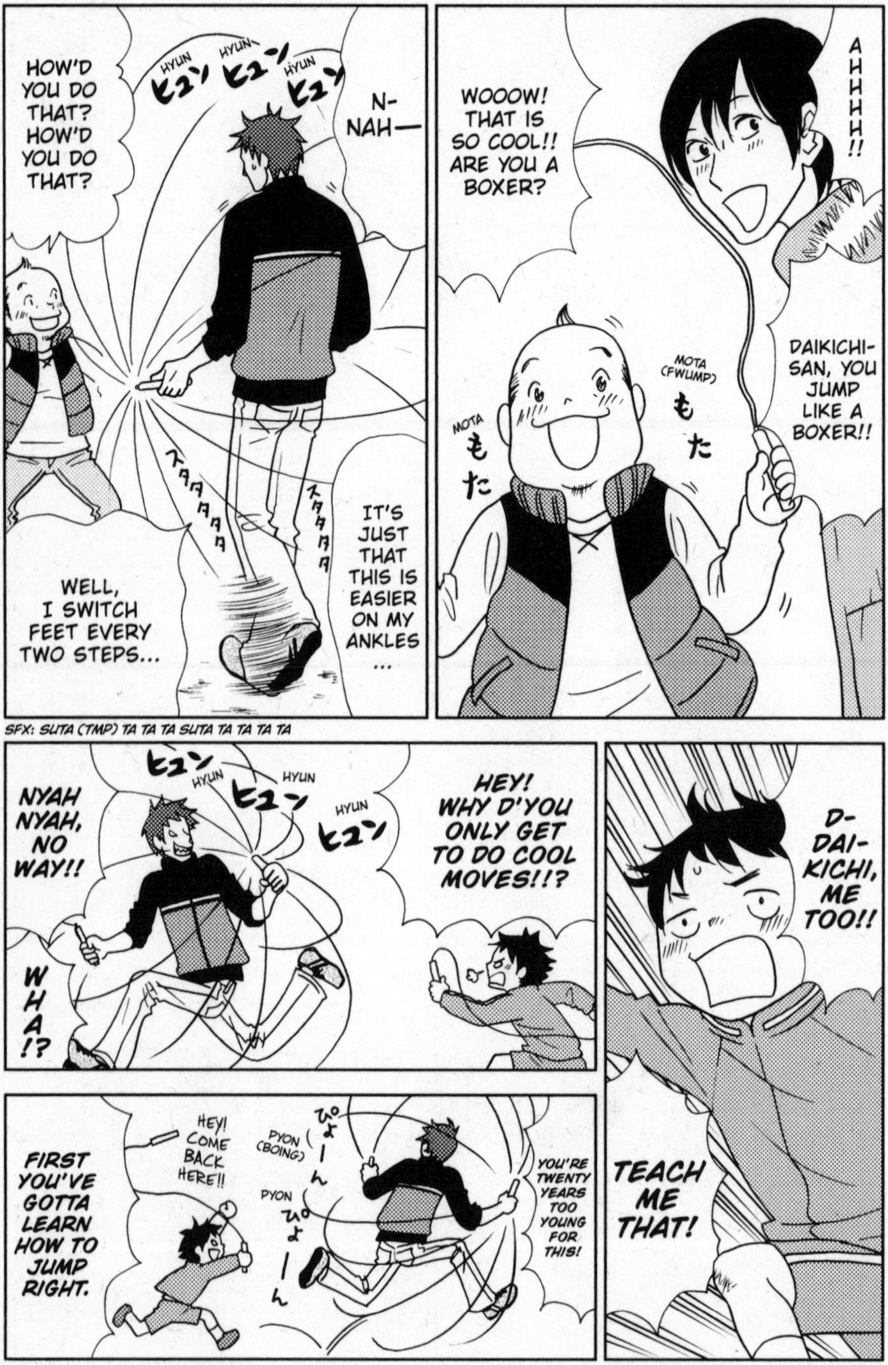
AHHHHH!!
WOOOW! THAT IS SO COOL!! ARE YOU A BOXER?
DAIKICHI-SAN, YOU JUMP LIKE A BOXER!!
MOTA (FWUMP) もた
MOTA もた
N-NAH—
HYUN ヒュン
HYUN ヒュン
HYUN ヒュン
HOW'D YOU DO THAT? HOW'D YOU DO THAT?
IT'S JUST THAT THIS IS EASIER ON MY ANKLES ...
スタタタタ
スタタタタ
WELL, I SWITCH FEET EVERY TWO STEPS...
SFX: SUTA (TMP) TA TA TA SUTA TA TA TA TA
D-DAIKICHI, ME TOO!!
TEACH ME THAT!
HEY! WHY D'YOU ONLY GET TO DO COOL MOVES!!?
HYUN ヒュン
HYUN ヒュン
HYUN ヒュン
NYAH NYAH, NO WAY!!
WHA!?
YOU'RE TWENTY YEARS TOO YOUNG FOR THIS!
PYON (BOING) ぴょーん
PYON ぴょーん
HEY! COME BACK HERE!!
FIRST YOU'VE GOTTA LEARN HOW TO JUMP RIGHT.

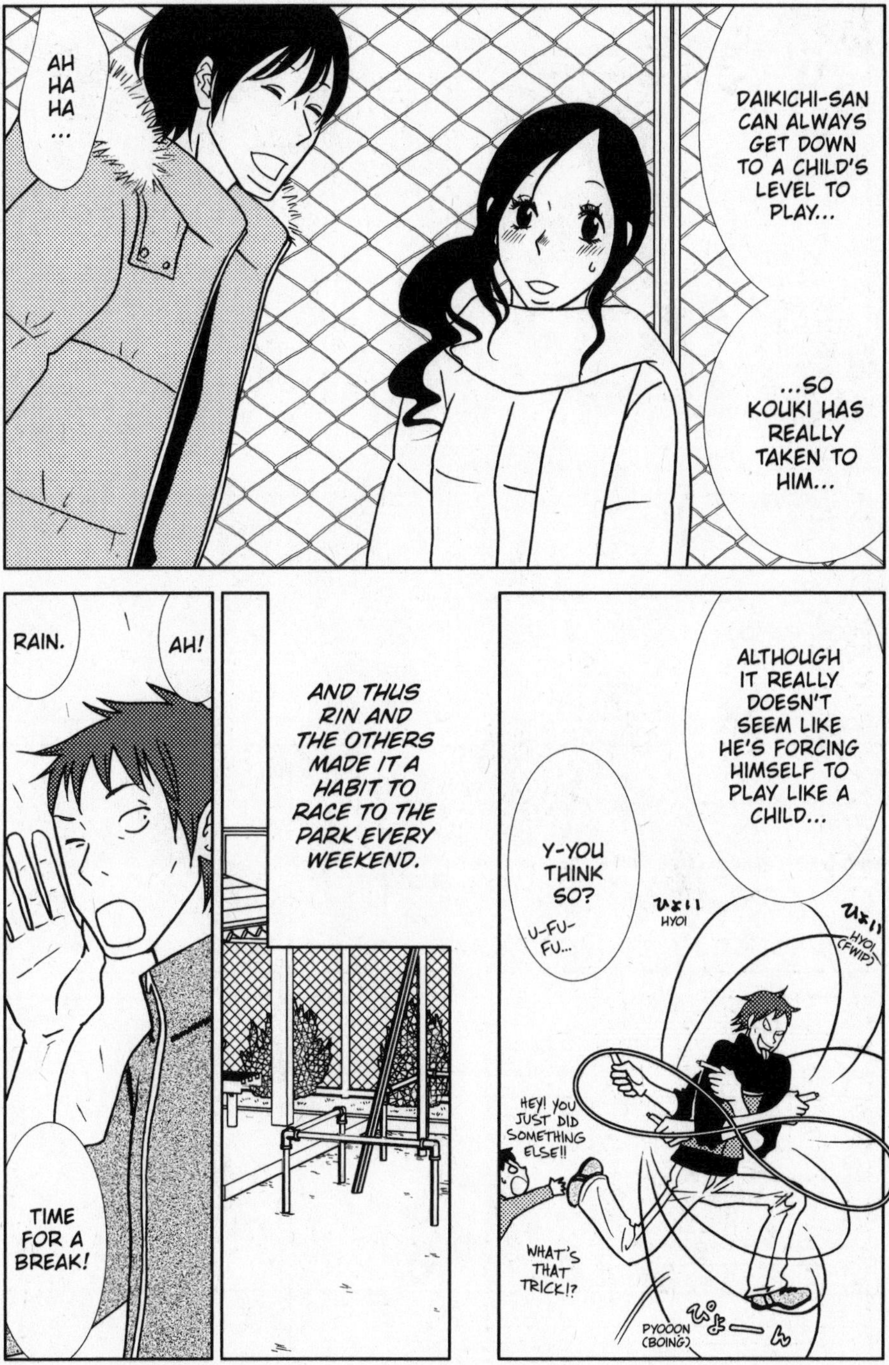

DAIKICHI-SAN CAN ALWAYS GET DOWN TO A CHILD'S LEVEL TO PLAY...
...SO KOUKI HAS REALLY TAKEN TO HIM...
AH HA HA ...
ALTHOUGH IT REALLY DOESN'T SEEM LIKE HE'S FORCING HIMSELF TO PLAY LIKE A CHILD...
Y-YOU THINK SO?
U-FU-FU...
ひょい HYOI (FWIP)
ひょい HYOI
HEY! YOU JUST DID SOMETHING ELSE!!
WHAT'S THAT TRICK!?
ぴょーん PYOOON (BOING)
AND THUS RIN AND THE OTHERS MADE IT A HABIT TO RACE TO THE PARK EVERY WEEKEND.
AH!
RAIN.
TIME FOR A BREAK!

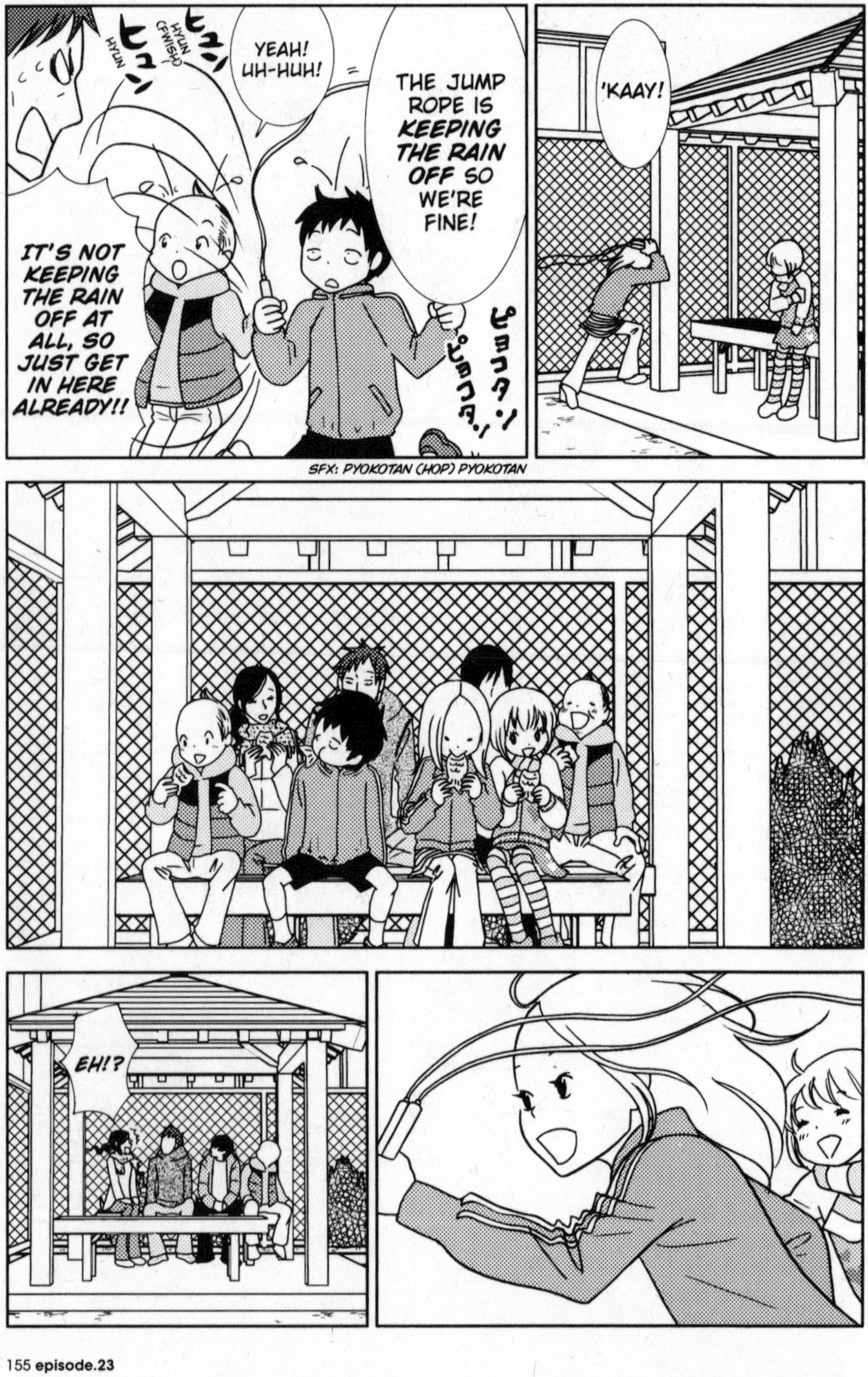
'KAAY!
THE JUMP ROPE IS KEEPING THE RAIN OFF SO WE'RE FINE!
ピョコタン ピョコタン
YEAH! UH-HUH!
ヒュン ヒュン
HYUN (SWISH) HYUN
IT'S NOT KEEPING THE RAIN OFF AT ALL, SO JUST GET IN HERE ALREADY!!
SFX: PYOKOTAN (HOP) PYOKOTAN
EH!?

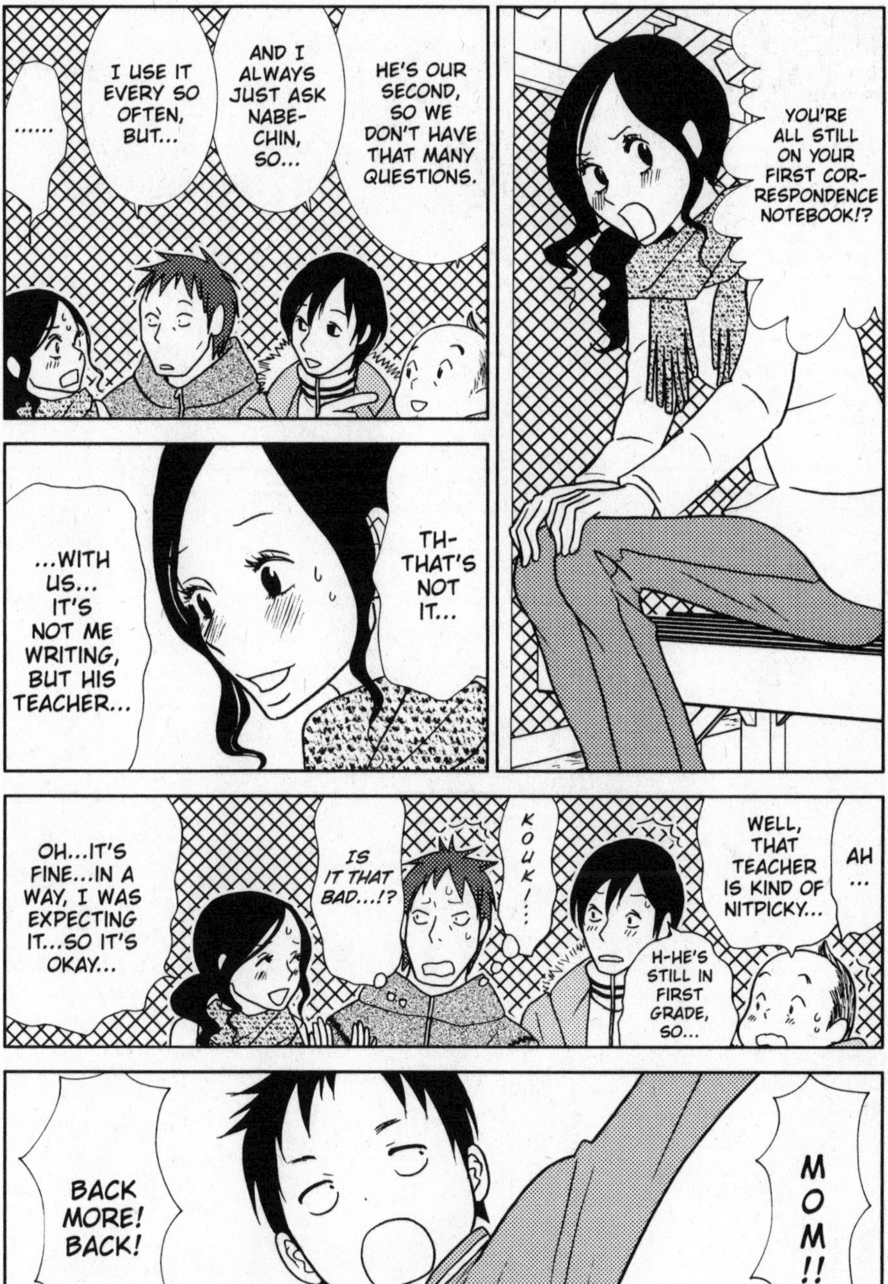
YOU'RE ALL STILL ON YOUR FIRST CORRESPONDENCE NOTEBOOK!?
HE'S OUR SECOND, SO WE DON'T HAVE THAT MANY QUESTIONS.
AND I ALWAYS JUST ASK NABE-CHIN, SO...
I USE IT EVERY SO OFTEN, BUT...
......
TH-THAT'S NOT IT...
...WITH US... IT'S NOT ME WRITING, BUT HIS TEACHER...
AH ...
WELL, THAT TEACHER IS KIND OF NITPICKY...
H-HE'S STILL IN FIRST GRADE, SO...
KOUK!...
IS IT THAT BAD...!?
OH...IT'S FINE...IN A WAY, I WAS EXPECTING IT...SO IT'S OKAY...
MOM!!
BACK MORE! BACK!

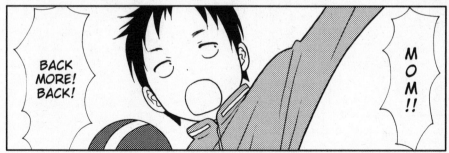

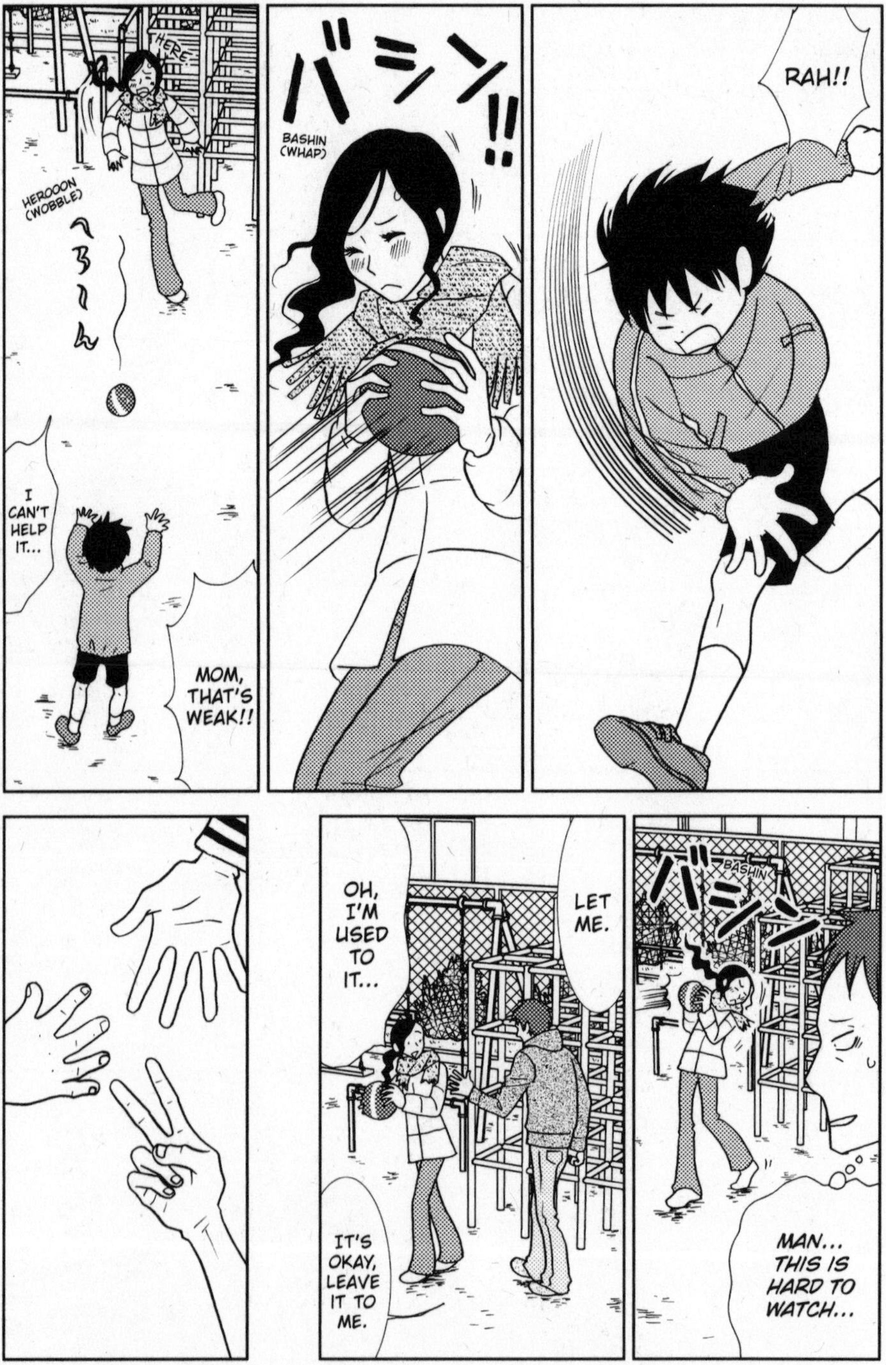
RAH!!
バシン!!
BASHIN (WHAP)
HERE!
HEROOON (WOBBLE)
へろ～ん
MOM, THAT'S WEAK!!
I CAN'T HELP IT...
バシン
BASHIN
MAN... THIS IS HARD TO WATCH...
LET ME.
OH, I'M USED TO IT...
IT'S OKAY, LEAVE IT TO ME.

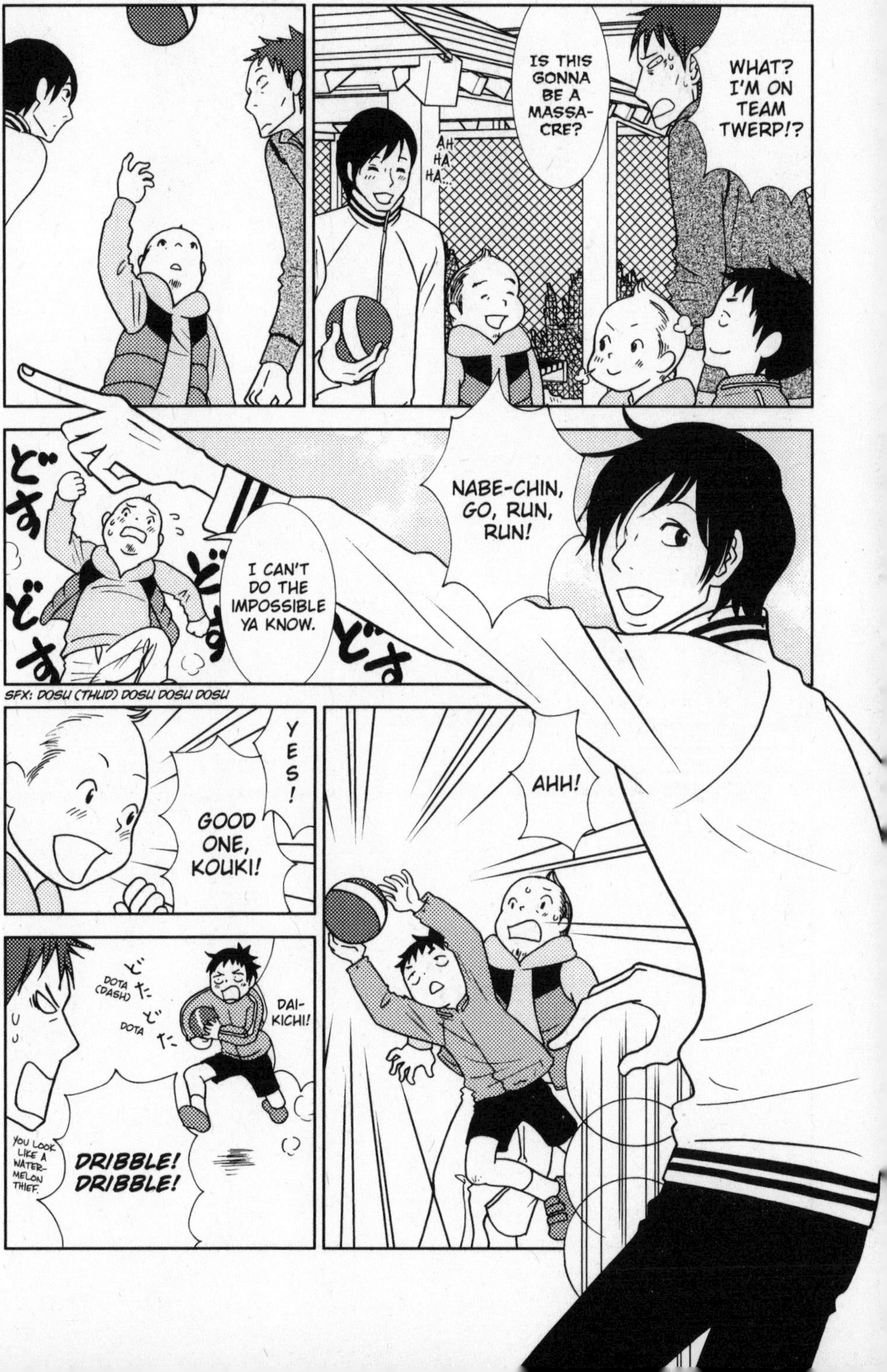
WHAT? I'M ON TEAM TWERP!?
IS THIS GONNA BE A MASSA-CRE?
AH HA HA...
NABE-CHIN, GO, RUN, RUN!
I CAN'T DO THE IMPOSSIBLE YA KNOW.
どす どす どす どす
SFX: DOSU (THUD) DOSU DOSU DOSU
AHH!
YES!
GOOD ONE, KOUKI!
DAI-KICHI!
どた どた
DOTA (DASH) DOTA
DRIBBLE! DRIBBLE!
YOU LOOK LIKE A WATER-MELON THIEF.

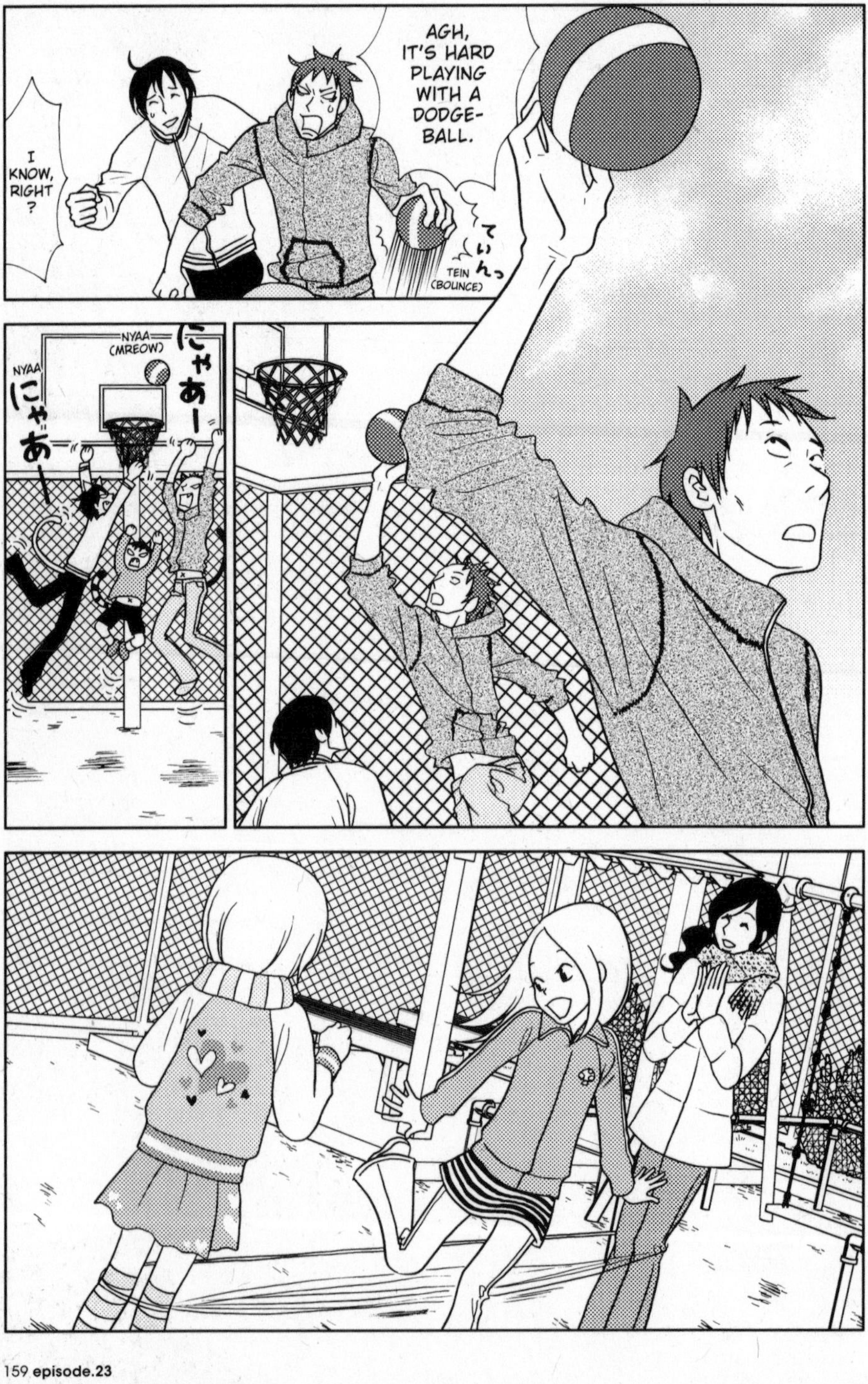
AGH, IT'S HARD PLAYING WITH A DODGE-BALL.
I KNOW, RIGHT?
ていんっ
TEIN (BOUNCE)
にゃあー
NYAA (MREOW)
NYAA
にゃあー

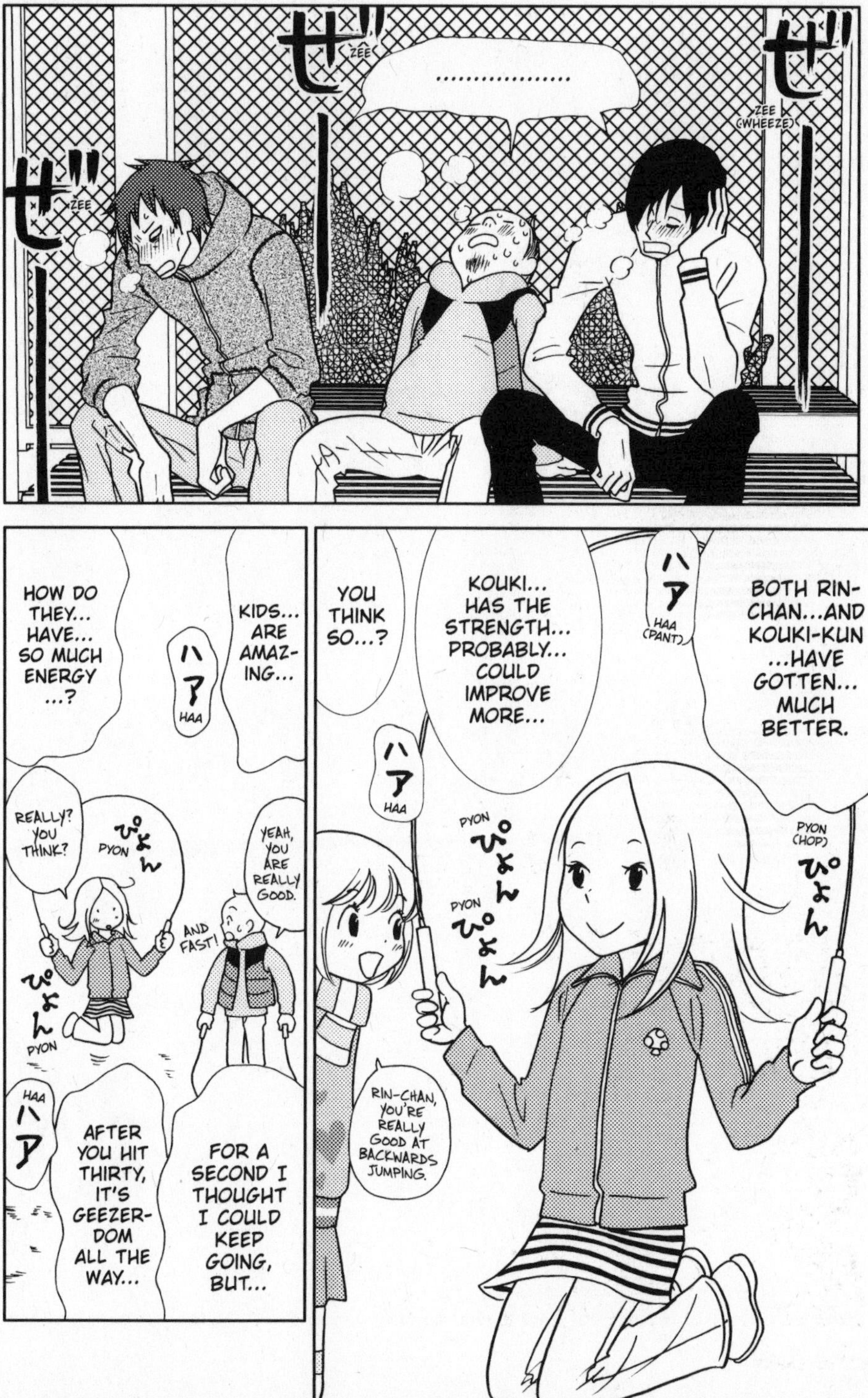
ゼ
ZEE (WHEEZE)
....
ゼ
ZEE
ゼ
ZEE
BOTH RIN-CHAN...AND KOUKI-KUN ...HAVE GOTTEN... MUCH BETTER.
ハア
HAA (PANT)
KOUKI... HAS THE STRENGTH... PROBABLY... COULD IMPROVE MORE...
YOU THINK SO...?
ぴょん
PYON (HOP)
ぴょん
PYON
ぴょん
PYON
ハア
HAA
RIN-CHAN, YOU'RE REALLY GOOD AT BACKWARDS JUMPING.
KIDS... ARE AMAZING...
ハア
HAA
HOW DO THEY... HAVE... SO MUCH ENERGY ...?
YEAH, YOU ARE REALLY GOOD.
AND FAST!
REALLY? YOU THINK?
ぴょん
PYON
ぴょん
PYON
FOR A SECOND I THOUGHT I COULD KEEP GOING, BUT...
AFTER YOU HIT THIRTY, IT'S GEEZERDOM ALL THE WAY...
ハア
HAA

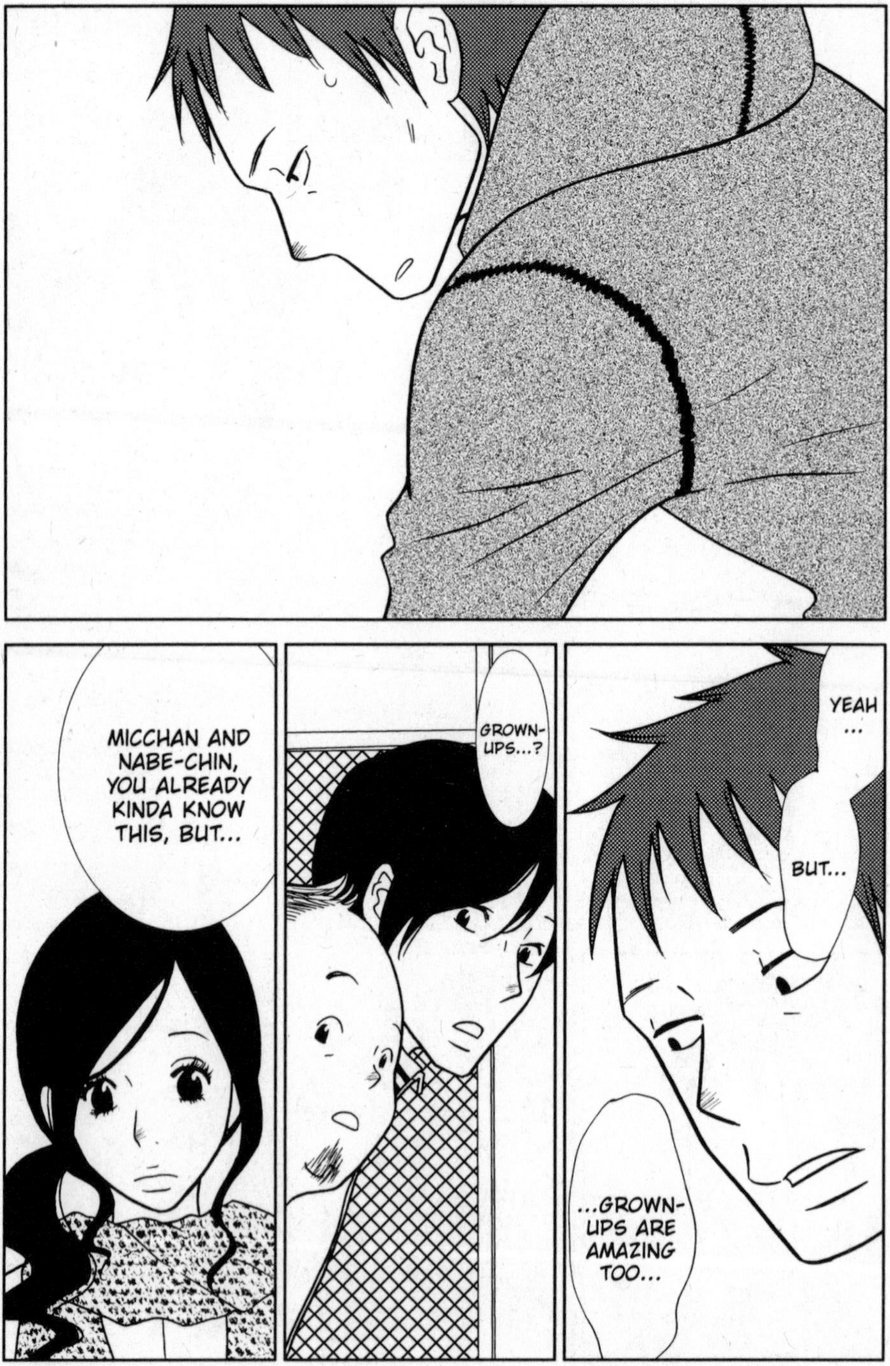
YEAH...
BUT...
...GROWN-UPS ARE AMAZING TOO...
GROWN-UPS...?
MICCHAN AND NABE-CHIN, YOU ALREADY KINDA KNOW THIS, BUT...

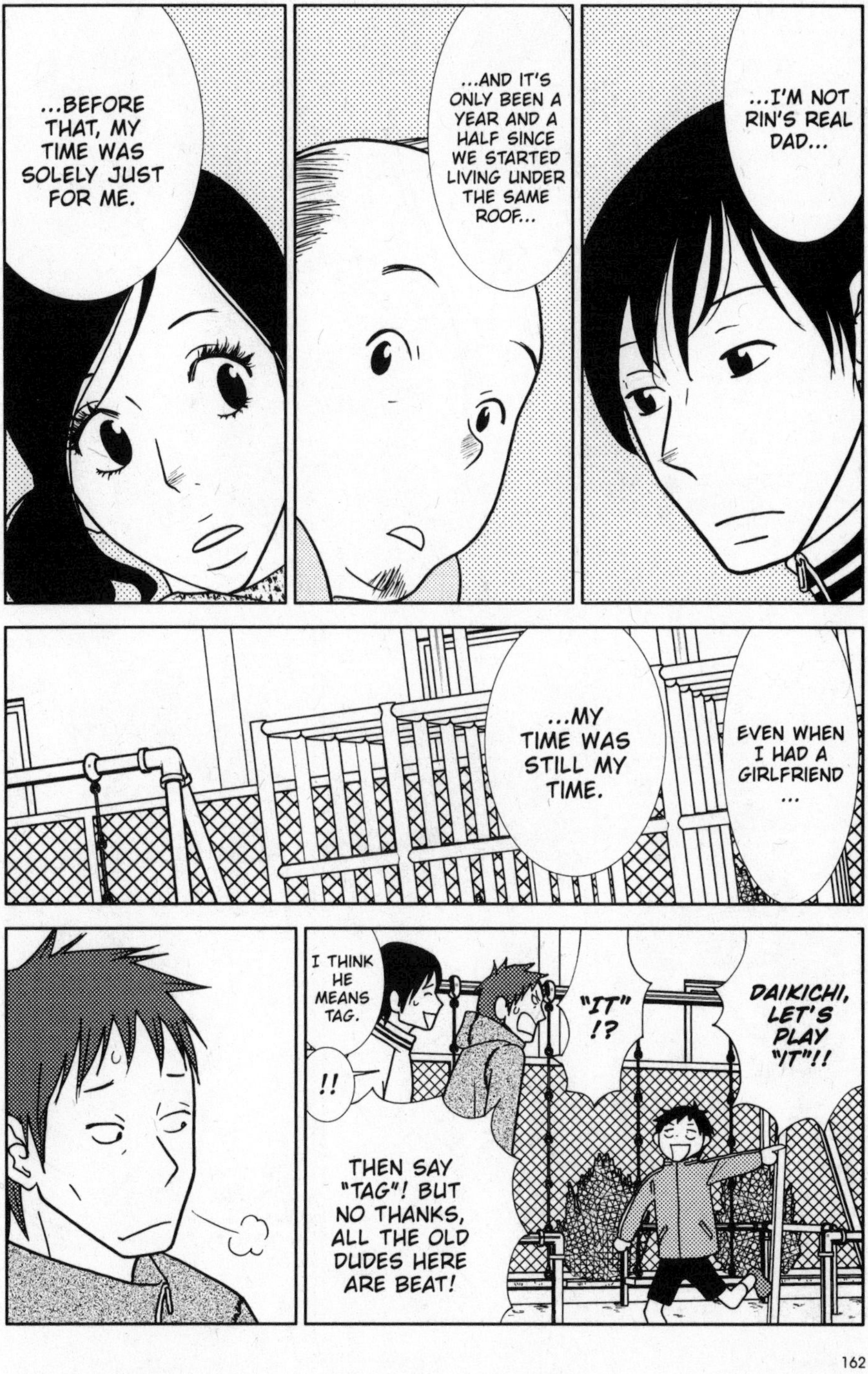
...I'M NOT RIN'S REAL DAD...
...AND IT'S ONLY BEEN A YEAR AND A HALF SINCE WE STARTED LIVING UNDER THE SAME ROOF...
...BEFORE THAT, MY TIME WAS SOLELY JUST FOR ME.
EVEN WHEN I HAD A GIRLFRIEND ...
...MY TIME WAS STILL MY TIME.
DAIKICHI, LET'S PLAY "IT"!!
"IT" !?
I THINK HE MEANS TAG.
!!
THEN SAY "TAG"! BUT NO THANKS, ALL THE OLD DUDES HERE ARE BEAT!

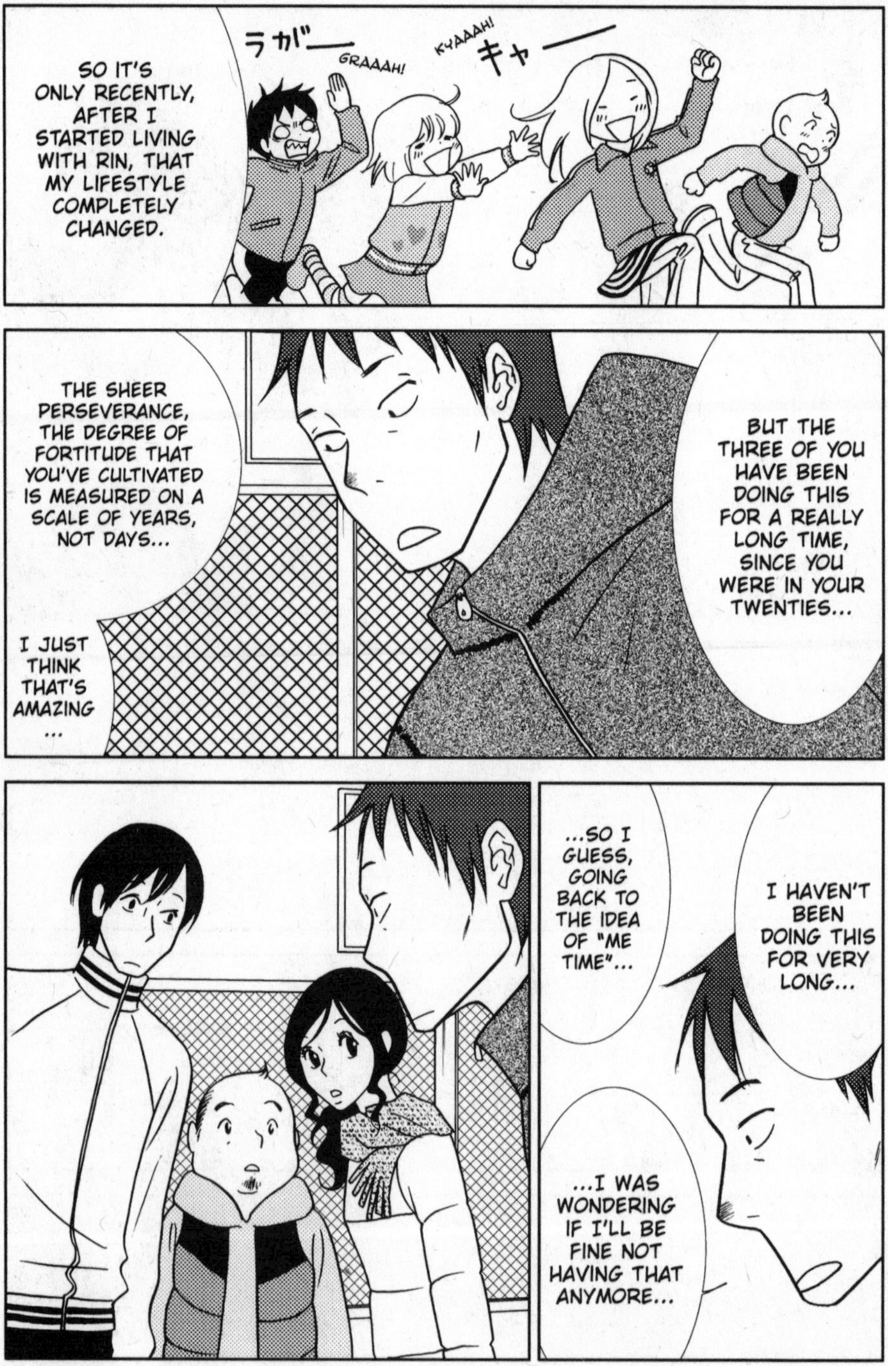
キャー
KYAAAH!
ラガー
GRAAAH!
SO IT'S ONLY RECENTLY, AFTER I STARTED LIVING WITH RIN, THAT MY LIFESTYLE COMPLETELY CHANGED.
BUT THE THREE OF YOU HAVE BEEN DOING THIS FOR A REALLY LONG TIME, SINCE YOU WERE IN YOUR TWENTIES...
THE SHEER PERSEVERANCE, THE DEGREE OF FORTITUDE THAT YOU'VE CULTIVATED IS MEASURED ON A SCALE OF YEARS, NOT DAYS...
I JUST THINK THAT'S AMAZING...
I HAVEN'T BEEN DOING THIS FOR VERY LONG...
...SO I GUESS, GOING BACK TO THE IDEA OF "ME TIME"...
...I WAS WONDERING IF I'LL BE FINE NOT HAVING THAT ANYMORE...

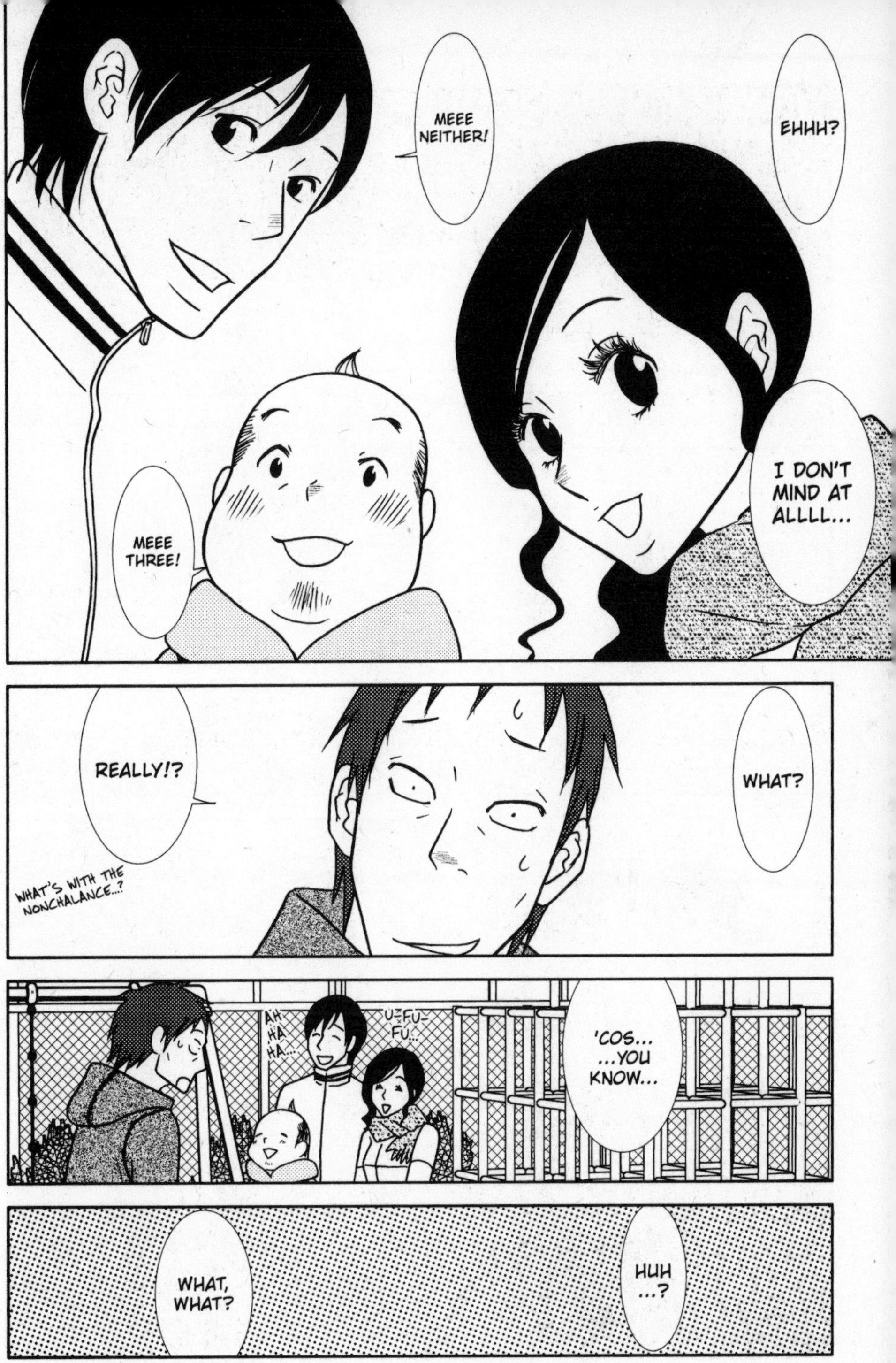
EHHH?
MEEE NEITHER!
I DON'T MIND AT ALLLL...
MEEE THREE!
WHAT?
REALLY!?
WHAT'S WITH THE NONCHALANCE...?
'COS... ...YOU KNOW...
U-FU-FU...
AH HA HA...
HUH ...?
WHAT, WHAT?

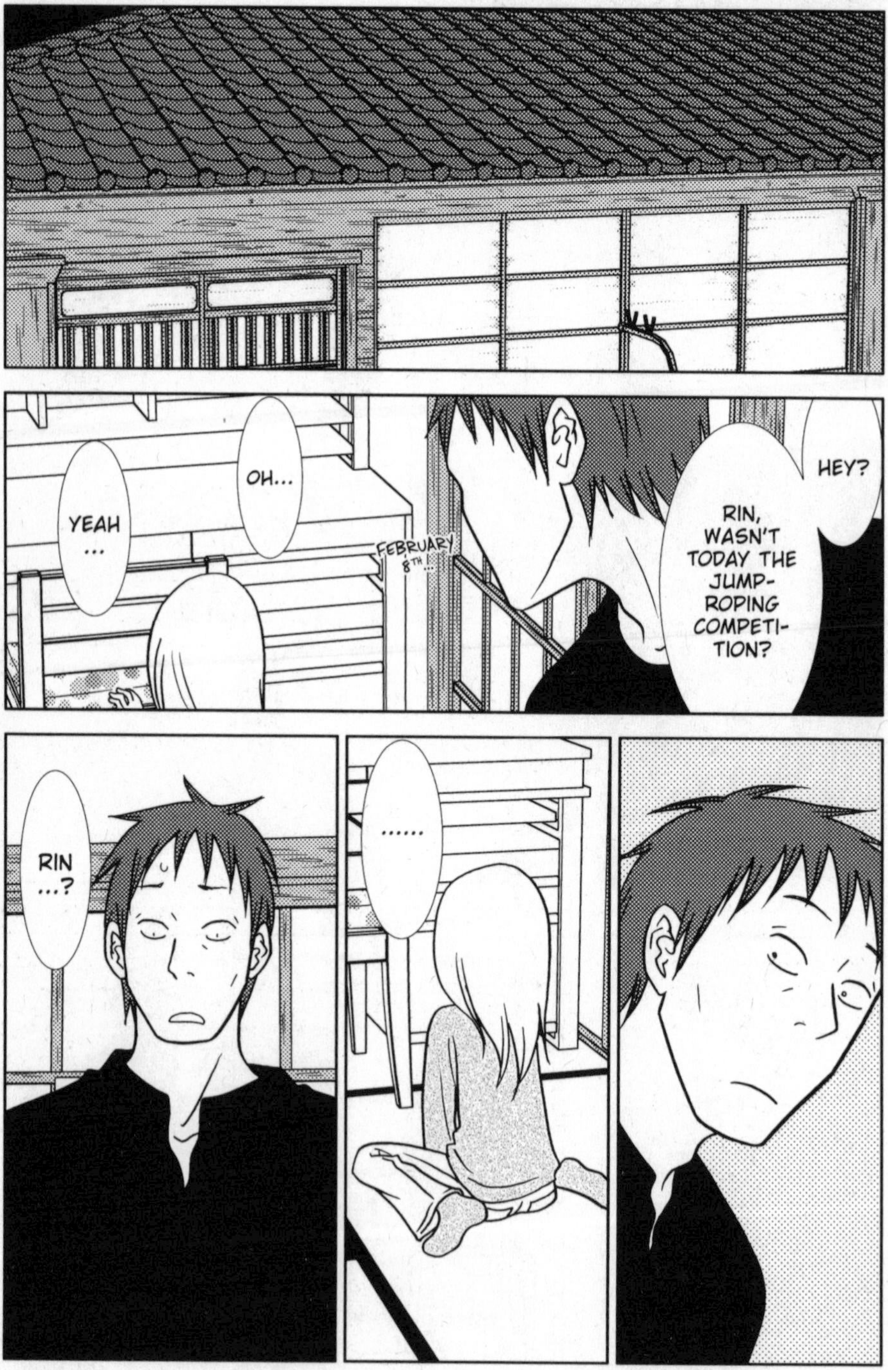
HEY?
RIN, WASN'T TODAY THE JUMP-ROPING COMPETITION?
FEBRUARY 8TH...
OH...
YEAH ...
......
RIN ...?

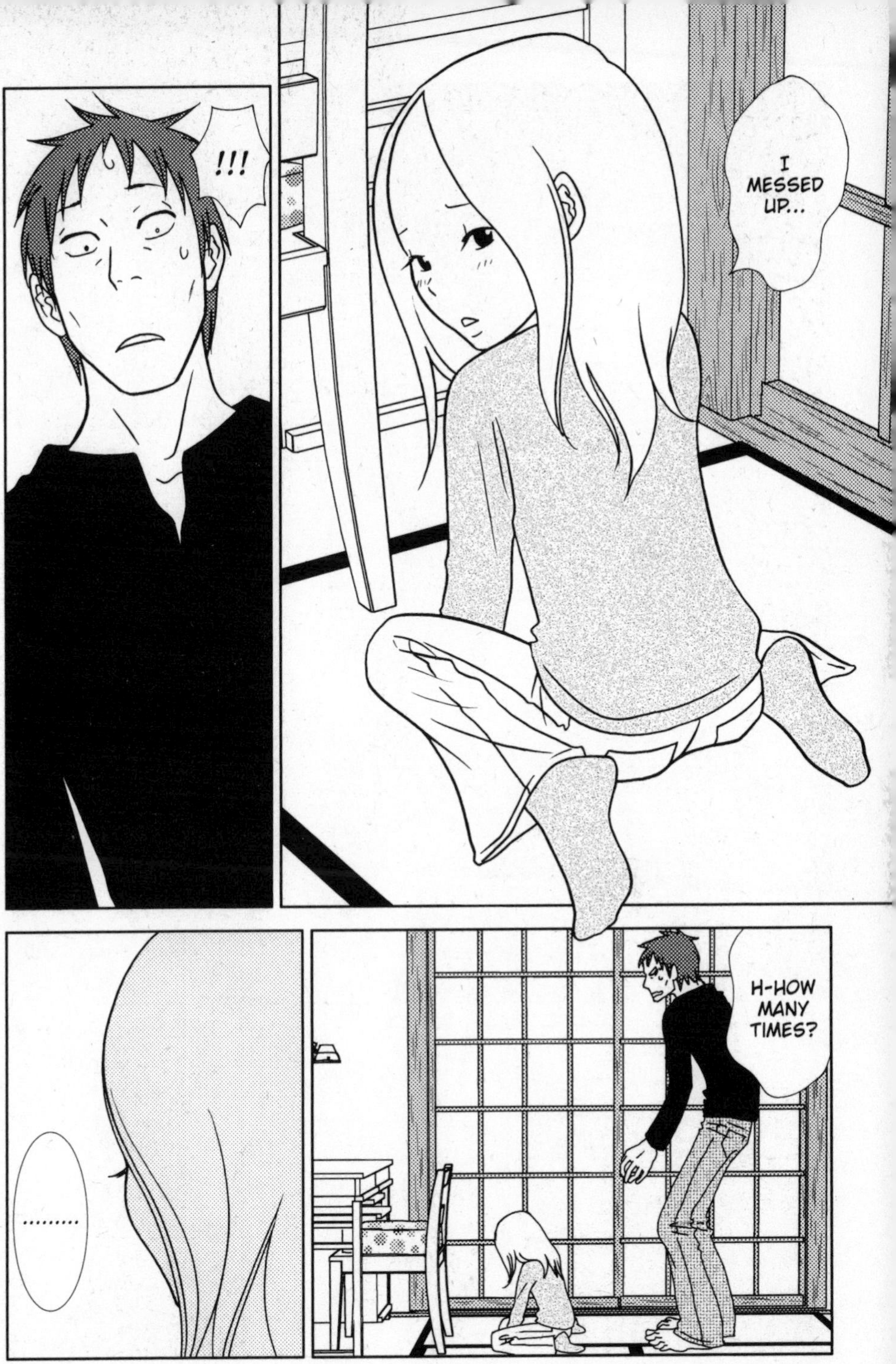
I MESSED UP...
!!!
H-HOW MANY TIMES?
....

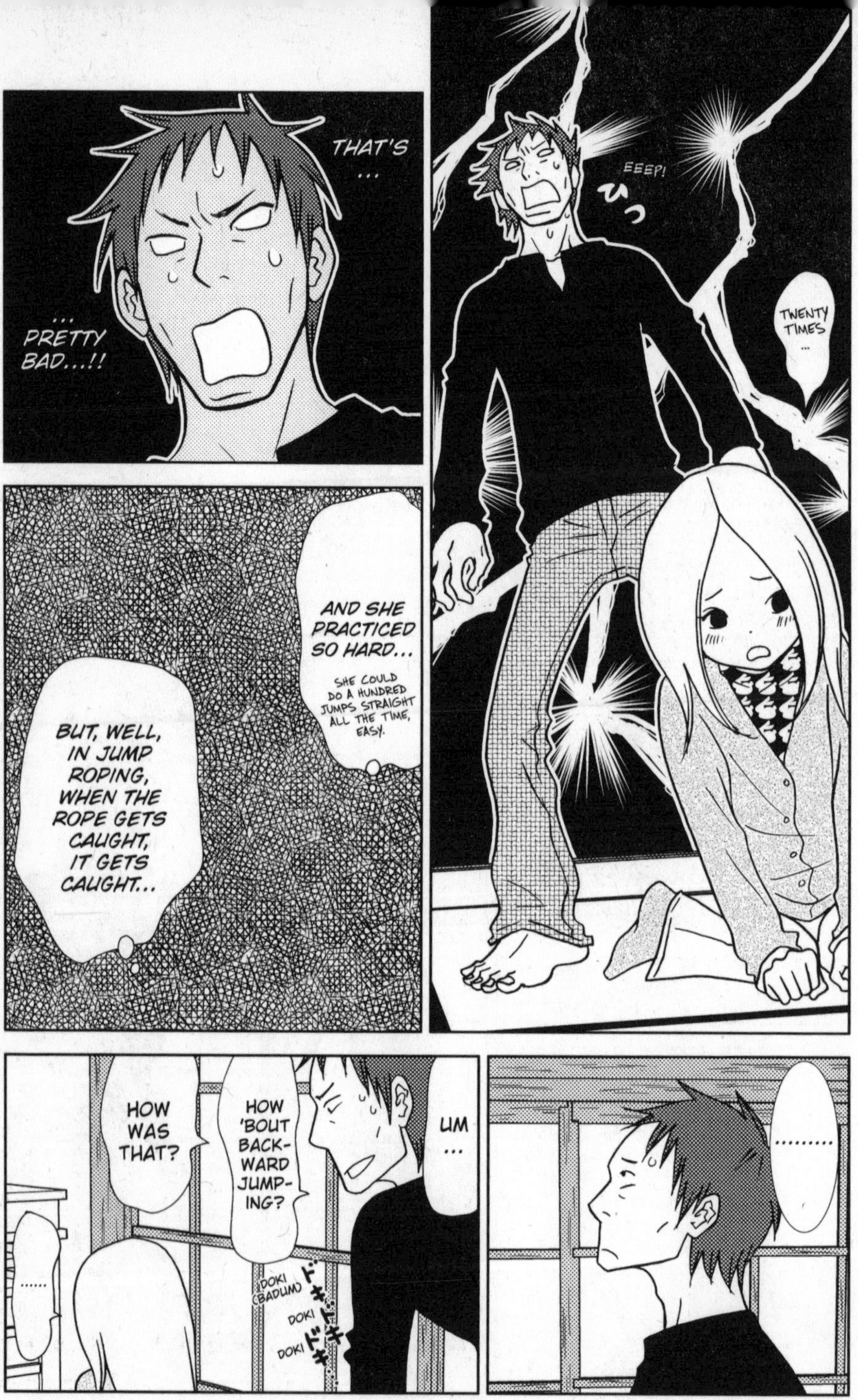
EEEP!
ひっ
TWENTY TIMES ...
THAT'S ...
... PRETTY BAD...!!
AND SHE PRACTICED SO HARD...
SHE COULD DO A HUNDRED JUMPS STRAIGHT ALL THE TIME, EASY.
BUT, WELL, IN JUMP ROPING, WHEN THE ROPE GETS CAUGHT, IT GETS CAUGHT...
....
UM ...
HOW 'BOUT BACKWARD JUMPING?
HOW WAS THAT?
......
ドキドキ
DOKI (BADUM) DOKI DOKI

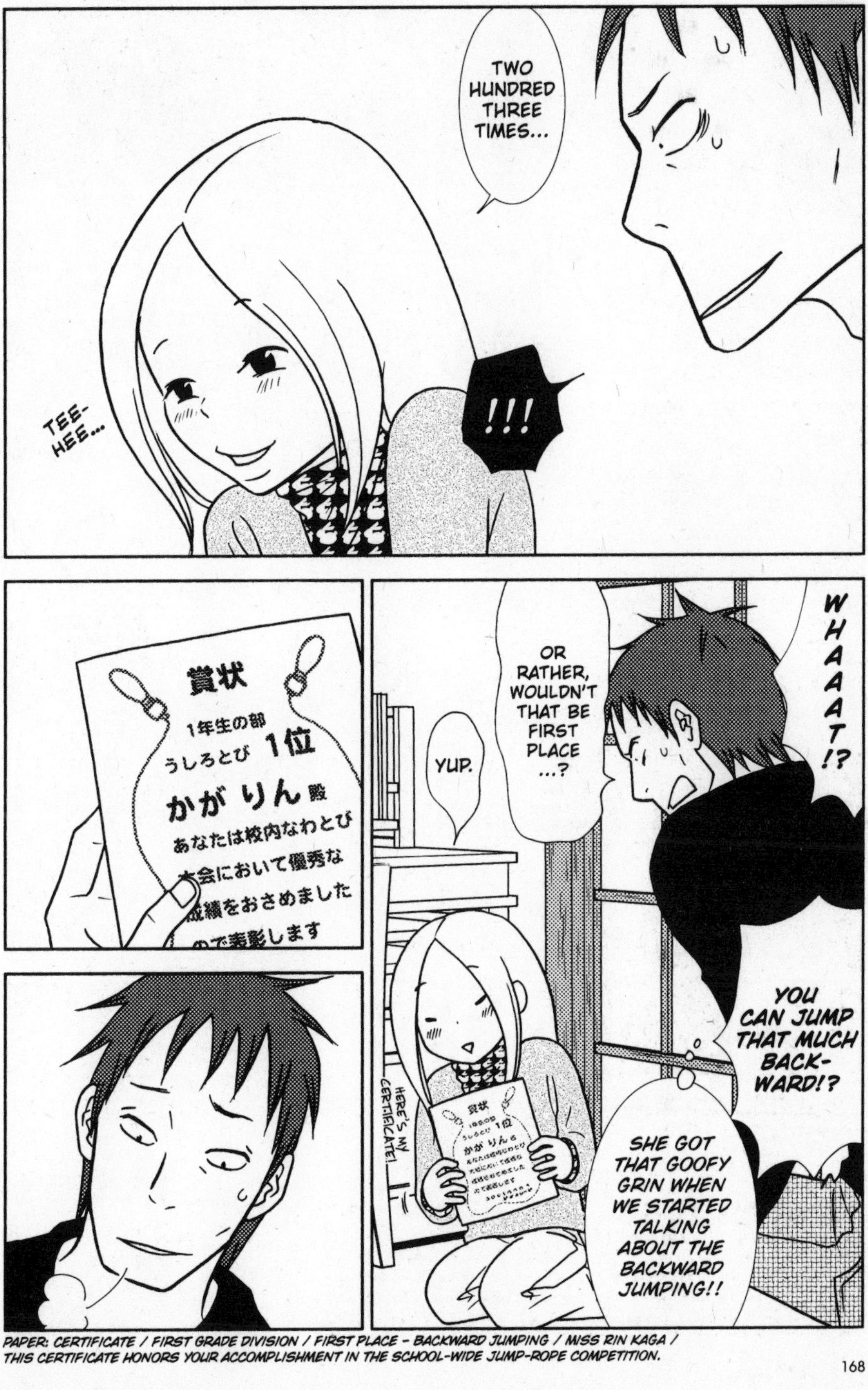
TWO HUNDRED THREE TIMES...
!!!
TEE-HEE...
WHAAAAT!?
OR RATHER, WOULDN'T THAT BE FIRST PLACE ...?
YUP.
YOU CAN JUMP THAT MUCH BACKWARD!?
SHE GOT THAT GOOFY GRIN WHEN WE STARTED TALKING ABOUT THE BACKWARD JUMPING!!
HERE'S MY CERTIFICATE!
賞状
1年生の部
うしろとび 1位
かが りん 殿
あなたは校内なわとび
大会において優秀な
成績をおさめました
ので表彰します

PAPER: CERTIFICATE / FIRST GRADE DIVISION / FIRST PLACE - BACKWARD JUMPING / MISS RIN KAGA / THIS CERTIFICATE HONORS YOUR ACCOMPLISHMENT IN THE SCHOOL-WIDE JUMP-ROPE COMPETITION.

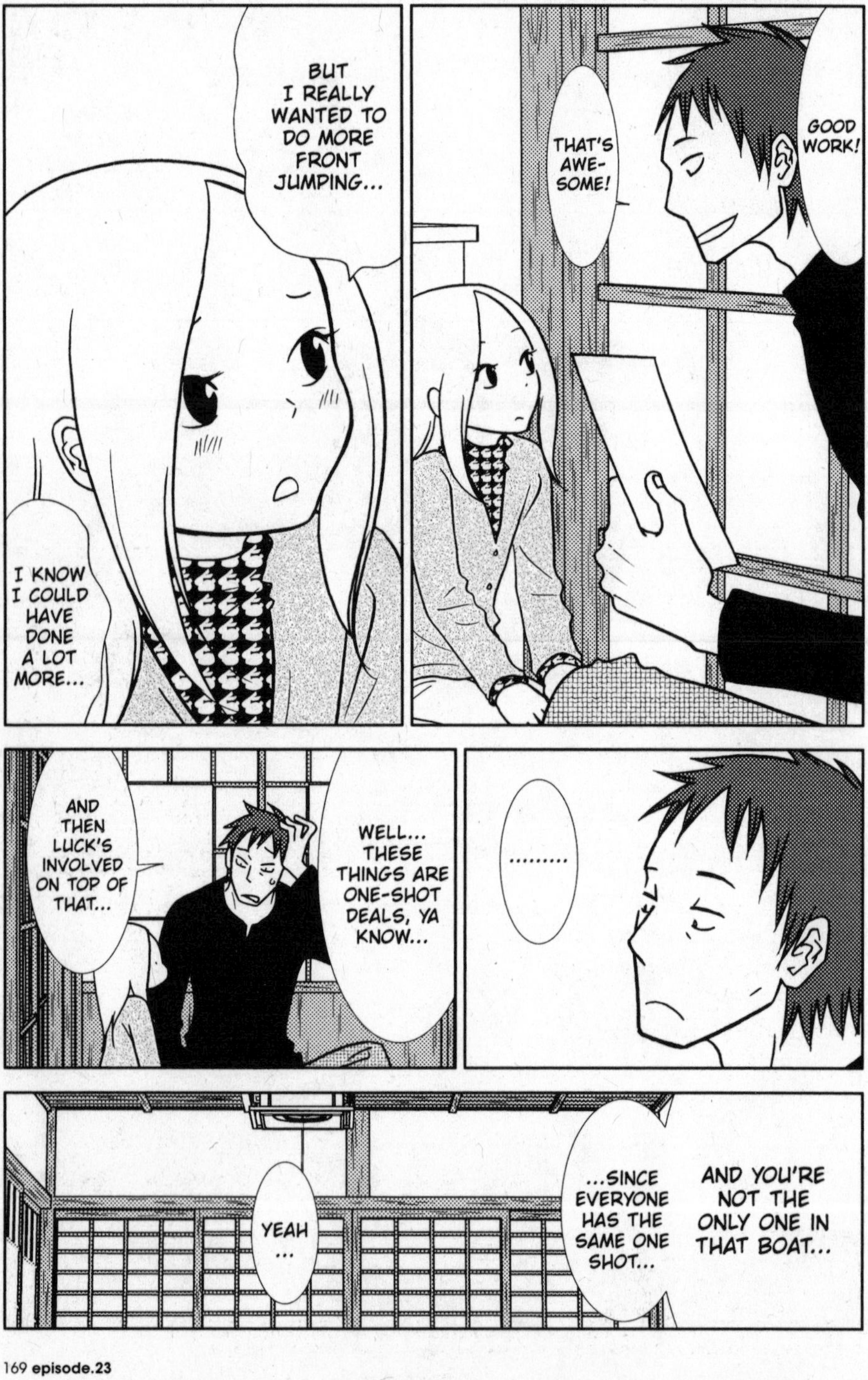
GOOD WORK!
THAT'S AWE-SOME!
BUT I REALLY WANTED TO DO MORE FRONT JUMPING...
I KNOW I COULD HAVE DONE A LOT MORE...
....
WELL... THESE THINGS ARE ONE-SHOT DEALS, YA KNOW...
AND THEN LUCK'S INVOLVED ON TOP OF THAT...
AND YOU'RE NOT THE ONLY ONE IN THAT BOAT...
...SINCE EVERYONE HAS THE SAME ONE SHOT...
YEAH ...

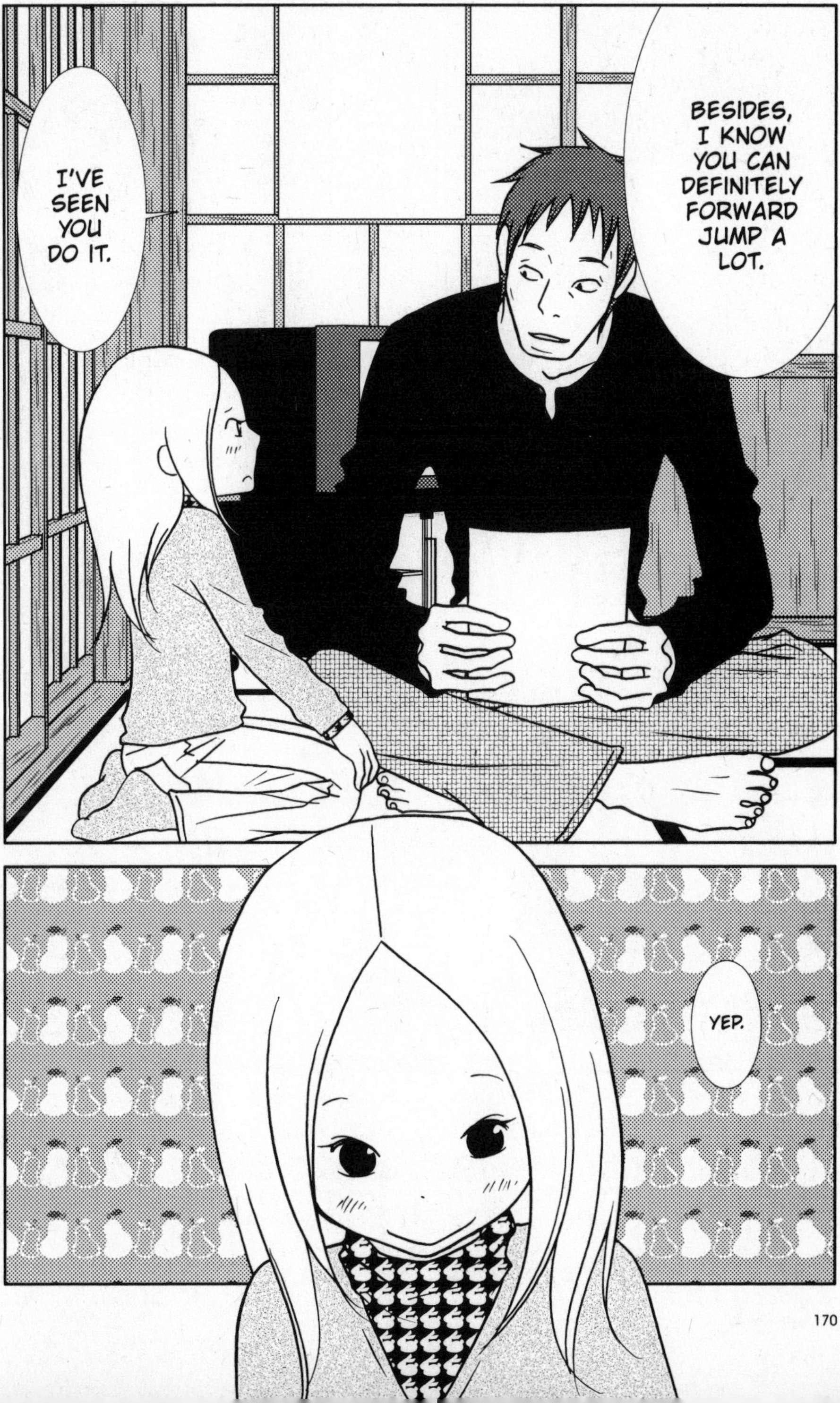
BESIDES, I KNOW YOU CAN DEFINITELY FORWARD JUMP A LOT.
I'VE SEEN YOU DO IT.
YEP.

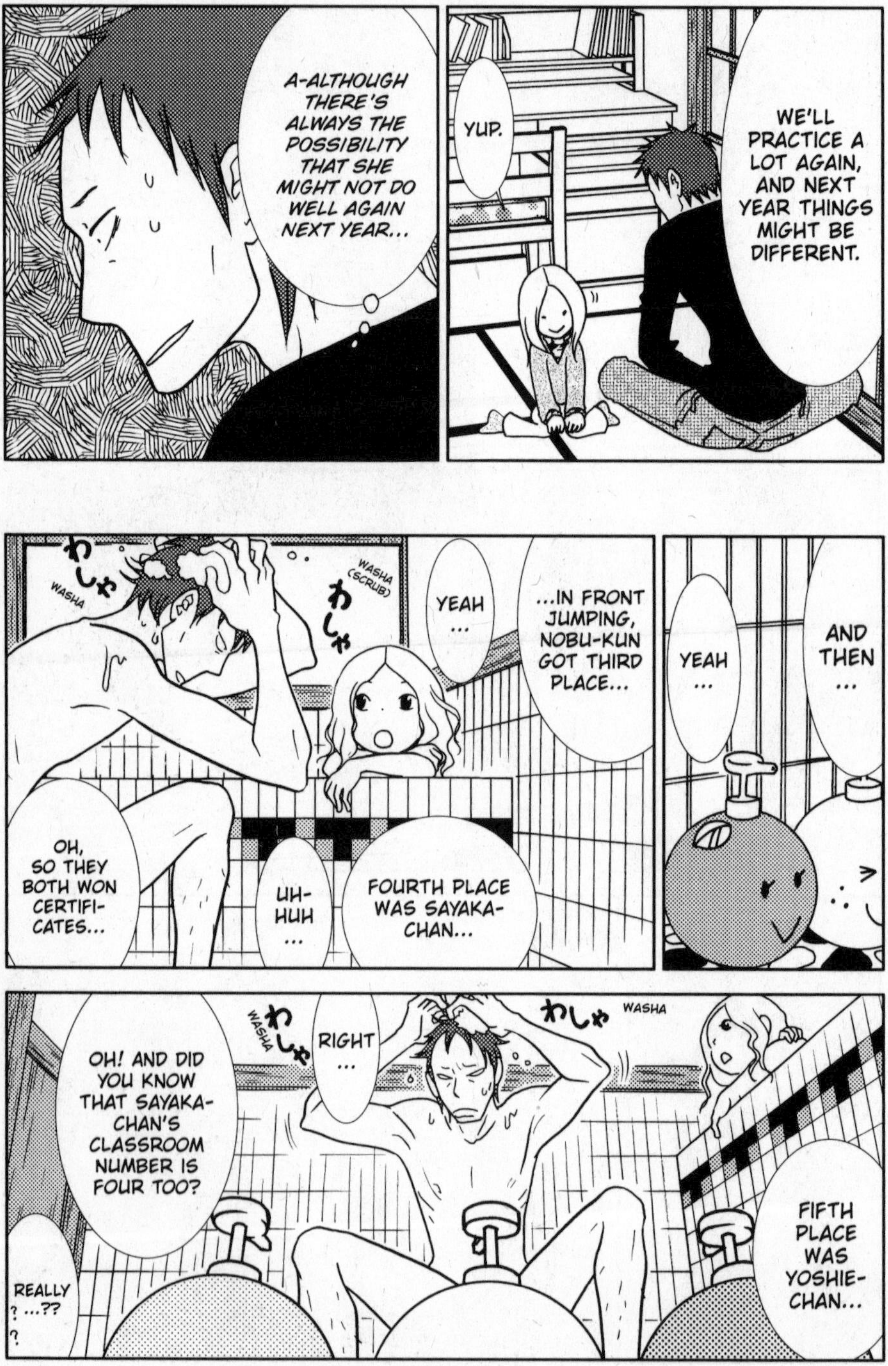
WE'LL PRACTICE A LOT AGAIN, AND NEXT YEAR THINGS MIGHT BE DIFFERENT.
YUP.
A-ALTHOUGH THERE'S ALWAYS THE POSSIBILITY THAT SHE MIGHT NOT DO WELL AGAIN NEXT YEAR...
AND THEN ...
YEAH ...
...IN FRONT JUMPING, NOBU-KUN GOT THIRD PLACE...
YEAH ...
わしゃ WASHA (SCRUB)
わしゃ WASHA
FOURTH PLACE WAS SAYAKA-CHAN...
UH-HUH ...
OH, SO THEY BOTH WON CERTIFICATES...
FIFTH PLACE WAS YOSHIE-CHAN...
わしゃ WASHA
RIGHT ...
わしゃ WASHA
OH! AND DID YOU KNOW THAT SAYAKA-CHAN'S CLASSROOM NUMBER IS FOUR TOO?
REALLY ? ...?? ?

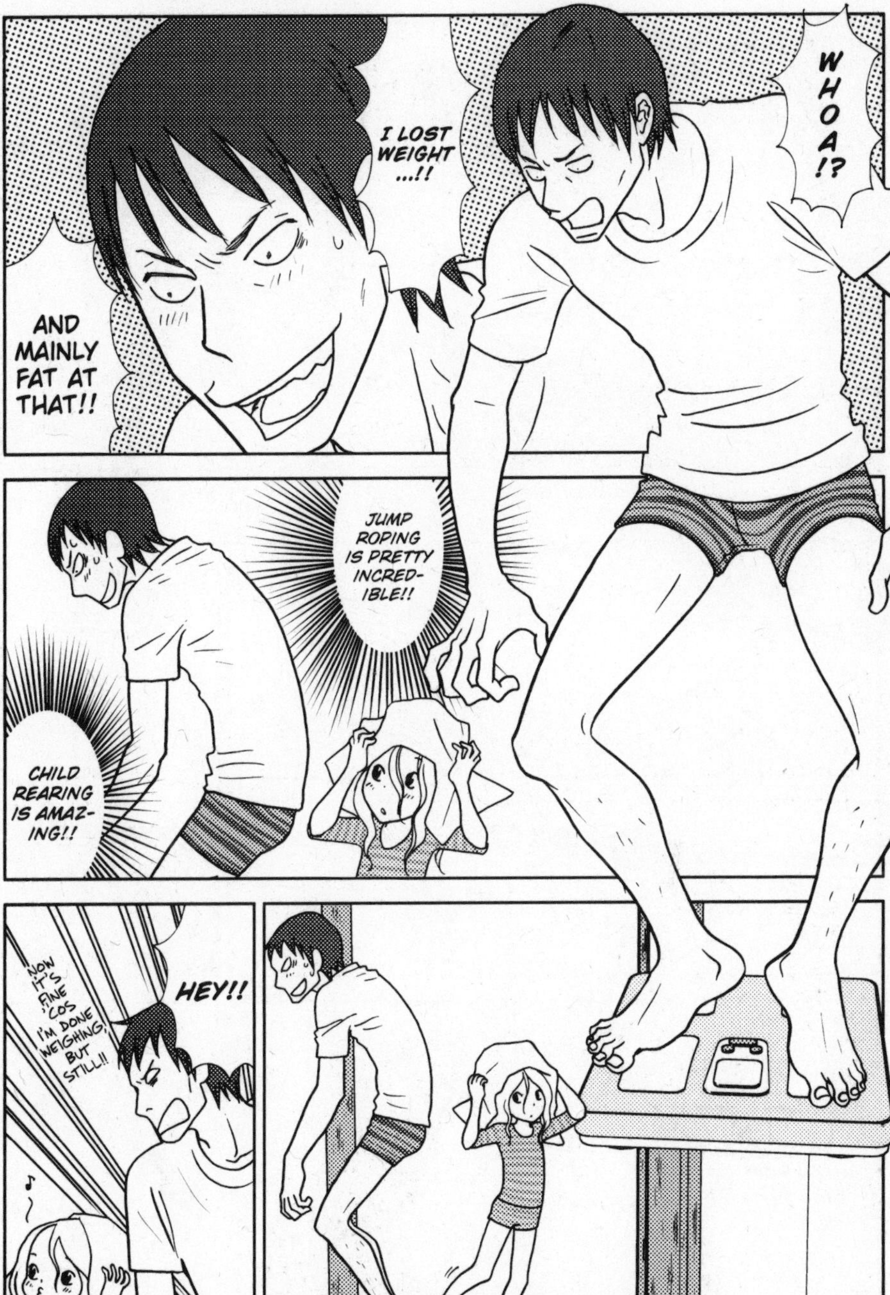
WHOA!?
I LOST WEIGHT ...!!
AND MAINLY FAT AT THAT!!
JUMP ROPING IS PRETTY INCREDIBLE!!
CHILD REARING IS AMAZING!!
HEY!!
NOW IT'S FINE 'COS I'M DONE WEIGHING, BUT STILL!!

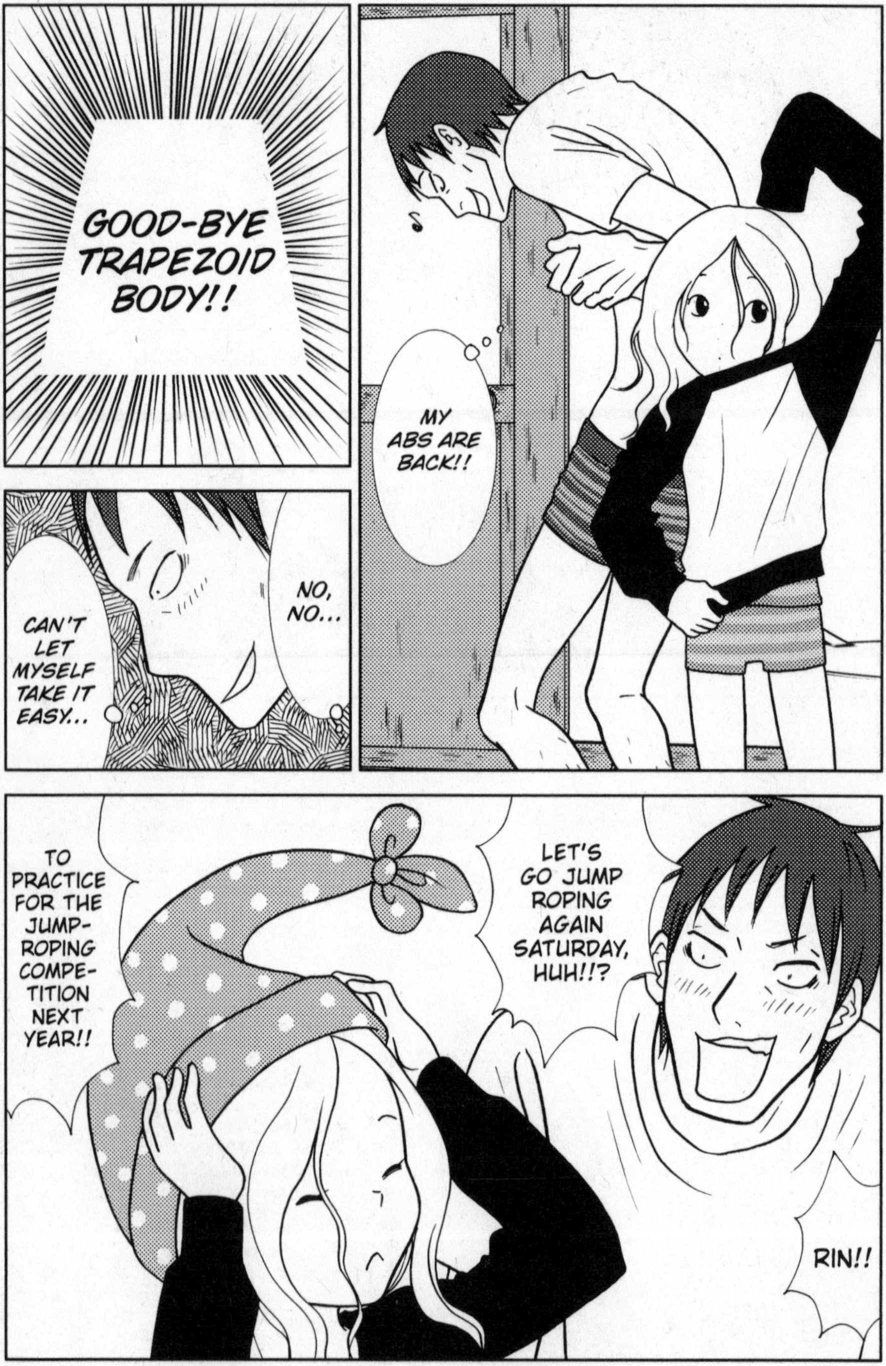
MY ABS ARE BACK!!
GOOD-BYE TRAPEZOID BODY!!
NO, NO...
CAN'T LET MYSELF TAKE IT EASY...
LET'S GO JUMP ROPING AGAIN SATURDAY, HUH!!?
TO PRACTICE FOR THE JUMP-ROPING COMPETITION NEXT YEAR!!
RIN!!

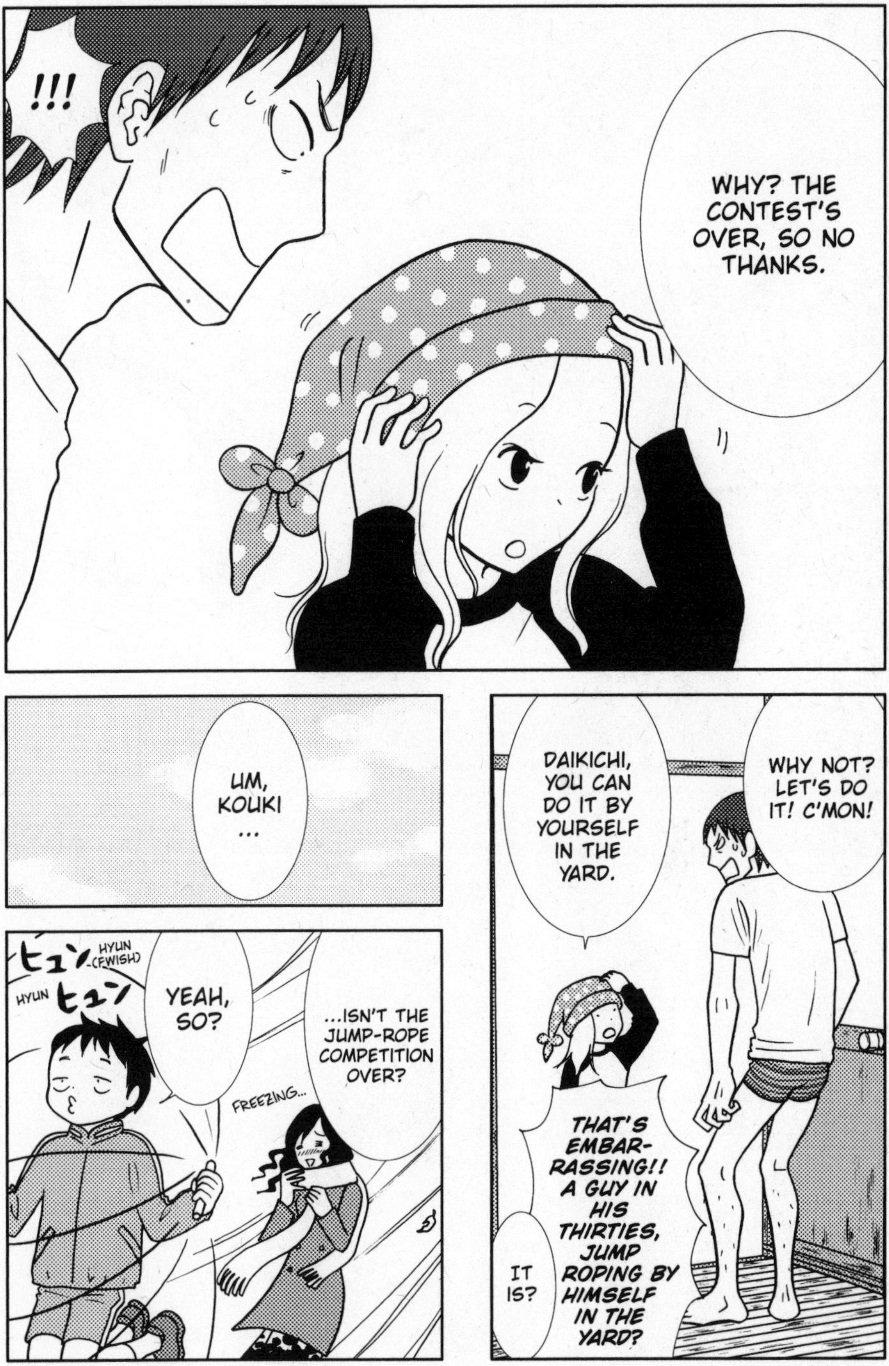
WHY? THE CONTEST'S OVER, SO NO THANKS.
!!!
WHY NOT? LET'S DO IT! C'MON!
DAIKICHI, YOU CAN DO IT BY YOURSELF IN THE YARD.
THAT'S EMBAR-RASSING!! A GUY IN HIS THIRTIES, JUMP ROPING BY HIMSELF IN THE YARD?
IT IS?
UM, KOUKI ...
...ISN'T THE JUMP-ROPE COMPETITION OVER?
FREEZING...
YEAH, SO?
ヒュン HYUN (FWISH)
ヒュン HYUN

BUNNY**DROP**
episode.24

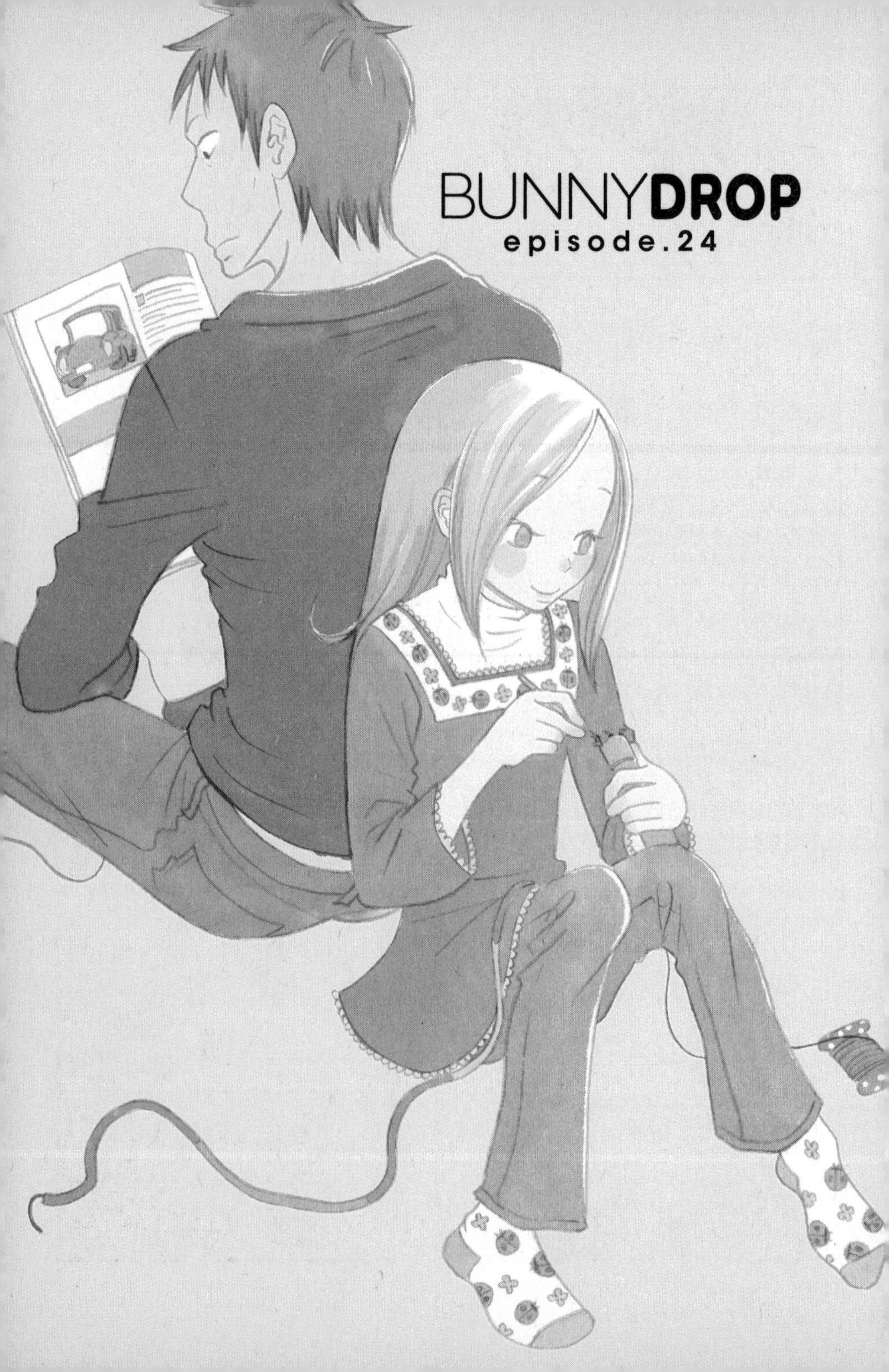

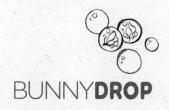

BUNNY**DROP**

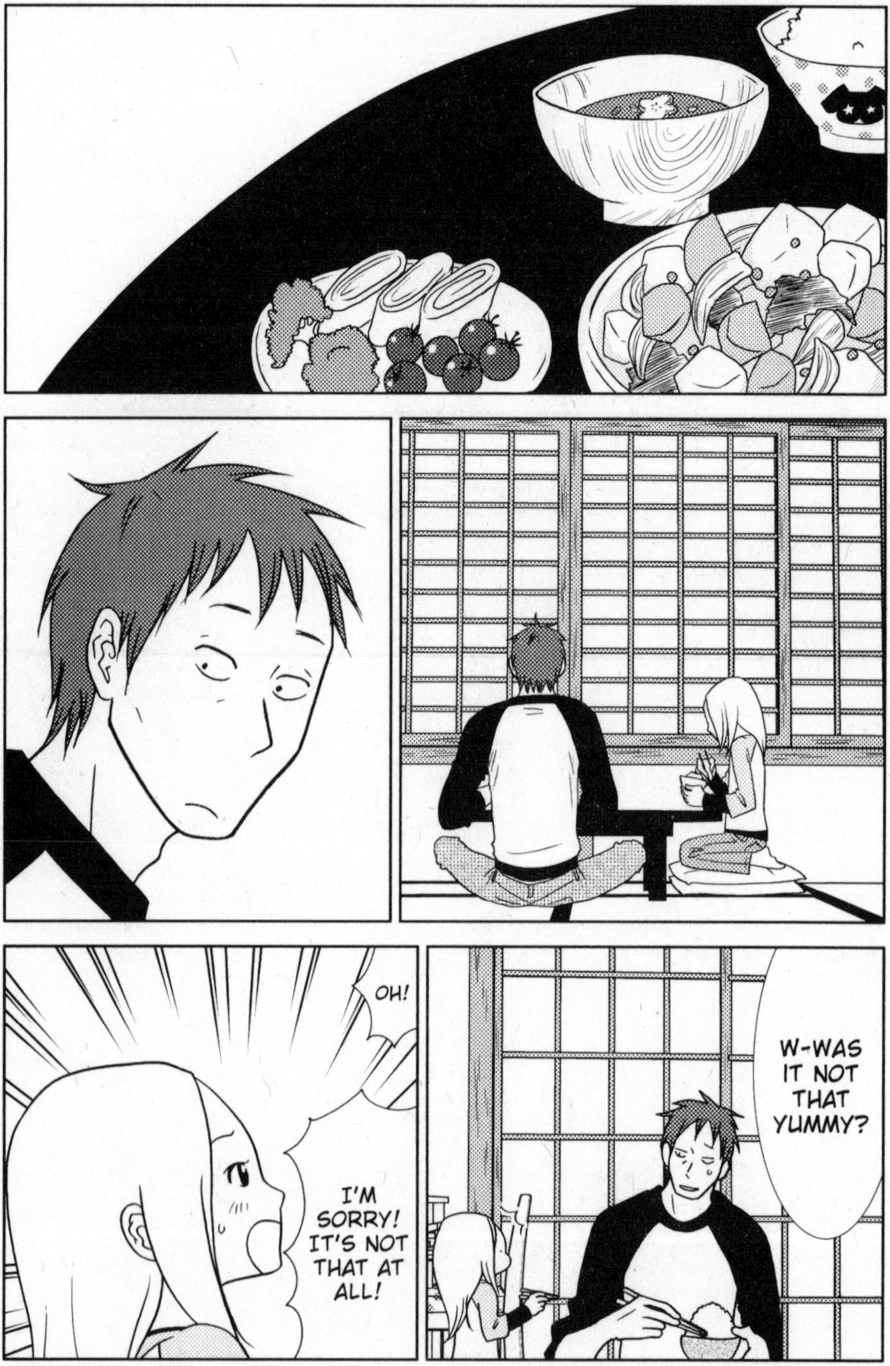
W-WAS IT NOT THAT YUMMY?
OH!
I'M SORRY! IT'S NOT THAT AT ALL!

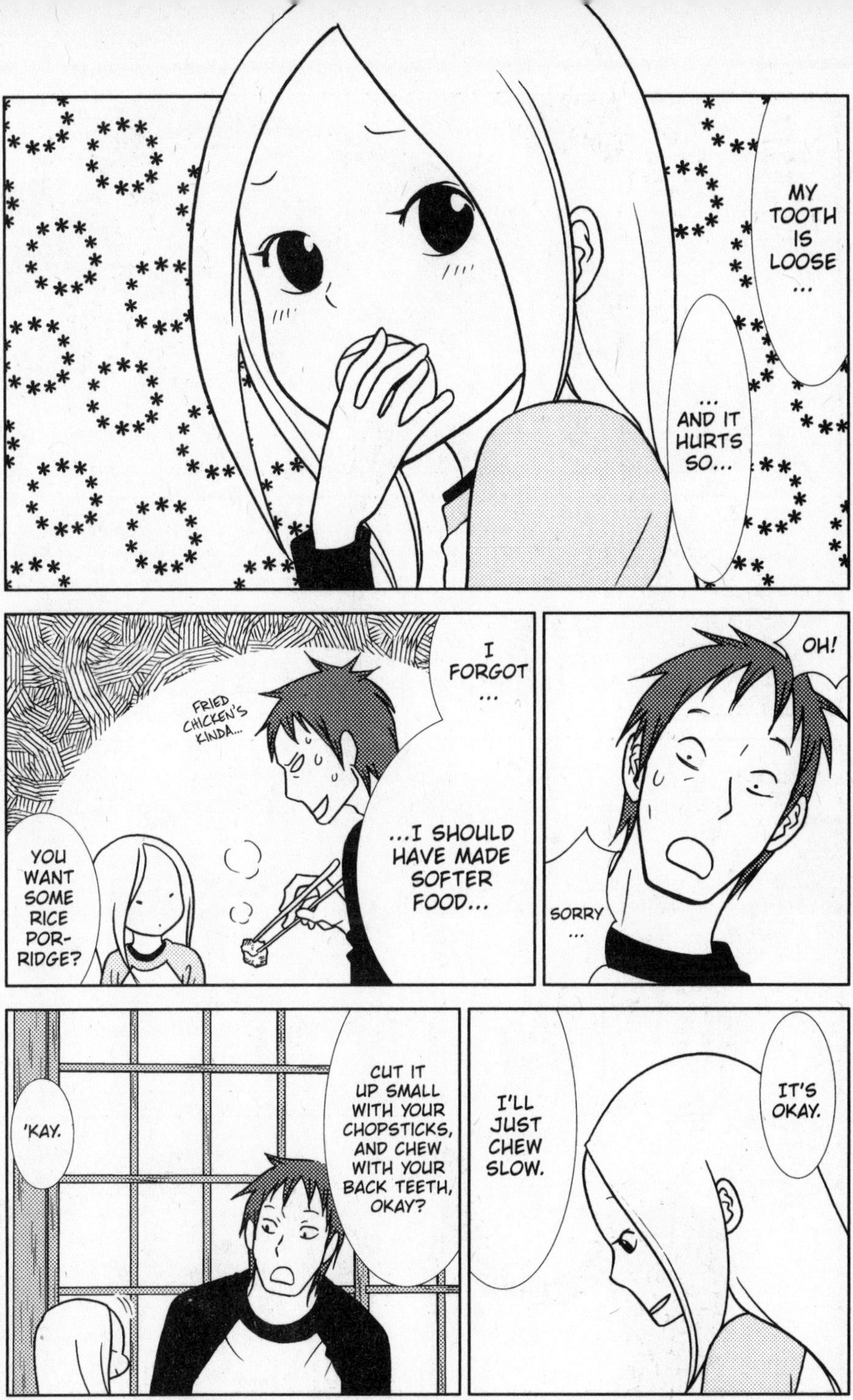
MY TOOTH IS LOOSE...
...AND IT HURTS SO...
OH!
SORRY...
I FORGOT...
...I SHOULD HAVE MADE SOFTER FOOD...
FRIED CHICKEN'S KINDA...
YOU WANT SOME RICE POR-RIDGE?
IT'S OKAY.
I'LL JUST CHEW SLOW.
CUT IT UP SMALL WITH YOUR CHOPSTICKS, AND CHEW WITH YOUR BACK TEETH, OKAY?
'KAY.

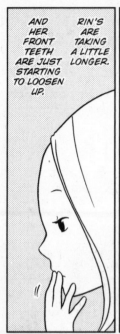

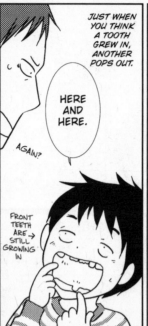

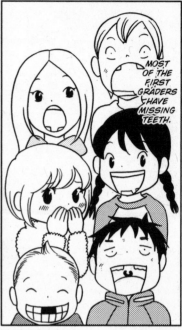

MOST OF THE FIRST GRADERS HAVE MISSING TEETH.
JUST WHEN YOU THINK A TOOTH GREW IN, ANOTHER POPS OUT.
HERE AND HERE.
AGAIN?
FRONT TEETH ARE STILL GROWING IN
RIN'S ARE TAKING A LITTLE LONGER.
AND HER FRONT TEETH ARE JUST STARTING TO LOOSEN UP.
AT FIRST RIN WAS TERRIFIED OF HER TEETH FALLING OUT...
MY TEETH ARE GOING TO FALL OUT?
WELL... NOT ALL AT ONCE...
AND THEY'LL GROW BACK...
...BUT AT THIS POINT, SHE'S GOTTEN USED TO THE IDEA.
いじ IJI
いじ IJI (JIGGLE)
ARE YOU PLAYING WITH YOUR TOOTH AGAIN...?
IT'LL FALL OUT IF YOU LEAVE IT ALONE.
AS THE ONE WATCHING THE SAGA UNFOLD, I'M NOT SURE IF I'M FEELING WORRIED OR JUST CAN'T KEEP WATCHING...
IT LOOKS LIKE IT HURTS!!
EVEN THOUGH WHEN I WAS GOING THROUGH THE SAME THING, I JIGGLED AND TWIRLED MY TEETH...

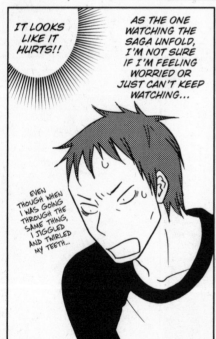

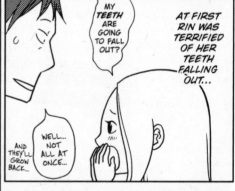

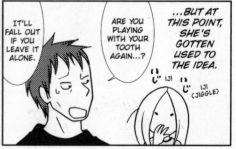

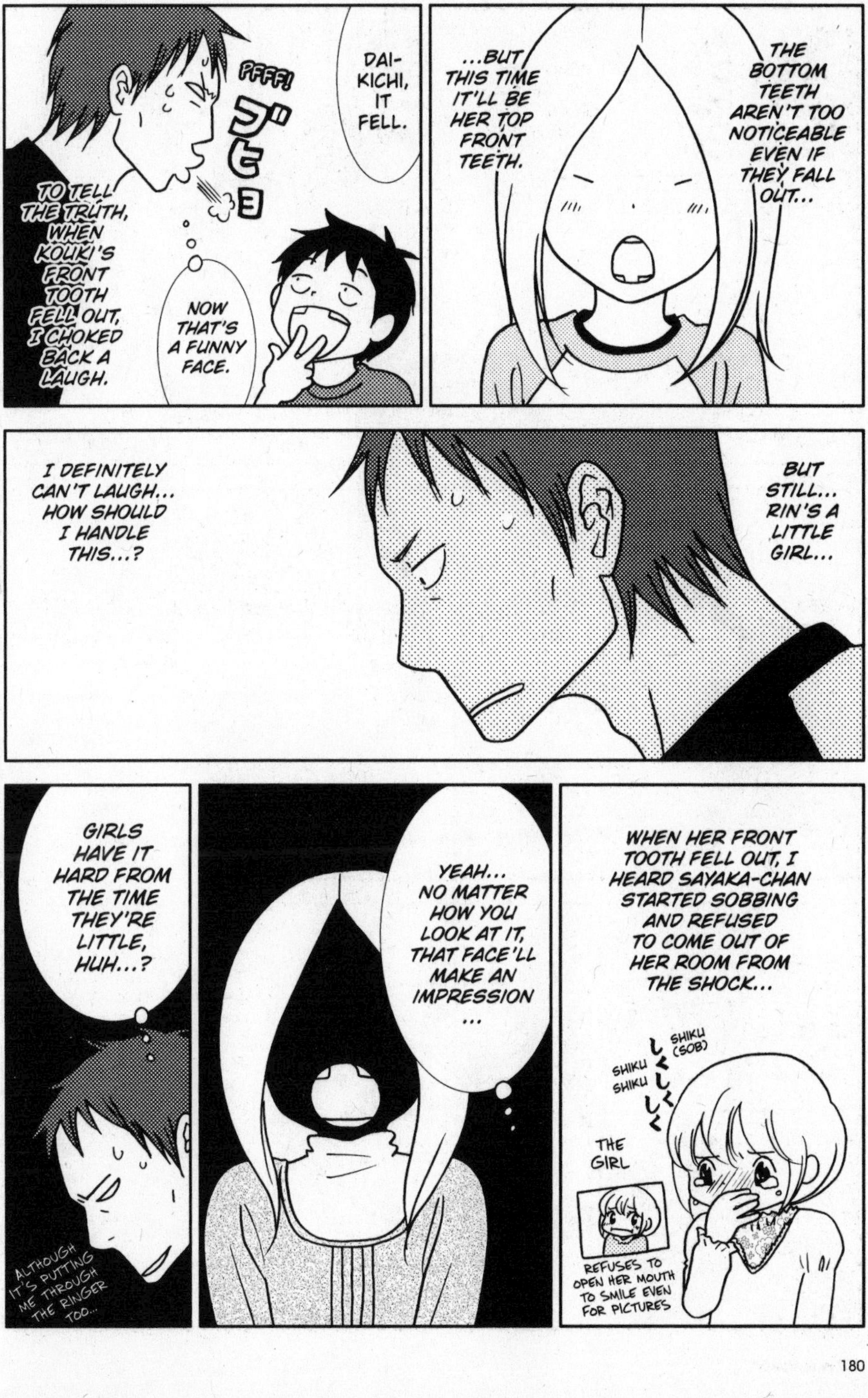
THE BOTTOM TEETH AREN'T TOO NOTICEABLE EVEN IF THEY FALL OUT...
...BUT THIS TIME IT'LL BE HER TOP FRONT TEETH.
DAI-KICHI, IT FELL.
PFFF! ブヒョ
NOW THAT'S A FUNNY FACE.
TO TELL THE TRUTH, WHEN KOUKI'S FRONT TOOTH FELL OUT, I CHOKED BACK A LAUGH.
BUT STILL... RIN'S A LITTLE GIRL...
I DEFINITELY CAN'T LAUGH... HOW SHOULD I HANDLE THIS...?
WHEN HER FRONT TOOTH FELL OUT, I HEARD SAYAKA-CHAN STARTED SOBBING AND REFUSED TO COME OUT OF HER ROOM FROM THE SHOCK...
SHIKU (SOB) しくしく
SHIKU SHIKU しく
THE GIRL
REFUSES TO OPEN HER MOUTH TO SMILE EVEN FOR PICTURES
YEAH... NO MATTER HOW YOU LOOK AT IT, THAT FACE'LL MAKE AN IMPRESSION ...
GIRLS HAVE IT HARD FROM THE TIME THEY'RE LITTLE, HUH...?
ALTHOUGH IT'S PUTTING ME THROUGH THE RINGER TOO...

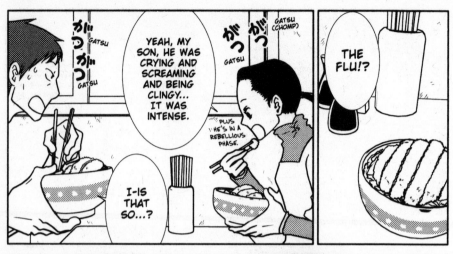

THE FLU!?
GATSU (CHOMP)
GATSU
YEAH, MY SON, HE WAS CRYING AND SCREAMING AND BEING CLINGY... IT WAS INTENSE.
GATSU
GATSU
PLUS HE'S IN A REBELLIOUS PHASE.
I-IS THAT SO...?
WERE YOU OKAY, GOTOU-SAN?
YEAH, I'M FREAKISHLY HEALTHY.
TEE-HEE.
LAID MY HUBBY OUT, THOUGH!
BUT I GUESS WHAT IT COMES DOWN TO IS THE FACT THAT I TOOK A LOT OF SICK DAYS TO CARE FOR MY SON. AND BEFORE THAT HE HAD THE STOMACH FLU AND SOME OTHER STUFF...
...SO I CAN'T CALL OUT EVEN IF I DIE.
AH-HA-HA...
I'LL EAT UP AND POWER MY WAY THROUGH!
GATSU
GATSU
MOGU
MOGU (MUNCH)
HA HA ...
SHE'S SMALL, BUT FORMIDABLE...
DO YOU GET A LOT OF CRITICISM FOR THAT?

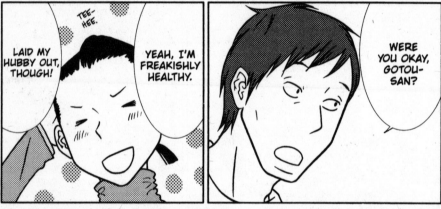

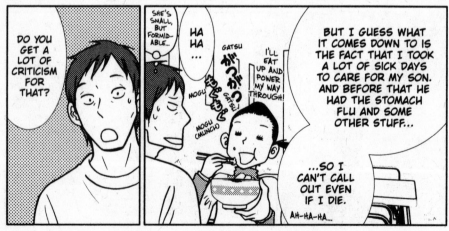

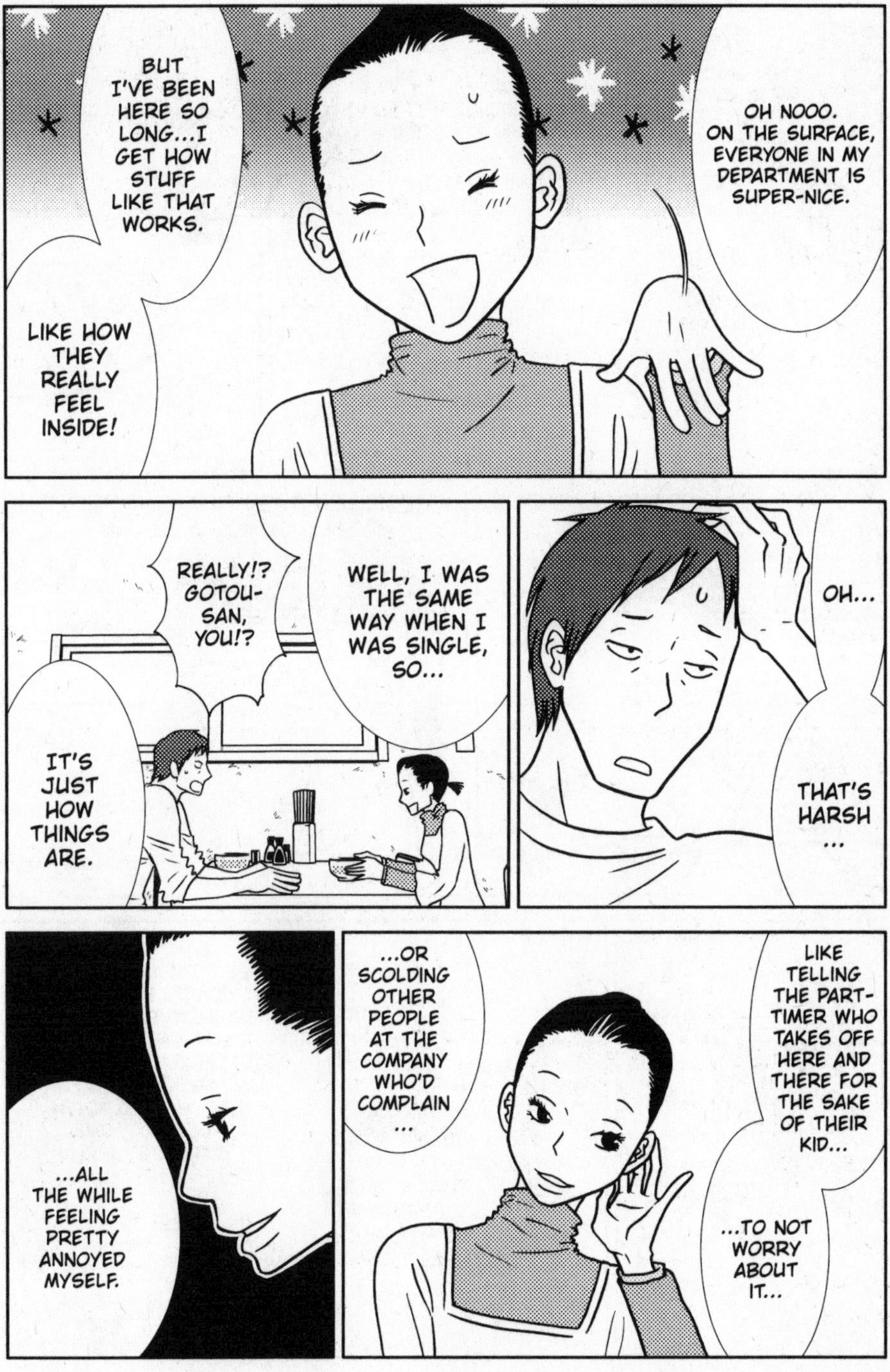
OH NOOO. ON THE SURFACE, EVERYONE IN MY DEPARTMENT IS SUPER-NICE.
BUT I'VE BEEN HERE SO LONG...I GET HOW STUFF LIKE THAT WORKS.
LIKE HOW THEY REALLY FEEL INSIDE!
OH...
THAT'S HARSH ...
WELL, I WAS THE SAME WAY WHEN I WAS SINGLE, SO...
REALLY!? GOTOU-SAN, YOU!?
IT'S JUST HOW THINGS ARE.
LIKE TELLING THE PART-TIMER WHO TAKES OFF HERE AND THERE FOR THE SAKE OF THEIR KID...
...TO NOT WORRY ABOUT IT...
...OR SCOLDING OTHER PEOPLE AT THE COMPANY WHO'D COMPLAIN ...
...ALL THE WHILE FEELING PRETTY ANNOYED MYSELF.

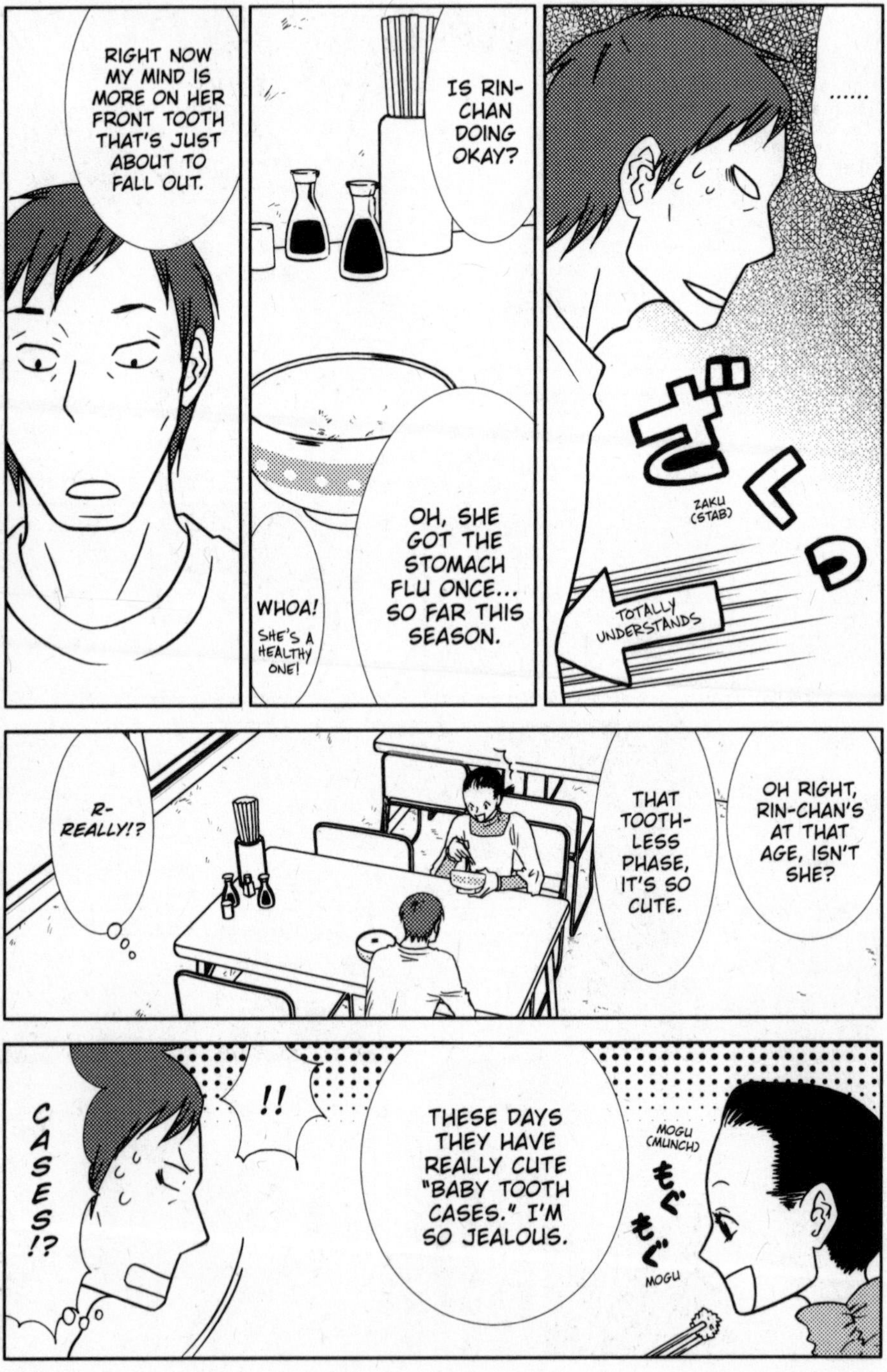
......
ざくっ
ZAKU (STAB)
TOTALLY UNDERSTANDS
IS RIN-CHAN DOING OKAY?
OH, SHE GOT THE STOMACH FLU ONCE... SO FAR THIS SEASON.
WHOA!
SHE'S A HEALTHY ONE!
RIGHT NOW MY MIND IS MORE ON HER FRONT TOOTH THAT'S JUST ABOUT TO FALL OUT.
OH RIGHT, RIN-CHAN'S AT THAT AGE, ISN'T SHE?
THAT TOOTH-LESS PHASE, IT'S SO CUTE.
R-REALLY!?
MOGU (MUNCH)
もぐもぐ
MOGU
THESE DAYS THEY HAVE REALLY CUTE "BABY TOOTH CASES." I'M SO JEALOUS.
!!
CASES!?

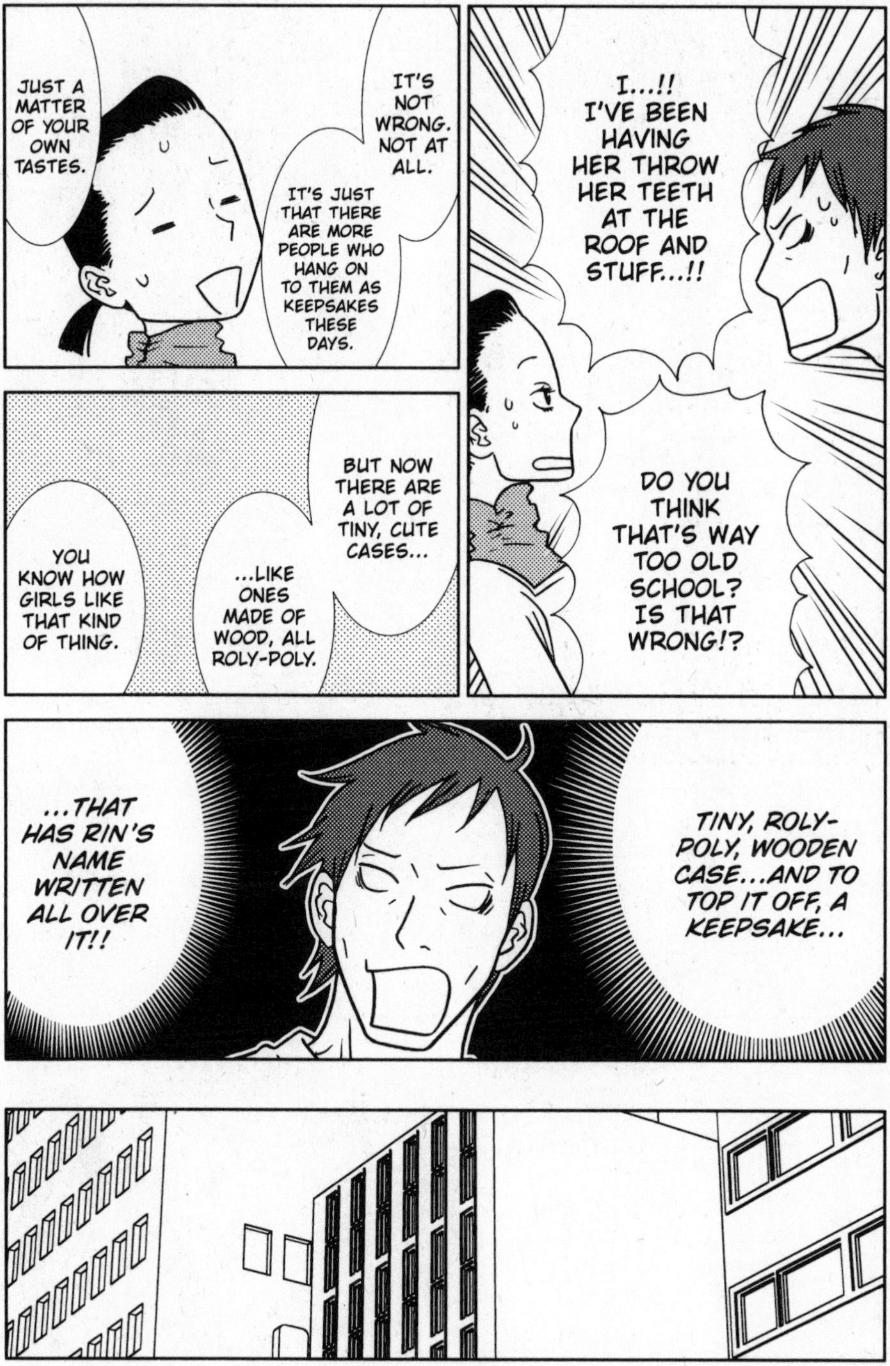
I...!! I'VE BEEN HAVING HER THROW HER TEETH AT THE ROOF AND STUFF...!!
DO YOU THINK THAT'S WAY TOO OLD SCHOOL? IS THAT WRONG!?
IT'S NOT WRONG. NOT AT ALL.
IT'S JUST THAT THERE ARE MORE PEOPLE WHO HANG ON TO THEM AS KEEPSAKES THESE DAYS.
JUST A MATTER OF YOUR OWN TASTES.
BUT NOW THERE ARE A LOT OF TINY, CUTE CASES...
...LIKE ONES MADE OF WOOD, ALL ROLY-POLY.
YOU KNOW HOW GIRLS LIKE THAT KIND OF THING.
TINY, ROLY-POLY, WOODEN CASE...AND TO TOP IT OFF, A KEEPSAKE...
...THAT HAS RIN'S NAME WRITTEN ALL OVER IT!!

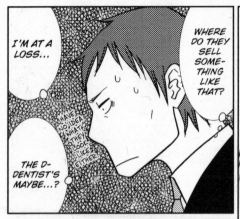

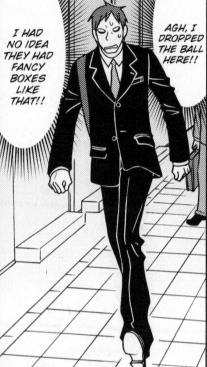

AGH, I DROPPED THE BALL HERE!!
I HAD NO IDEA THEY HAD FANCY BOXES LIKE THAT!!
WHERE DO THEY SELL SOMETHING LIKE THAT?
I'M AT A LOSS...
HAVE NO IDEA WHAT THEY LOOK LIKE EITHER
THE D-DENTIST'S MAYBE...?
!!!
WAIT, WHY AM I GETTING ALL WORKED UP ABOUT A TOOTH CASE!?
WHAT A DORK!!
......

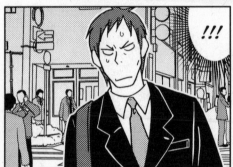

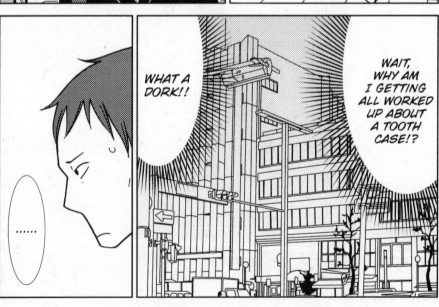

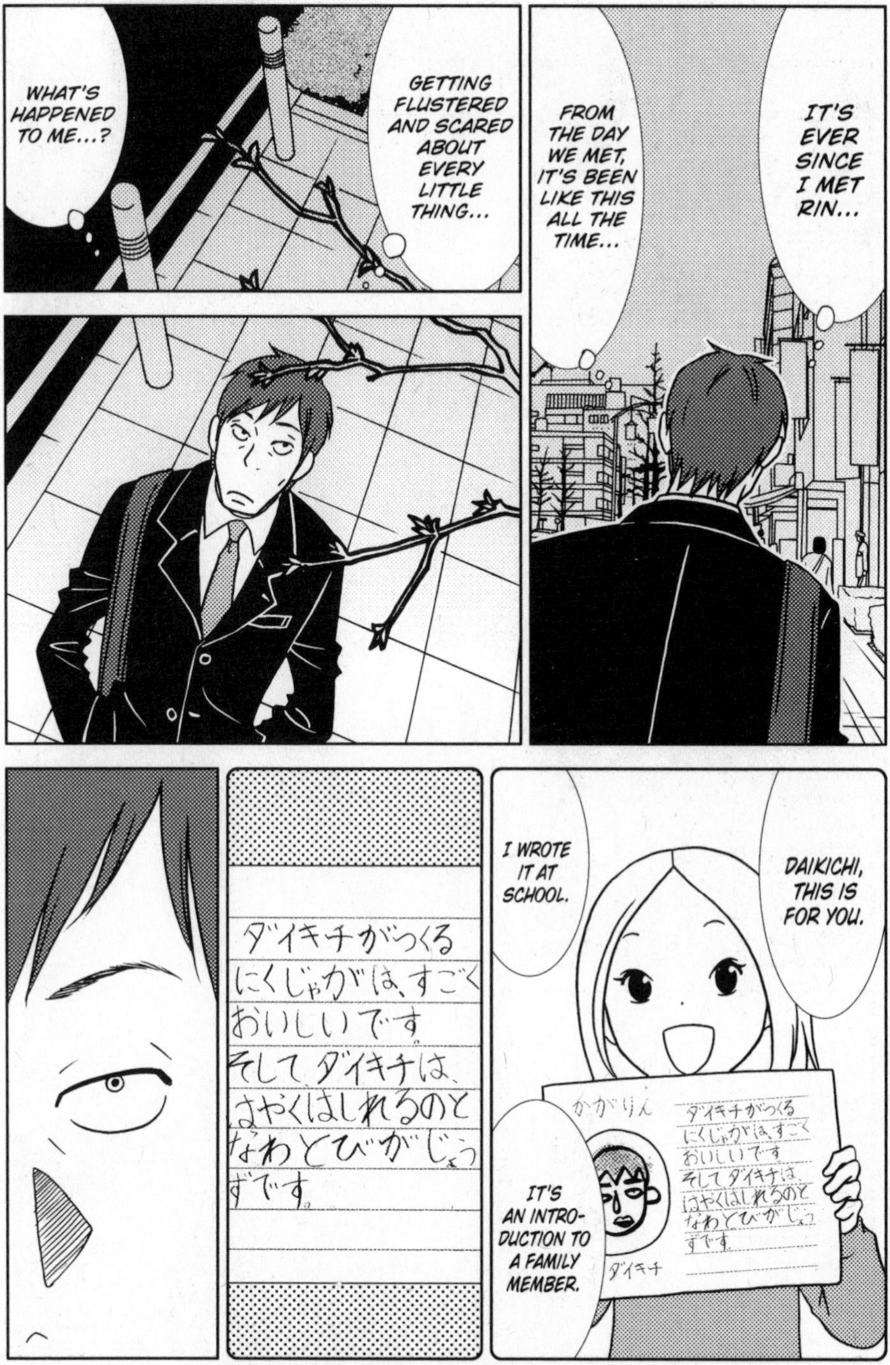
IT'S EVER SINCE I MET RIN...
FROM THE DAY WE MET, IT'S BEEN LIKE THIS ALL THE TIME...
GETTING FLUSTERED AND SCARED ABOUT EVERY LITTLE THING...
WHAT'S HAPPENED TO ME...?
DAIKICHI, THIS IS FOR YOU.
I WROTE IT AT SCHOOL.
IT'S AN INTRODUCTION TO A FAMILY MEMBER.
かがりん
ダイキチがつくるにくじゃがは、すごくおいしいです。そしてダイキチは、はやくはしれるのとなわとびがじょうずです。
ダイキチ
ダイキチがつくるにくじゃがは、すごくおいしいです。そしてダイキチは、はやくはしれるのとなわとびがじょうずです。

PAPER: RIN KAGA / DAIKICHI / THE MEAT-AND-POTATO STEW THAT DAIKICHI MADES IS SO DELICIOUS. AND DAIKICHI CAN RUN REALLY FAST AND IS GOOD AT JUMP ROPE.

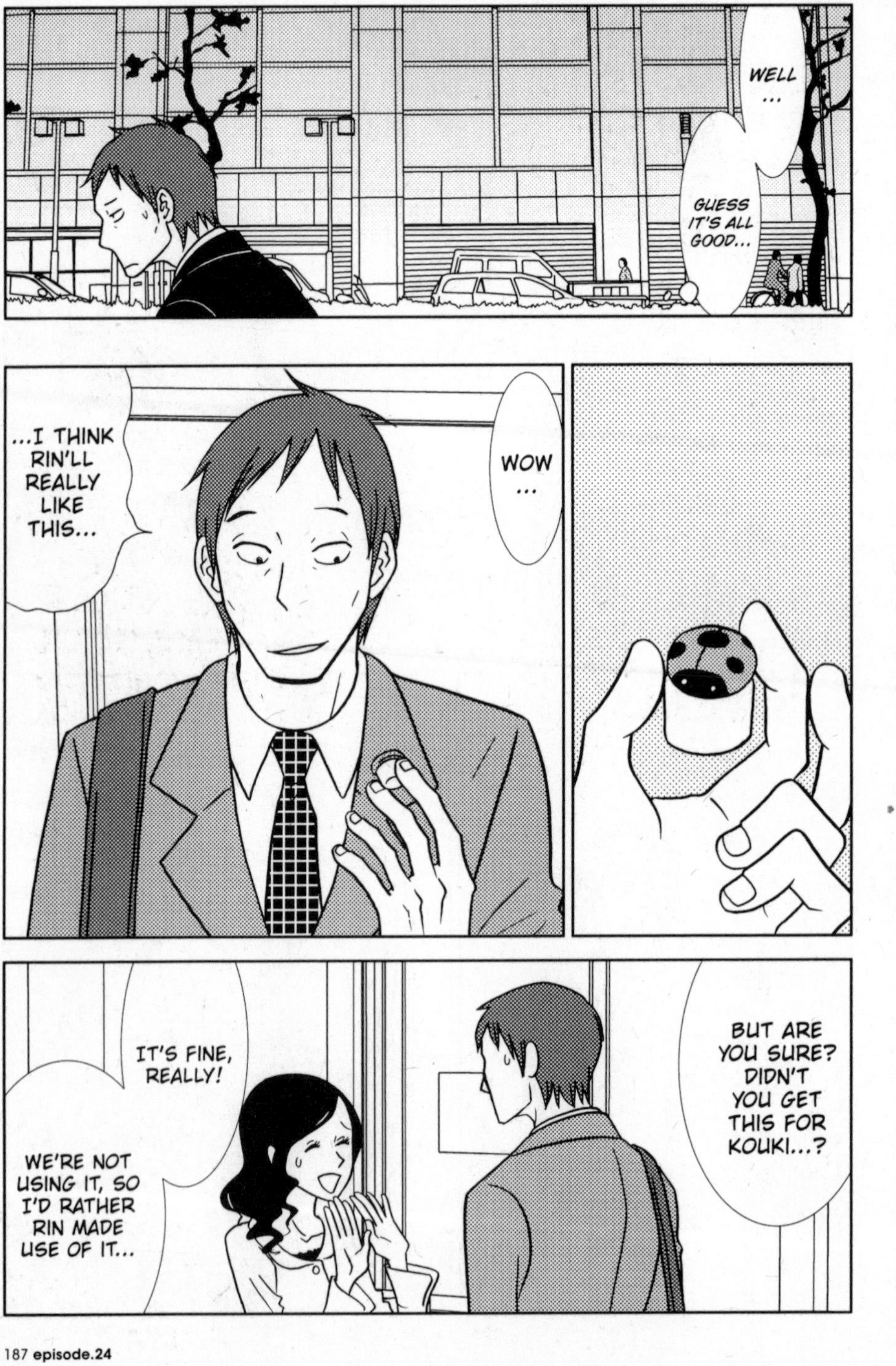
WELL...
GUESS IT'S ALL GOOD...
WOW...
...I THINK RIN'LL REALLY LIKE THIS...
BUT ARE YOU SURE? DIDN'T YOU GET THIS FOR KOUKI...?
IT'S FINE, REALLY!
WE'RE NOT USING IT, SO I'D RATHER RIN MADE USE OF IT...

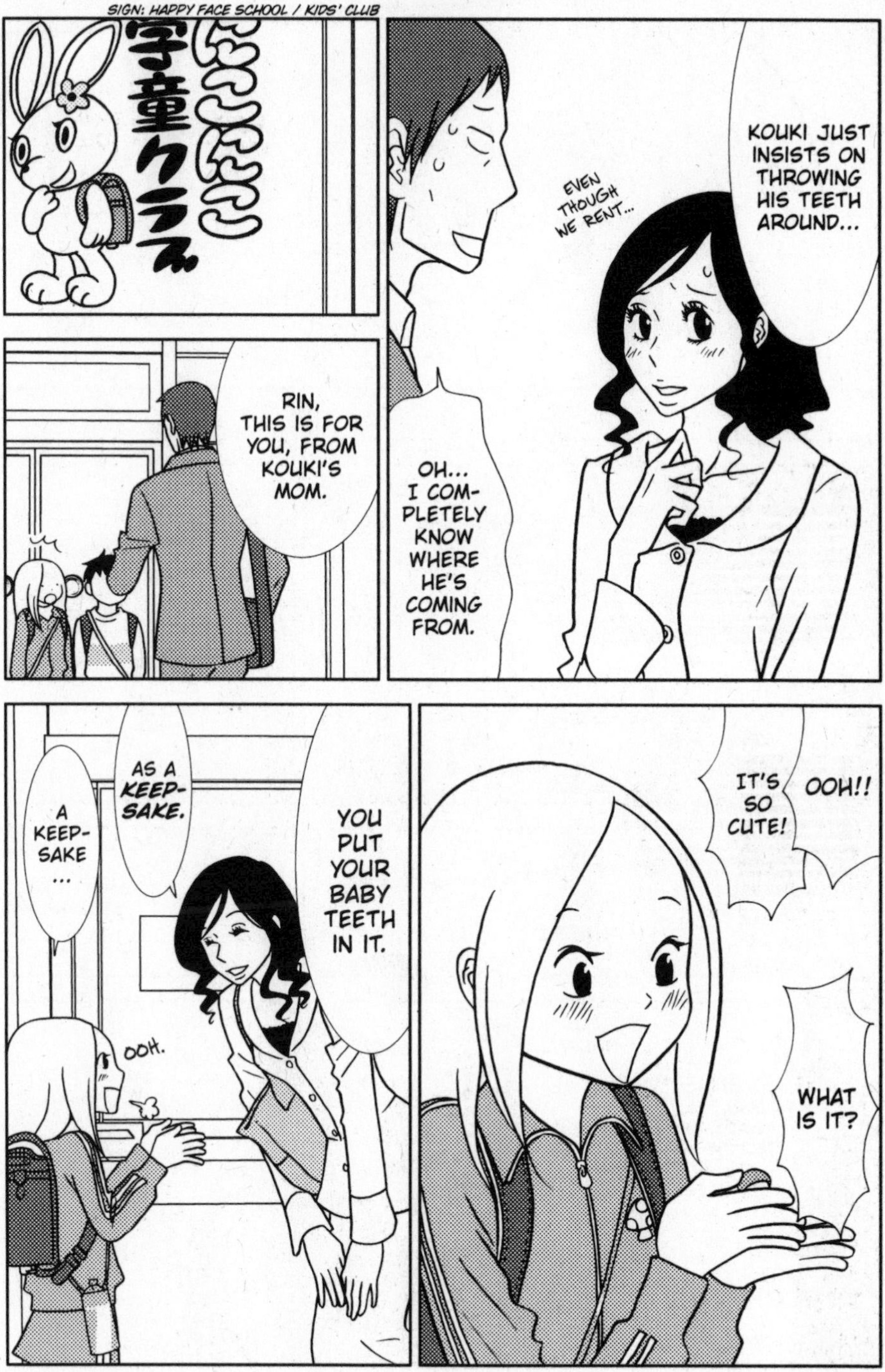
KOUKI JUST INSISTS ON THROWING HIS TEETH AROUND...
EVEN THOUGH WE RENT...
OH... I COMPLETELY KNOW WHERE HE'S COMING FROM.
SIGN: HAPPY FACE SCHOOL / KIDS' CLUB
RIN, THIS IS FOR YOU, FROM KOUKI'S MOM.
OOH!!
IT'S SO CUTE!
WHAT IS IT?
YOU PUT YOUR BABY TEETH IN IT.
AS A KEEPSAKE.
A KEEPSAKE...
OOH.

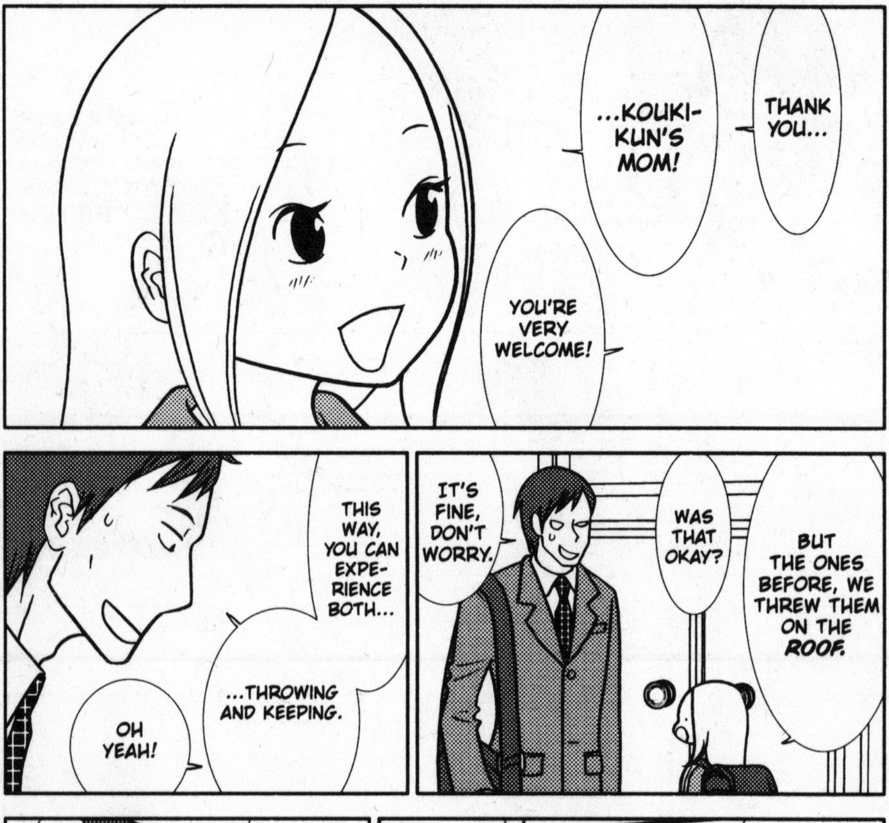

THANK YOU...
...KOUKI-KUN'S MOM!
YOU'RE VERY WELCOME!
BUT THE ONES BEFORE, WE THREW THEM ON THE *ROOF.*
WAS THAT OKAY?
IT'S FINE, DON'T WORRY.
THIS WAY, YOU CAN EXPERIENCE BOTH...
...THROWING AND KEEPING.
OH YEAH!
SO IF YOU STILL WANT TO KEEP THROWING THEM, YOU CAN DO THAT.
NOPE. I WANT TO KEEP THEM IN THIS.
IT'S SO CUTE, AND IT'S FOR MY KEEPSAKES.
I'M GONNA KEEP THROWIN' 'EM *FOREVER.*
IT'S PRETTY AMAZING FOR SAYAKA-CHAN, YOU KNOW!
HUH?
WHAT DO YOU MEAN?
IF SHE PUTS HER TOOTH UNDER HER PILLOW WHEN SHE GOES TO SLEEP...

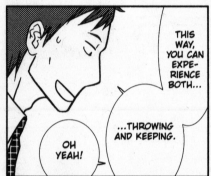

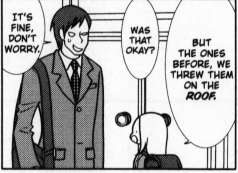

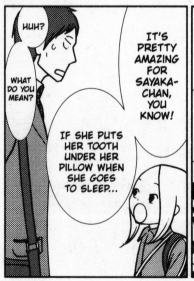

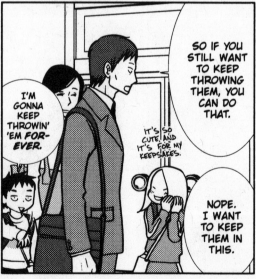

...THE MONEY FAIRY COMES, AND IN THE MORNING THE TOOTH'S TURNED INTO ¥50!!
WHAT!?
THAT REALLY HAP-PENS!?
I THINK THAT'S THE TOOTH FAIRY...
SERI-OUSLY!?
I TOTALLY LOST OUT!!

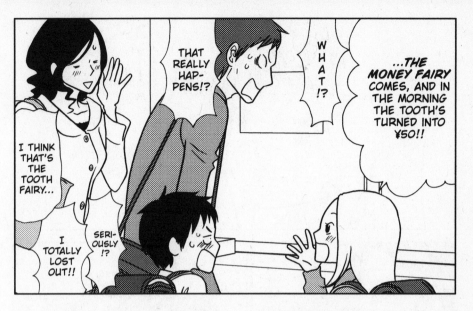

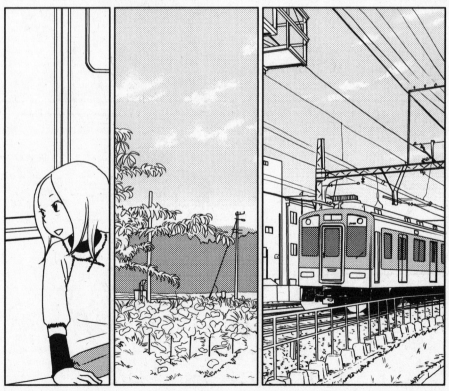

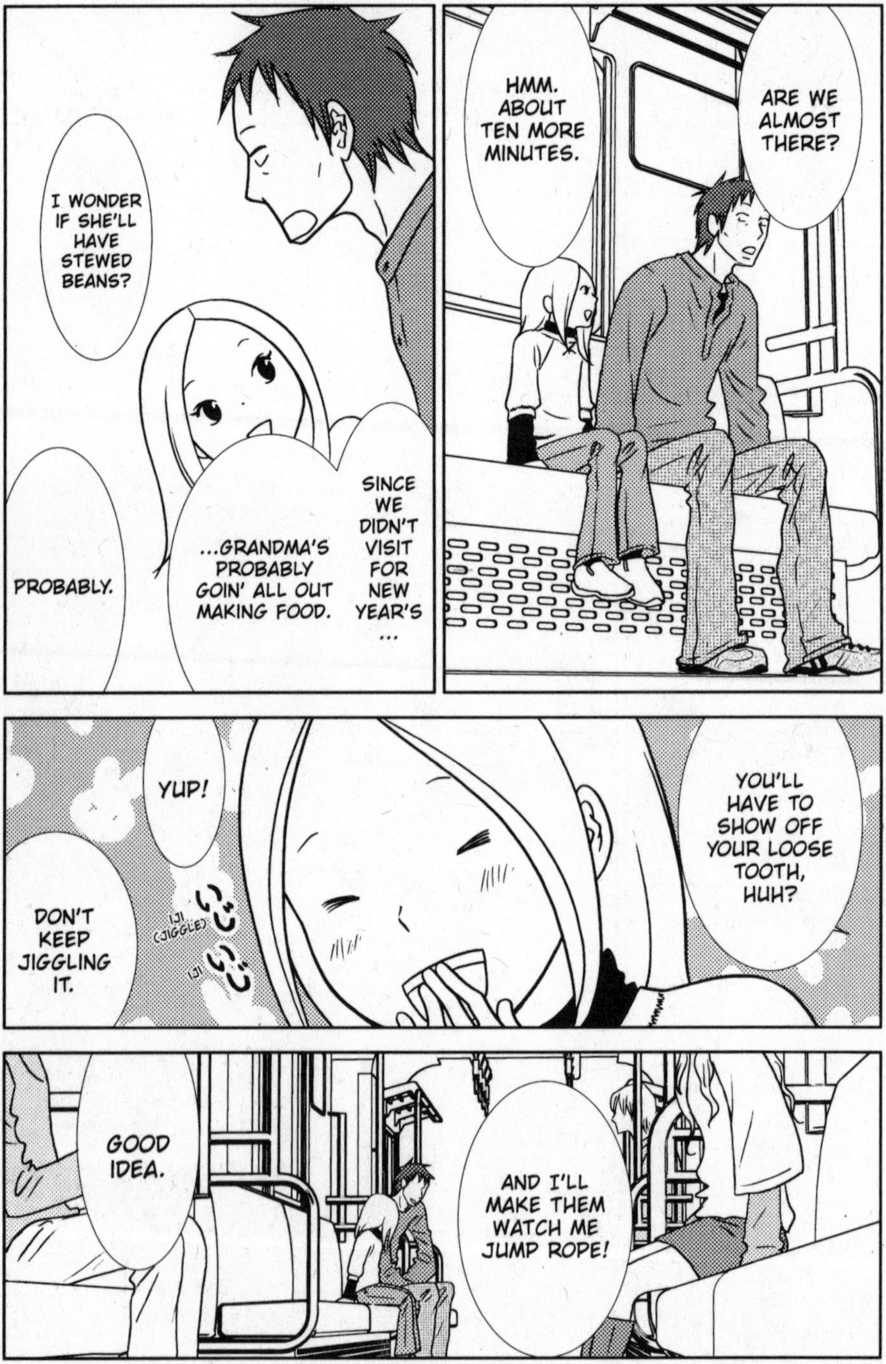
ARE WE ALMOST THERE?
HMM. ABOUT TEN MORE MINUTES.
SINCE WE DIDN'T VISIT FOR NEW YEAR'S...
...GRANDMA'S PROBABLY GOIN' ALL OUT MAKING FOOD.
I WONDER IF SHE'LL HAVE STEWED BEANS?
PROBABLY.
YOU'LL HAVE TO SHOW OFF YOUR LOOSE TOOTH, HUH?
YUP!
IJI (JIGGLE)
IJI
DON'T KEEP JIGGLING IT.
AND I'LL MAKE THEM WATCH ME JUMP ROPE!
GOOD IDEA.

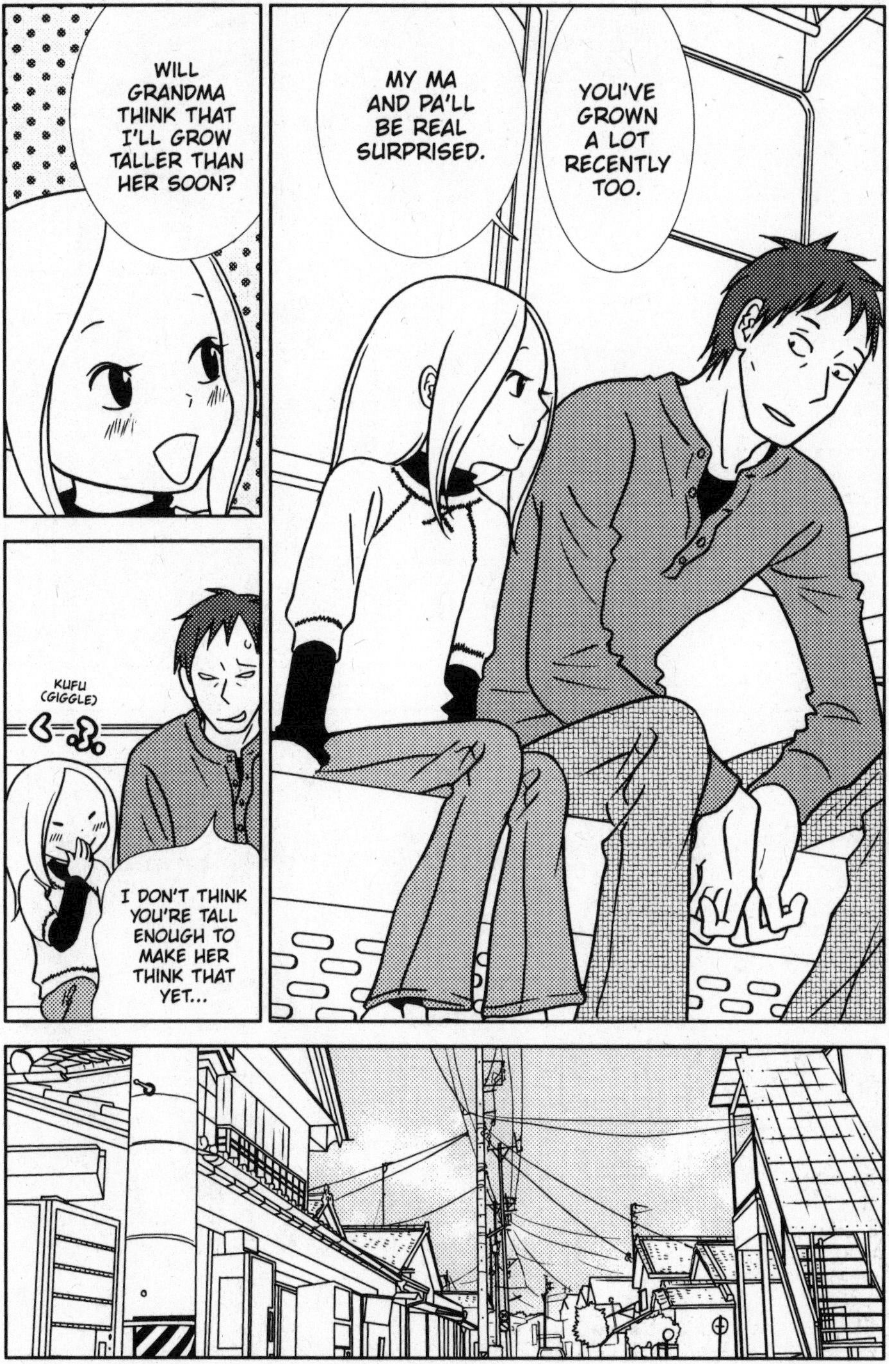
YOU'VE GROWN A LOT RECENTLY TOO.
MY MA AND PA'LL BE REAL SURPRISED.
WILL GRANDMA THINK THAT I'LL GROW TALLER THAN HER SOON?
KUFU (GIGGLE)
I DON'T THINK YOU'RE TALL ENOUGH TO MAKE HER THINK THAT YET...

WE'RE HOME!
WE'RE HOME!
OH MY! RIN-CHAN!
WELCOME! COME IN!!
YOU MIGHT HAVE CALLED! WE COULD'VE PICKED YOU UP!!
NAW. RIN'S PERFECTLY FINE WALKING TEN MINUTES.
OH DEAR, YOU REALLY HAVE GROWN TALLER...
ARE YOU ONE OF THE TALLER KIDS IN CLASS?
YUP!
YOU'LL BE TALLER THAN ME SOON.
I KNOW! RIN-CHAN, YOU COULD PROBABLY BECOME A MODEL WHEN YOU GROW UP!!
I'M SURE OF IT!!
DON'T TALK CRAZY, MA...

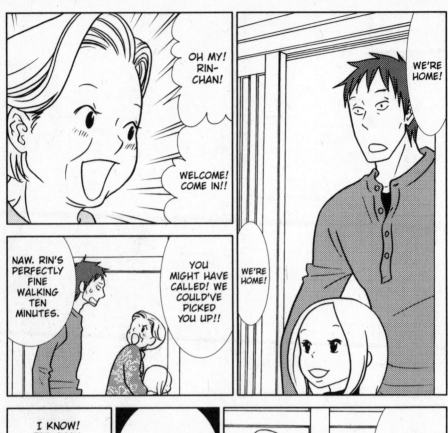

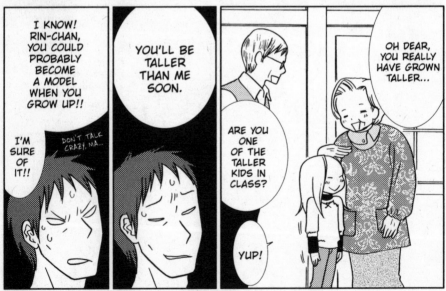

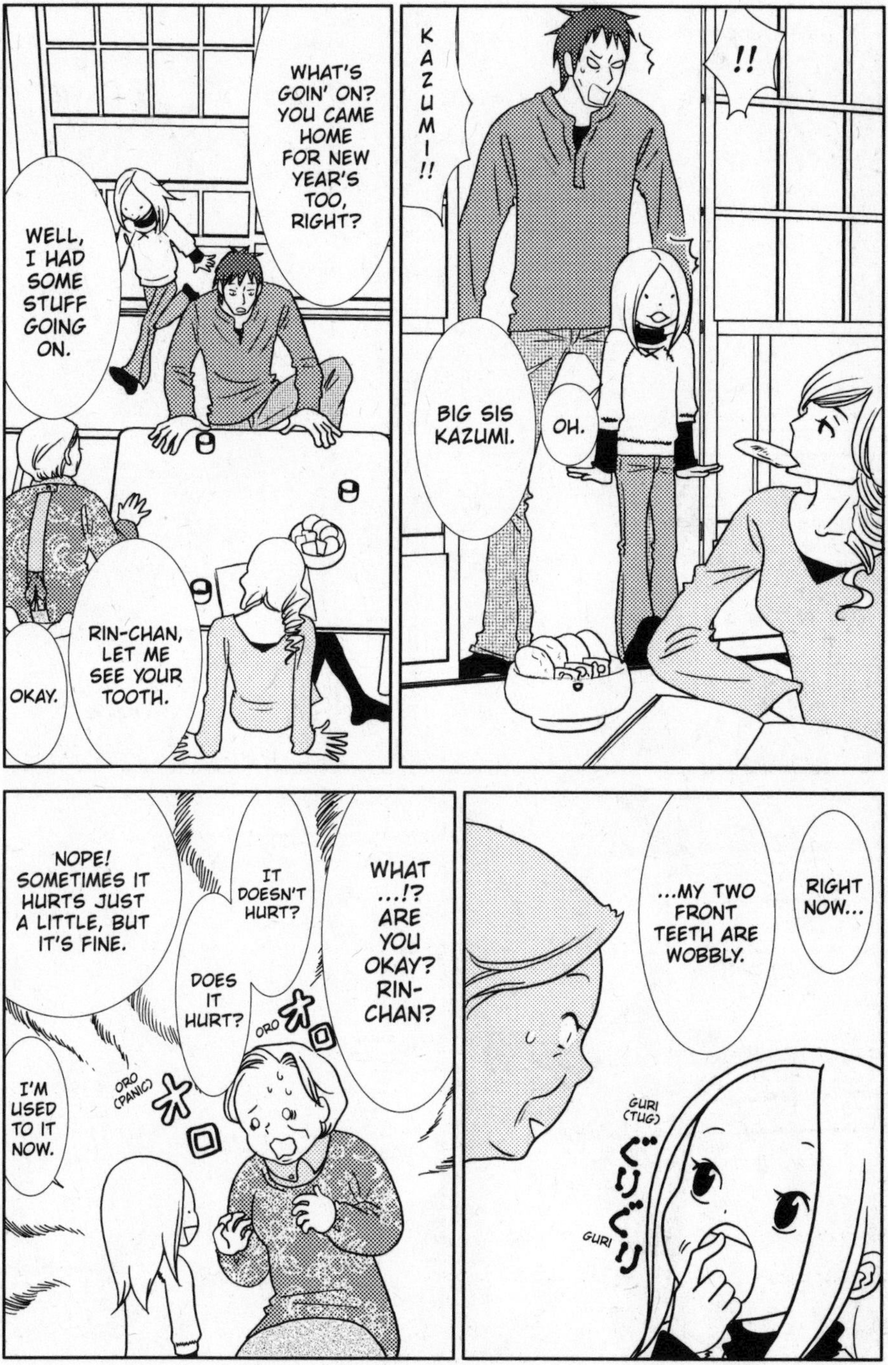

!!
KAZUMI!!
OH.
BIG SIS KAZUMI.
WHAT'S GOIN' ON? YOU CAME HOME FOR NEW YEAR'S TOO, RIGHT?
WELL, I HAD SOME STUFF GOING ON.
RIN-CHAN, LET ME SEE YOUR TOOTH.
OKAY.
RIGHT NOW...
...MY TWO FRONT TEETH ARE WOBBLY.
GURI (TUG)
ぐりぐり
GURI
WHAT ...!? ARE YOU OKAY? RIN-CHAN?
IT DOESN'T HURT?
DOES IT HURT?
ORO
オロ
NOPE! SOMETIMES IT HURTS JUST A LITTLE, BUT IT'S FINE.
ORO (PANIC)
オロ
I'M USED TO IT NOW.

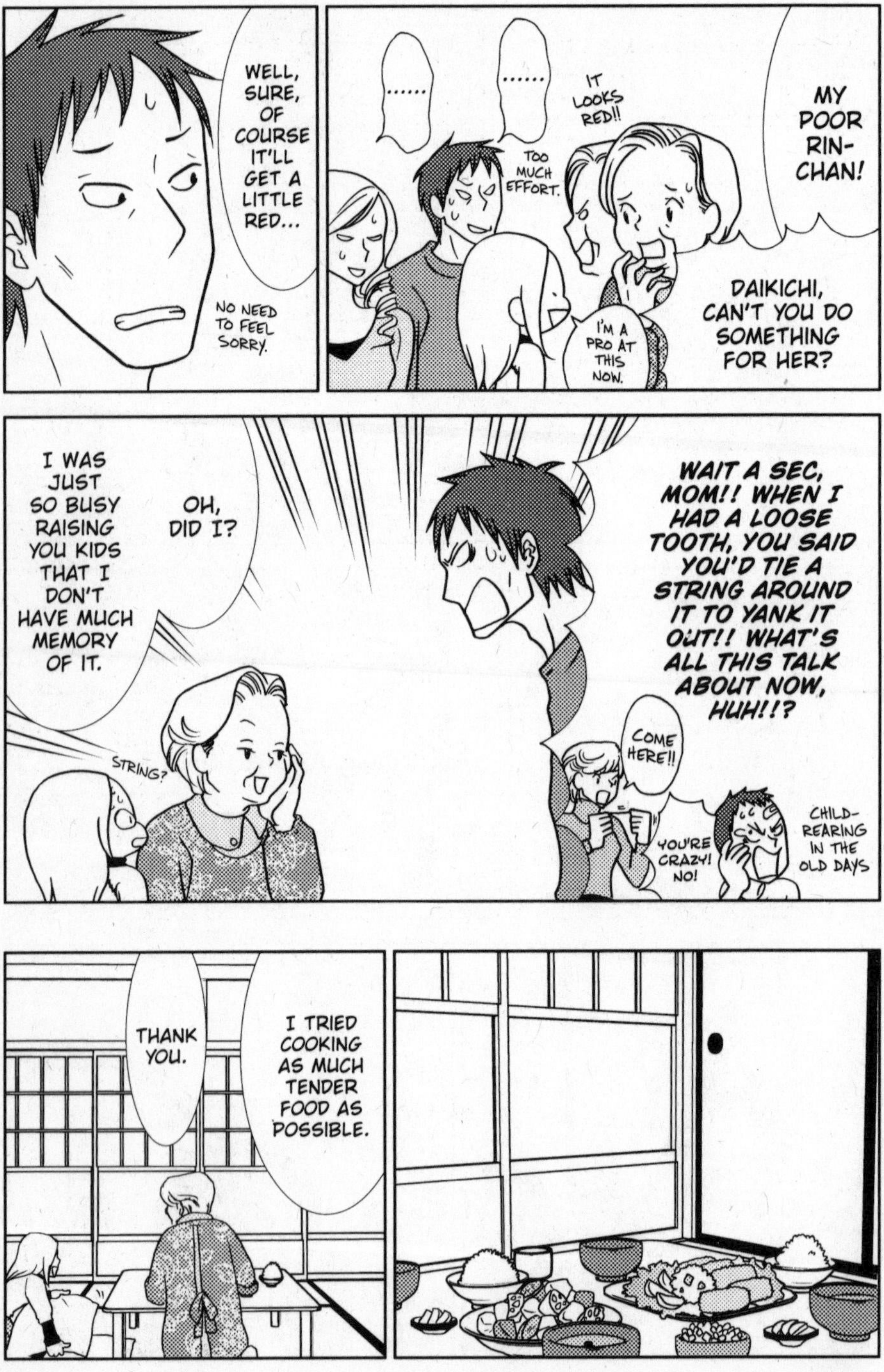
MY POOR RIN-CHAN!
DAIKICHI, CAN'T YOU DO SOMETHING FOR HER?
IT LOOKS RED!!
......
TOO MUCH EFFORT.
I'M A PRO AT THIS NOW.
......
WELL, SURE, OF COURSE IT'LL GET A LITTLE RED...
NO NEED TO FEEL SORRY.
WAIT A SEC, MOM!! WHEN I HAD A LOOSE TOOTH, YOU SAID YOU'D TIE A STRING AROUND IT TO YANK IT OUT!! WHAT'S ALL THIS TALK ABOUT NOW, HUH!!?
CHILD-REARING IN THE OLD DAYS
COME HERE!!
YOU'RE CRAZY! NO!
OH, DID I?
I WAS JUST SO BUSY RAISING YOU KIDS THAT I DON'T HAVE MUCH MEMORY OF IT.
STRING?
I TRIED COOKING AS MUCH TENDER FOOD AS POSSIBLE.
THANK YOU.

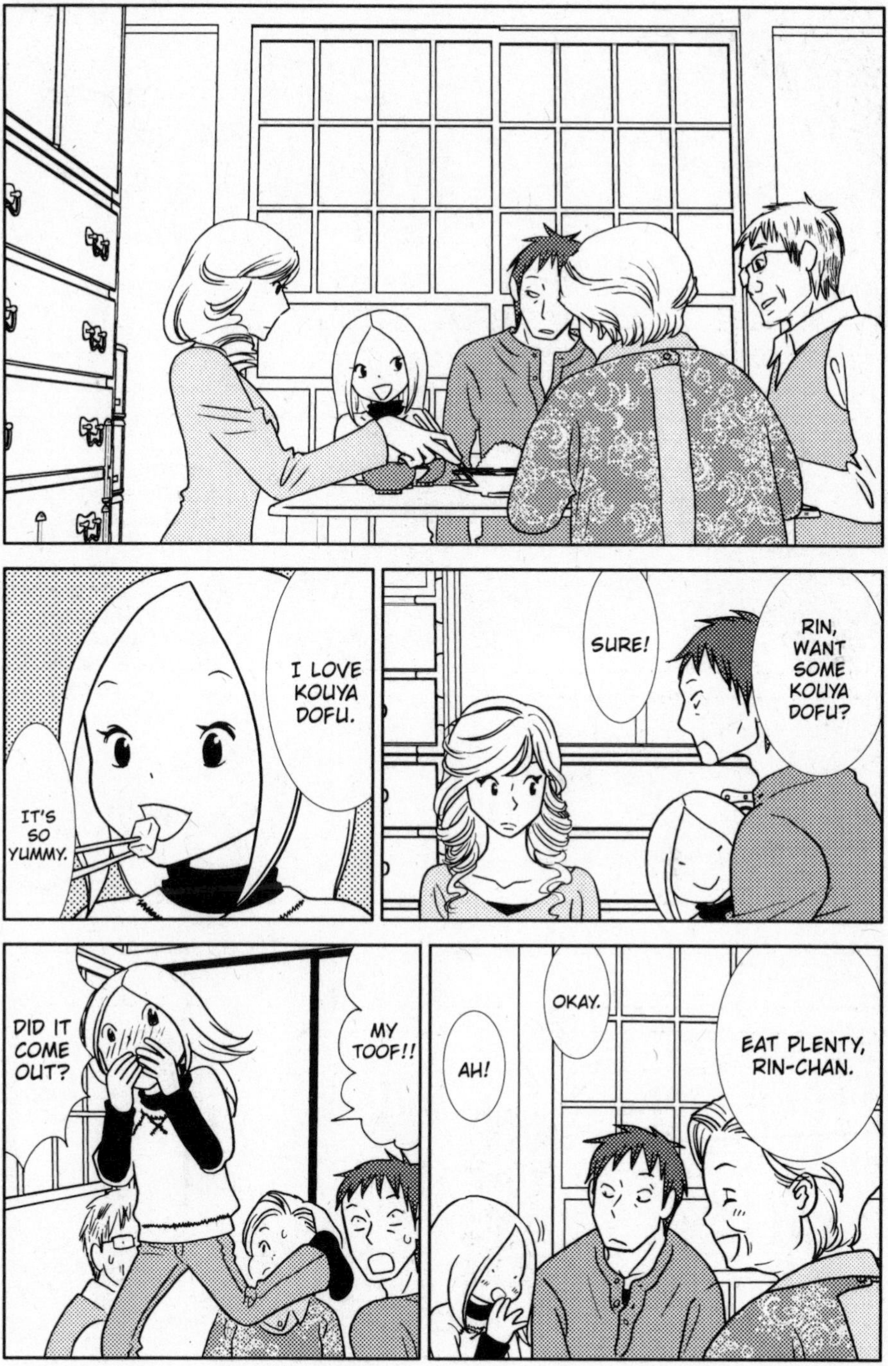
RIN, WANT SOME KOUYA DOFU?
SURE!
I LOVE KOUYA DOFU.
IT'S SO YUMMY.
EAT PLENTY, RIN-CHAN.
OKAY.
AH!
MY TOOF!!
DID IT COME OUT?

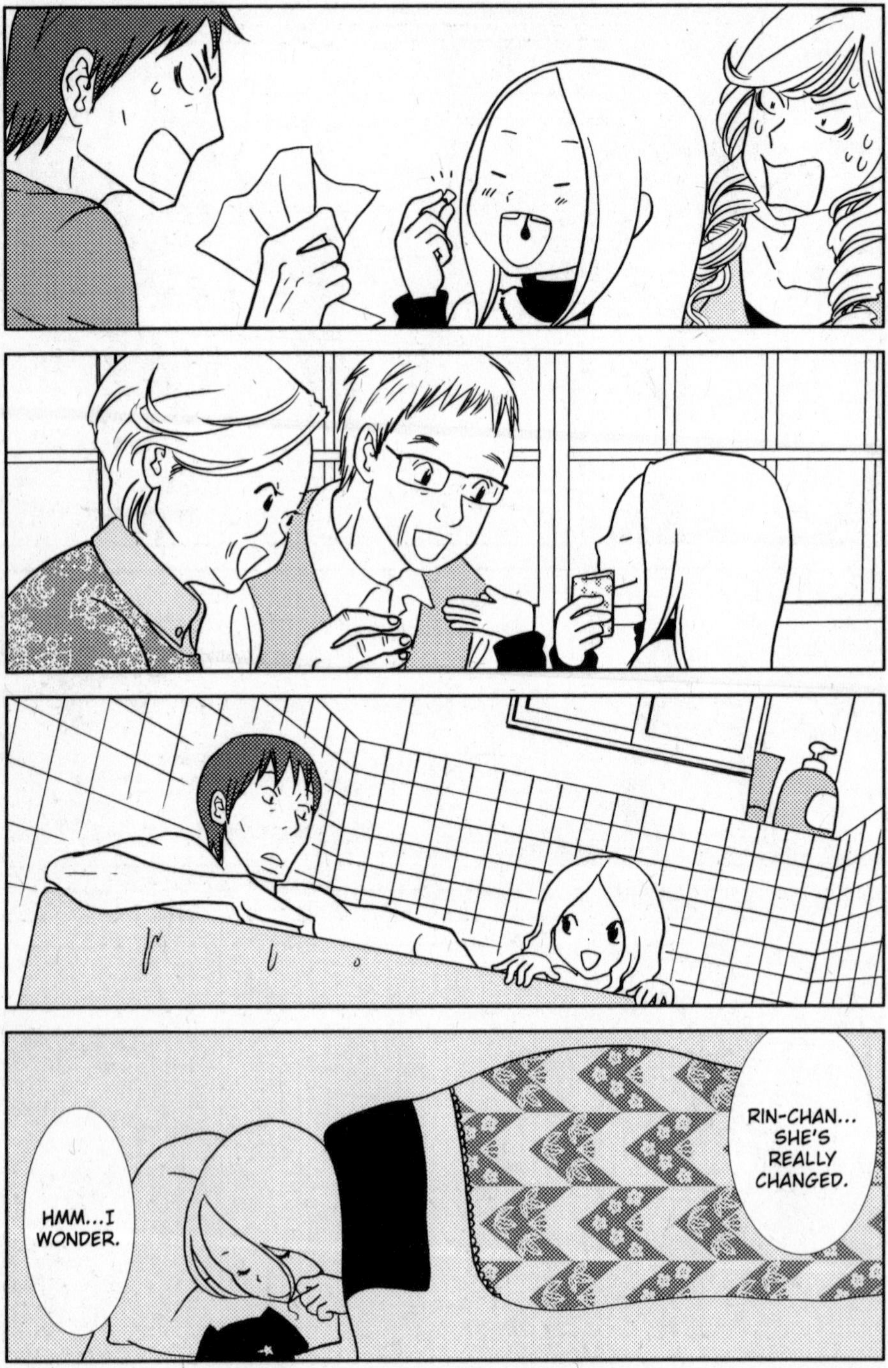
RIN-CHAN... SHE'S REALLY CHANGED.
HMM...I WONDER.

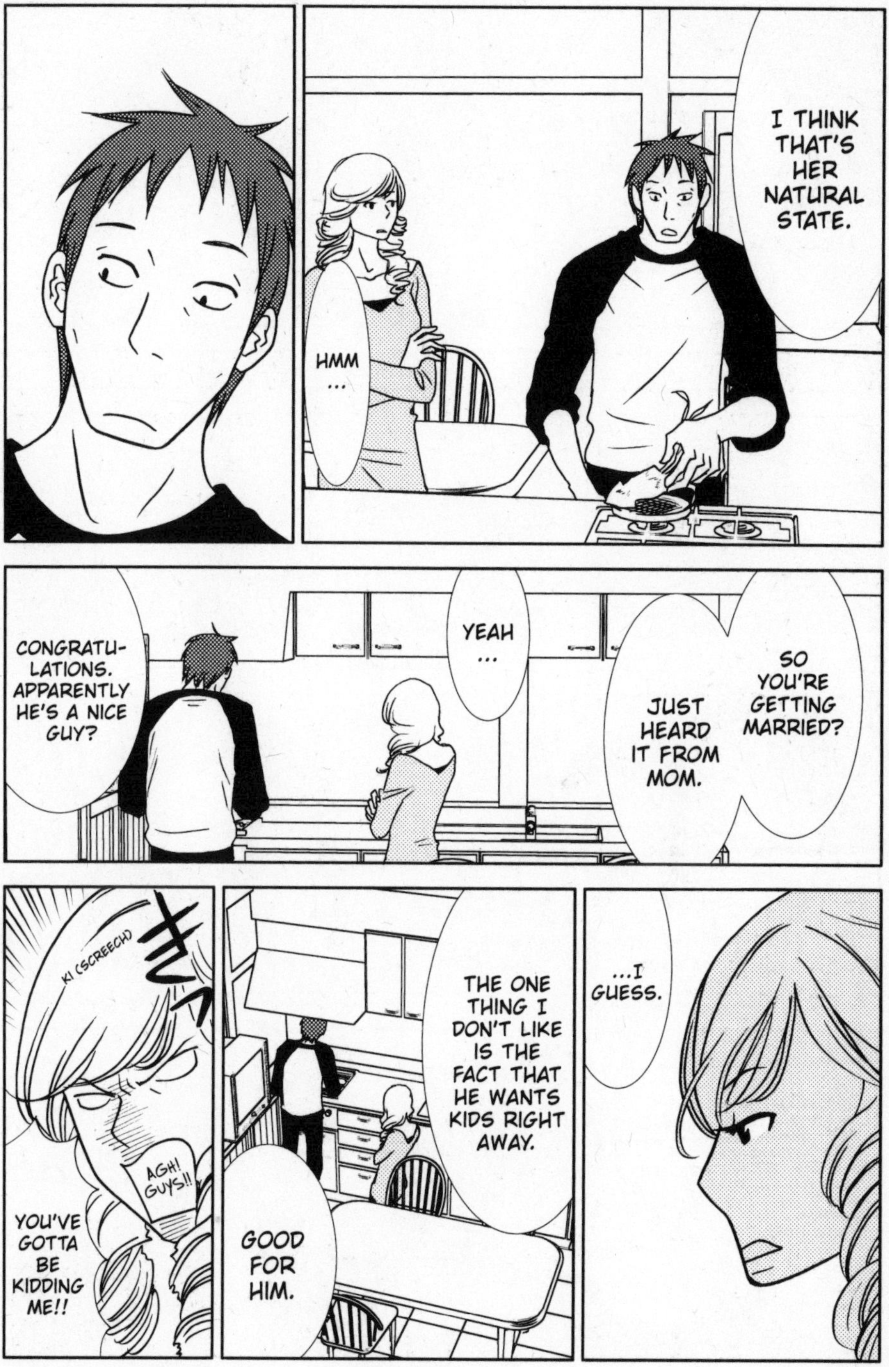
I THINK THAT'S HER NATURAL STATE.
HMM ...
SO YOU'RE GETTING MARRIED?
JUST HEARD IT FROM MOM.
YEAH ...
CONGRATULATIONS. APPARENTLY HE'S A NICE GUY?
...I GUESS.
THE ONE THING I DON'T LIKE IS THE FACT THAT HE WANTS KIDS RIGHT AWAY.
GOOD FOR HIM.
KI (SCREECH)
AGH! GUYS!!
YOU'VE GOTTA BE KIDDING ME!!

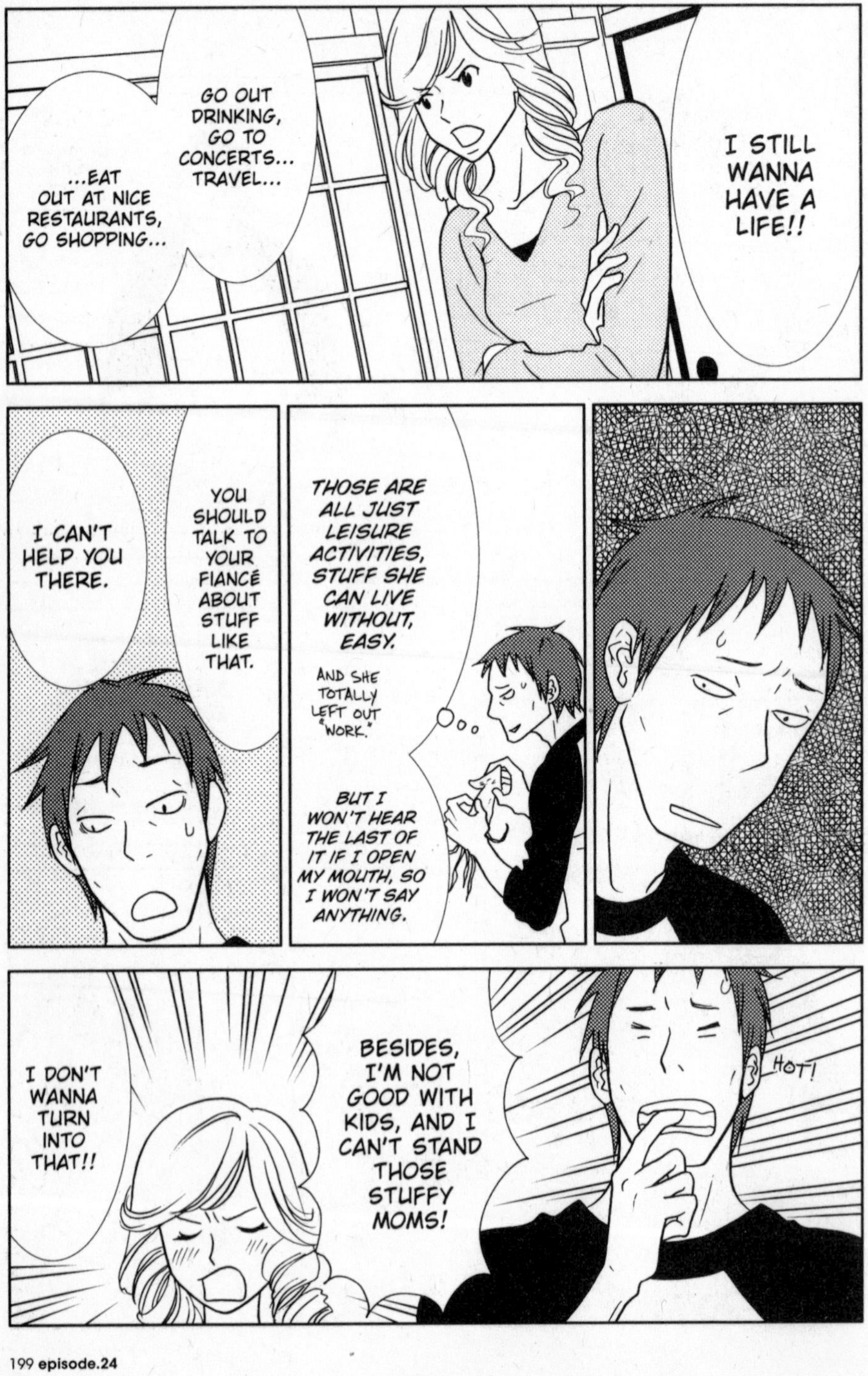
I STILL WANNA HAVE A LIFE!!
GO OUT DRINKING, GO TO CONCERTS... TRAVEL...
...EAT OUT AT NICE RESTAURANTS, GO SHOPPING...
THOSE ARE ALL JUST LEISURE ACTIVITIES, STUFF SHE CAN LIVE WITHOUT, EASY.
AND SHE TOTALLY LEFT OUT "WORK."
BUT I WON'T HEAR THE LAST OF IT IF I OPEN MY MOUTH, SO I WON'T SAY ANYTHING.
YOU SHOULD TALK TO YOUR FIANCÉ ABOUT STUFF LIKE THAT.
I CAN'T HELP YOU THERE.
BESIDES, I'M NOT GOOD WITH KIDS, AND I CAN'T STAND THOSE STUFFY MOMS!
HOT!
I DON'T WANNA TURN INTO THAT!!

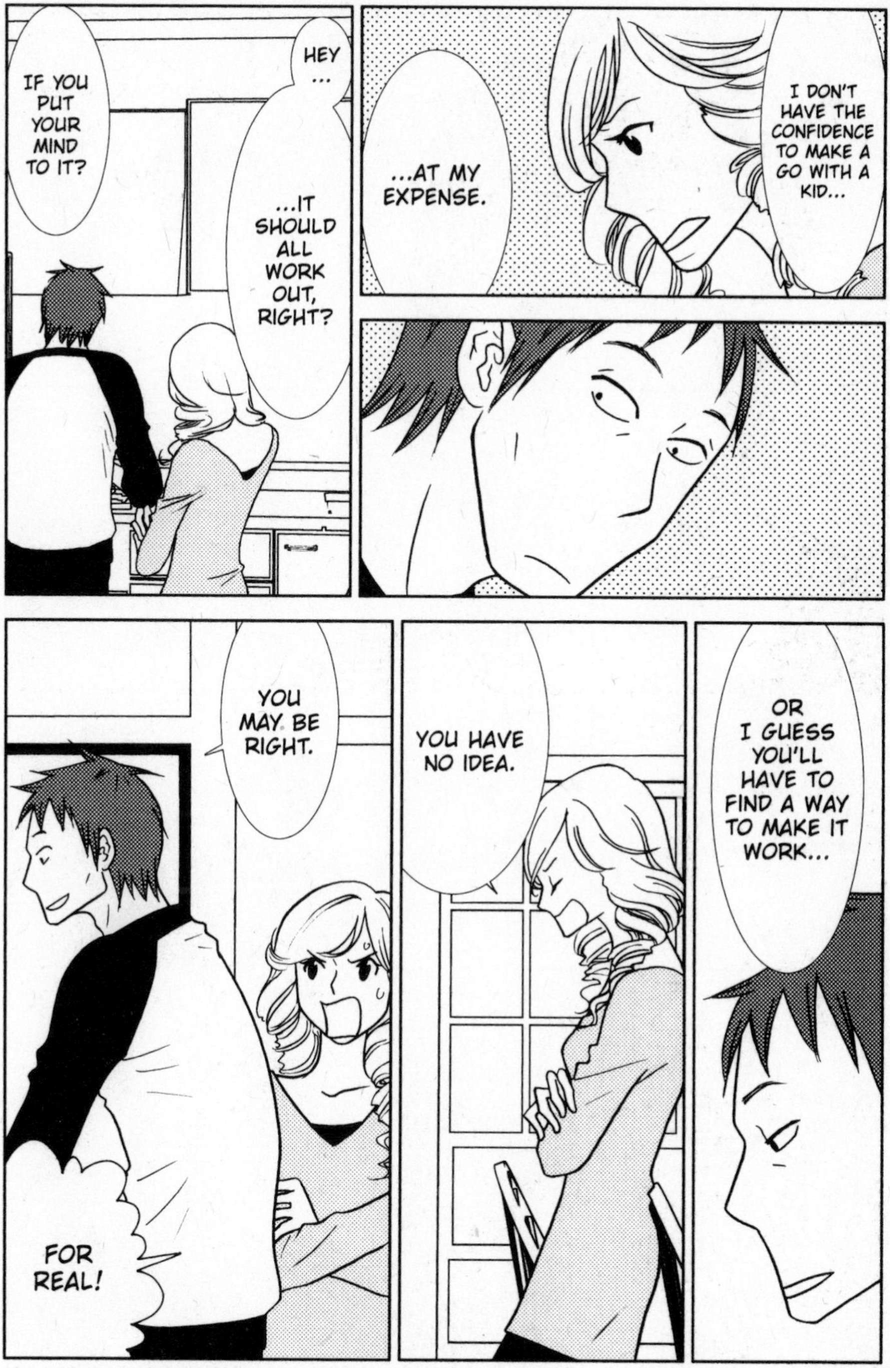
I DON'T HAVE THE CONFIDENCE TO MAKE A GO WITH A KID...
...AT MY EXPENSE.
HEY ...
...IT SHOULD ALL WORK OUT, RIGHT?
IF YOU PUT YOUR MIND TO IT?
OR I GUESS YOU'LL HAVE TO FIND A WAY TO MAKE IT WORK...
YOU HAVE NO IDEA.
YOU MAY BE RIGHT.
FOR REAL!

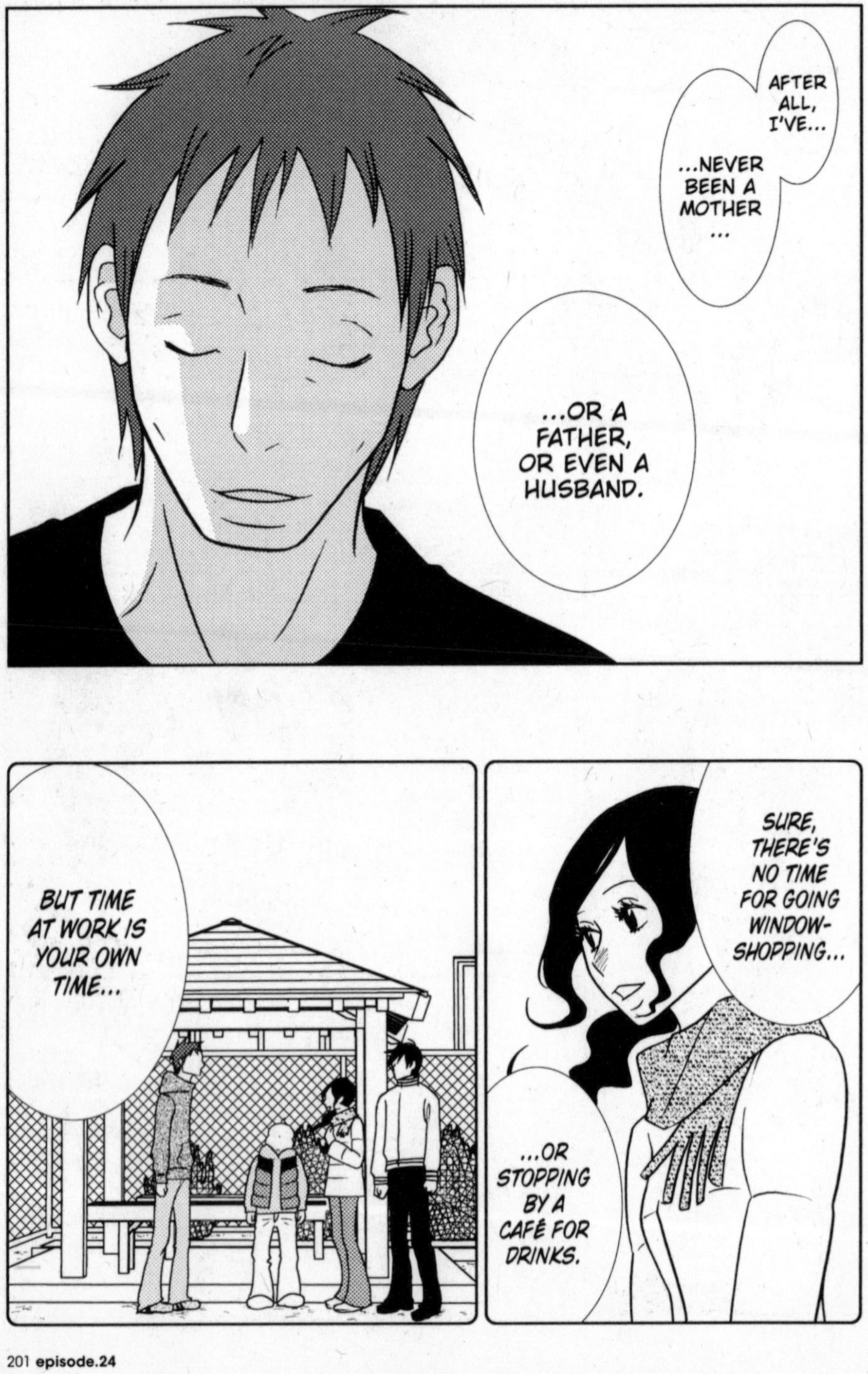
AFTER ALL, I'VE...
...NEVER BEEN A MOTHER...
...OR A FATHER, OR EVEN A HUSBAND.
SURE, THERE'S NO TIME FOR GOING WINDOW-SHOPPING...
...OR STOPPING BY A CAFÉ FOR DRINKS.
BUT TIME AT WORK IS YOUR OWN TIME...

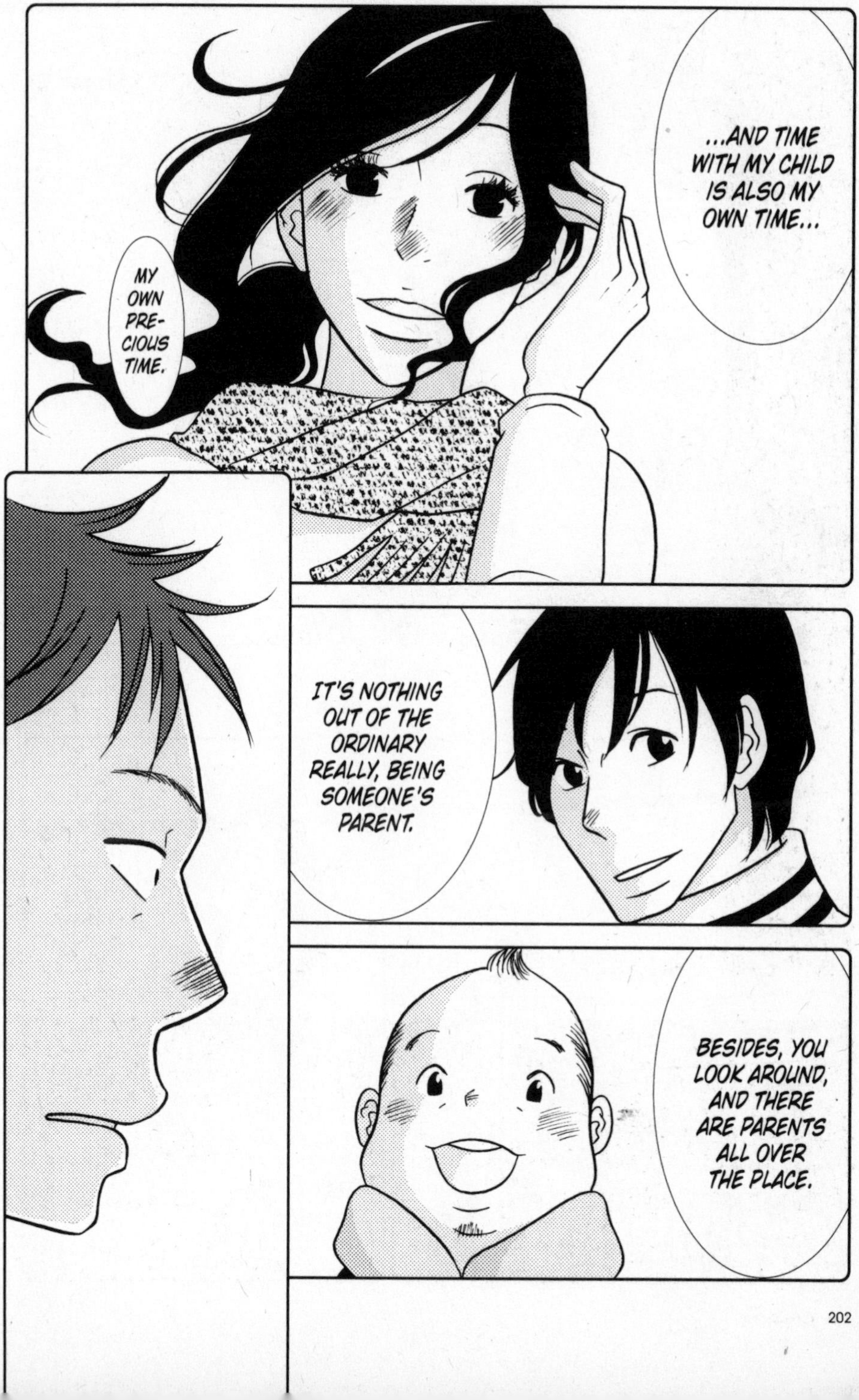
...AND TIME WITH MY CHILD IS ALSO MY OWN TIME...
MY OWN PRE-CIOUS TIME.
IT'S NOTHING OUT OF THE ORDINARY REALLY, BEING SOMEONE'S PARENT.
BESIDES, YOU LOOK AROUND, AND THERE ARE PARENTS ALL OVER THE PLACE.

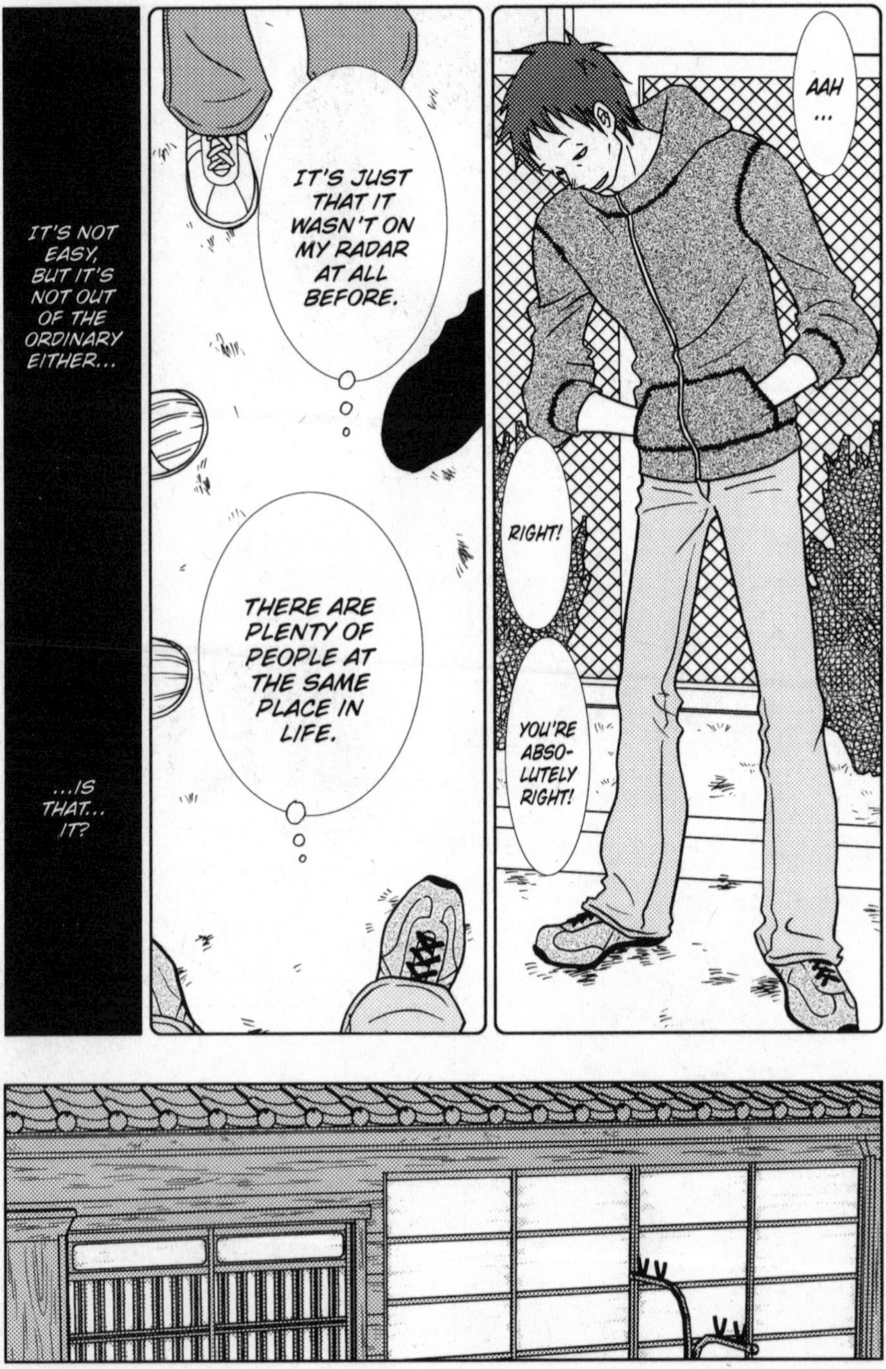
AAH ...
RIGHT!
YOU'RE ABSO-LUTELY RIGHT!
IT'S JUST THAT IT WASN'T ON MY RADAR AT ALL BEFORE.
THERE ARE PLENTY OF PEOPLE AT THE SAME PLACE IN LIFE.
IT'S NOT EASY, BUT IT'S NOT OUT OF THE ORDINARY EITHER...
...IS THAT... IT?

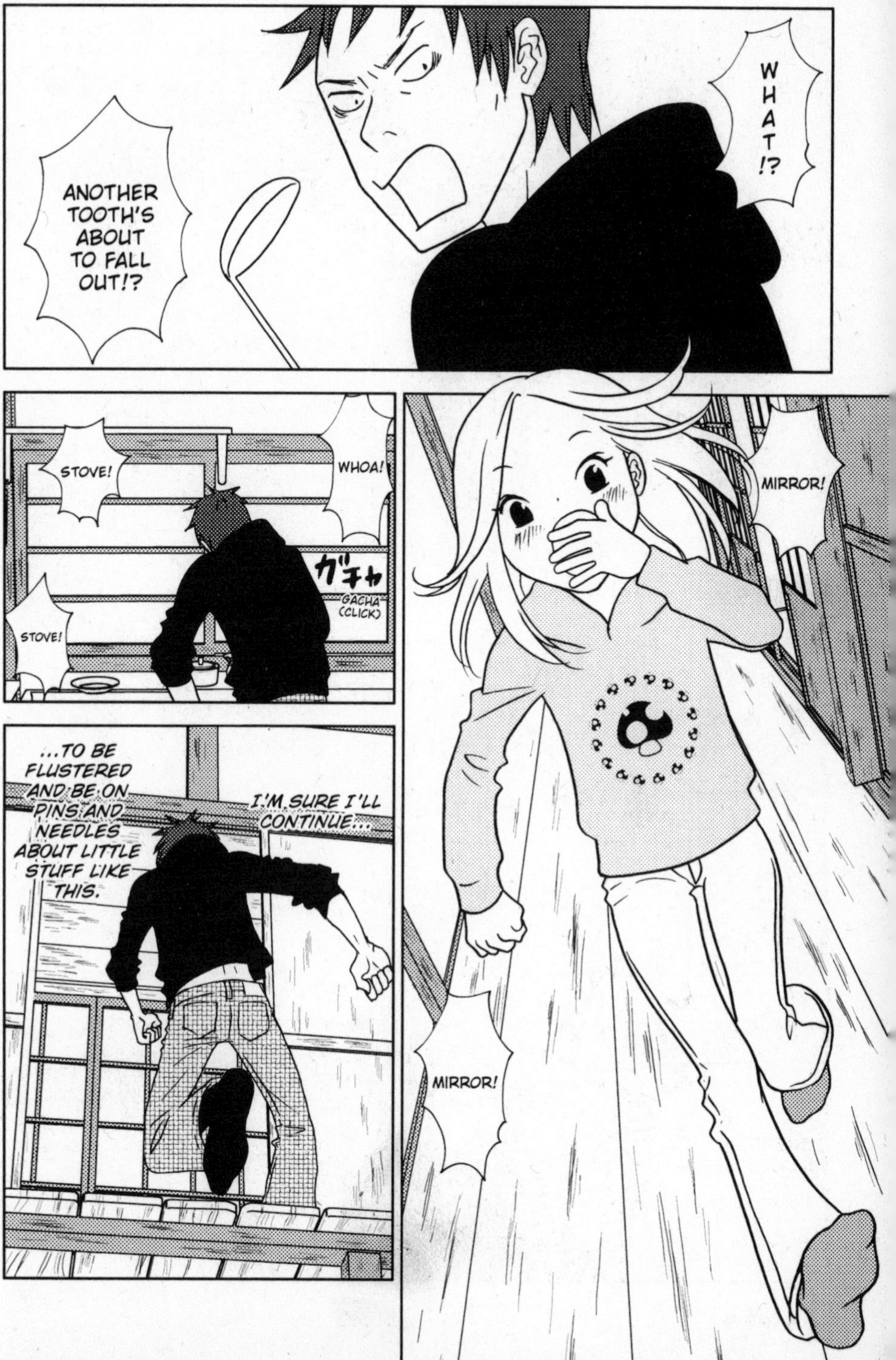
WHAT!?
ANOTHER TOOTH'S ABOUT TO FALL OUT!?
MIRROR!
MIRROR!
WHOA!
STOVE!
ガチャ
GACHA (CLICK)
STOVE!
I'M SURE I'LL CONTINUE...
...TO BE FLUSTERED AND BE ON PINS AND NEEDLES ABOUT LITTLE STUFF LIKE THIS.

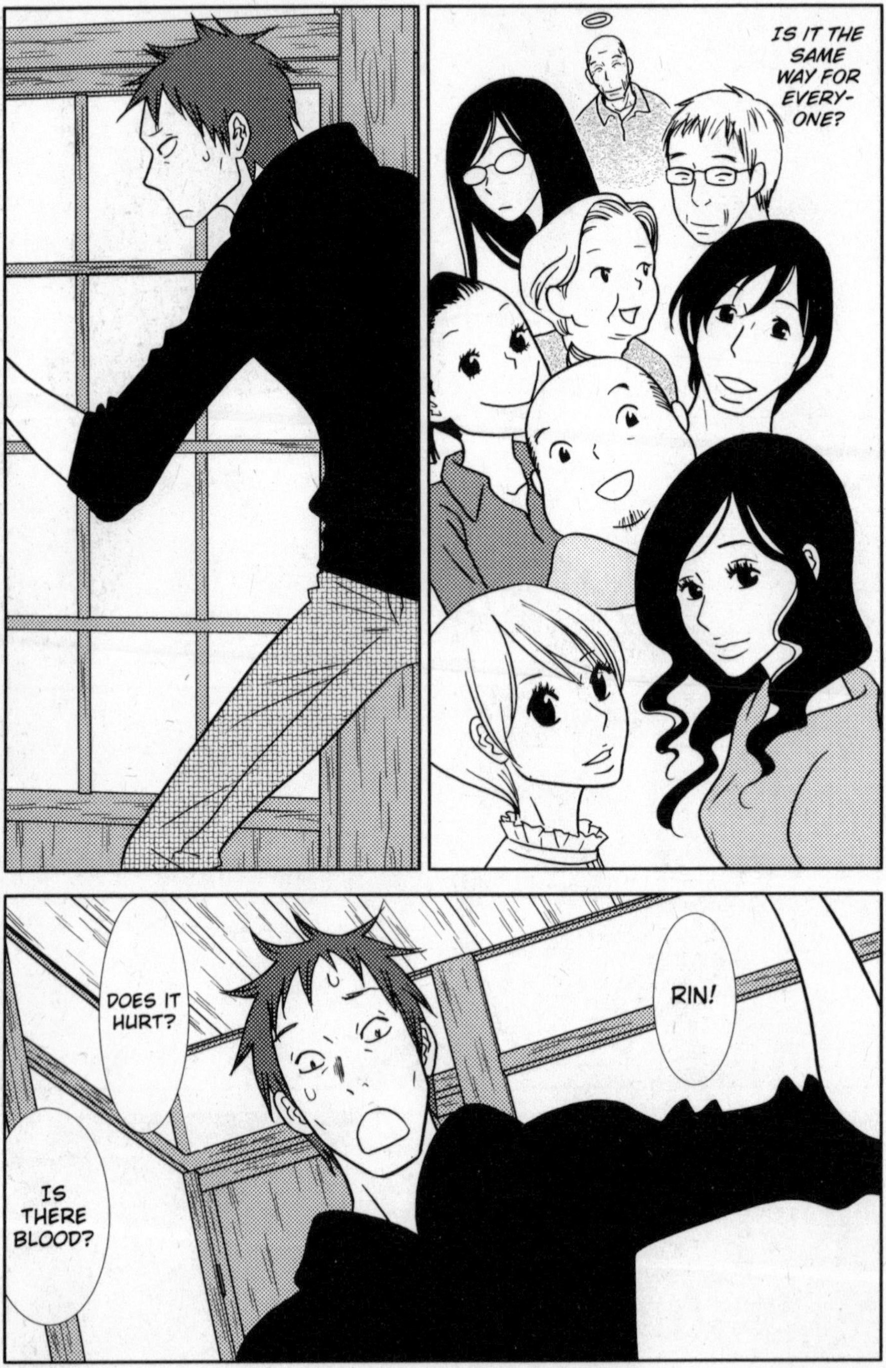
IS IT THE SAME WAY FOR EVERY-ONE?
RIN!
DOES IT HURT?
IS THERE BLOOD?

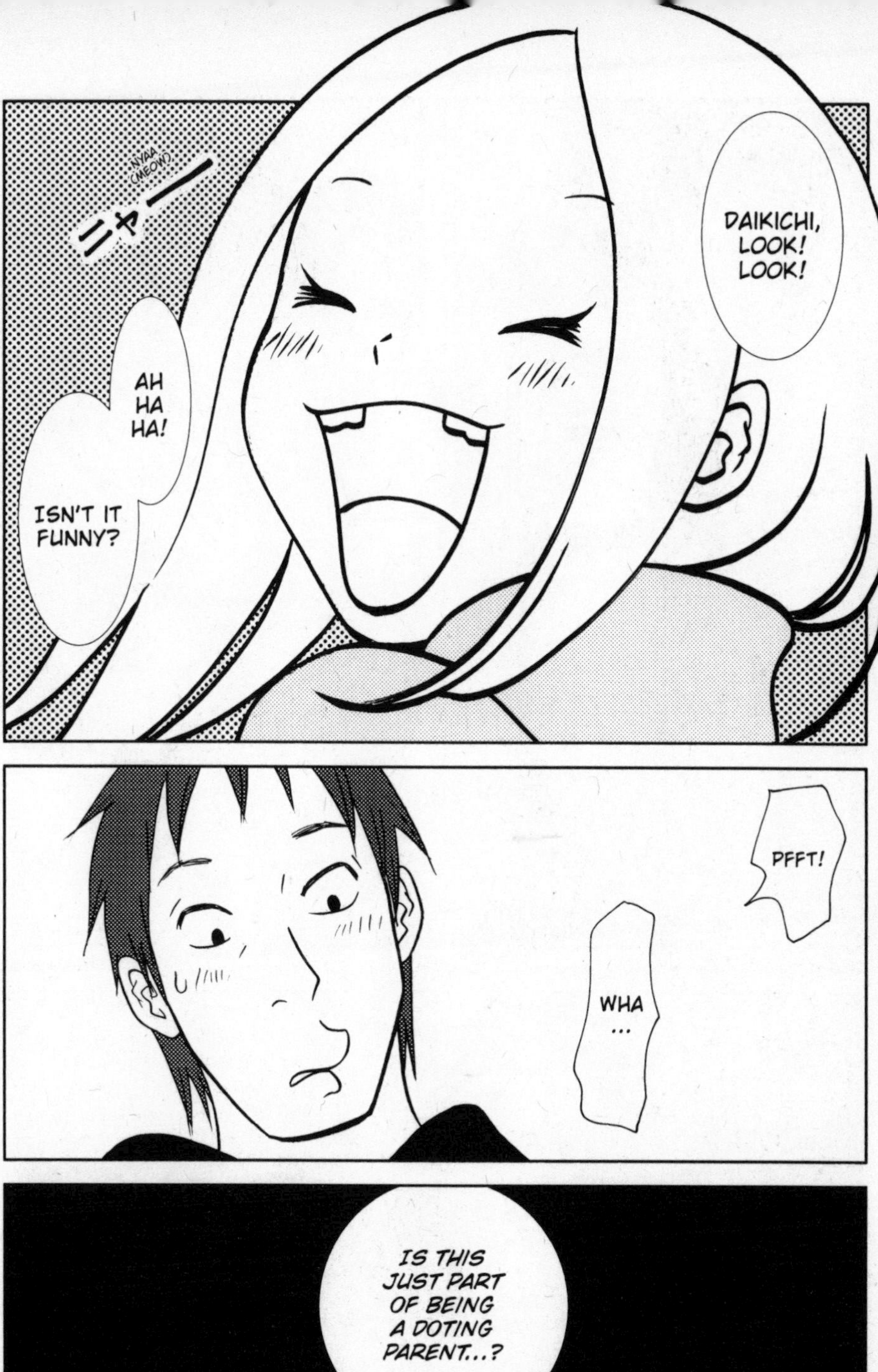
DAIKICHI, LOOK! LOOK!
ニャー
NYAA (MEOW)
AH HA HA!
ISN'T IT FUNNY?
PFFT!
WHA...
IS THIS JUST PART OF BEING A DOTING PARENT...?

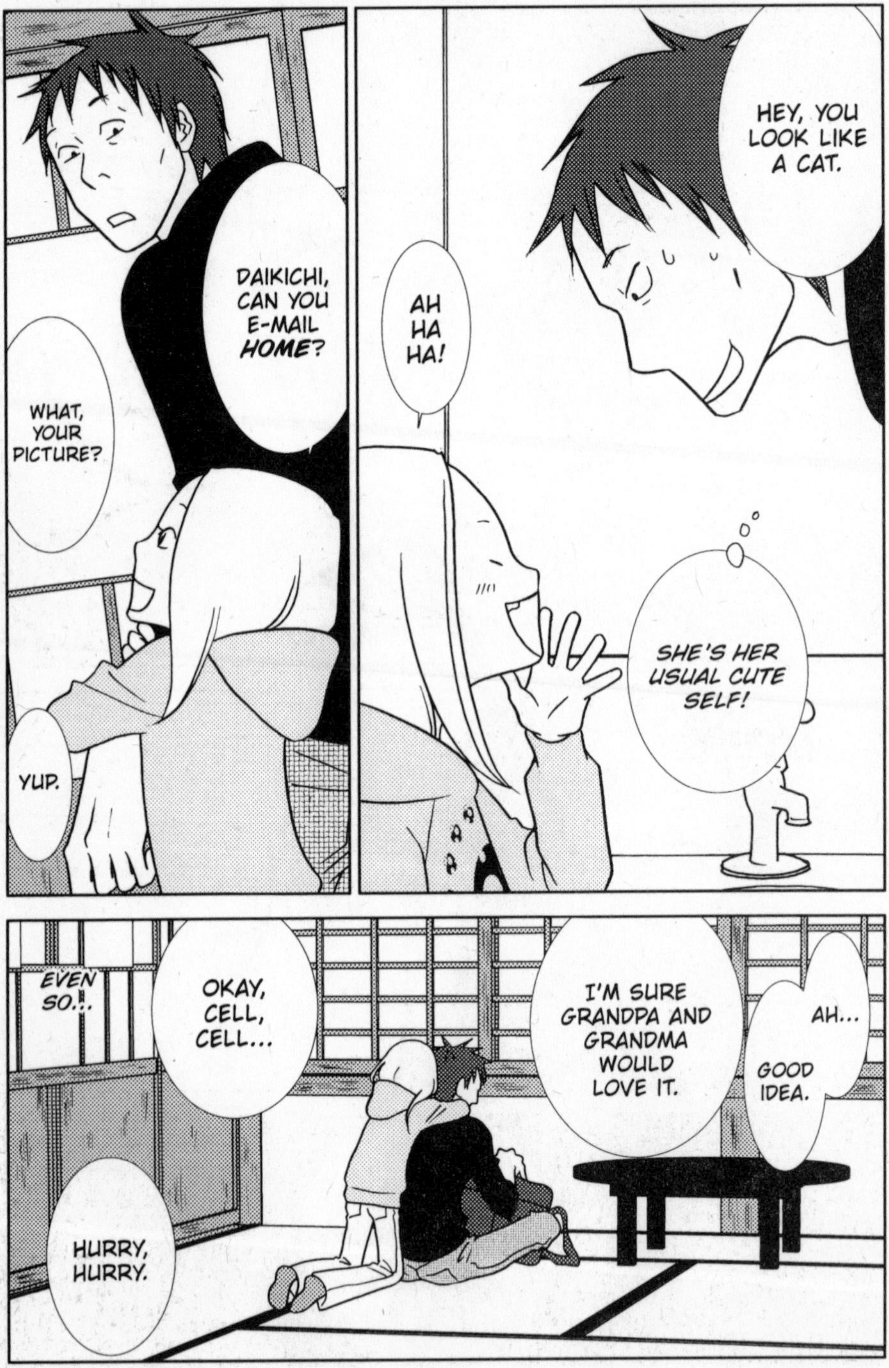
HEY, YOU LOOK LIKE A CAT.
AH HA HA!
SHE'S HER USUAL CUTE SELF!
DAIKICHI, CAN YOU E-MAIL HOME?
WHAT, YOUR PICTURE?
YUP.
AH...
GOOD IDEA.
I'M SURE GRANDPA AND GRANDMA WOULD LOVE IT.
OKAY, CELL, CELL...
EVEN SO...
HURRY, HURRY.

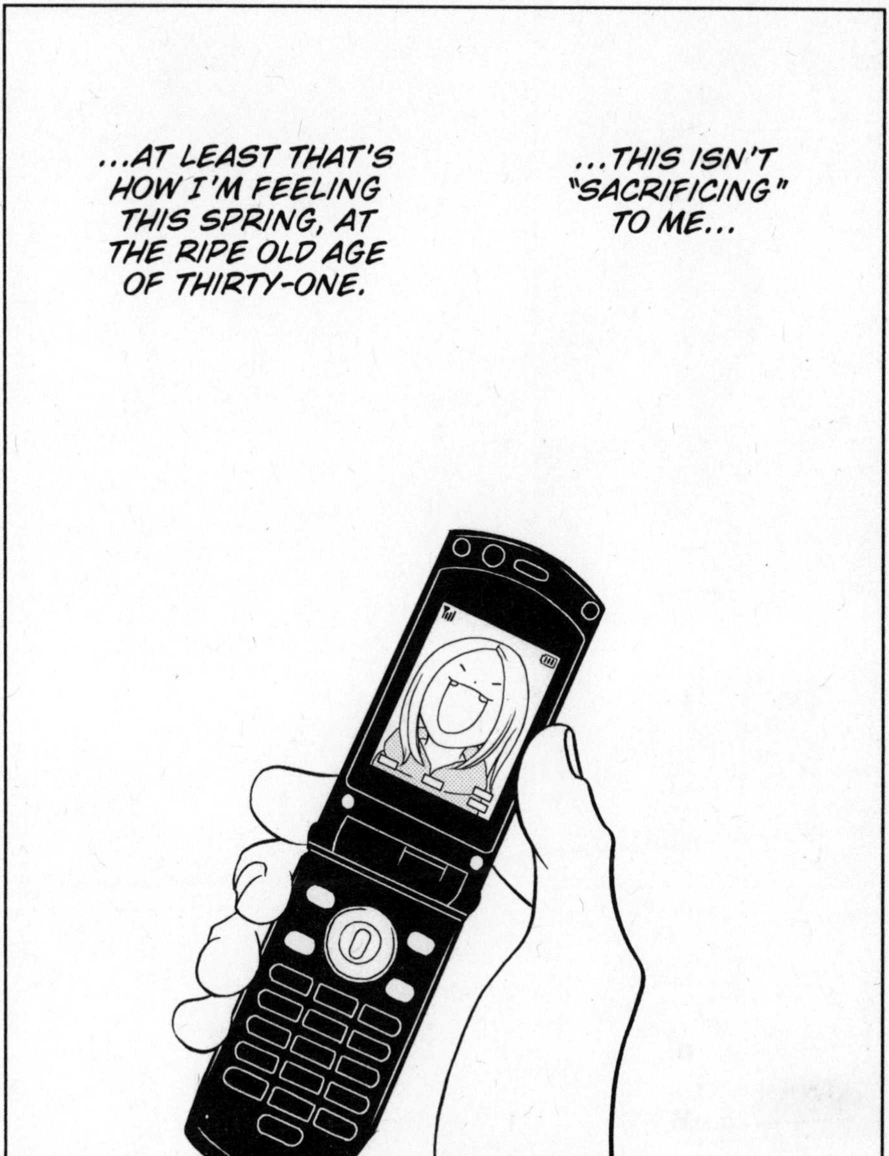
...THIS ISN'T "SACRIFICING" TO ME...
...AT LEAST THAT'S HOW I'M FEELING THIS SPRING, AT THE RIPE OLD AGE OF THIRTY-ONE.

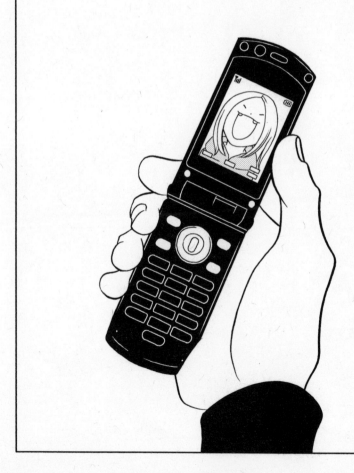

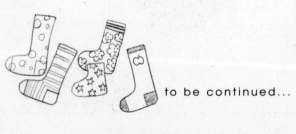

to be continued...

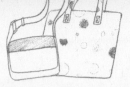
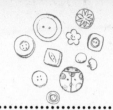

TRANSLATION NOTES

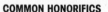

COMMON HONORIFICS
No honorific: Indicates familiarity or closeness; if used without permission or reason, addressing someone in this manner would constitute an insult.
-san: The Japanese equivalent of Mr./Mrs./Miss. If a situation calls for politeness, this is the fail-safe honorific.
-kun: Used most often when referring to boys (though it can be applied to girls as well), this indicates affection or familiarity. Occasionally used by older men among their peers, but it may also be used by anyone referring to a person of lower standing.
-chan: An affectionate honorific indicating familiarity used mostly in reference to girls; also used in reference to cute persons or animals of either gender.

Page 14
Amashoku: A dessert bun that looks like the top of a muffin split open at the peak, which is slightly dry in texture.

Page 14
Barley tea: A summer beverage, golden brown in color, generally served cold.

Page 25
Castella: A popular Japanese sponge cake of Portugese origin.

Page 49
Onigiri: A common Japanese food made of rice molded into a triangle or ball, which is wrapped in seaweed and has a savory filling like salmon or pickled plum inside.

Page 64
Crazy strength vs. superhuman strength: In the original edition, Haruko calls this *kajiba no baka chikara*, which translates literally to something like "crazy strength during a fire." This is the actual idiom in Japanese, while Daikichi's version, *kajiba no kuso chikara*, which means roughly the same thing, is the name given to the protagonist's power from the classic '80s manga *Kinnikuman* ("*Muscleman*").

Page 74
School festival: This event is held in most schools in Japan and showcases student achievements such as schoolwork, artwork, etc., and many also offer food, plays, concerts, and dances. It is also seen as an opportunity for students to see what life is like at other schools.

Page 80
-chin: Familiar, colloquial use of the honorific -chan.

Page 110
Udon: Thick wheat flour noodles, generally served hot in broth with a variety of toppings.

Page 139
Fools don't catch colds: A common Japanese saying that implies that stupid people are too stupid to realize when they've caught a cold and thus never do; i.e., "ignorance is bliss."

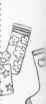

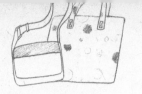

Page 184
Throwing teeth at the roof: In Japan, like in some other parts of the world, it is a traditional practice to throw lower baby teeth at the roof in the hopes that the adult teeth will grow in straight up and upper baby teeth under the floor so the adult teeth grow straight down.

Page 186
Meat-and-potato stew: Called *nikujaga* in Japanese, this dish is a bit different from a Western dish that might have the same name. In Japan, it is a common comfort food dish of thinly sliced meat, potatoes, onions and other vegetables in a sweetened soy sauce-flavored broth.

Page 196
Kouya dofu: Freeze-dried tofu.

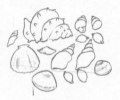
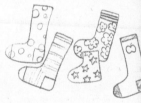
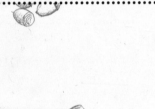
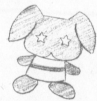
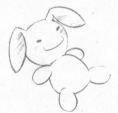
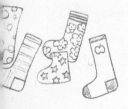

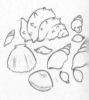

BUNNY**DROP**

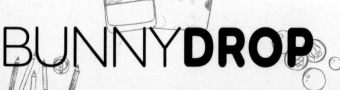

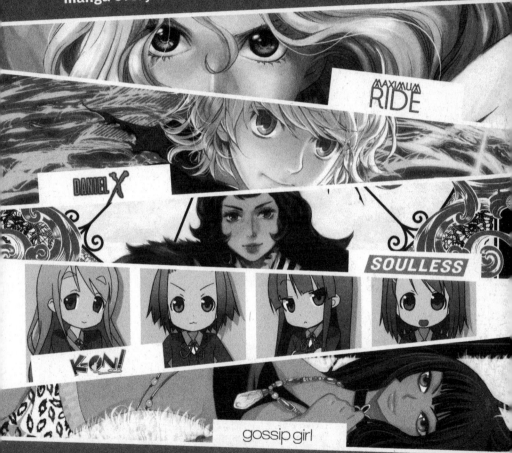

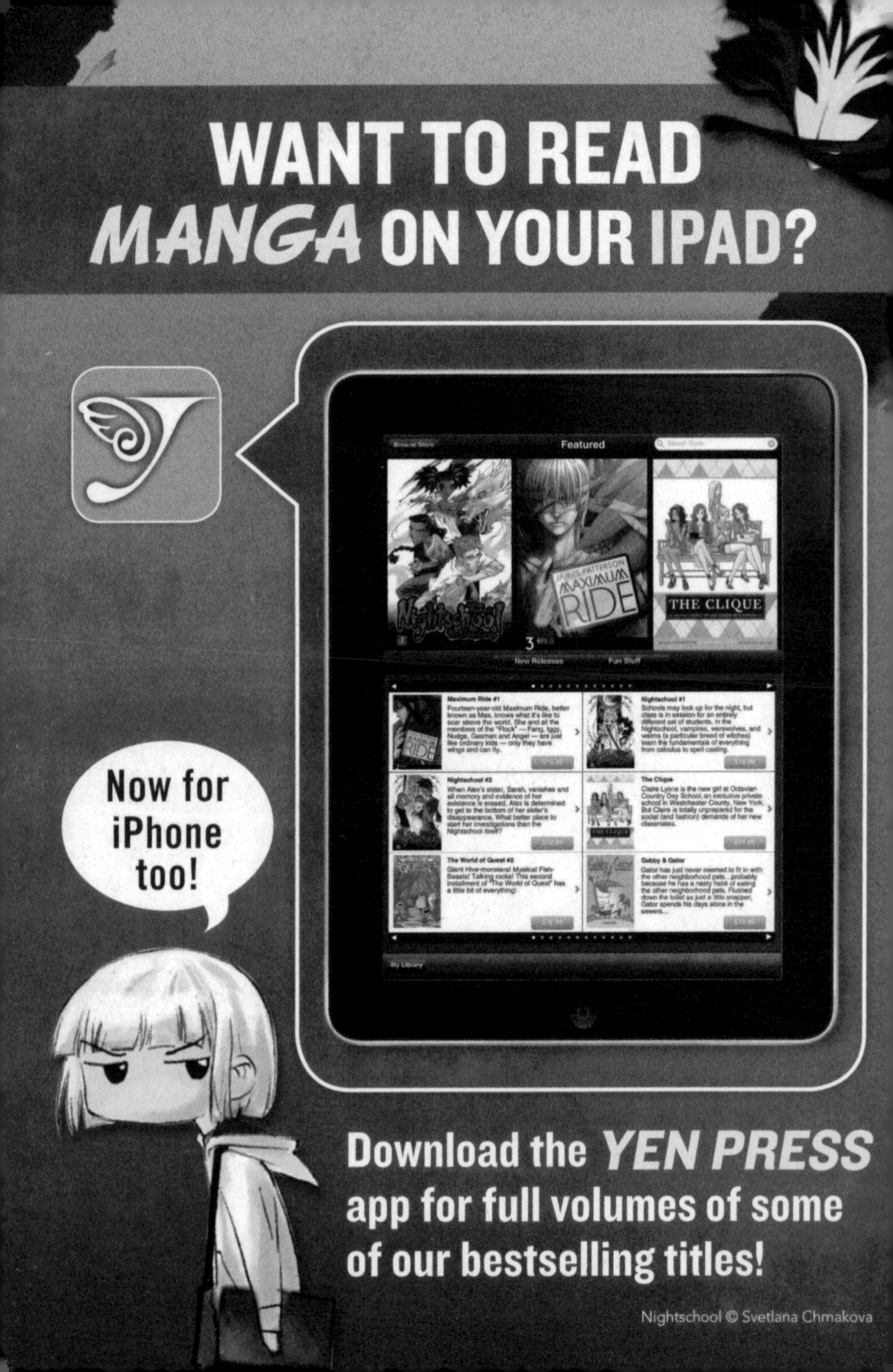
WANT TO READ
MANGA ON YOUR IPAD?
Now for iPhone too!
Download the YEN PRESS app for full volumes of some of our bestselling titles!
Nightschool © Svetlana Chmakova

Hello! This is YOTSUBA!

Guess what? Guess what?
Yotsuba and Daddy just moved here from waaaay over there!

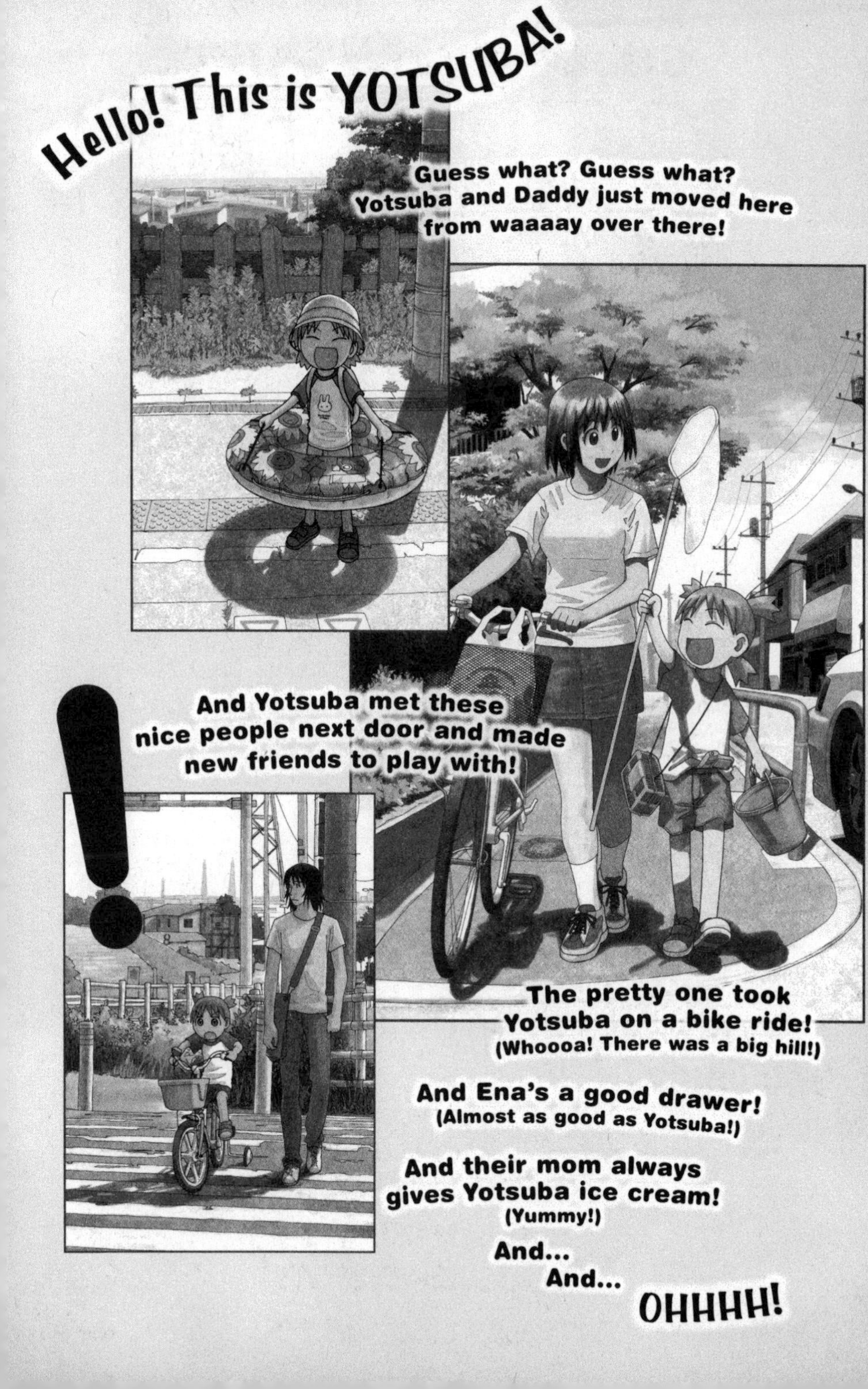

And Yotsuba met these nice people next door and made new friends to play with!

The pretty one took Yotsuba on a bike ride!
(Whoooa! There was a big hill!)

And Ena's a good drawer!
(Almost as good as Yotsuba!)

And their mom always gives Yotsuba ice cream!
(Yummy!)

And...
And...
OHHHH!

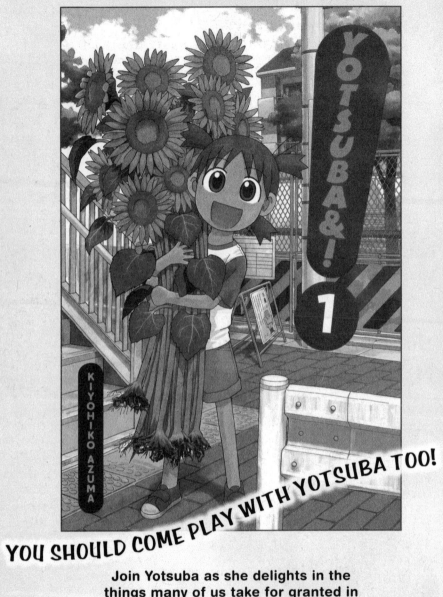

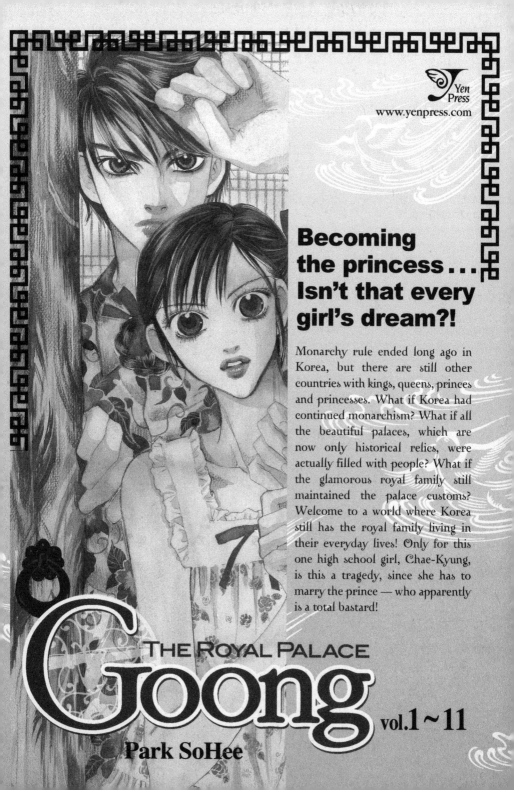

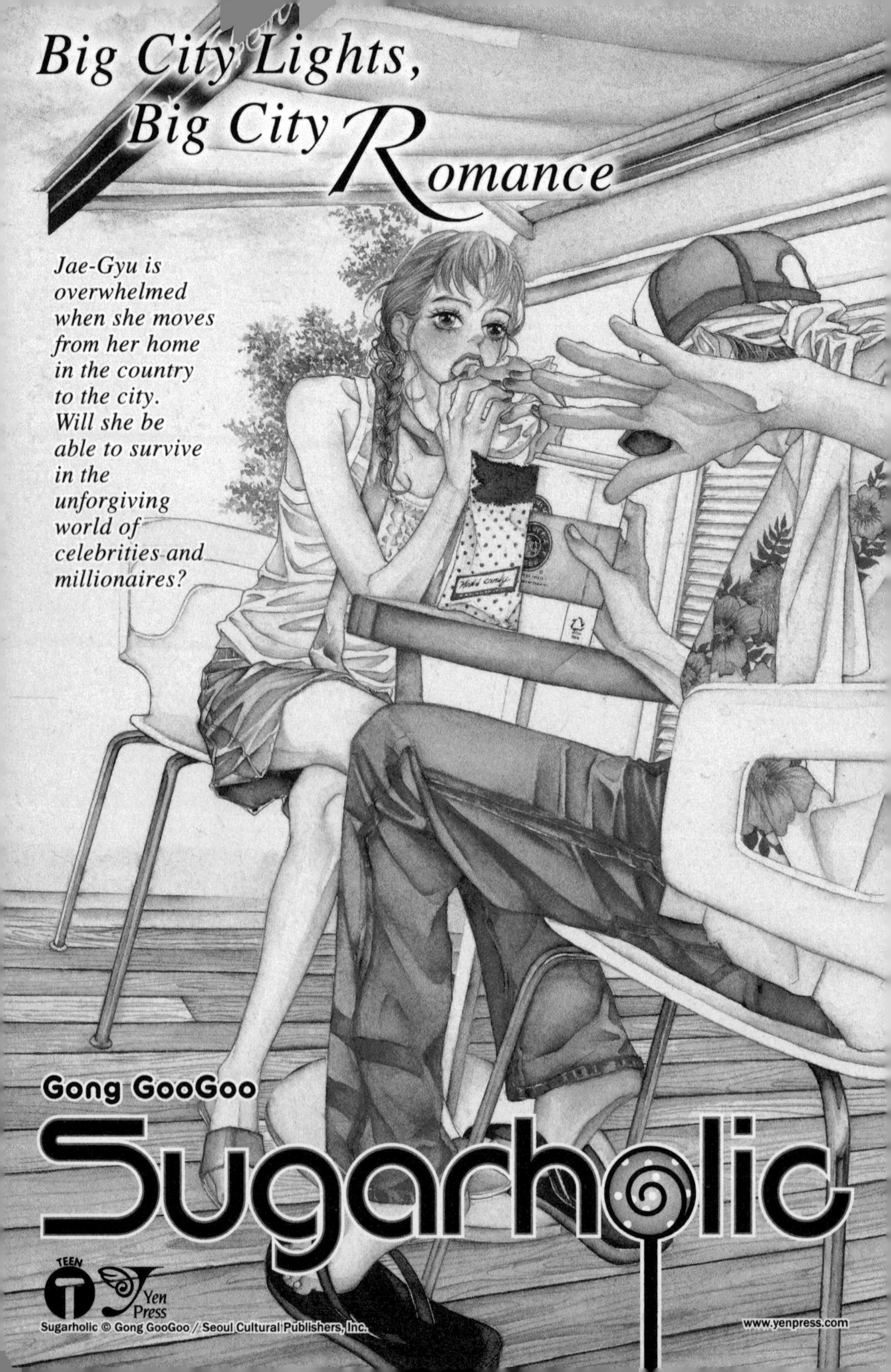
Big City Lights,
Big City Romance
Jae-Gyu is overwhelmed when she moves from her home in the country to the city. Will she be able to survive in the unforgiving world of celebrities and millionaires?
Gong GooGoo
Sugarholic
TEEN
Yen Press
Sugarholic © Gong GooGoo / Seoul Cultural Publishers, Inc.
www.yenpress.com

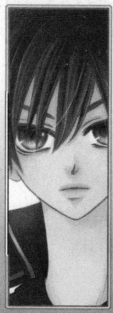
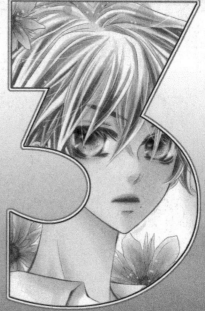

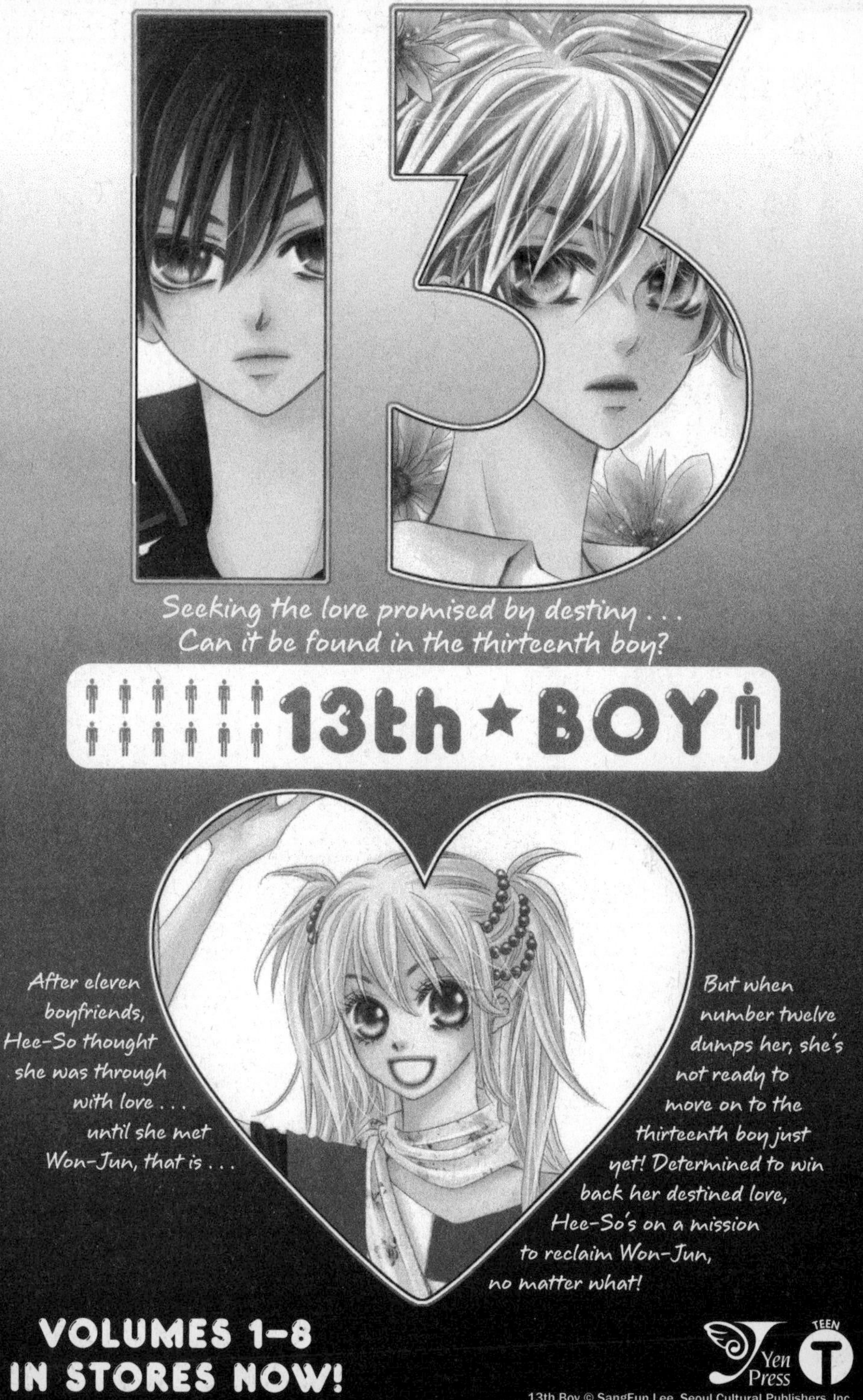

Seeking the love promised by destiny...
Can it be found in the thirteenth boy?

13th ★ BOY

After eleven boyfriends, Hee-So thought she was through with love... until she met Won-Jun, that is...

But when number twelve dumps her, she's not ready to move on to the thirteenth boy just yet! Determined to win back her destined love, Hee-So's on a mission to reclaim Won-Jun, no matter what!

VOLUMES 1-8
IN STORES NOW!

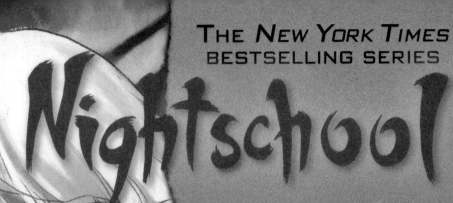
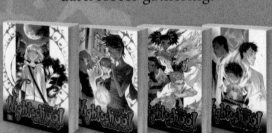

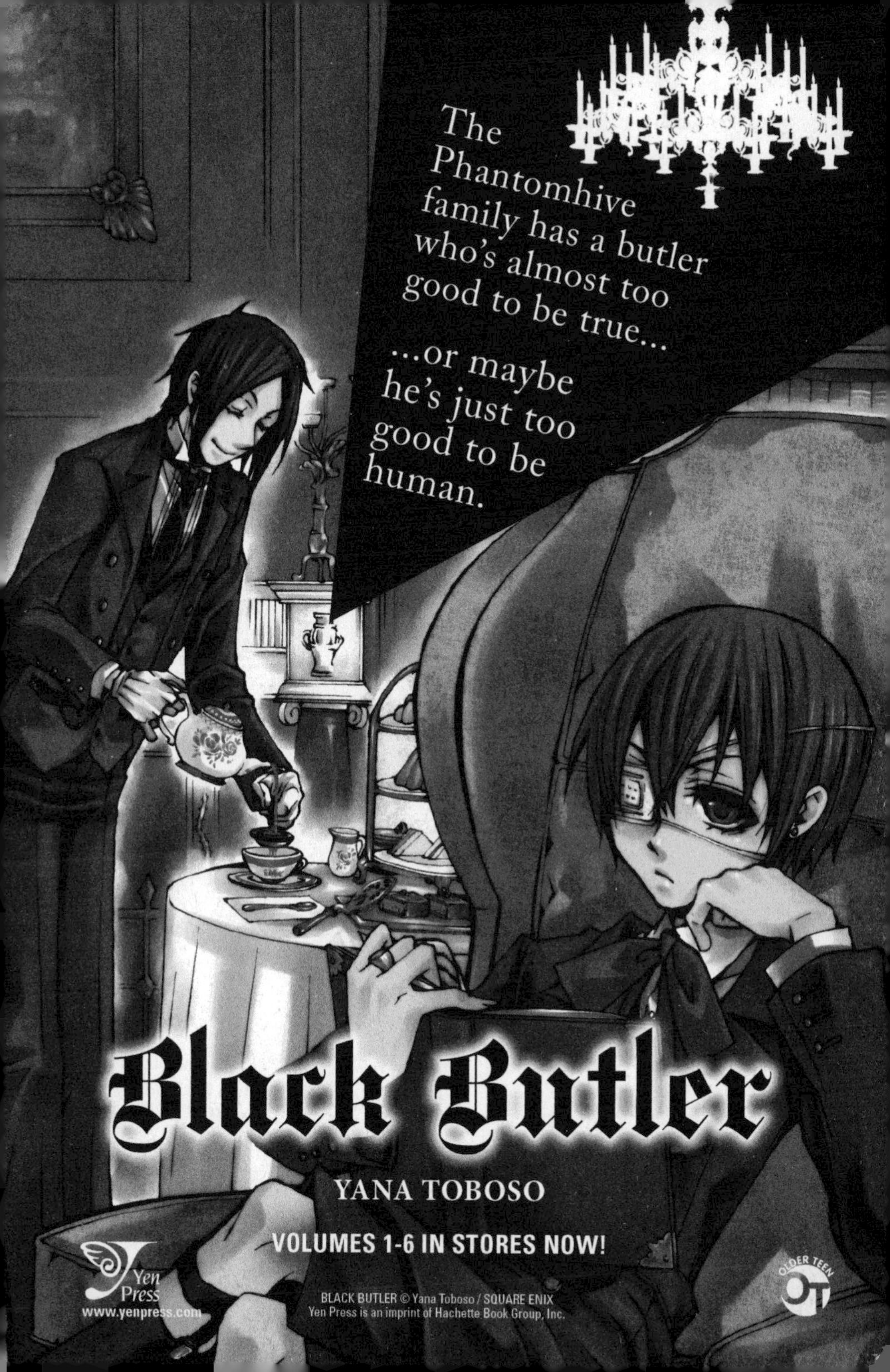
The Phantomhive family has a butler who's almost too good to be true...
...or maybe he's just too good to be human.
Black Butler
YANA TOBOSO
VOLUMES 1-6 IN STORES NOW!
Yen Press
www.yenpress.com
BLACK BUTLER © Yana Toboso / SQUARE ENIX
Yen Press is an imprint of Hachette Book Group, Inc.
OLDER TEEN
OT

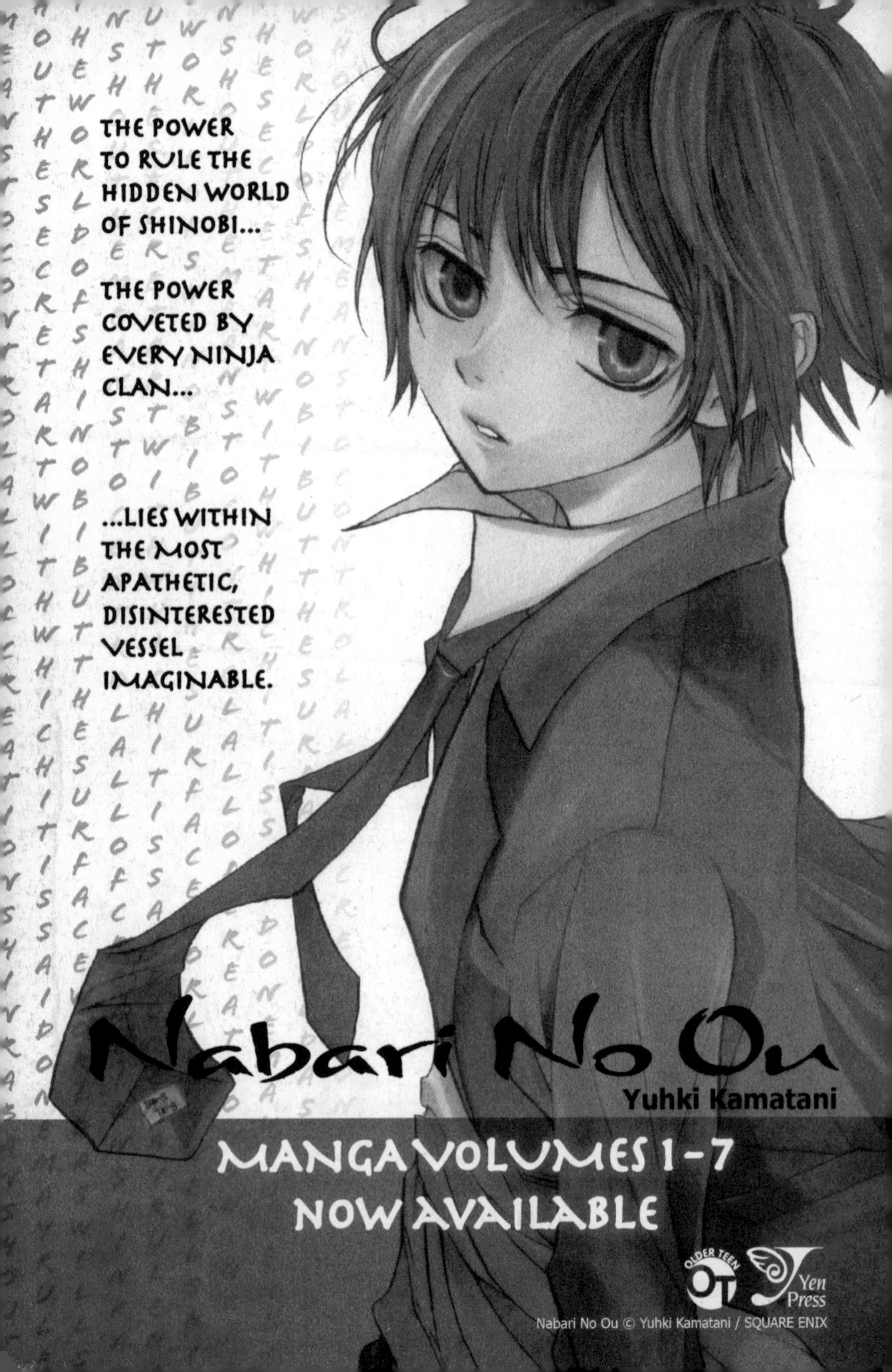
THE POWER TO RULE THE HIDDEN WORLD OF SHINOBI...
THE POWER COVETED BY EVERY NINJA CLAN...
...LIES WITHIN THE MOST APATHETIC, DISINTERESTED VESSEL IMAGINABLE.
Nabari No Ou
Yuhki Kamatani
MANGA VOLUMES 1-7
NOW AVAILABLE
OLDER TEEN
OT
Yen Press
Nabari No Ou © Yuhki Kamatani / SQUARE ENIX

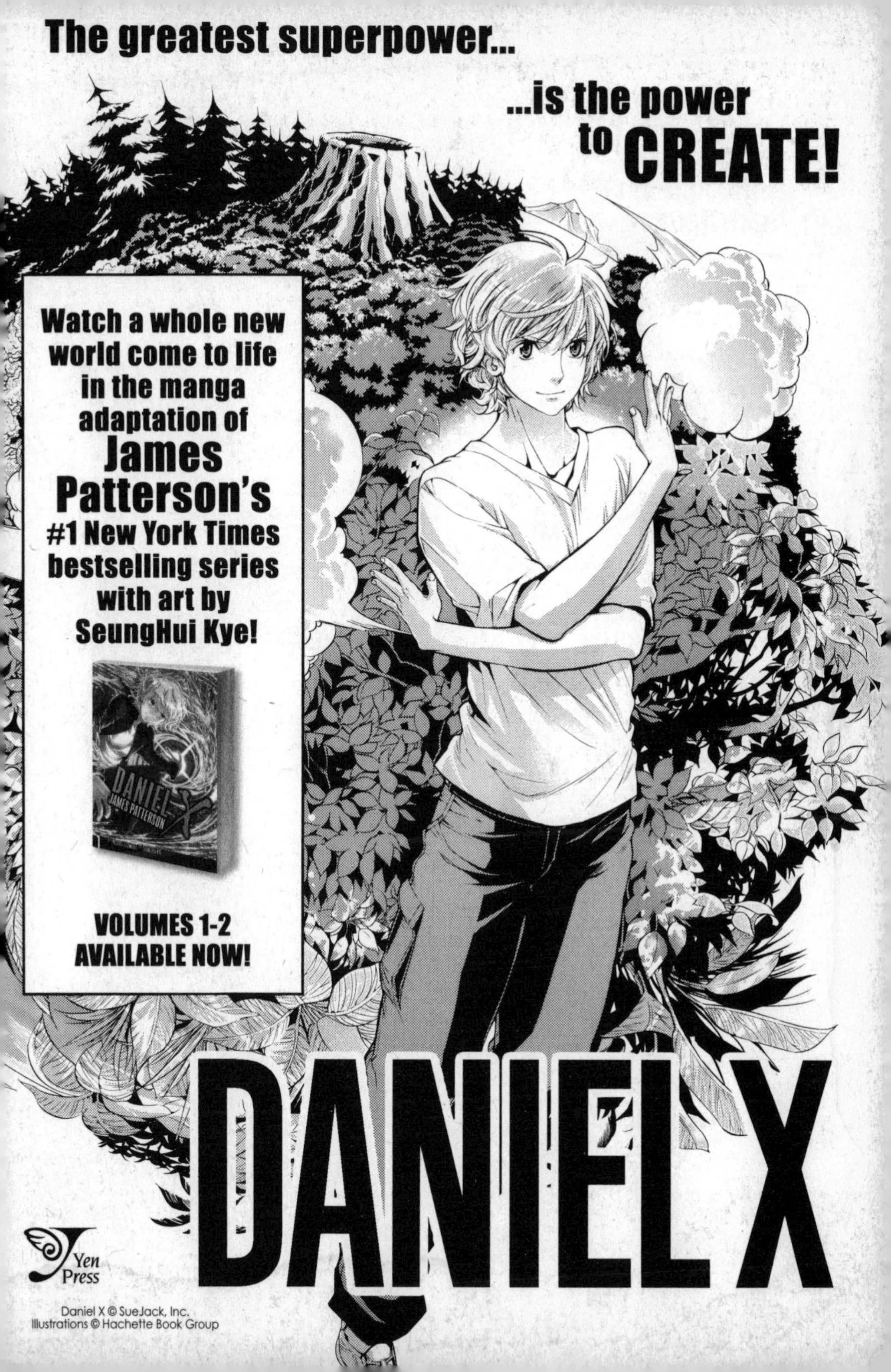

The greatest superpower...
...is the power to CREATE!
Watch a whole new world come to life in the manga adaptation of James Patterson's #1 New York Times bestselling series with art by SeungHui Kye!
DANIEL X
JAMES PATTERSON
VOLUMES 1-2 AVAILABLE NOW!
DANIEL X
Yen Press
Daniel X © SueJack, Inc.
Illustrations © Hachette Book Group

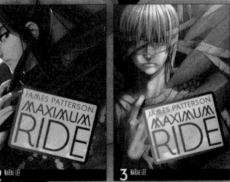

BUNNY DROP

Translation: Kaori Inoue • Lettering: Alexis Eckerman

BUNNY DROP Vol. 4 © 2008 by Yumi Unita. All rights reserved. First
published in Japan in 2008 by SHODENSHA PUBLISHING CO., LTD.,
Tokyo. English translation rights in USA, Canada, and UK arranged with
SHODENSHA PUBLISHING CO., LTD. and Hachette Book Group through
Tuttle-Mori Agency, Inc., Tokyo.

Translation © 2011 by Hachette Book Group, Inc.

Yen Press
Hachette Book Group
237 Park Avenue, New York, NY 10017

www.HachetteBookGroup.com
www.YenPress.com

Yen Press is an imprint of Hachette Book Group, Inc. The Yen Press name
and logo are trademarks of Hachette Book Group, Inc.

First Yen Press Edition: September 2011

ISBN: 978-0-7595-3121-5

10 9 8 7 6 5 4 3

BVG

Printed in the United States of America